CISTERCIAN STUDIES SERIES: NUMBER ONE HUNDRED NINETY-THREE

Praise No Less Than Charity

Studies in Honor of M. Chrysogonus Waddell
Monk of Gethsemani Abbey

D1194655

Photograph by Eileen Klee Sweeny

CISTERCIAN STUDIES SERIES: NUMBER ONE HUNDRED NINETY-THREE

Praise No Less Than Charity

Studies in Honor of M. Chrysogonus Waddell
Monk of Gethsemani Abbey

Contributions from Colleagues, Confrères,
and Friends on the Occasion of the Fiftieth
Anniversary of His Monastic Profession

Edited by E. Rozanne Elder

Cistercian Publications
Kalamazoo, Michigan

Cistercian Publications

Editorial Offices & Customer Service
The Institute of Cistercian Studies
WMU Station 1903 W. Michigan Avenue
Kalamazoo, MI 49008-5415

Cistercian Publications UK
A Service of Mount Saint Bernard Abbey
Customer Service:
97 Loughborough Road
Thringstone, Coalville, Leics. LE67 8LQ

www: spencerabbey.org/cistpub

The work of Cistercian Publications
is made possible in part by support from Western Michigan University
to The Institute of Cistercian Studies

Typeset by Bookcomp, Inc.
Printed in the United States of America

Table of Contents

Table of Abbreviations

7

Pre   Bernard of Clairvaux, *De preceptione et dispensatione*
RH   Repertorium hymnologicum. 4 volumes. Louvain 1892–1922.
SBOp   *Sancti Bernardi Opera.* 8 volumes. Rome: Editiones Cistercienses, 1957–1977.
SC   Sermones in Cantica canticorum
SCh   Sources chrétiennes series
SI   *Sermones inediti B. Aelredi abbatis Rievallensis.* C. H. Talbot, ed. Series Scriptorum S. Ordinis Cisterciensis 1. Rome: Apud Curiam Generalem Sacri Ordinis Cisterciensis, 1952.
RB   Benedict's Rule for Monasteries
RM   The Rule of the Master

Preface

THOMAS EDWARD WADDELL was a student at the Philadelphia Conservatory of Music when he sensed a call to monastic life. On the second day of August 1950, he entered Gethsemani Abbey, a young man of twenty. One month and one day later he was formally received into a large novitiate with a new name, Maria Chrysogonus. 'There are two recollections that stand out for me', recalls one of his fellow novices:

> One is that he always had a stack of books with him. In those days, we had a strong common life, but in the Scriptorium, he would have his stack of books in front of him, reading and studying several things at a time. The rest of us—around eighty-five choir novices—would be reading just one book at a time. I realize now that this 'pre-school' work was preparing him for the tremendous work and contributions he would be making to the Order.
>
> The other is an occasion when the Novice Director asked us some questions and reflections on the spirituality of the common life. I think, if I recall correctly, that we had to write these down. I clearly remember that Father Chrysogonus wrote something to the effect that the spirituality of the common life begins or has its origin in the common life of the three persons of the Trinity. This impressed me—although at that tender age I wasn't quite sure what it meant. Much later I would come

to know of Baldwin of Ford's treatise on the common life and see that Father Chrysogonus was 'right on'. Perhaps he had been reading it in Latin or French, for in those days, one could count on one's fingers the number of english translations of the Cistercian Fathers available.

He had the same personality then as he does now. He hasn't changed—just deepened![1]

The ebullient Frater Chrysogonus made his simple (temporary) profession on the Feast of the Nativity of Mary, 1952. It was perhaps a portent that this day, 8 September, also marks the commemoration of a great twelfth-century Cistercian, William of Saint Thierry, a scholar and a monk whose thought this new American Cistercian would one day study with the same infectious and erudite enthusiasm with which he would track down the origins of early cistercian liturgy, ruminate the works of Saint Bernard of Clairvaux and those of his nemesis, Peter Abelard, pore over the books and letters of the seventeenth-century reforming abbot of la Trappe, lay bare the monastic theology underlying apparently unsophisticated *exempla* and hagiography, and seek out and edit the early documents from the very first Cistercian monastery, that 'New Monastery' which became the centre of a european—and now world-wide—family. But this is to get ahead of the story.

Frater Maria Chrysogonus persevered in monastic life and made his solemn profession on All Saints' Day, 1 November 1955. Committing his life to God under the benedictine vows of obedience, stability, and conversion of life, he became a member of an Order noted for its austerity and its silence, an Order which, in the words of one of its earliest members, 'means learning to be silent, to fast, to keep vigil, to pray, to work with our

---

1. Thomas X. Davis, abbot of New Clairvaux Abbey, Vina, California.

hands, and—above all—to cling to that most excellent
way, which is charity. . . .'[2]

Ordained priest on the Feast of the Visitation, 31 May
1958, the young Trappist continued his studies at the
Collegio Sant'Anselmo in Rome. From 1962 to 1964,
he concentrated on liturgical studies and devoted the
following year to the study of theology. 'He was a good
companion,' writes a confrère, 'always running around
with lots of books, going from one library to another'.[3]

When he returned home to Gethsemani, he was made
Choir Master, a post he was to hold for over thirty years
while providing most of the organ accompaniment to the
monastic liturgy, the Work of God to which nothing is
to be preferred.[4] The assignment challenged his musical, liturgical, and theological training, for his studies
in Rome had coincided with the sessions of the Second
Vatican Council which—among many other things—
authorized the use of the vernacular in liturgical wor-
ship. When the Order of Cistercians of the Strict Observance began the process of changing the latin chant—
antiphons, psalm tones, and hymns hallowed by generations of monks and nuns—into modern languages, the
enormous task of adaptation at Gethsemani Abbey fell to
Father Chrysogonus. Not content simply to translate both
chant and lyrics for the daily office and liturgical cycle
into an american-english idiom, he explored the origins of
early cistercian liturgical practices and traced the twelfth-
century monks' zeal for authentic chant backwards to pre-
cistercian usages. In his zeal for authenticity and accuracy,

2. Bernard of Clairvaux, Ep. 142.1 (Bruno Scott James translation, Letter
151,1; CF 62: 220): Ordo noster abjectio est, humilitas est, voluntaria
paupertas est, obedientia, pax, gaudium in Spiritu sancto. Ordo noster est
esse sub magistro, sub abbate, sub regula, sub disciplina. Ordo noster est
studere silentio, exerceri jejuniis, vigiliis, orationibus, opere manuum; et
super omnia, excellentiorem viam tenere, quae est charitas. . . .
3. Armand Veilleux, abbot of O.L. of Scourmont, Belgium
4. RB 43.3

he asked for and gained permission to scour Europe for manuscripts on early cistercian, and related, liturgies. With dazzling energy, he then edited, keyboarded, and published much of this material in the Cistercian Liturgy Series of books and in numerous articles in the journal he single-handedly produces, *Liturgy OCSO*.

As he delved ever deeper into the patrimony of the Cistercians, he came to know and love the great monks of the 'Golden Age'—the eloquent Bernard of Clairvaux, the erudite William of Saint-Thierry—and no less the twelfth-century 'monks in the stall' known only through the edifying tales of the *Exordium Magnum*, and the thirteenth-century nun-mystics memorialized in *Lives* whose surface piety covers great theological depths. His fascination extended to the life, letters, and thought of the great seventeenth-century reformer, the abbé de Rancé. Neither the first nor the only person to be fascinated by the abbot of la Trappe,[5] Chrysogonus—unlike most of the others—developed a deep attachment to the man to whom most others react with romantic adulation. Those of us who know him best through his annual visits to the Medieval Studies Congress at Kalamazoo would look forward each year to the inevitable and inevitably spirited debate between Father Chrysogonus and Father Louis Lekai, a monk of the Order of Cistercians, a professor at the University of Dallas, and the author of a masterly study on *The Rise of the Strict Observance*. A no-nonsense Hungarian, Fr Lekai tempered his respect for Rancé with patent disapproval of his excessive austerities. The more Father Chrysogonus read the works of Rancé, on the other hand, the greater became his esteem and genuine

5. Henri Bremond, *L'abbé Tempête Armand de Rancé, réformateur de la Trappe*. Paris 1929. ET: *The Thundering Abbot, Armand de Rancé, Reformer of La Trappe*. London 1930. L. J. Lekai, *The Rise of the Cistercian Strict Observance in Seventeenth-century France*. Washington D.C. 1968. A. J. Krailsheimer, *Armand-Jean de Rancé, Abbot of La Trappe : His Influence in the Cloister and the World*. Oxford 1974.

affection for an abbot he regarded as compassionate and lovable.

It was at the Kalamazoo Congress that I first met Father Chrysogonus. He first attended, along with Father Basil Pennington, when I was a lowly graduate student visiting from Toronto. From a respectful distance I observed the first Trappist monks I had ever met—and the last I ever expected to meet—not knowing what to say and not at all sure, despite their obvious humor and informality, that conversation with a young woman would be met with encouragement. When, on the second or third day of the Conference, it came time for this (I was sure) austere and (I knew) learned trappist monk to present his paper, he gathered up a bulky but untidy pile of papers from a tattered briefcase barely capable of containing them. Straightening the straying pages as he approached the podium, he lay them on it and paused as he began speaking to gesture modestly to his audience. Papers flew across the desk and on to the floor. 'Oh dear', he exclaimed, gathering them up in random order. 'Well, it doesn't matter, really. I have only a few simple remarks to make.' And then, without so much as glancing at the hastily recovered but now throughly disorderly pages, he launched into the most compelling twenty-minute presentation I had ever heard.

As years passed and Kalamazoo became a sort of annual family reunion, I discovered—from other 'non-papers' and from conversations—that his knowledge of the history, the members, and the ethos of the Cistercians was both detailed and encyclopaedic. His subjects have ranged from a meticulous catalogue of the night office readings of the early Cistercians to the office propers for Marie d'Oignies at the abbey of Villers; from the 'exploited, forgotten, romanticized' twelfth-century cistercian lay brothers to the seventeenth-century lay sisters in the Constitutions of Port Royale. The eastertide devotions of an unknown fifteenth-century flemish nun intrigued him no less than a brief letter of Stephen Harding, the third abbot of Cîteaux, or the books and voluminous correspondence of Rancé.

In addition to his immense scholarly contributions to our understanding of the cistercian tradition, he has over the years shared his deep love for and unparallel knowledge of that patrimony with young monks and nuns at home and around the world and with students and young scholars. No Congress paper has ever been too abstruse or too inane to elicit a question or a comment from Chrysogonus. His remarks, like his homilies, are always educational and always profound. Many young scholars have been saved from error, and many senior scholars pointed to new interpretations and new sources by his interventions.

The range of subjects covered by his insights is vast and his command of them extensive. Unexpectedly and unpreparedly asked to fill in at a workshop for a visiting scholar who had developed laryngitis, a colleague, John Sommerfeldt, and I once found ourselves facing a size-able and expectant monastic audience with far more time than we had material. 'What are we going to talk about?', I asked an unnervingly calm John, 'What are we going to do to fill all this time?' His answer was as effective as it was simple: 'We're going to ask Chrysogonus a question'.

Nor has his help been confined to conferences. Fairly early in my stint as editor of Cistercian Publications, I faced what seemed to me the daunting task of generating an introduction to translations of the fairly disparate marian sermons of Bernard of Clairvaux and his younger contemporary, Amadeus of Lausanne. The two homily series could not have been more different. The christocentric homilies of Bernard pointed unwaveringly from the Mother of God to her Son. In the mariocentric sermons of Amadeus, the Son's words and actions were referred back to the mother. Between their theologies of Our Lady,

there yawned to my eye the great gulf between scrip-
turally rooted patristic/monastic theology and the senti-
mental and largely unscriptural extravagances of nascent
late medieval piety. As I often would, I turned for counsel
to Chrysogonus. When his introduction arrived, as it did
in short order, it spanned the devotional and ecumenical
void. Prescinding from historical developments and theological sensitivities, his stunning exegesis of the texts of
both preachers rested on a single word:

> Praise. Skip over this word in the general title of
> Bernard's four Marian homilies, and you are off to
> a bad start. *In PRAISE of the Virgin Mother*, we read.
> Praise, then, is what provides the proper focus for
> our reading of these texts; praise is what renders
> the content of these homilies clear and limpid and
> undistorted.

Praise, I have come to realize over the intervening
thirty years, is the very word which best expresses
Chrysogonus' own christian committment. Whether
preaching to his brother monks or exchanging learned
theories with scholars, whether traversing Europe in
search of manuscripts or teaching the rudiments of plain-
song to young monks or unmusical academics, whether
writing learned articles or typing mailing labels for abbey
fruitcakes, he does whatever he does in praise of God.

In searching his own many and varied contributions
to historical, theological, and liturgical scholarship for
an appropriate title for this volume of papers written by
confrères, colleagues, and friends to honor this remarkable monk, I re-discovered—in an article which probably
few people have read about a medieval nun of whom few
have likely even heard—a brief passage which sums up the
cistercian vocation I have come to recognize and respect
in Chrysogonus Waddell.

> Talk about mysticism in any context other than that
> of love and desire of God because God is God, and

you pervert the cistercian experience in its very
essence. *Praise, no less than charity*, is the very form
of cistercian existence. Work at the contemplative
experience in any other context, and you will end
up frantically whirling in ever diminishing circles
around the still point of your own little ego.[6]

E.R.E.

---

6. 'The Inconveniences of Ecstasy', *Hidden Springs. Cistercian Monastic Women*. Kalamazoo 1995. 2:451 (my italics).

One Last Trace of Psalm Prayers?

FOR MANY YEARS, Father Chrysogonus Waddell, in his goodness, has been regularly sending me the always interesting issues of his magazine *Liturgy OCSO*. In addition, I remember having received from him precious documentation on Abelard and the Paraclete.[1] Thus, this Festschrift in his honor is a welcome opportunity to show him my gratitude by dealing once again with a liturgical practice which has interested me for the past thirty years: the silent prayer which the ancient monks offered after each psalm in the Office. Without revisiting the entire question[2] or the dozens of varied witnesses we can glean from the writings of the Fathers[3] I would like to examine one of the last texts in which there still remains a trace of this usage which had once been universal: the

1. Cf. my article 'Échos de Philon dans la Vie de saint Sulpice de Bourges et dans la Règle d'Abélard sur le Paraclet', *Analecta Bollandiana* 103 (1985) 359–365 (see p. 363, n. 32).
2. See our insights in *La Règle de saint Benoît*, vol. V, Sources Chrétiennes 185 (Paris 1971) 577–588; vol. VII (Paris 1977) 206–221; translation: *The Rule of Saint Benedict, A Doctrinal and Spiritual Commentary* CS 54 (Kalamazoo 1983) 139–149.
3. A. de Vogüé, 'Psalmodie et prière. Remarques sur l'office de saint Benoît', *Collectanea Cisterciensia* 44 (1982) 274–292; 'Psalmodier n'est pas prier', *Ecclesia Orans* 6 (1989) 7–32; 'Le psaume et l'oraison. Nouveau florilège', *Ecclesia Orans* 12 (1995) 325–349. The two first articles are reprinted in *Études sur la Règle de saint Benoît. Nouveau Recueil*, Vie monastique 34 (Bellefontaine 1996) 251–275 and 277–303. The third is reprinted in *Regards sur le monachisme des premiers siècles. Recueil d'articles*, Studia Anselmiana 130 (Rome 2000) 855–878.

Life of Saint Benedict of Aniane, written in the first half
of the ninth century by his disciple and friend, Ardo.[4]

We know that the couplet psalm-prayer appeared at
the origins of the monastic Office, as the basic cell of
the entire *opus Dei*, whether celebrated privately or in
common. Each psalm recited or sung was followed by
a period of silence, during which the person who had
recited the psalm drew from his own heart a personal
response to the Word of God heard in the sacred text;
the latter often offered the monk a formula or model
of prayer ready to be repeated or imitated. But human
weakness and 'abhorrence of the void' made this silent
prayer particularly vulnerable. In fact, it would disappear
completely by the end of three or four centuries, with
the result that the choral office came be reduced to a
simple succession of psalms recited one after the other,
as we have known and practiced it until timid efforts at
restoration in recent years.

This decline of postpsalmic prayer can be glimpsed as
early as the beginning of the sixth century, when the
Rule of Saint Benedict is much less explicit about it than
was the Rule of the Master, so much so that one may
even doubt that it was still practiced at Monte Cassino.[5]
At the end of this century, it is true, Columban clearly
attests that each psalm of the office was followed by
the prostration characteristic of prayer, but the details
he provides on this subject clearly show the diminution
and deformation psalm prayer had undergone: instead of
being a spontaneous prayer, comparable in length to the

4. *Vita Benedicti Abbatis Anianensis et Indensis auctore Ardone*, ed. G. Waitz (*MGH,
Scriptorum*, XV/I:200–220 (Hannover 1887). A translation by Allen Cabaniss,
The Emperor's Monk, was published in England in 1979 (Il Francombe, Devon:
Stockwell). The passage which interests us here (*Vita* 38, p. 216, 21–37) is
reproduced in *Corpus Consuetudinum Monasticarum*, ed. K. Hallinger (Siegburg
1963) 1:313, 19–315, 4. See also PL 103:378 B-379 A (*Vita* 52). We will
quote the *Corpus* from now on.
5. See *La Règle de saint Benoît*, vol. 5:577–588, as well as 'Le psaume et
l'oraison' (above, note 3), 280–289.

psalm, it now consisted only in repeating quietly three times the verse *Deus in adiutorium meum intende, Domine ad adiuuandum me festina*.[6] A little later, Columban's disciple, Donatus of Besançon reproduces this prescription of the Master, but with a significant omission: instead of being recited three times (*ter*), the *Deus in adiutorium* is said only once.[7] Visibly, psalm prayer was dying. It will come as no surprise that we hear nothing more of it.

Thus, in the first half of the seventh century, when Donatus wrote his Rule for the nuns of Jussa Moutier, the gallic monasticism renewed by Columban was preparing to abandon a practice which had originally been the essential act of the office, the very thing which made of it a word addressed to God, a prayer. However, in Spain at the same time, the Rules of Isidore and of Fructuosus still required a prostration after each psalm, and this moment where one 'adores' as Isidore says,[8] is followed in Fructuosus' Rule by another moment where each one 'prays' standing, with hands lifted towards heaven.[9]

Returning to Gaul, let us see how, two centuries later, Benedict of Aniane kept a faint trace of these prayers after the psalms. This vestige is found, not in

---

6. Columban, *Reg. coen.* 9, in *Sancti Columbani Opera*, ed. G.S.M. Walker, *Scriptores Latini Hiberniae* 2:158, 13–21(Dublin 1957). Cf. Saint Colomban, *Règles et pénitentiels monastiques*, ed. A. de Vogüé, *Vie monastique* 20 (Bellefontaine 1989) 130–131 (*Reg. coen.* 9, 9–13). Columban quotes Psalm 69:2.

7. Donatus, *Reg. uirg.* 34, 7–8. See A. de Vogüé, 'La Règle de Donat pour l'abbesse Gauthstrude', *Benedictina* 25 (1978) 219–313, especially p. 274.

8. Isidore, *Reg.* 6, 181–184: *post consummationem singulorum psalmorum prostrati omnes humo pariter adorabunt, celeriterque surgentes psalmos sequentes incipiant.* See *San Leandro, San Isidoro, San Fructuoso, Reglas monásticas de la España visigoda*, ed. J. Campos Ruiz-I. Roca Melia, *BAC, Santos Padres Españoles* (Madrid 1971) 2:100–101.

9. Fructuosus, *Reg.* 2, 68–73, Campos, 140–141: *Sane in omnibus horarum singularum orationibus nocturno ac diurno tempore ad omnem psalmorum finem gloriam canentes Domino prosternantur in terram, eo scilicet ordine ut nemo prius seniore aut incuruetur aut iterum surgat, sed omnes summa aequitate consurgant extensisque ad caelum palmis orando persistunt sicut et aequaliter merguntur.* Cf. Cassian, *Inst.* 2.7.2–3.

the communal office, but in the private psalmody which precedes the nocturns. Each monk was to recite fifteen psalms privately before the office proper began. To this end, three successive signals were given at the end of the night: first a loud bell (scilla) was sounded in the dormitory to wake the brethren; then a bell (signum) announced to the guests that the church doors were open to them; finally a third signal marked the beginning of the choral office, intoned by the hebdomadary priest.[10]

The private recitation of the fifteen psalms took place in silence between the second and third signals. As soon as they had risen, the brothers entered the church and after signing themselves with holy water, they visited all the altars 'humbly and with reverence'. That done, each went to his place in choir, where he recited 'secretly' the psalms prescribed before the office. This preliminary psalmody was not to be performed in any corner of the church whose doors had just been opened to seculars. It was 'seated in choir' that the monks said their fifteen psalms, before standing at the third signal to await the intonation of the priest who was presiding the Office.[11]

This is how Ardo describes the custom instituted by Benedict of Aniane:[12]

10. Ardo, *Vita Benedicti Anianensis* 38 = *Ordo diurnus Anianensis*, in CCM 1:313, 19–314, 9.

11. *V. Ben. An.* 38; CCM 1:314, 5–7: *sintque parati ut, cum tertium pulsauerit signum, absque mora surgentes* (cf. RB 22.6) *adtonitis auribus* (cf. RB Prol. 9) *sacerdotem expectent, qui officium incipiendi sortitus est.* Ardo applies to a choir movement (seated, the monks rise) what Benedict said about rising in the dormitory (RB 22.6), and he transposes into this liturgical context (silence before the intonation of the nocturns) Benedict's invitation to listen to the Word of God transmitted by the Rule (*RB* Prol. 9). After this *adtonitis auribus audiamus* Benedict's Prologue quotes a verse of Psalm 94, which is the Invitatory of the night office (RB Prol. 10, quoting Ps 94:8 *Hodie si uocem eius audieritis, nolite obdurare corda uestra*; cf. RB 9.3 which places Ps 94 at the beginning of nocturns).

12. CCM 1:314, 10 -315, 4: *Psalmos autem cantare iussit quinque pro omnibus fidelibus in toto terrarum orbe uiuis, quinque etiam pro omnibus fidelibus defunctis; pro eis quoque qui nuper defuncti sunt, quia ad noticiam singulorum non statim causa*

He prescribed five psalms to be sung for all the faithful living on the whole earth, and five also for all the faithful departed. In addition, for those who have died recently and whose departure has not yet been made known to all, he established that five psalms would also be sung perpetually.

After reciting five psalms, one should prostrate to pray, recommending to God those for whom one has prayed, and only then does one begin again [to sing psalms] to intercede in favour of other souls. Laziness must not prevent anyone from supplicating the Eternal King, prostrate on the ground, after the number of psalms fixed by the rule, since we do not fear bowing our heads at every word before powerful men, and especially because by doing this we provoke divine grace and arouse fervent compunction.

Ardo does not say from which part of the psalter these three groups of five psalms recited in turn for all the living, all the dead, and those who have just died, are taken. We might think of the only set of fifteen consecutive psalms in the Psalter, namely Psalms 119–133, each of which bears the title 'Song of Ascents' (*Canticum graduum*). Almost all of them are very short— only Psalm 131 is slightly longer—and they would be very suitable for a supplementary recitation, not adding much to the choral psalmody. Moreover, the third group of five psalms, those recited for the recently deceased, would begin with the *De profundis* (Ps 129), which seems highly appropriate.

In fact, however, and despite the name *Psalmi graduales*

peruenit, ut iugiter canerentur instituit nichilominus quinque. Decursos uero psalmos quinque, pronus orationi incumbat, eos pro quibus cecinit deo commendans, et tunc demum pro aliis rogaturus initium sumat. Nec pigritandum est pro certis defixisque psalmodiis aeterno regi dimerso in terra corpore supplicare, cum potentibus ad singula uerba non reuereatur quis inflectere caput, maximeque quia hoc modo gratia prouocetur diuina et compunctionis suscitetur feruor.

given here and there to the fifteen psalms recited before the nocturns,[13] it is not these 'Songs of Ascents' which Benedict of Aniane and his biographer seem to have in mind, but a discontinuous series of psalms taken from here and there. A list of them is given by several documents of the carolingian reform, particularly by the 'Collection of Saint Martial of Limoges', which gives the following incipits:[14]

76.	Miserere mei deus secundum	Ps	50
	Deus in nomine tuo		53
	Miserere mei deus miserere		56
	Deus misereatur nostri		66
	Deus in adiutorium meum		69
77.	Verba mea		5
	Domine ne in furore tuo		6
	Dilexi quoniam		115
	Credidi		116
	De profundis		129
78.	Dominus regit me		22
	Ad te domine leuaui		24
	Dominus illuminatio mea		26
	Domine exaudi II		142
	Lauda anima mea dominum		145

As for the prescription to pray after each group of psalms, this rubric—which is of chief interest to us here—leads to several observations. Let us note first that Ardo uses an expression from the Benedictine Rule. *Pronus orationi incumbat* recalls an 'instrument of good works' of the Master and Benedict: *Orationi frequenter incumbere.*[15] Here, as in the two sixth-century Rules, we

13. See for example the notes in CCM 1:314, 9 and 561, 18–29.
14. *Collectio Sancti Martialis Lemovicensis* 76–78; CCM 1:561. After the first five psalms (76), another is said *pro rege specialiter*. This is Psalm 19 (*Exaudiat te dominus*).
15. RM 3:62 = RB 4:55. See our article '*Orationi frequenter incumbere*. Une invitation à la prière continuelle', in RAM 41 (1965) 467–472. Translated in *Cistercian Studies Quarterly* 20 (1986) 29–45.

have translated *incumbere* by 'prostrating oneself'. The latin verb does not always have this concrete meaning, it is true, and Cæsarius of Arles, a contemporary of Benedict and the Master, clearly uses it at least on two occasions to mean 'to devote oneself to'.[16] But here we cannot doubt that it means to prostrate oneself, as is demonstrated first by the adjective *pronus* which accompanies *incumbere*, then by the justification which the legislator felt he had to add to gain acceptance for the tiring gymnastics: it is 'with our body lying on the ground' (*dimenso in terram corpore*) that we must 'make supplication to the eternal king'.

We will speak later about the objections which this insistence on the obligation to prostrate supposes. But first, let us take note of the main point which most interests us: the prayer comes not after each psalm, but only at the end of each group of five psalms. The original observance, which said a constant alternation of psalm and prayer, is therefore represented only by a vestige: the psalmody remains intact, but the silent prayer has been reduced to one-fifth of what it had been. An enormous disproportion exists where there had been equality between the two elements. The psalms have devoured prayer.

Moreover, this vestige of postpsalmic prayer remains no longer within the community's Office, but only in the framework of the semi-private practice of the recitation of the fifteen psalms before Nocturns. And what is more, prayer here does not have the free and spontaneous character prayer earlier had, aroused by the psalm one had just recited and more or less inspired by it. Now, it becomes a matter of praying for a very specific intention: for the living, then for the dead, and finally for the recently departed. Like the psalmody which precedes it, this prayer

---

16. Cæsarius, *Ep.* '*Vereor*' (PL 67:1132 C: *lectioni et meditationi . . . incumbere*); *Serm.* 184.6 (CCL 104:751 [711, 5–6]): *ieiuniis et orationibus frequenter incumbat*. The letter '*Coegisti*', which I quoted in SCh 181:461 (*Ep.* I, PL 67:1128 A) is not authentic.

is directed to a specific end. This obligatory intention is the only element which unites the five psalms with the subsequent prayer. Without any intrinsic relationship to the texts just recited, silent prayer crowns only the act of pious charity towards the living or the dead which this recitation was intended to be.

Let us move on to the phrases which indicate a certain repugnance to practicing this prayer, however truncated. From the very first phrase about it, the words *tunc demum* rule out one temptation: the brother who has said his first five psalms is tempted to continue immediately with the next five without pausing to pray, and he must be reminded that it is 'only' after prayer that he may continue the psalmody. One of the reasons for this temptation, and perhaps the main one, is revealed immediately afterwards: 'laziness' which resists the great movement of prostration which prayer requires.

The same instinctive repugnance to prayer, particularly because of the physical exercise which it supposes, had shown up already two centuries previously in the insistent prescriptions of several monastic legislators: Columban, Isidore, and Fructuosus all agree in specifying that *all* must prostrate, *every* day, at *every* Office, at the end of *each* psalm, and Columban adds that this must be done 'cheerfully and willingly' (*aequo animo*).[17]

To this physical lassitude which Cæsarius and Columban took into account in their exhortations,[18] one can surely add intellectual poverty which renders difficult prayer not undergirded by formulas. Reciting psalms one knows by

17. Columban, *Reg. coen.* 9.9–11: *In commune autem omnes fratres omnibus diebus ac noctibus tempore orationum in fine omnium psalmorum genua in oratione, si non infirmitas corporis offecerit, flectere aequo animo debent, sub silentio dicentes: Deus in adiutorium meum intende, domine ad adiuuandum me festina. Quem uersiculum postquam ter in oratione tacite decantauerint, aequaliter a flexione orationis surgant.* . . . Isidore and Fructuosus: see notes 8 and 9 above.

18. Cæsarius, *Serm.* 76, 1 and 77, 1: 'If one cannot kneel, let him bend down'; Columban, *Reg. coen.* 9.9: *si non infirmitas corporis offecerit* (see previous note).

heart requires little effort. Producing a request is more demanding, especially if supplication is prolonged.

Coming back to the physical act of prostrating, let us note that Cassian mentioned another kind of laziness in this regard: after the effort required to prostrate on the ground, the brothers are tempted to remain in this position as long as possible and to doze off.[19] Hence the prescription that all rise together at the presider's signal, which was already formulated in the Rule of Pachomius and will be found in Benedict's.[20]

Let us conclude our examination of Ardo's text by observing that, when he compares prayer directed to God with a conversation where one addresses a 'powerful' man, he also reminds us of the Benedictine Rule.[21] Once again we think of Benedict of Nursia when we hear of the 'divine grace' that another Benedict, of Aniane, hoped to 'provoke' by the prostrate monk's humble supplication in this remark about prayer: an 'inspiration of divine grace' which prolongs prayer, also envisioned by the Rule.[22] It is true that Ardo might have been thinking of the graces given by God to those for whom the monk is praying—the living and the dead—but what follows indicates instead that he had in mind a grace of prayer similar to that mentioned in the Rule: his 'provoke divine grace' parallels 'arouse the fervor of compunction'.

This last phrase—*compunctionis suscitetur fervor*—in its turn evokes the 'tears of compunction' thanks to which the monk's prayer is heard, according to the Rule.[23] The 'fervor' which Ardo associated with compunction, Bene-

---

19. Cassian, *Inst.* 2.7.2–3.

20. Pachomius, *Praec.* 6; RB 20.5.

21. RB 20.1–2: *Si cum hominibus potentibus uolumus aliqua suggerere, non praesumimus nisi cum humilitate et reuerentia, quanto magis Domino Deo universorum cum omni humilitate et puritatis deuotione supplicandum est.*

22. RB 20.4: *nisi forte ex affectu inspirationis diuinae gratiae protendatur.*

23. RB 20.3: *in puritate cordis et conpunctione lacrimarum nos exaudiri sciamus.* Cf. RB 49.4: during Lent one practices 'compunction of heart'.

dict of Nursia did not connect especially to compunction
or to prayer,[24] but *feruor* and *compunctio*, as well as the
verbs and adjectives related to these two nouns, are found
together more than once in Cassian's writings on prayer.[25]

So it is that a material prescription—to prostrate
three times during the private psalmody preceding the
nocturns—brings Ardo, the spokesman for Benedict of
Aniane, to open limitless spiritual perspectives: those of
divine grace and of the fervor which grace arouses in the
hearts of persons touched by compunction. The vestige
of psalm prayer preserved here causes the experiences
described by Cassian in his most beautiful passages on
prayer to reappear for a moment. This passing remark
provides a glimpse of all that monasticism and the Church
lost when they gave up praying between the psalms, which
were henceforth recited one after the other without
interruption, under the pretext that they are themselves
a prayer and that it is enough to 'pray the psalms'.

To conclude, we would like to situate Ardo's witness
within the framework of contemporary documents by
comparing it to two practices attested at the same period:
recitation of the psalms not followed by prayer; and processions where everyone pauses to pray after psalmody.

By prescribing prayer after each group of five psalms,
the legislation related by Ardo differs from several *ordines*
which do not mention this silent prayer. The *Collection
of Saint Martial of Limoges*, from which we reproduced
above the list of fifteen psalms, requires only that one
'sing' these psalms—before Prime in summer, 'after
the interval' in winter—and says nothing about any
prayer which might conclude each group of five.[26] Is

---

24. RB 1.3: *conuersationis feruore nouicio*; 66.3: *cum feruore caritatis*.
25. Cassian, *Conl.* 9.15.1 (*feruentissime*) and 3 (*compungitur*); 9.26.1 (*compunc-
tionum; feruentissimas*) and 2 (*feruoris . . . conpunctionem*). 'Fervor' in prayer:
Cassian, *Inst.* 2.10.1 and 3; 'compunction': *Conl.* 9.27.1 and 28.1; 10.11.4.
26. CCM 1:561. The word 'to sing' *(canantur)*, which this text uses three
times, does not mean that the psalmody has become collective or public,

this omission simply editorial—it was not necessary to mention prayer—or does it mean that they did not, in fact, stop to pray?

The same paralipsis of *oratio* is observed in the *Ordo officii* collected by the famous Monte-Cassino manuscript 175 (tenth century). There, in a different form,[27] we find psalmody for the deceased and the living, but nothing is said about prayer which may have followed the psalms.

Similarly, the nuns' *Memoriale Qualiter* of the twelfth-century Montpellier manuscript H 85 contains seven psalms to be recited: three psalms for the deceased, two for the abbess and community, and two for whomever one wishes, but these seven penitential psalms apparently succeed one other without interruption.[28] A prayer was said by each sister when she entered the church, before taking her place in choir where she recited the seven psalms,[29] but these do not seem to have been punctuated by prayers. Later on, there is no further mention of prayers with regard to the fifteen psalms, also divided into three groups, which the nuns added during the summer.[30]

Once again, we may ask ourselves whether these silences about psalmic prayer mean its real disappearance or whether they occur simply because of the concise composition of the text. In either case, they make us appreciate

---

because Ardo similarly says that Benedict of Aniane had the fifteen psalms, which are certainly said privately, 'sung' (*cantare*) before Nocturns. *Cantare* is the verb used for every recitation of the psalms, even quietly. Cf. Columban *Reg. coen.* 9.11: *Quem uersiculum (Deus in adiutorium) postquam ter in oratione tacite decantauerint. . . .*

27. *Ordo Cassinensis* II; CCM 1:123: at each hour, psalm 50 is said for the deceased, psalm 69 for the living, psalm 129 for the Empress, and so on.

28. *Memoriale Qualiter* II.1; CCM 1:267, 30–35 (added text).

29. *Ibid.*, p. 267, 18–29 (ancient text) and 267, 35–268, 6 (added text).

30. *Memoriale Qualiter* II.4; CCM I:273, 7–13 (added text). Nothing about prayer address in *Synodi secundae Aquisgranensis decr.* (817), 12 and *Regula S. Benedicti Anianensis* 43 (CCM 1:475 and 528), which prescribe *psalmi speciales*, but these are only mentioned, too briefly for the absence of prayers to be significant.

the explicit and insistent witness of Benedict of Aniane's biographer.

In line with his indications, let us finally note the beautiful description of the *Circuitus orationum* with which Angilbert, abbot of Saint-Riquier ends his *Institutio*.[31] This was a procession made every day after Vespers. When the brothers had sung Vespers in the church of Saint-Riquier, they went in procession to the sanctuary of the Passion, singing psalms. There, after a prayer, they divided into two choirs. One went to the sanctuary of the Resurrection, the other to the sanctuary of the Ascension. Another prayer followed, and the procession continued *psallendo et orando*, as the text says three times about the various routes taken according to the day.[32] The itinerary varied, but the procedure was always the same: psalmody while walking, then a pause to pray when the holy place had been reached.

This alternation of sung psalmody while walking and prayers for which one stopped and remained motionless reminds us of the Rule of the Master. In a chapter on the celebration of the Office during travel, it prescribed that the travelling brothers 'walk with a psalm', then 'stop awhile to pray, with head bowed'.[33] Nothing suggests that Angilbert was remembering the Rule of the Master, but the same instinct, guided by tradition, led him to join psalmody to walking in procession and prayer to standing before an altar. Between the psalmody and the prayers which punctuated it, there is a kind of hierarchy. While singing psalms, one can do something else—walk, in this case—but when it comes to praying to God, one must suspend every other occupation and give oneself

---

31. *Institutio Angilberti Centulensis* 17; CCM 1:302–303. The date is around 800 (*Ibid.*, p. 288–289).
32. CCM 1:302, 17 and 34; 303, 9.
33. *RM* 56, 1–10, *SC* 106, p. 262–264; *The Rule of the Master*, CS 6 (Kalamazoo 1977) 221–222.

completely to this supreme act which mobilizes the whole person.

Singing psalmody while walking: the pairing of these two actions resembles the pairing of scriptural 'meditation' and manual labor, to which monks consecrate a large portion of their time. For the ancient monks, psalmody was, in a special form, a continuation of what they did all day long: recite texts of Scripture. First, they recite the Bible during the hours of *lectio*, to memorize it, then one does so during the hours of work, to continue hearing the Word of God. Let us remember the young Theodore, disciple of Pachomius, whom the Bohairic *Vita Pachomii* pictures for us this way[34] at the beginning of his monastic life: 'One day—it was the first year—Theodore was sitting in his cell, braiding ropes and reciting passages of Holy Scripture he had learned by heart; each time his heart prompted him, he would stand up and pray.'

Recitation while working and psalmody while walking: these two combinations are analogous. In both, the divine voice heard in the recitation or the psalmody calls for the response of prayer, for which from time to time one abandons every other task.

Coming back to our texts by Angilbert and Ardo, we may conclude that the alternation of psalmody and prayer of which they speak is an evident vestige of the primitive structure of the Offices. Thanks to a particular rite, at the monastery of Saint-Riquier the carolingian period also preserved what had been general usage in antiquity. Shortly before Benedict of Aniane, Angilbert is one of the final witnesses to the pairing of *psalmus-oratio*. What the abbot of Centula (Saint-Riquier) has his monks do together after Vespers, the abbot of Aniane will prescribe they do individually before Nocturns. In

---

34. L. Th. Lefort, *Les Vies coptes de saint Pachôme et de ses premiers successeurs* (Louvain 1943) p. 105, 9–12 (Bo 34); A. Veilleux, *Pachomian Koinonia*, vol. I (Kalamazoo 1980) p. 58.

both cases, the originally universal norm survives in some way in a special system, whereas current usage almost everywhere dissociates these two acts originally destined to be united without merging: psalmody and prayer.

La liturgie et le récit. L'exemple
du Grand Exorde de Cîteaux[*]

PLUS QUE LA DIFFUSION, la réception d'une œuvre médiévale, qu'elle soit d'ordre littéraire, technique, etc. est essentielle pour en comprendre la portée mais également pour saisir les motivations de son rédacteur. L'oeuvre qui relate les «grands débuts cisterciens» n'échappe pas à cette question.[1] Lorsque Conrad, moine de l'abbaye rhénane d'Eberbach, rédige son *Exordium magnum cisterciense* dans les années 1190–1210, son but est autant de fixer les débuts prestigieux de l'ordre cistercien que de répondre à tous les ennemis des moines blancs.[2] Pour cela, Conrad fait oeuvre de compilation en s'inspirant fortement de toute une tradition littéraire cistercienne antérieure (*Petit Exorde*, *Liber miraculorum* d'Herbert de Clairvaux . . .) sur laquelle il applique le riche fonds de sa culture biblique et profane.[3]

---

[*] Jacques Berlioz (CNRS, Lyon) et le Fr. Placide Vernet (Abbaye de Cîteaux) m'ont, chacun dans leur domaine, apporté une aide précieuse: qu'ils lisent ici l'expression de mes remerciements amicaux.

1. Voir Brian P. McGuire, «Introduction», dans Conrad d'Eberbach, *Le Grand Exorde de Cîteaux ou Récit des débuts de l'ordre cistercien*, Jacques Berlioz (dir.) *et alii* (Turnhout: Brepols-Cîteaux: *Commentarii cisterciense*, 1998), xxxv + 556 pages. Lorsque sera cité désormais *Le Grand Exorde de Cîteaux*, éd. cit., je fais référence à la traduction française citée ci-dessus; *Exordium magnum cisterciense . . .* , éd. cit., renvoie à la réédition du texte latin de Bruno Griesser (1960) CCCM, 138 (Turnhout, Brepols, 1994) [édition parue en fait en 1998].

2. *Ibid.*, p. XI.

3. Sur cette question, cf. Placide Vernet, «Les sources de Conrad d'Eberbach», dans *Le Grand Exorde de Cîteaux*, pp. 405–409 (*supra* n. 1).

S'il ne faut pas oublier de mentionner à côté de ces sources classiques, la place importante de la tradition orale dans la rédaction de cet ouvrage, l'influence de la liturgie, de ses textes, de ses rituels a marqué de son empreinte le fonds même du récit.[4] À relire l'ensemble du texte, de nombreuses références intéressent les rituels —baptême, confession, mariage, funérailles; les acteurs de la liturgie—prêtres, curés de paroisse, sacristains, chantres; les objets—cloches, habits, livres; ou bien encore les lieux de la liturgie—autel, chapelle, cimetière, cloître, pupitre, stalle. Même si ceci n'est pas pour étonner—l'auteur est un cistercien qui écrit dans un cadre monastique, pour des lecteurs imprégnés d'une culture liturgique qu'ils vivent (ou sont censés vivre) quotidiennement—il convient tout de même de signaler et de s'arrêter sur l'importance et la place que le *Grand Exorde de Cîteaux* laisse à la liturgie, dans ses objets, ses pratiques, ses rituels et ses textes. Schématiquement, les éléments liturgiques sont de quatre ordres:

1) les mentions touchant au calendrier et à l'organisation du temps liturgique;
2) celles portant sur les rituels liturgiques: offices, messes, sacrements, processions.
3) les termes faisant référence aux objets, à l'architecture, aux vêtements liturgiques: ce que l'on pourrait rassembler sous la désignation d'«environnement liturgique»;
4) les citations liturgiques: oraisons, antiennes, bénédictions, péricopes bibliques, etc.

Partant de cette constatation, il faut poser la question de la fonction, du rôle, qu'occupent ces nombreux

---

4. Récemment, Chrysogonus Waddell a donné une étude sur la liturgie cistercienne médiévale dans le cadre des 54e rencontre session de la Société française d'études mariales (Orval, 1998) Ê: «La Vierge Marie dans la liturgie cistercienne au XIIe siècle», dans Jean Longère (dir.), *La vierge dans la tradition cistercienne* (Paris: Médiaspaul-Études mariales, 1999) 348 pages, spéc. pp. 123–136.

éléments liturgiques qui émaillent le *Grand Exorde de Cîteaux*. Pourquoi citer tel ou tel *incipit* liturgique dans le cours du texte? Comment interpréter l'utilisation—volontaire ou non?—d'expressions liturgiques dans le travail d'écriture? Les pièces liturgiques cités, les vêtements, les objets, les gestes liturgiques décrits, apportent-ils réellement une connaissance nouvelle de ces rituels en question? Quel est le rôle, la fonction, de ces textes, mais aussi de ces rituels décrits avec soin? Peut-on connaître, peut-on approcher la réalité liturgique cistercienne vécue à la fin du XIIe siècle par la lecture et l'étude du *Grand Exorde de Cîteaux*? Ce dernier est-il le «miroir littéraire» d'une liturgie cistercienne présentée et codifiée dans les *Ecclesiastica officia*[5] de quelques années son aîné (1185–1186) ou plus généralement dans le manuscrit-type[6] cistercien donnant l'ensemble de la liturgie de l'ordre cistercien et rédigé dans les années 1173–1191? Peut-on aller jusqu'à interpréter le *Grand Exorde de Cîteaux* comme un des instruments de cette réforme liturgique qui se met en place dans le dernier tiers du XIIe siècle?

Pour se construire, le récit impose à son auteur de rassembler pour sa rédaction l'ensemble des sources qui sont à sa disposition. Nombre d'entre elles—sans que ceci soit exclusif—proviennent du domaine liturgique: que ce soit les citations textuelles annoncées et données comme telles, les références aux pièces liturgiques plus diffuses ou bien encore l'ensemble des rituels. Pour ma part, je pense que ces éléments liturgiques servent un but. En effet, s'ils permettent, par leur emploi constant,

---

5. Danièle Choisselet et Placide Vernet (éd.), *Les Ecclesiastica officia cisterciens du XIIe siècle*, La documentation cistercienne, 22 (Reiningue: Abbaye d'Œlenberg, 1989) 623 pages (désormais cité *Ecclesiastica officia*). Cette date (1185–1186) est la date retenue par les éditeurs des Ecclesiastica officia d'après le manuscrit de base: Dijon, Bibl. mun. MS 114; cf. *Ibid.*, pp. 49–50.
6. Sur le Dijon, Bibl. mun., MS 114 (écrit entre 1173 et 1191), cf. DACL, III/2 (Paris: Letouzey & Ané, 1914) col. 1784–1785 et Philippe Guignard, *Les monuments primitifs de la règle cistercienne publiés d'après les manuscrits de l'abbaye de Cîteaux* (Dijon, 1878).

la lente et patiente construction de l'oeuvre, tous ces éléments (pièces, rituels . . .) donnent une véritable identité cistercienne au récit. En se les appropriant, le *Grand Exorde* peut alors être perçu comme un enseignement vrai et acquérir ainsi une réelle légitimité et une dimension historique authentique aux yeux de ses lecteurs. Il s'agit alors de repérer et de comprendre maintenant les différentes citations textuelles données comme telles, c'est-à-dire annoncées dans le cours du récit; en second lieu, d'analyser quelques références employées de manière plus diffuse dans le *Grand Exorde de Cîteaux*.[7]

DU BON USAGE DES CITATIONS LITURGIQUES

Peu nombreuses (une vingtaine), les pièces explicitement citées sont représentatives, pour chacune d'entre elles des différents types de textes qui sont soit chantés, soit lus à la messe et/ou à l'office. On y relève des mentions d'hymnes, de psaumes, de répons, d'antiennes . . . ou bien encore des pièces moins caractéristiques d'une solennité, comme les *Pater noster*, *Gloria patri*, *Alleluia*. Le tableau n° 1 (cf. Annexe ci-après) permet de repérer quelles sont ces pièces, leur emplacement dans le récit mais aussi dans leur emploi dans le cadre de la liturgie cistercienne.

Lorsqu'il désire rapporter la fin du maître des novices de la maison de Grandselve (II.24), Conrad d'Eberbach construit son récit à l'aide de citations choisies fort justement en relation avec le calendrier et la liturgie du moment. Les derniers jours précédant sa mort, l'acteur principal se plaît à invoquer Dieu en le priant de bientôt lui permettre de le rejoindre:

Ce vieillard, comme un soldat émérite qui a beaucoup combattu, commença de penser au repos de

---

7. Il faut rendre ici hommage au Fr. Placide Vernet qui a repéré nombre de ces citations discrètes dans le *Grand Exorde de Cîteaux*.

l'éternelle félicité; n'ayant plus que mépris pour
toutes les choses du monde et de la chair, il soupirait
du plus profond de son cœur vers la bienheureuse
présence du Christ notre Seigneur, et souhaitait
ardemment de se dissoudre pour être avec lui, car
c'est de beaucoup le meilleur. Pendant qu'il subissait
l'assaut douloureux de ce désir spirituel et qu'il di-
sait chaque jour dans ses oraisons: 'Quand viendrai-
je et paraîtrai-je devant la face de Dieu?' [Ps. 41:
3], survint le jour sacré de la Cène du Seigneur;
selon la coutume, la communauté devait s'approcher
solennellement de la table sainte pour participer au
sacrement de vie. (II.24, 7–8).

L'insertion du verset psalmique (Ps 41:3) à ce moment
là du récit n'est pas innocente. Non seulement ce Ps
41:3 est tout à fait désigné pour signifier le désir de
rejoindre l'au-delà (*Quando veniam et apparebo ante faciem
Dei?*), mais il s'inscrit également dans la tradition de
la liturgie pascale occidentale. Ce passage est en effet
communément employé dans la liturgie du Samedi Saint
depuis les VIIIe–IXe siècles.[8] La liturgie cistercienne suit
le même usage.[9] Le choix de ce verset psalmique à cet
endroit répond à un double sens: liturgique puisqu'il
reprend un texte de la liturgie pascale, mais également
théologique, puisque la Pâques, c'est avant tout le passage
vers l'au-delà. Choisir ce texte pour évoquer sa propre
mort à venir inscrit la mort du maître des novices dans le
schéma classique de la mort du saint, qu'une seule issue,
forcément heureuse, vient couronner. L'aboutissement
de cet épisode trouve son dénouement dans ce même
temps pascal puisque la mort du maître survient le Samedi

8. René-Jean Hesbert, *Antiphonale missarum sextuplex* (Bruxelles: Vromant et
Cie, 1935) CXXVI + 256 pages (désormais abrégé *Sextuplex*), spéc. 79b,
pp. 98–99: *Sicut cervus desiderat ad fontes aquarum ita desiderat anima me ad te
Deus. Sitivit anima mea ad Deum usum quando veniam et apparebo ante faciem dei
mei [. . .] (Ps 41) [C'est moi qui souligne]*.
9. Dijon, Bibl. mun., MS 114, fol. 132vc (*Sicut cervus . . .*).

Saint. Si ce texte (Ps 41:3) provient bien de la liturgie
cistercienne pascale, il n'en va pas de même de la prière
qu'adressat le Jeudi Saint le mourant au moment de
recevoir «l'hostie salutaire» (II.24, 10):

> Seigneur Jésus-Christ, Fils du Dieu vivant, Sauveur
> du genre humain, tu as daigné prendre dans le sein
> de l'immaculée et intacte Vierge Marie, pour nous
> pécheurs, cette chair très pure et très innocente
> que j'ai osé recevoir malgré mon indignité; si la
> requête de ton pauvre petit serviteur ne te déplaît
> pas, je prie et je supplie ta clémente bonté de ne plus
> jamais permettre que le pain de la terre ou aucune
> substance terrestre passe par mon gosier où je dois
> faire passer maintenant la nourriture céleste, le pain
> de la vie éternelle.[10]

En effet, si elle ne semble pas être issue du répertoire
liturgique cistercien mais relève plutôt d'une composition personnelle, on peut y trouver une forte con-
notation cistercienne dans sa construction. Si l'*incipit*
Domine Jesu Christe, fili Dei vivi n'est pas une formule
très répandue dans le répertoire des grandes traditions
liturgiques occidentales,[11] il convient cependant de le rap-
procher d'une oraison issue de l'*ordo* de la messe que les

---

10. *Exordium magnum cisterciense*, Lib. II.24, l. 46–55: *Domine Jesu Christe, fili
Dei vivi, salvator generis humani, qui hanc purissimam et innocentissimam carnem,
quam indignus sumere praesumpsi, ex immaculatae et intemeratae Mariae virginis utero
pro nobis peccatoribus sumere dignatus es, si tibi non displicet ista petitio qualiscumque
servuli tui, precor et supplico pietatis tuae clementiam, quatenus per meatum gutturis
huius, per quod nunc cibum caelestem, panem vitae aeternae traicere debeo, terrenum
panem seu quamcumque aliam terrenam substantiam de cetero nullo modo transire
permittas.*
11. Une recherche dans les différentes traditions des grands sacramentaires
occidentaux confirme la relative rareté de cet *incipit*. On le trouve employé
à deux occasions pour une oraison. La première, pour la bénédiction du
feu nouveau à Pâques: *Domine Iesu Christe, fili Dei vivi, qui hodierna die pro
salute nostra crucis passionem sustinuisti nosque tua temporali morte a vinculis nostris
perpetue liberans misericorditer aripuisti, adesto nunc, quaesumus, nostris affectibus
et tua gratuita bonitate benedicere et sanctificare hujus ignis incrementa dignare, ut
nobis qui eum nunc in nomine tuo secuturi sumus atque omnibus in te sperantibus,
fugato demoniaco fantasmate, lumen et calorem saluberrimum infundat. Per.* (Il m'est

Ecclesiastica officia du XIIe siècle décrivent,[12] oraison que le
prêtre doit prononcer avant la communion. Alors que le
maître des novices est en train de mourir et que son seul
souhait est de goûter le corps du Christ, l'emploi de cette
formule de la liturgie de la messe pour faire débuter la
prière de l'acteur principal permet à Conrad d'Eberbach
de rappeler le parallèle classique entre viatique et communion et de rattacher en même temps son récit à une
quotidienneté vécue par l'ensemble de la communauté
cistercienne.

Les deux exemples suivants renforcent cette idée d'une
narration puisant ses sources dans le terreau du rit cistercien. Lorsqu'aux confins du Danemark et de la Saxe, un
saint moine parvient à l'heure de la mort, c'est tout le
rituel de la *commendatio animae* qui est décrit avec soin.[13]
Dans un dernier souffle, le mourant entonne l'antienne
Subvenite sancti dei[14] qui, selon les *Ecclesiastica officia*, doit

agréable de saluer ici la mémoire du Rd P. Robert Amiet [† 23 janvier 2000]
qui m'a donné ce texte.) R. Amiet, *La veillée pascale dans l'Église latine*. I.
Le rite romain, coll. Liturgie, n° 11 (Paris: Le Cerf, 1999) p. 152 [n° 20] en
donne la traduction française. La seconde fois, elle permet de faire débuter
une pièce utilisée comme collecte pour la Passion, dans le missel de Sarum
de 1487: éd. F. H. Dickinson, *Missale ad usum insignis et praeclarae ecclesiae
Sarum* (Oxford-London, 1881–1883 [réimpr. Farnborough, 1960]) spéc. col.
927*; sur ce missel cf. W. H. I. Weale et H. Bohatta, *Catalogus missalium ritus
latini ab anno MCCCCLXXIV impressorum* (Londres, B. Quarritch, 1928) xxxii
+ 380 pages, spéc. pp. 228–229 [n° 1387]. On trouvera le texte intégral
de cette pièce dans Eugenio Moeller, Joanne Maria Clement et Bertrandus
Coppieters't Wallant, *Corpus orationum*, t.III (Turnhout: Brepols) n° 2315, p.
277. Dans les deux cas, l'emploi de cet *incipit* se rattache à une tradition
liturgique pascale évidente.
12. *Ecclesiastica officia*, (*supra*, n. 5) Annexe: Section 9 [*Ordo de la messe*], pp.
368–369, n° 39–40. On retrouve cet *incipit* dans l'*ordo* de la messe tel que le
décrit le Dijon, Bibl. mun., MS 114, fol. 134vb [*Missale*].
13. *Exordium magnum cisterciense*, IV.35. Sur la mort du moine cistercien, cf.
Pl. Vernet, dans *Le Grand Exorde de Cîteaux . . .*, pp. 431–432 et *Id.*, art.
«Recommandation», *Ibid.*, p. 502.
14. Texte complet de cette antienne dans René-Jean Hesbert, *Corpus an-
tiphonalium officii*. 6 vol. (Roma: Herder, 1963–1979) (désormais abrégé
CAO), spéc. t. 4:7716. Sur cette antienne *Subvenite dei*, cf. Thierry Maertens
et Louis Heuschen, *Doctrine et pastorale de la liturgie de la mort* (Bruges:

être chantée dès après le dernier soupir du moine ago-
nisant par le chantre alors présent.[15] Dans ce cas de figure,
Conrad, en faisant chanter le mourant lui-même, insiste
par ce simple procédé, sur la sainteté du moine cistercien, mais permet surtout de *renforcer* l'obéissance et le
respect des règles codifiées et édictées quelques années
auparavant.[16] Une fois la célébration achevée, le *Grand Exorde* fournit la suite du rituel avec l'inhumation du cadavre
d'un moine défunt à l'abbaye de Clairvaux:[17] tous les
frères, assemblés autour de la tombe, chantent l'antienne
Clementissime Domine.[18] En conformité avec les prescriptions du statut de 1154, les frères doivent se prosterner
aux mots *Domine miserere super peccatore,*[19] derniers mots de
l'antienne. Ces deux récits intègrent parfaitement dans
leur déroulement les différentes prescriptions statutaires
de l'ordre qui réglementent et encadrent la liturgie de la
mort dans le monde cistercien dès la deuxième moitié du
XIIe siècle. Par ce biais, l'efficacité du récit est d'autant
plus forte qu'elle renforce encore chez ses lecteurs et/ou
ses auditeurs une impression de proximité immédiate
avec ces acteurs exemplaires d'une liturgie connue et
vécue.

Apostolat liturgique-Abbaye de Saint-André [Paroisse et liturgie; coll. de
pastorale liturgique, n° 28], 1957, 135 pages, spéc. pp. 42–43.
15. *Ecclesiastica officia*, Annexe 18, pp. 380–381. Cf. également J.-M. Canivez, «Le rite cistercien», dans *Ephemerides liturgicae*, 63 (1949) 276–311,
spéc. p. 303.
16. *Ecclesiastica officia*, 94.15.
17. *Exordium magnum cisterciense*, VI.3.
18. D'après Pl. Vernet, dans *Grand Exorde de Cîteaux . . .* , p. 379, note n° 25,
cette antienne fait partie du répertoire cistercien dès avant 1150. Cf. J.-M.
Canivez, «Le rite cistercien», p. 303. Antienne récente, absente du CAO.
19. *In antiphona Clementissime Domine, ad Domine miserere super peccatore, petat conventus veniam super genua. Si autem in luteo loco steterit, super
articulos tantum inclinet*: Statuts de 1154, n° 14, dans J.M. Canivez (éd.),
Statuta capitulorum generalium ordinis cisterciensis ab anno 1116 ad annum 1786,
(Bibliothèque de la revue d'histoire ecclésiastique, 9–14B Louvain, 1933–
1941) spéc. T.I: p. 57, §14, cité également dans *Ecclesiastica officia*, p. 459,
note n° 212. Sur cette antienne de la liturgie de la mort, cf. aussi J.-M.
Canivez, «Le rite cistercien», p. 303.

Le dernier récit choisi utilise, pour sa mise en scène, la liturgie pascale.[20] Une mise en scène qui est double: d'une part, Conrad place cet épisode lors des vigiles de la fête de Pâques et d'autre part, il utilise les répons de ces mêmes vigiles comme trame pour la construction de son histoire. Alors qu'un jeune frère assiste aux vigiles pascales, le Christ lui apparaît pendant que l'assemblée présente chante le répons *Angelus Domini*.[21] Une fois les blessures de la crucifixion montrées au frère en question, le Christ disparaît pendant que sont chantées les dernières paroles du répons: *Jam surrexit, venite et videte*. Inspiré de Mt 28:5–6, ce répons permet à l'auteur une construction de son récit intéressante. Non seulement faire apparaître le Christ lors de la fête de Pâques renforce la grandeur et la magnificence de cette solennité, mais en retour, cette propre apparition acquiert, par l'imminence sacrée de Pâques, un caractère de véracité qui ne peut être mis en doute. En second lieu, Conrad utilise le répons pour faire apparaître

20. *Exordium magnum cisterciense*, III.18, l. 127–155: *Et ecce secunda lectione iam lecta, cum responsorium* Angelus Domini *a conventu cantaretur repente is, qui in corde eius devotionis ignem accenderat, Dominus Jesus Christus vigilanti et flenti apparens stetit ante illum in medio chori manus suas expandens et quasi ostendens ei. Porro in eius beatissimis palmis loca clavorum evidentissime apparebant, ita ut de ipsis plagis recentibus sanguis manare videretur. Viso itaque Domino frater ille gavisus est gaudio magno valde ; sed obstupescens et quasi extra se factus nesciebat in arto temporis, quid agere deberet. Volebat namque in medium prosilire et pedes apprehendere salvatoris, sed retinebat eum pudor et reverentia conventus, ne velut insaniens reputaretur. Nam et hoc ignorabat, utrum videlicet apparens Dominus ab ipso solummodo, an et ab aliis pariter videretur. Flebat autem uberrime eratque cor eius in semetipso pietate liquescens prae immensa dulcedine amoris illius, quem intuebatur. Eadem vero apparitio Domini tamdiu duravit, quousque in responsorio, quod tunc cantabatur, dictiones istae* Iam surrexit, venite et videte *tanta morositate, quanta a sancto conventu illo cantari solebat, perdicerentur: Quis autem digne explicare valeat, quantum de visione illa profecerit, quomodo cunctis motibus universisque affectionibus animae ipsius recreatis et renovatis in amorem illius, quem viderat, totus incanduerit? Solius dantis et accipientis nosse est, quam festivos exinde cum dilecto suo duxerit dies, cum sponsa non tam vocibus oris quam affectibus cordis exclamans*: Inveni, quem diligit anima mea ; tenui illum nec dimittam. *Et cum patriarcha Jacob*: Vidi Dominum facie ad faciem et salva facta est anima mea.
21. CAO 4:6095A; cf. Claire Maître, *Un antiphonaire cistercien pour le temporal, XIIe siècle* (Poitiers 1998), fol. 96^v.

et disparaître le Christ: alors «l'ange du Seigneur s'adressant aux femmes [venues au tombeau] leur dit: 'Qui cherchez-vous? Est-ce Jésus que vous cherchez? Mais déjà, il est ressuscité. Venez et voyez'.»[22] L'épisode se clôt selon le même procédé. Pour mettre un terme à cette vision, Conrad cite un texte biblique (Gen 32:30) qu'il puise, non directement dans la Bible elle-même, mais sans doute dans le répertoire de la liturgie de préparation au temps pascal, répertoire connu et utilisé depuis les VIIIe-IXe siècles: «J'ai vu le Seigneur face à face et mon âme est sauve».[23] Il faut souligner ici l'habileté de Conrad qui réussit à assembler récit d'apparition et liturgie pascale en un texte court et qui, grâce à ces subtilités, dut obtenir une réelle efficacité auprès de ses lecteurs et/ou auditeurs.

Au coeur du même récit (III.18), l'acteur principal a une nouvelle vision lors de la célébration des vigiles de la Pentecôte.[24] Cette fois, il s'agit d'une vision de la

22. *Angelus Domini locutus est mulieribus, dicens: Quem queritis? An Jesum queritis? Nam surrexit: venite et videte. Alleluia. Alleluia.* (CAO 4:6095A).

23. CAO 4:7874: *Dominica II Quadragesimae.* Cf. *Ecclesiastica officia,* 39.5, pp. 130–131; également Cl. Maître, *Un antiphonaire cistercien* (*supra,* n. 21), cf. spéc. fol. 68[r].

24. *Exordium magnum cisterciense,* III.18, l. 163–188: *Factum est namque in die sancto Pentecosten, dum a fratribus alacri instantia sacrae vigiliae celebrarentur et iam divinus ille ymnus Te Deum laudamus, in quo evangelicae gratiae praenuntia laus figuratur, cantaretur, ut universitas fratrum mystica illa verba, quibus sub distinctione trium personarum unus Deus praedicatur et adoratur, scilicet Sanctus, sanctus, sanctus Dominus Deus Sabaoth, ob honorem sanctae Trinitatis cum summa reverentia inclinis, sicut est consuetudinis, cantaret. In ipsa vero inclinatione praedictus servus Dei non quidem scrutans seu commissum fidei secretum irrumpere gestiens, sed pavendo, tremendo et admirando coepit in simplicitate cordis sui meditari, quam sublime et incomprehensibile esset tantae maiestatis arcanum, quam nosse vita et vita aeterna est, secundum quam sapere sapientia sine errore est, in qua delectari voluptas sine comparatione est, cui conformari similitudinem Dei, quam in Adam perdidimus, recuperare est, cui servire regnare est, sine cuius gratia omnes gentes quasi non sint, sic sunt Coram ipsa, quae in futura vita erit sanctis omnibus pax exsuperans omnem sensum et gaudium sine interpolatione seu temporis decursione. Inclinatione vero illa divinae reverentiae exhibita, cum frater isdem se erigeret, subito aperti sunt intellectuales oculi eius et quasi totus extra se raptus vidit visionem quandam gloriosam atque mirabilem*

Trinité qui intervient au moment de la récitation de la très célèbre invocation trinitaire *Sanctus, sanctus, sanctus*,[25] qui fait suite à la récitation de l'hymne *Te deum*.[26] Provenant d'une formulation hébraïque (marque d'un superlatif), cette triple invocation, expliquée et comprise dans le sens de la prière à la Trinité,[27] convient parfaitement à «la vision glorieuse et admirable de la Trinité qui est Dieu».[28]

LES CITATIONS IMPLICITES

Ce chapitre (III.18) est décidément riche et particulièrement intéressant pour l'observation et la compréhension de ces «éléments» liturgiques dans le récit. Car si nous abandonnons le terrain des citations liturgiques explicites pour nous tourner vers les emplois diffus de ces mêmes sources,[29] nous pouvons noter à la suite de

---

de *Trinitate, quae Deus est, quam mirabiliorem, digniorem atque excellentiorem esse omnibus visitationibus, quibus unquam a Domino visitari meruerat, intelligebat.*

25. C'est un usage ancien de la liturgie occidentale que d'invoquer la Trinité à la fin d'une hymne; cf. Aimé-Georges Martimort (dir.), *L'Église en prière. Introduction à la liturgie* (Paris: Desclée, 1983–1984) (nouvelle éd.), 4 volumes, spéc. t. I: p. 158.

26. Ulysse Chevalier, *Repertorium hymnologicum* (Louvain, 1892–1922) 4 vol. (désormais cité RH), spéc. n° 20086. Abondante bibliographie sur cette hymne. Cf. DACL, XV-2: 2028–2048, où H. Leclercq rapporte les débats qui agitèrent la communauté scientifique à propos de l'auteur du *Te deum*.

27. Les exemples de la tradition médiévale donnant cette interprétation sont nombreux: cf. par exemple le *Liber Quare*, Georges Polycarpe Götz (éd.) CCCM, 60 (Turnhout: Brepols, 1983) 260 pages, spéc. App. II, 23e, spéc. p. 157, l. 114–118: *Hymnus videlicet Sanctus, sanctus, sanctus, a beato Sixto papa institutus non incongrue potest significare fidem Sanctae Trinitatis* [. . .]. À la fin du XIIIe siècle, Guillaume Durand lui consacre un chapitre dans son *Rationale*: Guillelmus Durantus, *Rationale divinorum officiorum*, par Anselme Davril et Timothy M. Thibodeau (éd.), CCCM, 140–140A–140B (Turnhout: Brepols, 1995–2000) 3 vol. (t. I: Lib. I–IV, t. II : Lib. V–VI et t. III : Lib. VII–VIII): ici, cf. Lib. IV, cap. 33, 3, dans t. I: p. 410, l. 28–29: *Illud etiam advertandum est quod ter dicitur Sanctus, ut notetur trinitas, seu distinctio personarum* [. . .].

28. *Exordium magnum cisterciense*, III.18, 51: [. . .] *visionem quandam gloriosam atque mirabilem de Trinitate, quae Deus est* [. . .].

29. Comme le montre aisément la lecture du tableau ci-après (Annexe, n° 2), nombreuses sont les expressions provenant de la liturgie que l'on peut repérer çà et là dans l'écriture du texte du *Grand Exorde*.

l'exemple précédant, l'utilisation caractéristique de la formule *cui servire, regnare est*. Appelée à trois reprises dans le corps du texte (III.5, 19; 18, 50 et 29, 9), la sentence «le servir, c'est régner» est représentative de cette constante imbrication des éléments de la prière liturgique dans l'écriture de Conrad d'Eberbach. Cette citation, qui connaît un succès certain dans la littérature patristique,[30] tire ses origines de la liturgie et plus particulièrement d'une oraison pour la paix (*pro pace*), dans laquelle sont demandées l'aide et la protection divine.[31] Sans entrer dans les détails de l'histoire de la tradition et de la filiation de cette pièce liturgique, disons simplement qu'on la voit apparaître dans le sacramentaire gélasien ancien,[32] pour passer ensuite dans les traditions ultérieures représentées par les sacramentaires gélasiens du VIIIe siècle,[33] dans le Supplément d'Aniane[34]

30. Sur les différentes références aux littératures de spiritualité, de théologie et de morale, on se reportera à la note (n° 19) que j'ai consacrée à cette expression dans *Le Grand Exorde de Cîteaux*, pp. 136–137.

31. Jean Deshusses et Benoît Darragon, *Concordances et tableaux pour l'étude des grands sacramentaires*, t. I, *Concordance des pièces*, Spicilegium friburgensis subsidia, n° 9, (Freiburg 1982) n° 749 (désormais abrégé Conc.); Placide Bruylants, *Les oraisons du missel romain*, (Rome) t. II, n° 204, p. 64. Voici le texte de cette oraison: *Deus auctor pacis et amator quem nosse vivere, cui servire regnare est, protege ab omnibus inpugnationibus supplicis* [*supplices*, dans Sp] *tuos, ut qui defensione tua fidimus* [*confidimus*, dans Sp] *nullius humilitatis* [*hostilitatis*, dans Sp] *arma temeamus* [*timeamus*, dans Sp]. *Per Dominum.*

32. Leo Cunibert Mohlberg, Leo Eizenhöfer und Petrus Siffrin (éd.), *Liber sacramentorum romanae aeclesiae ordinis anni circuli*, Coll. Rerum Ecclesiasticorum Documenta, Series maior, fontes IV (Roma: Herder, 1960). 315 pages + x. ill., spéc. n° 1476.

33. Ne citons que le plus fameux témoin représentatif de cette tradition liturgique qu'est le sacramentaire de Gellone: André Dumas, Jean Deshusses (éd.), *Liber sacramentorum Gellonensis*, CCSL, 159 et 159A (Turnhout, Brepols, 1981), 2 volumes, spéc. n° 2767.

34. Jean Deshusses, *Le sacramentaire grégorien. Ses principales formes d'après les plus anciens manuscrits,* coll. Spicilegium Friburgense, n° 16, 24 et 28 (Freiburg: Universitätsverlag, 1971–1982) 3 volumes (désormais abrégé Sp), spéc. t. I, n° 1345. Sur l'attribution du Supplément à Benoît d'Aniane, cf. J. Deshusses, «Le "Supplément" au sacramentaire grégorien: Alcuin ou saint Benoît d'Aniane?», dans *Archiv für Liturgiewissenschaft*, IX/1 (1965) 48–71;

au grégorien hadrianique ou bien encore dans la liturgie
ambrosienne du IXe siècle.³⁵ On retrouve bien entendu
cette pièce liturgique comme oraison de postcommunion
dans cette même messe pour la paix dans le manuscrit-
type cistercien.³⁶ À observer les trois emplois successifs
de cette citation dont on a souligné l'origine liturgique
indéniable, cette expression permet à Conrad d'Eberbach
de désigner le Christ (III.5, 12: «celui dont il est dit
que le servir, c'est régner») et d'affirmer l'importance
de la majesté de la Trinité divine dans la spiritualité du
moine cistercien.³⁷ Le troisième emploi, plus général,
est consigné dans le chapitre consacré à la conversion et
à la vie exemplaire du noble Gunnarus.³⁸ Faisant suite
à un long passage de «conclusion» comportant nombre
de *topoi* de la littérature médiévale monastique (aban-

tout récemment, le débat sur ce problème a été à nouveau ouvert par Philippe
Bernard, «Benoît d'Aniane est-il l'auteur de l'avertissement "Hucusque" et du
Supplément au sacramentaire "Hadrianum"?» dans *Studi medievali*, 3e série,
fasc. 1 (1998) 1–120.
35. Angelo Paredi (éd.), *Sacramentarium Bergomense* (Bergamo: edizioni Monumenta Bergomensia, 1962) 559 pages, Monumenta Bergomensia, VI, spéc
n° 1374.
36. Dijon, Bibl. mun., MS 114, fol. 139vc.
37. *Grand Exorde de Cîteaux*, III.18, 50: «Le serviteur de Dieu, tandis qu'il était
ainsi incliné, n'osait scruter ce mystère ni chercher à pénétrer le secret de
cet article de foi, mais plein de crainte, de respect et d'admiration, il se mit à
penser dans la simplicité de son coeur combien sublime et incompréhensible
est cette divine Majesté: la connaître, c'est la vie, et la vie éternelle; savoir
selon elle, c'est une sagesse qui ne trompe pas; prendre en elle ses délices, une
jouissance incomparable; se conformer à elle, c'est retrouver la ressemblance
de Dieu que nous avons perdu par la faute d'Adam; la servir, c'est régner.
Sans sa grâce, toutes les nations sont devant elle comme si elles n'étaient
pas. Dans la vie future, elle sera pour tous les saints la paix qui surpasse tout
sentiment, et la joie sans mélange et sans fin.»
38. *Grand Exorde*, III.29, 9: «Ne pouvant souffrir aucun retard, il établit son
fils aîné pour gouverner à sa place; quant à lui, qui était encore dans toute la
vigueur du corps et de l'âme, étant agé de quarante ans, il quitta la Sardaigne
et méprisant toute la gloire du monde entra pauvre et humble à Clairvaux.
Il y combattit sous la discipline de l'Ordre jusqu'à l'âge le plus avancé ou
plutôt jusqu'à la mort, se réjouissant d'avoir échangé un royaume terrestre
pour celui du ciel.»

don des vanités du monde, amour de la pauvreté), cette
expression, «le servir, c'est régner», vient, comme en
point d'orgue, manifester l'idéal du moine cistercien
exemplaire. Les termes-mêmes de cette citation sont
d'un usage particulièrement constant dans la tradition
textuelle de la prière chrétienne. Sans faire l'inventaire
des occurrences de *servire*, ni de *regnare*, le premier de
ces deux termes renvoie au culte divin, à l'adoration de
Dieu, mais aussi à la nécessaire acceptation et soumis-
sion de l'homme aux commandements divins. C'est
par cette adoration perpétuelle, par la célébration—
ininterrompue—du culte et le respect des préceptes divins que l'homme, pécheur par nature, pourra accéder
enfin au royaume de Dieu (*regnum*). Quant au terme
regnare, il n'est guère besoin de s'y attarder pour en
souligner l'importance dans la construction et la pensée
de la théologie chrétienne de l'espérance.

Un second exemple permettra d'insister encore sur
l'importance et la valeur de ces éléments liturgiques
dans le texte de Conrad d'Eberbach. Dans l'épisode qu'il
consacre au suicide d'un frère prémontré[39] le jour de la
Pentecôte,[40] Conrad d'Eberbach ouvre son récit par un
long préambule dans lequel il rappelle la question des
faiblesses humaines et de la justice divine, ainsi que le
rôle de la grâce de Dieu dans le rachat des péchés.

. . . je te prie, lecteur, d'accepter avec patience
que je te présente brièvement un exemple, très
nécessaire à ce que je crois, touchant le sacrement
de pénitence: tu y verras clairement à quelle ruine
lamentable est exposée dans son aveuglement l'âme
humaine qui a été corrompue par son libre arbitre
et inversement combien la grâce est puissante et

39. Sur le problème du suicide au Moyen Âge, cf. Alexander Murray, *Suicide in the Middle Ages*. T. 1. *The Violent against Themselves* (Oxford: Oxford University Press, 1999) xxii + 485 pages.
40. *Exordium magnum cisterciense*, V.13, l. 25–182.

efficace pour sauver ce qui était perdu; elle aurait
même pu nous préserver de cette ruine si, comme
le dit très bien saint Ambroise, *le péché d'Adam, que le*
Christ a effacé par sa mort, n'avait été nécessaire, afin que
la noble nature créée à l'image de Dieu, apprenant
ce qu'elle est par elle-même et ce qu'elle est par la
grâce, n'oublie jamais les miséricordes du Seigneur.
(V.13, 2–5).

Conrad utilise là une citation qu'il attribue à saint
Ambroise (*Necessarium fuisset Adae peccatum, quod Christi*
morte deletum est) mais qu'il convient en réalité de rattacher à l'*Exultet* pascal.[41] Il faut relever ici l'influence
de la liturgie cistercienne[42] qui, à la suite de la tradition issue des sacramentaires gallicans,[43] gélasiens du
VIIIe siècle[44] et du grégorien supplémenté[45] a conservé
dans le texte de son *Exultet* cette citation louant la
«faute nécessaire d'Adam» comme ayant entraîné en

41. Sur la question de l'*Exultet*, cf. entre autres, R. Amiet, *La veillée pas-*
cale . . . , (*supra* n. 11) spéc. pp. 204–206 et pp. 208–209.
42. Une fois de plus, le manuscritÊ114 (fol.Ê122va) de la Bibliothque
municipale de Dijon vient confirmer la présence de cette citation dans l'*Exultet*
tel qu'il devait être chanté dans tout l'Ordre cistercien, au moins dès le
quatrième quart du XIIe siècle. Je remercie ici le Fr. Placide Vernet (Abbaye de
Cîteaux) de m'avoir communiqué photocopie du texte de l'*Exultet* cistercien
(Lettre du 4 juillet 2000); cf. aussi, par exemple, le missel cistercien imprimé
à Paris en 1529, feuillet LX, col. a; sur cette édition de 1529, cf. W. I. H.
Weale et H. Bohatta, *Catalogus missalium ritus latini* . . . , spéc. p. 301 [n°
1765]; Robert Amiet, *Missels et bréviaires imprimés.* (*Supplément aux catalogues*
de Weale et Bohatta). *Propre des saints* (Paris: CNRS, 1990) 623 pages, spéc.
p. 112 [n° 1765].
43. Leo Cunibert Mohlberg, Leo Eizenhöfer und Petrus Siffrin, *Missale*
gallicanum vetus, Rerum ecclesiasticarum documenta, Series major, Fontes
III (Roma: Herder 1958) 167 pages + vii. ill., spéc. 25, n° 134, p. 35, l.
31–33; Leo Cunibert Mohlberg, *Missale gothicum*, Rerum Ecclesiasticorum
Documenta, Series maior, fontes V (Roma: Herder, 1961) 141 pages + vi
ill., spéc. n° 225, p. 60, l. 21–22.
44. Patrick Saint-Roch (éd.), *Liber sacramentorum Engolismensis*, CCSL, 159C
(Turnhout: Brepols 1987) spéc. n° 734, p. 109, l. 19–20.
45. J. Deshusses, *Le sacramentaire grégorien* . . . , spéc. 1022a, p. 361, l.
19–21.

conséquence la «mort» nécessaire du Christ.[46] L'attribution de cette citation à saint Ambroise pose un problème. En effet, une recherche dans les oeuvres ambrosiennes ne permet pas d'en retrouver la trace. En revanche, il faut savoir que seuls les témoins liturgiques gallicans du VIIIe siècle donne l'évêque de Milan comme étant l'auteur de l'*Exultet*,[47] attribution qui disparaît ensuite complètement de l'ensemble des grandes traditions liturgiques ultérieures. En conséquence, il est légitime de penser que Conrad d'Eberbach put avoir sous les yeux—ou dans sa culture liturgique—une source ancienne (gallicane?) qui lui fasse attribuer la paternité de cette citation à l'évêque de Milan.

CONCLUSION

Les cas de citations liturgiques participant activement à l'écriture et à la construction du récit sont nombreux et permettraient de multiplier les exemples à l'envie. S'attarder sur certains d'entre eux permet de les dégager de leur gangue littéraire et de les faire apparaître comme les témoins privilégiés de la culture liturgique de leur auteur et de son milieu. En utilisant des répons, des

---

46. Il faut savoir que seul le *Pontifical romano-germanique* rhénan (*circa* 960, rédigé à Mayence) a expurgé le texte de l'*Exultet* de cette citation et de la suivante (*O felix culpa, quae talem ac tantum meruit habere redemptionem*). Ce fait est à mentionner car le *Pontifical romano-germanique*, rédigé à Mayence près de l'abbaye d'Eberbach (*Grand Exorde*, éd. cit., V, 17, 6, mentionne Mayence comme ville toute proche), eut une importante diffusion. Cf. Cyril Vogel et Reinhard Elze, *Le pontifical romano-germanique du dixième siècle*, (Studi e testi, 226–227 [Texte] et 269 [Introduction et Tables] (Città del Vaticano: Biblioteca apostolica vaticana, 1963) 3 volumes, spéc. 99, 347 (t. II: p. 98, l. 18 et suivantes).

47. L. C. Mohlberg, *Missale gothicum* . . . , n° 225; L. C. Mohlberg, L. Eizenhšfer und P. Siffrin, *Missale gallicanum vetus* . . . , éd. cit., n° 25. Sur le problème de l'auteur de l'*Exultet*, cf. Eligius Dekkers, *Clavis patrum latinorum* (Turnhout: Brepols, 1995 [3e éd.]), 968 pages, spéc. n° 162; Michel Huglo, «L'auteur de l'*Exultet* pascal», dans *Vigiliae Christianae*, 7 (1953) 72–88 et M. Testard, «Virgile, saint Ambroise et l'*Exultet*», dans *Revue d'études latines*, 60 (1982) 282–297.

antiennes ou des fragments d'oraison, Conrad d'Eberbach peut bâtir son récit en faisant s'appuyer ses personnages sur le message de ces citations liturgiques. Cette méthode va certes de soi puisque bien souvent ces héros sont des personnages du monde monastique cistercien et que les lecteurs et/ou auditeurs de ces mêmes histoires sont eux-mêmes imprégnés de cette culture liturgique cistercienne. Le message peut alors d'autant mieux passer: la valeur de la liturgie et du culte cisterciens est telle qu'elle permet la manifestation de bien des faits extraordinaires et forcément vrais puisque s'adossant sur l'expression d'une culture commune et reconnue.

Le *Grand Exorde de Cîteaux* ne se contente pas de rapporter fidèlement les exploits quotidiens des moines blancs: il permet de voir que les prescriptions liturgiques contenues notamment dans le manuscrit-type (Dijon, Bibl. mun. MS 114) sont bien intégrées dans la quotidienneté de l'Ordre, permettant même des manifestations miraculeuses régulières. Comme nombre de documents «primitifs»[48] cisterciens (*Carta caritatis*, *Parvum exordium* . . .), le *Grand Exorde de Cîteaux* apparaît comme un instrument efficace au service de la profonde vague de réforme de l'ordre cistercien de la seconde moitié du XIIe siècle. Le dialogue constant entre les frères et Dieu est d'autant plus riche puisque la liturgie et ses textes sont bien adaptés pour chacune de ces occasions. Par ces références à la liturgie, par son ancrage dans la réalité quotidienne monastique et par ces manifestations divines, l'écrit acquiert une sacralité indéniable que nul ne saurait remettre en cause.

48. Sur cette question des documents primitifs, on lira *Cîteaux. Documents primitifs. Texte latin et traduction française*, François de Place, Gabriel Ghislain et Jean-Christophe Christophe (éd.), *Cîteaux-Commentarii cistercienses* (Textes et documents), 1988, 221 pages. Plus récemment, *Origines cisterciennes. Les plus anciens textes* (Paris: le Cerf, 1998), 190 pages [traduction française; sans le texte latin]; Ch. Waddell, *Narrative and Legislative Texts of Early Cîteaux* (Cîteaux. Commentarii cistercienses, 1999) 634 pages, ill.; H. Brem, A.M. Altermatt (éd.), *Einmütig in der Liebe: die frühesten Quellentexte von Cîteaux* (Langwaden: Bernardus Verlag–Turnhout: Brepols 1998) xv–341 pages.

ANNEXES

1-. Les citations liturgiques dans le *Grand Exorde de Cîteaux*

Incipit	E MC	Identification	Temps liturgique	Références
Te deum laudamus …	II. 4, 1–3; III.18, 49	RH, 20086	—	RB 11.8
Pater noster …	II. 19, 17; III.19, 15–16; IV.20, 4	—	Ad missam	B. Botte, *L'ordinaire de la messe* …, 1953, p. 86–87. *Eccl. off.* 70.43–62
Domine Jesu Christe …	II. 24, 10	—	Ad missam (ante Co.)	*Eccl. off.*, Ann. 9.40 (p. 368)
Benedicite …	II. 25, 12	—	—	*Eccl. off.*, p. 572.
Quando veniam et apparebo ante faciem dei	II. 24, 8	*Sextuplex*, 79b	Samedi saint	Ps 41:3
Angelus Domini …	III. 18, 39	CAO, IV, 6095A	2ᵉ Rep. Vig. paschae	—
Jam surrexit, venite et videte …	III. 18, 45	CAO, IV, 6095A	2ᵉ Rep. Vig. paschae (fin du Rep. *supra Angelus Dni.*)	—
Sanctus, Sanctus, Sanctus …	III. 18, 49	—	Vig. Pentecost.	Is 6:3
Gloria Patri et Filio et Spiritui Sancto …	III. 19, 23; 19, 25; V. 15, 21; 16, 6–10	—	Doxologie chantée à la fin de chaque psaume.	—

Continued

1-. Les citations liturgiques dans le *Grand Exorde* *Continued*

Incipit	EMC	Identification	Temps liturgique	Références
Domine deus virtutem ... in te	III. 25, 15	—	Noct. II Vig. dedicat. eccl.	Ps 83:13
Beatus ... atriis ejus	III. 25, 16	—	Noct. I Vig. dedicat. eccl.	Ps 64:5
Et introibo ... juventutem meam	III. 25, 19	—	Noct. I Vig. dedicat. eccl.	Ps 42:4
Miserere mei ...	III. 27, 15	—	—	Ps 50:2
Igne illo ... accendi	III. 29, 8	Conc., 1855	Oratio post Lectio I, IV temp. pentec.	Lc 12:49
Ecce Christus salvatori ...	IV. 1, 10	CAO, III, 1074	Ant. Invitat. Vig. Dnica I[a] Adv. Dni.	
Subvenite, sancti dei ...	IV. 35, 13	CAO, IV, 7716	Commendatio animae	*Eccl. off.*, 94, 15 et Ann. 15 (p. 380)
Te coeli regina ...	V. 9, 15; 9, 24	AH, LIII, 180*	Assumptio BMV	—
Alleluia	V. 17, 2	—	Ad missam	—
Benedicite omnia opera Dni....	V. 18, 4	—	Ad laud. (Pentec.)	Dn 3:57–88
Benedicamus patrem et filium ...	V. 18, 6	CAO, IV, 7966	Doxologie	—
Clementissime Dne....	VI. 3, 25	—	Ant.	*Eccl. off.*, 98.9 (n° 212, p. 459)
Requiescant in pace ...	VI. 7, 1–7	—	Ad sepulturam	—

* *AH* = Guido Maria Dreves, Clemens Blume, Henry Mariott Bannister, *Analecta hymnica medii aevi* (Leipzig, 1886–1922) 55 volumes.

2-. Les citations liturgiques implicites dans le *Grand Exorde de Cîteaux*

Texte	EMC	Identification	Temps liturgique	Références
Deus creator omnium …	I. 1,2	CAO, IV, 8292; RH 4426; AH,50,13	—	*Hymn. cist.*, n°8, p. 17*
in spiritu humilitatis …	I. 4,10	CAO, III, 3288	Ant. I^a Domca. IV	—
deus medium silentium …	I. 10,13	CAO, III, 2461	Intr. Dom. Oct. Nat. Dni. + Ant. *Magnificat.*	Sg 18:15
redemptionis novae …felicitatis eterne	I. 13,7	CAO, IV, 6859B	2^e R. Vig. Nat. Dni.	—
a porta inferi …	II. 15,7	CAO, III, 1191	Ant. ad VI^a in Sab. sanct.	Ps 88:49 Is 38:12
de cujus angeli ….	II. 23,5	*Sextuplex*, 30	Intr. ad miss. S. Agath. + fest. BMV	—
beati quos eledisti Domine …	II. 23,8	CAO, III, 1593/94	Ant. Vig. Omnium Sanct.	Ps 64:5
benedictus … misericordiis suis	II. 30,20	—	Post prandium	—
soli polique …	II. 30,20	AH 2, 93; 43; 281; 50, 285; RH 2824	Hymn. paschal. (*Chorus novae Jerusalem*)	*Hymn. cist.*, n°26, p. 44.
mediae noctis silentio …	II. 31,6	CAO, III, 2461	Intr. ad miss. Dnica in Oct. Nat. Dni.	Sg 18:14

Continued

2-. Les citations liturgiques implicites dans le *Grand Exorde*   *Continued*

Texte	EMC	Identification	Temps liturgique	Références
peccata … dissimulantem	II. , 31,24	Cf. CAO, III, 3193	Ant. Fer. IVᵃ in cin.	Sg 11:24
Nequaquam immemor existat …	II. 31,27	—	Ant. *Magn.* ad Vesp. Assumptio BMV	—
cui servire regnare est	III .5,19; 18,50; 29,9	Conc., 749	Oratio pro pace	—
visio pacis …	III .7,8	CAO, IV, 8405; AH, 51, 110; RH, 20918	Hymn. in dedicat. eccl.(*Urbs Ierusalem beata, dicta pacis visio …*)	—
tunsionibus et pressuris …	III .8,13	CAO, IV, 8405; AH, 51, 102; RH, 20933	Hymn. in dedicat. eccl.(*Urbs Ierusalem beata, dicta pacis visio …*)	—
mortuus erat …	III .11,16	*Sextuplex*, 52	Comm. *Oportet* in Sabb. post Dnica. IIᵃ in XLᵃ.	Lc 15:24; 15:32
carnis spuratias impolluto …	III .13,4	CAO, IV, 7318	4ᵉ R. in vig. S. Agnet.	—
locum illum refrigerii …	III .27,8; 28,19; V,19,5	—	Ad missam (*Memento*)	B. Botte, *Le canon …*, 1935, p. 44–45 (n°XIII).

Continued

2-. Les citations liturgiques implicites dans le *Grand Exorde*   *Continued*

Texte	EMC	Identification	Temps liturgique	Références
reginam caelorum …	III.27,9	CAO, III, 1542	Ant. fest. BMV	—
natus est nobis …	III.31,3	CAO, III, 3586/87	Ant. Invit. Vig. Nat. Dni.	—
Ingrediar in locum …	III.32,17	CAO, III, 3335	Ant. pro defunctis	Ps. 41:5
Ingrediente Domino …	IV.1,11	CAO, IV, 6961	6e R. Vig. Dnca in Palm.	—
Splendor paternae gloriae …	IV.30,12	CAO, IV, 8394; RH,19349; AH,50,11	Hymn. ad laud.	Hymn. cist., n°3, p. 8–9.
Necessarium fuisset Adae peccatum …	V.13,5	—	*Exultet* (Bened. cerae paschal. Vig. paschae)	—
paradisis portas … accepit	VI.5,9	Cf. CAO, III, 1886	Ant. S. Agnetis	—
O eterna … prodisti … disponens … suaviter	VI.8,2–2	Cf. CAO, III, 4081	Ant. 'O' (Adv. Dni.)	Si 24:5; Sg 8:1

* *Hymn. cist.* = John Michael Beers (éd.), *A Commentary on the Cistercian Hymnal. Explanatio super hymnos quibus utitur ordo cisterciensis. A Critical Edition of Troyes, Bibl. mun., MS 658,* (Gainsborough: Henry Bradshaw Society [vol. 102], 1982) liv + 94 pages.

Claire Maître

Institut de Recherche et d'Histoire des Textes

A propos des chants du célébrant dans le manuscrit Dijon, 114[1]

L E MANUSCRIT CONSERVÉ à la Bibliothèque municipale de Dijon sous la cote 114 (82)[2] est connu de tous les médiévistes qui s'intéressent aux débuts de l'ordre cistercien; il comporte les textes originaux qui servent de référence pour tous les manuscrits liturgiques de cet Ordre. Copié à la fin du XIIe s., entre 1185 et 1191, il comprenait à l'origine les parties suivantes, selon la table au f. 1v: *Breviarium* (2–102v, leçons et oraisons de nocturnes), *Epistolare* (102v–114v), *Textus evangeliorum* (114v–129v), *Missale* (129v–140v, sacramentaire), *Collectaneum* (140v–151, calendrier, capitules et collectes), *Kalendarium* (151–162v, martyrologe); *Regula* (*sancti Benedicti*, 162v–167v); *Consuetudines* (167v–185v), *Psalterium, Cantica, Hymnarium, Antiphonarium, Gradale*. Malheureusement, depuis 1480 au moins,[3] le manuscrit se termine par les *Consuetudines*, c'est à dire que toutes les parties chantées ont disparu. Pour connaître la pratique du chant dans les débuts de cet Ordre, il

1. La contribution qui va suivre a bénéficié de plusieurs discussions avec Dom Jean Claire, ancien Maître de choeur à l'abbaye Saint-Pierre de Solesmes, qu'il trouve ici l'expression de mes très sincères remerciements.
2. Sur ce ms. on peut voir V. Leroquais, *Bréviaires* II, 26–27, n° 218; Idem, *Sacramentaires* I:333–336, n° 166; Edition, Ph. Guignard, «Les monuments primitifs de la règle cistercienne», *Analecta divionensia* X (1878).
3. Cf. catalogue de Jean de Cirey (1480), qui décrit cette lacune. Édition: *Catalogue général des manuscrits des bibliothèques publiques de France* V, n° 445, pp. 385–386.

MS Dijon, BM 114, fol. 122 recto (jacquette 6438).

faut consulter les antiphonaires et les graduels cisterciens conservés depuis cette époque,[4] et, au XIIIᵉ siècle, une copie fautive du traité qui fonde la réforme cistercienne du plain-chant.[5]

Il est cependant une partie notée conservée dans le manuscrit de Dijon, à laquelle on ne prête guère attention, ce sont les chants du célébrant ou, éventuellement, de ses ministres. En effet, celui-ci n'est pas un chanteur professionnel, ses capacités vocales sont limitées, et les parties qui lui sont réservées ne donnent pas lieu à une musique très complexe. Ce sont: les oraisons, les lectures, la préface et le canon, le *Pater*, l'*Exultet*, les bénédictions pontificales.

Or le ms. 114 donne, en notation neumatique, l'intonation des lectures des épîtres et des livres bibliques, (f. 102v), puis, (ff. 122r–v) le chant complet de l'*Exultet*, ou bénédiction du cierge dans la nuit pascale, enfin, (ff. 133v–134v), les préfaces et le *Pater* sont également notés. Cette dernière partie ne sera pas ici abordée, elle nécessiterait une étude de trop vastes dimensions, mais l'analyse des intonations des livres bibliques et du chant de l'*Exultet* s'est révélée fructueuse et il a semblé particulièrement approprié d'en faire l'hommage au père Chrysogone.

LES TITRES DES LECTURES AVANT L'ÉVANGILE
(cf. exemple 1)[6]

Il s'agit de celles de l'ancien Testament et des épîtres des apôtres.

---

4. En particulier, pour les fonds français, les manuscrits: Charleville, Bibl. mun. 155; Colmar, Bibl. mun. 226 ; Paris, BnF, latin 17328, nouv. acq. lat. 1410, 1411, 1412, 1414; Troyes, Bibl. mun., 574.
5. Ms. Paris, Bibl. Sainte-Geneviève, *2204*. Édition, traduction et commentaire in Cl. Maître, *La réforme cistercienne du plain-chant* (Brecht 1995).
6. Les transcriptions musicales ont été faites d'après microfilms. Enfin, l'accentuation latine a été notée, pour permettre d'établir le rapport entre texte et musique.

Dijon, ms. 114, f. 102v

EXEMPLE 1

Lêc - ti - o e - pìs - to - le be - à - ti Pàu - li a - pòs - to - li ad Ro - mà - nos

ad Co - rìn - thi - os, ad E - phè - si - os, ad He - brè - os, ad Phi - lip - pèn-ses,

ad Thes-sa - lo - ni - cèn-ses, ad Gà - la-thas, ad Co - lo-sèn-ses, ad Tì - tum,

ad Thi - mò - te - um.

Lêc - ti - o ìì - bri Gè - ne - sis, lêc - ti - o ìì - bri Le - vì - ti - cì,

lêc - ti - o ìì - bri Èx - o - di, lêc - ti - o ìì - bri Nù - me - rì,

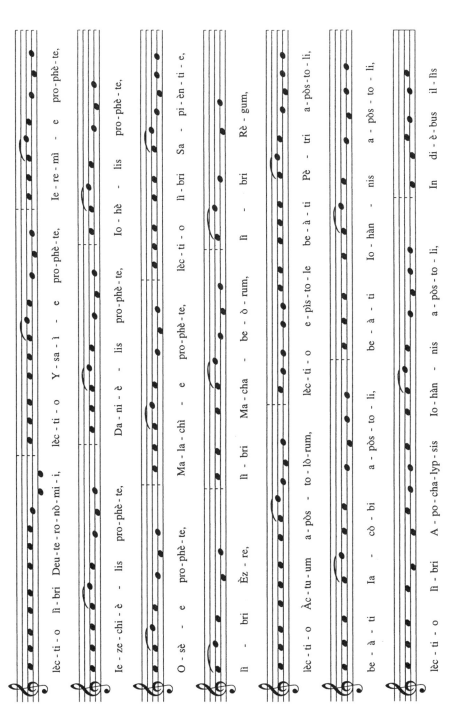

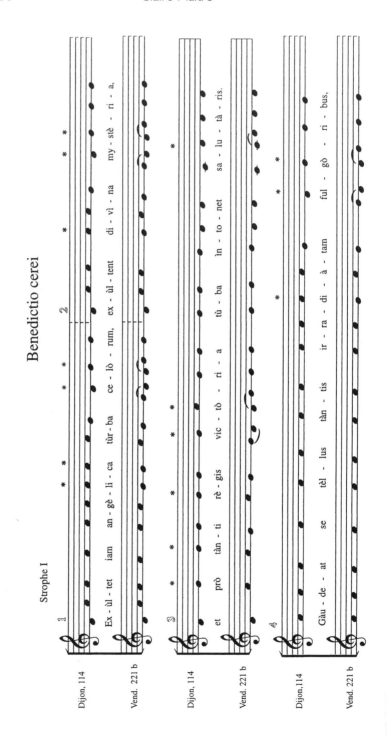

Benedictio cerei

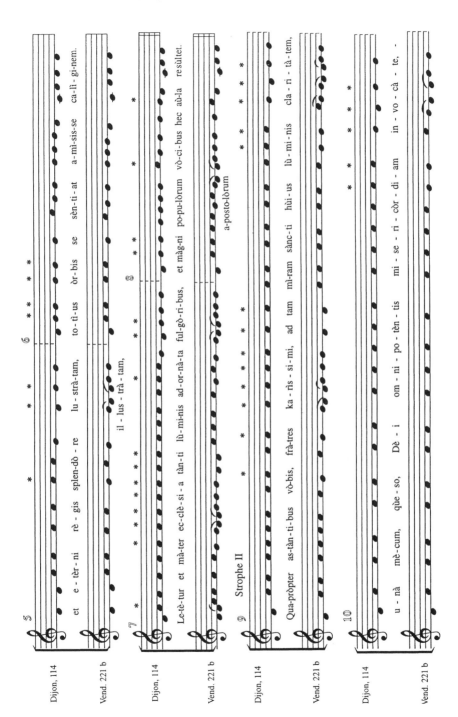

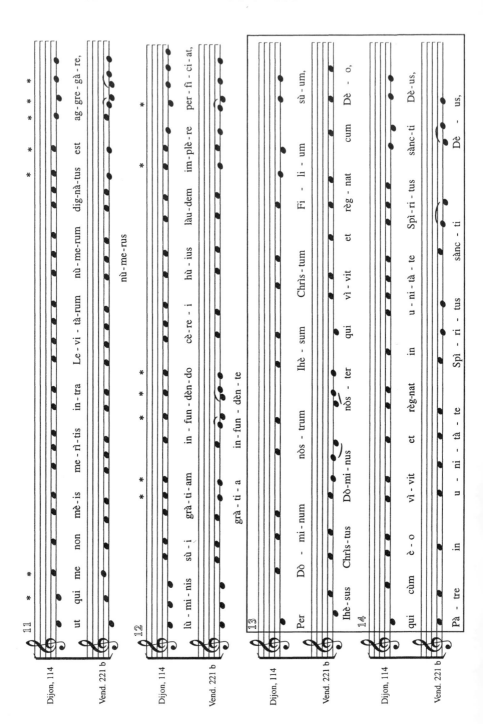

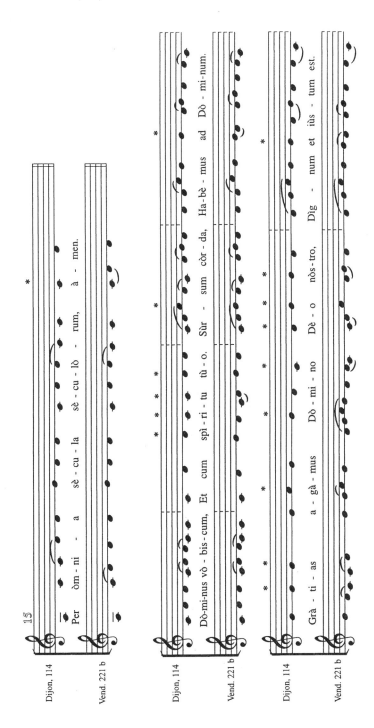

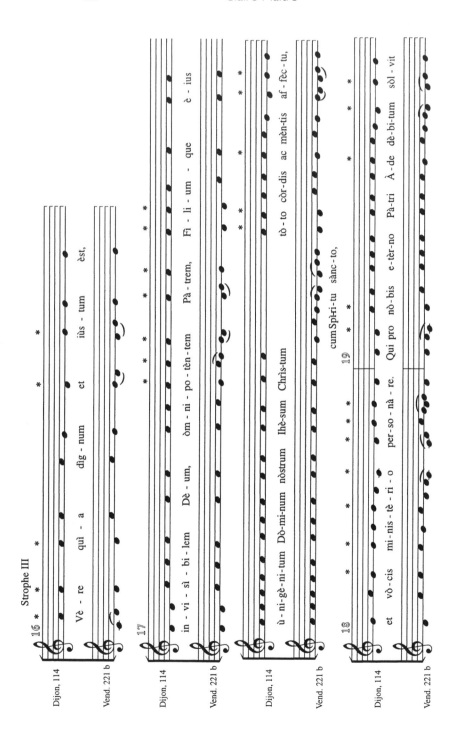

Strophe III

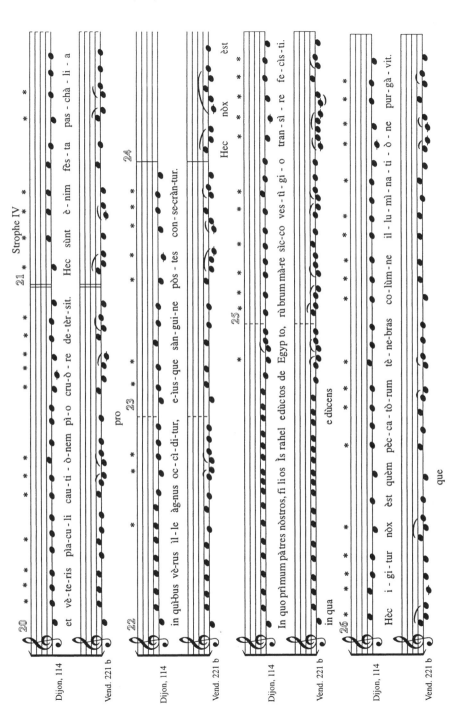

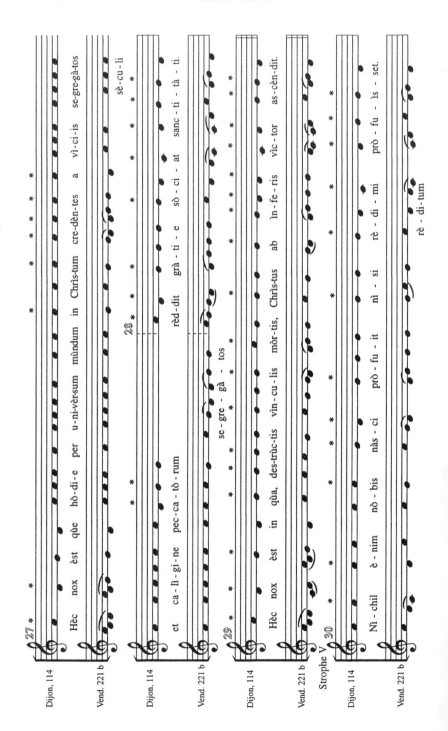

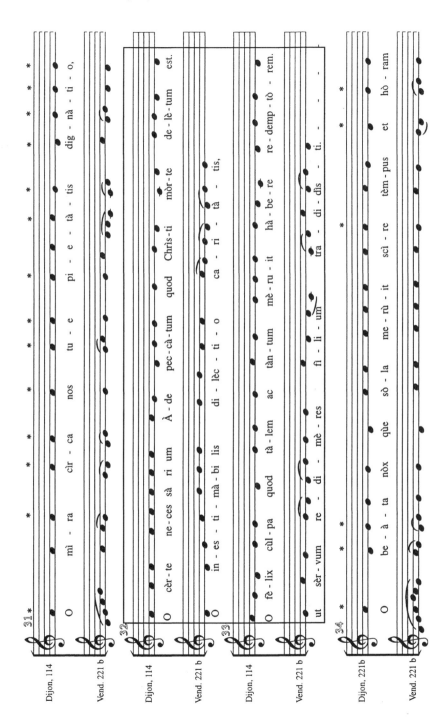

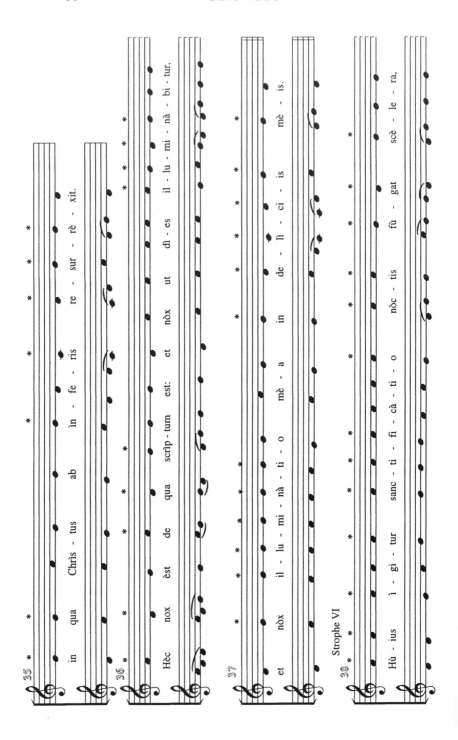

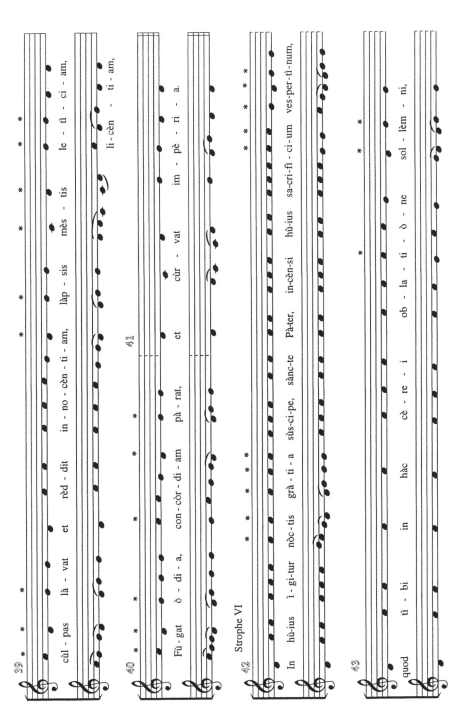

68   Claire Maître

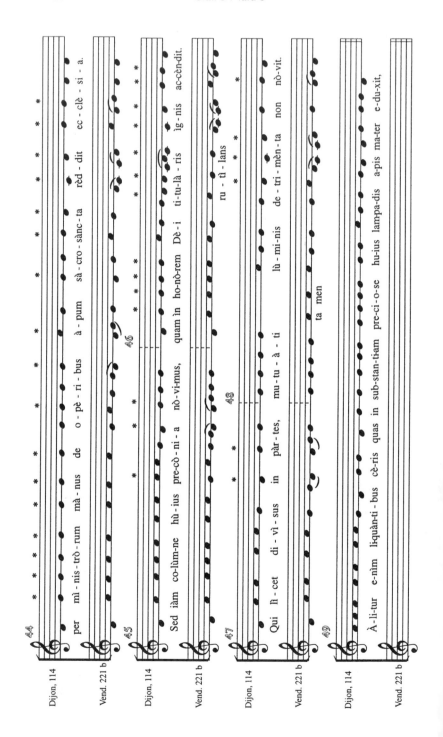

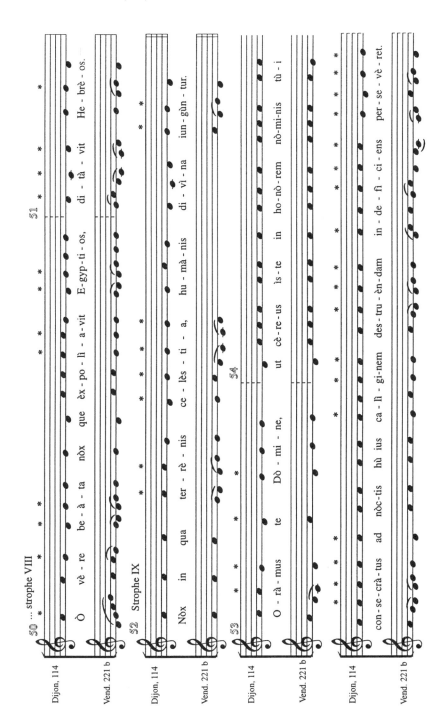

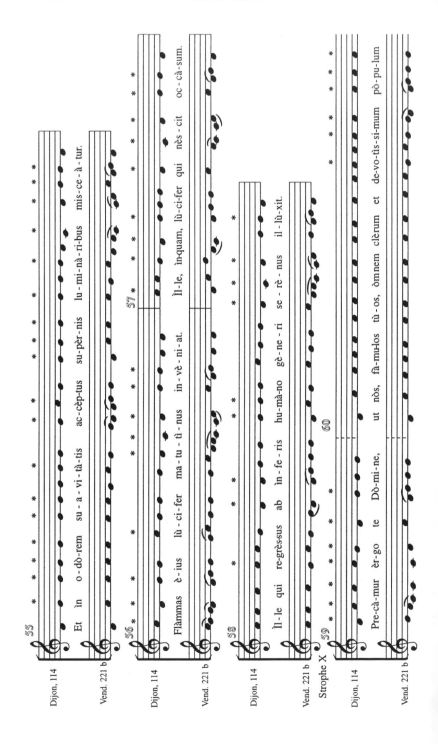

Dijon, 114 — 55 — Et in o-dò-rem su-a-vi-tà-tis ac-cèp-tus su-pèr-nis lu-mi-nà-ri-bus mis-ce-à-tur.

Vend. 221 b

Dijon, 114 — 56 — Flàmmas è-ius lù-ci-fer ma-tu-tì-nus in-vè-ni-at. Ìl-le, ìnquam, lù-ci-fer qui nès-cit oc-cà-sum.

Vend. 221 b — 57

Dijon, 114 — 58 — Ìl-le qui re-grèssus ab ìn-fe-ris hu-mà-no gè-ne-ri se-rè-nus il-lù-xit.

Vend. 221 b

Strophe X

Dijon, 114 — 59 — Pre-cà-mur èr-go te Dò-mi-ne, — 60 — ut nòs, fà-mu-los tù-os, òmnem clèrum et de-vo-tìs-si-mum pò-pu-lum

Vend. 221 b

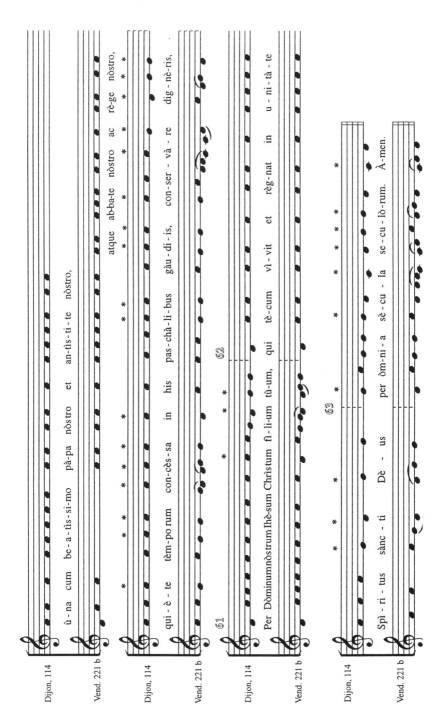

1 – L'intonation des épîtres. C'est une corde de La, qui s'infléchit sur Sol à la cadence et à la médiante (*Lectio epistole beati Pauli*), avec la double broderie de ces deux degrés forts au Si et au Fa, intervalle de quarte augmentée attaqué parfois directement (*Galathas*). Or, ce ton de La (= Ré), habituel pour l'intonation des évangiles, est très rare, voire inconnu, pour celle des épîtres. La dernière édition du *Graduale romanum* ne mentionne que sa pâle imitation en Do.[7] Il renvoie à une pratique non romaine et probablement gallicane. Cette 'exception' cistercienne mériterait une recherche à elle seule.

D'autre part, si l'on met en regard les mouvements mélodiques avec l'accentuation du texte latin, on s'aperçoit que la broderie au Fa[8] coïncide toujours avec l'accent latin, à l'exception d'un seul cas: *ad Thimoteum*, que l'on peut interpréter soit comme une erreur, soit comme un déplacement de l'accent latin au XIIᵉ siècle, de la pénultième à l'antépénultième syllabe.

	Ad	Ro -	mà	-	nos
	Ad	Co -	rìn -	thi -	os
	Ad	E -	phè -	si -	os
	Ad	He -	brè	-	os
Ad	Phi-	lip -	pèn	-	ses
Ad Thessa	- lo	ni -	cèn	-	ses
	Ad		Gà -	la -	thas
Ad	Co-	los -	sèn	-	ses
	Ad		Tì	-	tum
Ad	Thi-	mò -	te	-	um.

2 – L'intonation des autres livres bibliques. La formule musicale est identique: une corde de La, infléchie au

7. *Graduale romanum Pauli VI cura recognitum*, Solesmis (1974) 804.
8. La traduction musicale de l'accent latin par une broderie inférieure est également souvent considérée comme une pratique gallicane, différente de Rome où l'on accentuait par une broderie supérieure.

degré inférieur pour la cadence, ce noyau étant orné par deux broderies, aux degrés supérieur et inférieur. Considérons l'adéquation de la musique au latin:

	Lì	-	bri	Gè -	ne	sis
	Lì	-	bri Le	vì -	ti -	ci
	Lì	-	bri	Èx -	o -	di
	Lì	-	bri	Nù -	me -	ri
Ysa-	ì -	e	pro -	phè	-	te
Iere-	mì -	e	pro -	phè	-	te
Iezechi-	è -	lis	pro -	phè	-	te
Dani-	è -	lis	pro -	phè	-	te
Io -	hè -	lis	pro -	phè	-	te
O -	sè -	e	pro -	phè	-	te
Mala-	chì -	e	pro -	phè	-	te
	Sa	-	pi -	èn -	ti -	e
	Lì -	bri		Èz	-	re
Ma	chà	-	be -	ò	-	rum
	Lì	-	bri	Rè	-	gum
Actuum a -	pòs	-	to -	lò	-	rum
	Pè -	tri	a -	pòs -	to -	li
	Ia -	còbi	a -	pòs -	to -	li
Io-	hàn -	nis	a -	pòs -	to -	li

L'accent latin du dernier mot est toujours placé sur la broderie inférieure Fa, avec parfois la survenante Sol, en cas de mot proparoxyton. La broderie supérieure est également placée sur l'accent latin, sauf dans un cas *Iacòbi*, un mot étranger. Après cet accent, une survenante, sur La, est également insérée en cas de besoin. On remarque une hésitation au livre d'Esdras: la broderie retombe sur le degré de la survenante, alors que l'on aurait attendu le Sol; et un mouvement mélodique différent au livre du Deutéronome: la note conclusive s'abaisse jusqu'au Ré, une évolution modale qui laisse préfigurer le futur premier mode authente.

Ces intonations des livres de l'Ancien Testament sont habituelles, l'usage de la corde de La (*i.e.* Ré) y est la norme, et, comme pour les intonations des Épîtres, on y trouve cette corrélation de la musique et du latin qui caractérise le plain-chant bien écrit.

Exultet iam angelica

Il s'agit de la prière dite par le diacre le Samedi-Saint, au début de la vigile pascale, au moment de la bénédiction du cierge.[9] Attestée dès le IVe siècle,[10] elle est cantillée sur une mélodie très ancienne, dont il existe plusieurs traditions. Le texte de l'*Exultet* varie également: «Autrefois une certaine variété paraît avoir été la règle, et pendant plusieurs siècles. Et même si le texte littéraire a été adopté définitivement par le missel romain de st Pie V (14 juillet 1570) et généralement suivi depuis lors, la mélodie, elle, semble n'avoir trouvé l'unité que depuis les dernières réformes de la fin du XIXe et du début du XXe siècle».[11]

Cette *benedictio cerei* comporte deux grandes parties: le *praeconium pascale* et une préface. Dans cette dernière, deux incises (32 et 33 de la transcription), ont parfois fait scandale et n'apparaissent pas dans toutes les versions.

Dans une étude consacrée aux récitatifs liturgiques,[12] dom Claire consacre un chapitre aux diverses traditions de l'*Exultet*, dont les deux composantes sont, d'une part «une sorte d'oraison dans laquelle le diacre demande qu'on prie pour lui au moment où il va exercer son ministère, et d'autre part une véritable préface de bénédiction du cierge, précédée du dialogue habituel, et qui contient l'annonce des fêtes pascales: *praeconium*

9. Sur les différentes traditions littéraires et musicales de ce chant, cf. G. Benoît-Castelli, «Le praeconium pascale», *Ephemerides liturgicae* LXVII (1953) 309–334.

10. Cf. H. Leclercq, art. «Pâques», *Dictionnaire d'Archéologie Chrétienne et Liturgique* 13/2 (Paris, 1938) col. 1559–1571.

11. *Ibidem*, 310.

12. Jean Claire, «L'évolution modale dans les récitatifs liturgiques», *Revue grégorienne* 41 (1963/6) 127–151 plus 8 tableaux musicaux.

pascale».[13] Le tableau *Jc* donne «douze étapes esthétiques et modales . . . de la mélodie du prologue qui, partie du ton d'oraison a fini par aboutir à un ton de préface, très évolué et agrémenté de quelques fantaisies».

Pour résumer rapidement, ce tableau montre en premier lieu cinq familles de manuscrits qui conservent le même degré, Ré comme corde de récitation et finale (éventuellement écrite Sol ou La) : Lyon, Chartres, Dijon, Arezzo, Aquitains, avec des niveaux divers d'ornementation. Deux familles infléchissent la finale au degré inférieur: Bénévent et Mâcon. Les manuscrits de Milan abaissent la finale à la quarte inférieure dans cette écriture de protus quarte qui leur est si coutumière.[14] Les familles de Vendôme et d'Angers élèvent la teneur à la tierce mineure et récitent sur Fa, pour revenir conclure sur Ré. Enfin les manuscrits de Saint-Amand et les versions modernes font monter la teneur au Fa et descendre la finale au La, combinant ainsi les deux évolutions déjà identifiées.

La tradition cistercienne s'apparente étroitement à celle de Vendôme, les cadences se font sur Ré, la récitation sur un mélange de Ré et de Fa (Voir la transcription aux pages suivantes). Ce rapprochement des monastères de la Trinité de Vendôme et de Cîteaux paraît au premier abord inattendu, mais les histoires respectives de ces abbayes fournit un possible éclaircissement.

L'abbaye de la Trinité de Vendôme fut fondée, entre 1032 et 1038, par Geoffroy Martel, comte de Vendôme, et son épouse, Agnès de Bourgogne. Les premiers abbé et prieur, ainsi que vingt cinq moines, vinrent de Marmoutier,[15] qui, à la même époque, était appelée à réformer l'abbaye de Montier-la-Celle, où deviendra moine quelques années plus tard un certain Robert, futur fondateur

---

13. *Ibidem*, 139.

14. Sur ce sujet, on peut voir: Cl. Maître, «Le protus quarte dans le répertoire ambrosien», *Cantus planus*, 3 (Budapest, 1995) 517–527.

15. Cf. Penelope D. Johnson, *Prayer, Patronage and Power. The Abbey of la Trinité, Vendôme, 1032–1187* (New York & London, 1981) 37–38.

de Molesme, puis de Cîteaux. [16] La parenté des traditions
de l'*Exultet* entre les abbayes de Cîteaux et de la Trinité de
Vendôme s'expliquerait donc par une origine commune:
l'antique et prestigieuse abbaye de Marmoutier. [17]
     La transcription (pp. 58ff) comparée des deux versions
de Cîteaux et de Vendôme [18] montre quelques variantes
textuelles et de plus nombreuses dans la musique, [19] celles-
ci relevant le plus souvent du domaine de l'ornementation.
     Si l'on regarde la structure générale de ces deux ver-
sions, on observe un degré fondamental, Ré, qui s'élève
d'une seconde ou d'une tierce mineure pour la récitation.
Le discours est organisé en incises, conclues par des repos
suspensifs sur Mi ou conclusifs sur Ré, que l'on nommera
demi-cadences et cadences. A Cîteaux, une récitation sur
Mi se termine toujours par une cadence, une récitation
sur fa sur une demi-cadence.

Les demi-cadences

Les demi-cadences peuvent se rapporter à deux modèles
mélodiques. Le texte est toujours accentué à l'arrivée
sur la teneur Fa, à l'avant-dernière syllabe Mi, et, dans le
deuxième modèle, au repos médian sur Mi:

Demi-cadence A – Après une intonation qui fait entendre les deux degrés structurels Ré-Fa, [20] la voix ne
s'abaisse qu'à la demi-cadence, introduite par la broderie
inférieure:

16. Cf. Chrysogonus Waddell, «La Vierge Marie dans la liturgie cistercienne au XIIe siècle», *La Vierge dans la tradition cistercienne*, Communications
présentées à la 54e session de la Société Française d'Études Mariales, Abbaye
Notre-Dame d'Orval, 1998, réunies par Jean Longère (Paris 1999) 125.
17. L'étude de G. Benoît-Castelli effectuait déjà le rapprochement entre la
tradition de Cîteaux et celles de Vendome et d'Angers (cf. *supra* n. 9).
18. L'*Exultet* de Vendôme a été transcrit d'après un graduel du XVe siècle,
Vendôme, Bibl. mun. 221 bis, ff. 46v–49.
19. Ces dernières sont matérialisées par une astérisque, l'accent latin est
indiqué et un rectangle entoure les variantes textuelles importantes.
20. A trois exceptions près: 4, 16 et 38 qui commencent directement sur le
Fa et par une syllabe accentuée.

N														
1		Ex-	ul-	tet	iam	an-	ge-	li-	ca	tur-	ba		lò-	rum
2		Ex-	ul-	tent	se				di-	vi-	ce-		tè-	a
4	Et	e-	Gau-	deat	re-	gis	ti-	ir-	radi-	a-	mys-		gò-	bus
5		Le-	ter-	ni	et		mi-	a-	splen-	do-	ful-		trà-	tam
7		Qua-	te-	tur	as-	tan-		se-	dor-	na-	lus-		gò-	bus
9		U-	prop-	ter	cum			bus	ri-	lu-	ful-	minis	tà-	tem
10		qui	na	me-	me-	is	mi-	se-	dig-	cor-	ri-	diam	cà-	te.
11	Ut	minis	me	non	i	is		Chris-	im-	na-	vo-	tus est	gà-	re
12	Lu-	Per	su-	i	num			qui-	tum	ple-	gre-		fì-	at,
13		Qui	Do-	mi-	vi-		et	le		fi-	per-	ritus	sù-	um
14		Invi-	cum	eo	lem	Ve-	re		a	Spi-	um		Dè-	us
16		pro	si-	bis	e-	De-	um	qui-	ac	dig-	ti		ius-	est
17		Hec	no-	bis	nim	ter-	no	:	:	men-	et		fèc-	tu
19	Qui	In	sunt	e-	ve-	rus	il-	le	e-	de-	af-		sòl-	vit
21		In	qui-	bus	mum	pa-	tres	pi-	cri-	fes-	tum	tos	chà-	a
22		O	quo	pri	ca	cir-	nos…	sa-	ti-	ag-	pas-		cì-	tur
24		In	mi-	ra	gi-	gi-	tur…	bla-	di-	duc-	oc-	tis	gyp-	to
31		Quod	hu-	ius	i-	gi-	o-	ius	:	ta-	E-	cium	nà-	o
38		Sed	hu-	ius	hac-	in	hu-		:	noc-	dig-		scè-	ra
42		Qui	ti-	bi	in	ne	ius	pre-	cri-	fi-	gat		tì-	num
43	Ut	Ut	iam	co-	lum-		in-	di-	ti-	o-	per-		lèm-	ni
45		Pre-	li-	cet	ne	te		de-		co-	sol-	ciens	nò-	mus
47		Ut	ce-	reus	is-		con-	ser-	:	vi-	a		pàr-	tes
54		Per	ca-	mur		te	trum	:	:	fi-	in		vè-	ret.
60		Qui	nos	fa-	los	los	et		:	er-	se-	ritus	Dò-	ne
61			Do-	mi-	nos-	nos-			:	va-	te		nè-	ris
62			te-	mi-	num				:	fi-	dig-		tù-	um
63	Qui		te-	cum	vi-	vit			:	Spi-	ti		Dè-	us

Demi-cadence B – La même formule mélodique est précédée d'une introduction dont le squelette: Fa-Ré-Mi, dans une forme un peu mouvante, est une annonce concentrée des degrés de la déclamation:

27	Hèc	nox			èst	que	hò-	di-	e	...	pec-	–	ca-	tò-	rum
34	Ò	be-	a -	ta	nòx	que	sò-	la...	sci -	re	tem-	pus	et	hò-	ram
36	Hèc	nox	est	scriptum	èst	et	nòx	ut	di-	es	il-	lu-	mi-	nà-	bitur
40	Fù-	–	gat		òdia	que	èx-	in		con-	cor-	di-	am	pà-	rat
50	O vè-	re	be-	a -	nòx		Nòx		po-	li-	a-	vit	E-	gyp-	tios
52								qua	ter-	re-	nis	ce-	lès-	tia
54								O-		ra-	mus	te	Dò-	mine

Les cadences

Les phrases cadentielles sont de trois types, le plus souvent construites en deux parties. L'on trouve toujours une syllabe accentuée à l'arrivée sur la teneur Mi (cadences A, A') ou l'intonation au degré supérieur Fa (cadence B), sur la broderie de fin de première partie et sur l'avant-dernière syllabe.

Cadence A – Après un repos sur le degré suspensif Mi brodé au ton supérieur, la conclusion sur le Ré est introduite simplement par la broderie au ton inférieur:

3	Et	prò-	tan-	ti	re-	gis	vic-	tò-	ri-	a	...	in-	tonet	sa-	lu-	tà-	ris
6	To-	ti-	us	or-	bis	se	sèn-	ti-	at	a-	misis-	se	ca-	li-	gi-	nem
8	Et	màg-	nus	po-	pu-	lo-	rum	vò-	ci-	bus	hec	au-	re-	sùl-	—	tet

Cadence A' — La différence d'avec A réside dans la conclusion, maintenant à double broderie:

	Texte (syllabé)
20	Et vè- te- ris … cau- ti- ò- nem pi- o cru- ò- re de- tèr- sit
25	Et Rù- brum ma- re … ves- ti- gio tran- si- re fe- cis- ti
37	nòx il- lu- mi- na- tio mè- a in de- li- ci- is mè- is.
41	Per mì- nis- tro- rum … ope- ribus à- pum Et cùr- rit vat im- pè- ria
44	Quam in ho- no- rem a- ti sa- cro- sanc- ta ta rèd- dit ec- clè- sia
46	… Dè- i … ti- tula- ris ig- nis ac- cèn- dit.
48	Mu- tu- a- ti de- tri- mèn- ta non nò- vit.
51	lù- minis Di- ta He- brè- os.
18	E- … que … et vò- cis mi- nis- tè- ri- o per- so- nà- re
23	ius- que … sàn- guine … pòs- tes con- se- cràn- tur
35	in … qua Chris- tus ab in- fe- ris re- sur- rè- xit.
55	Et in o- do- rem … ac- cèp- tus … mis- ce- à- tur

Dans ce dernier exemple, les cadences ont été regroupées selon qu'elles relevaient d'un *cursus planus-tardus* ou *velox*. En effet, même si les formules ont connu des altérations, le mouvement de la phrase latine laisse entendre une attention à ce rythme particulier.

Cadence B – La première incise commence sur Fa, comme dans la demi-cadence de même type, et s'infléchit immédiatement sur Mi, teneure des formules conclusives. La chute se fait sur la double cadence qui affirme bien la corde de Ré, entourée de deux tons.

Exemple musical (Cadence B). Les syllabes des différentes pièces alignées sous la même mélodie :

n°																	
26	Héc	i-	gitur	nox	est	quem	peccato-	rum	tè-	nebras…	illumina-	ti-	ò-	ne	pur-	gà-	vit.
29	Héc			nox	est	in	…vincu-	lis	mòr-	tis	ab in-	feris	vic-	tor-	as-	cén-	dit
33	Ò-	fe-	lix	culpa	quod	talem	ac		tàn-	tum…	ha-	bè-	re	re-	demp-	tò-	rem

n°																	
52	Nòx…			terre-	nis	ce-	lestia	hu-	mà-	nis		di-	vi-	na	iun-	gun-	tur.
56					Flàm-	mas	e-	ius	lu-	cifer	ma-	tu-	ti-	nus	in-	vé-	niat
58	ìlle	qui regres-	sus		ab	in-	feris		gè-	neri		se-	rè-	nus	il-	lù-	xit
63								Per	òm-	nia	se-	cù-	la	se-	cu-	lò-	rum

n°																	
28	Réd-	dit…								gràtie	so-	ci-	at	sanc-	ti-	tà-	ti
30	Nichil	…	nas-	ci						…	re-	di-	mi	pro-	fu-	is-	set
32	Ò	certe					pec-	cà-	tum	…	Chris-	ti	mòr-	te	de-	lè-	tum est
57	il-	le	in-	quam						lucifer		qui	nès-	cit	oc-	cà-	sum

Le classement établit trois variantes, selon le développement donné à la première partie de la phrase. La cadence
elle-même se divise en *cursus planus-tardus* (26, 29, 32,
52, 56, 57, 58) et *cursus velox* (28, 30, 33, 63).

Enfin, dans cette analyse, la conclusion de la première
partie (15) et le dialogue qui précède la préface, n'ont pas
été pris en compte. La conclusion, anhémitonique, fait
intervenir un nouveau degré: le La grave, et des cadences
suspensives sur Do, degré de repos provisoire des chants
évoluant sur la corde de Ré.

*Comparaison entre les versions de Cîteaux
et de la Trinité de Vendôme*

La variante musicale la plus fréquente est la préparation
d'un degré, à Vendôme, par son appogiature; elle n'a
aucune incidence sur la modalité. On remarque à trois
reprises, à Vendôme une montée à la quarte Sol, absente
de Cîteaux (11, 31, 38). En 11 et 31, le diacre parle
en son nom personnel, ceci expliquerait-il cela? Enfin,
Vendôme interrompt plus volontiers le discours musical:
en 31, 54 et 60 des cadences conclusives sont entendues,
des cadences suspensives à Cîteaux.

Plus intéressante est la fluctuation de la corde de
récitation, Mi pour Fa et inversement, alors que le Ré est
plus stable, illustration de la différence de nature entre
ces deux degrés structurels: Ré est le pôle d'origine,[21]
centre de gravité de la récitation, Mi et Fa sont des degrés
d'évolution de cette teneur archaïque. On remarque ainsi
des exemples de récitation sur Ré à Vendôme, montée au
Mi et même au Fa à Cîteaux, cette variante musicale
rejoint les données historiques: l'abbaye de Vendôme
est plus ancienne que celle de Cîteaux, en outre cette
dernière a été soucieuse, dans la réforme de son chant,
d'écrire dans les modes évolués à deux pôles structurels,

---

21. La corde-mère, telle qu'elle a été définie par Dom Claire au volume XV
des *Études Grégoriennes* (1975).

synonymes pour elle et, par une erreur de perspective, de langue musicale des origines.

Cette rapide analyse du chant, à Cîteaux, des titres des lectures et de l'*Exultet*, montre le respect d'une tradition ancienne, relativement peu évoluée. En cela, elle tranche sur nombre d'autres qui se sont rapprochées de la langue de l'octoéchos, assimilant ainsi l'*Exultet* à un chant, dans le sens classique du terme. Les réformateurs cisterciens ont conservé à cette pièce son caractère de cantillation, de lecture solennelle, qui est un genre propre au moyen âge. Nous l'identifions parfois mal, car, même s'il n'a pas disparu (récitatif classique, *Sprechgesang* contemporain), il n'est plus exploité comme forme autonome. C'est à l'honneur des chantres cisterciens d'avoir choisi de maintenir cette écriture dans son caractère *sui generis*.

Giles Constable

The Institute for Advanced Study, Princeton

Herman of Tournai and the Monastery of Saint Vincent at Valencia[*]

T
HE HISTORIAN AND HAGIOGRAPHER Herman of Tournai entered the monastery of Saint Martin of Tournai, together with his father and three brothers, while he was still a boy, probably about 1095, and established himself rapidly as a trusted member of the community.[1] Among other things, he was an

---

[*] The following abbreviations are used in the notes:

AASS   *Acta sanctorum*, 3rd ed. (Paris, 1863–1870)

BHL   *Bibliotheca hagiographica latina* (Brussels, 1898–1899) and *Novum supplementum*, Subsidia hagiographica, 70 (Brussels 1986)

Documen- José Ma. Lacarra, 'Documentos para el estudio de la reconquista y
tos, 1, 2, repoblación del Valle del Ebro', *Estudios de Edad Media de la Corona de*
and 3   *Aragón*, 2 (1946) 469–574 (=Publicaciones de la Escuela de estudios medievales: Trabajos y documentos, 2), 3 (1947–1948), 499–727, and 5 (1952), 511–668 (=Consejo superior de l'investigaciones cientificas. Escuela de estudios medievales. Publicaciones de la seccion de Zaragoza, 3 and 6).

Esp. sag. *España sagrada*, ed. Henrique Florez a.o. (Madrid, 1747 f.)

GC   *Gallia christiana* (Paris, 1715 f.)

JL   Philip Jaffé, *Regesta pontificum Romanorum*, 2nd ed. (Leipzig, 1885–1888)

MGH   *Monumenta Germaniae historica*

PL   *Patrologia latina*, ed. J.P. Migne (Paris, 1841–1864)

PU   *Papsturkunden*

1. The most thorough works on Herman, or Heriman, are (in chronological order) *Histoire littéraire de la France*, 12, ed. Paulin Paris (Paris, 1869) 279–288 (and 289–292 on Herman of Laon, who was considered here as a separate figure); Georg Waitz, 'Hermann von Tournai und die Geschichtschreibung der Stadt', *Forschungen zur deutschen Geschichte*, 21 (1881) 431–448; *idem*, in

85

accomplished scribe and copied several works by Saint
Augustine and at least four breviaries.[2] He became abbot in 1127 and remained in that position until 1136 or
1137, when he resigned for reasons of health or, perhaps,
of temperament, since there are suggestions that he preferred writing to administration. Although he remained
involved in ecclesiastical affairs and travelled extensively
during the following years, he devoted himself primarily
to writing, and all his known works date from this period.[3]
He joined the Second Crusade in 1147 and is not heard of
again. He may have returned, but most scholars assume
that he died in the East.[4]

He went to Rome on two occasions, in 1140/1 and
1141/2, in order to win the support of the papacy for
the efforts of the clergy of Tournai to win independence
from the bishop of Noyon.[5] During his second visit he
began work on his *Book on the restoration of the monastery of*

the introduction to his edition of the *Monumenta historiae Tornacensis*, in *MGH,
Scriptores* in fol., 14:266–270; Max Manitius, *Geschichte der lateinischen Literatur
des Mittelalters,* Handbuch der Altertumswissenschaft, IX.2.1–3 (Munich,
1911–1931) 3:531–5; and Gerlinde Niemeyer, 'Die Miracula S. Mariae
Laudunensis des Abtes Hermann von Tournai', *Deutsches Archiv*, 27 (1971)
135–74, who showed conclusively that Herman of Tournai and Herman of
Laon were the same man, though some doubt on the point is still expressed in
the entry on Herman in the *Repertorium fontium historiae Medii Aevi*, 5 (Rome,
1984) 451, which has a useful bibliography on Herman.

2. A. Boutemy, 'Odon d'Orléans et les origines de la bibliothèque de l'abbaye
de Saint-Martin de Tournai', in *Mélanges dédiés à la mémoire de Félix Grat* (Paris,
1949) 2:193–194.

3. On Herman's writings see the entries, with editions and bibliographies, in
Michael McCormick, *Index scriptorum operumque Latino-Belgicorum Medii Aevi*,
ed. Léopold Genicot and Pierre Tombeur, 3:1–2 (Brussels, 1977–1979),
who cataloged, in addition to the five works mentioned below, three other
works attributed to Herman: *Vita secunda Eleutherii Tornacensis* (3:1, 61), *De
antiquitate urbis Tornacensis* (3:2, 292), and *Status imperii Judaici* (3:2, 293).

4. Cf. Waitz, 'Hermann' (cited n. 1) 434 and 437, who pointed out that
since the Continuation said only that Herman wanted to see (not necessarily
visit) the sepulchre of Christ, he may have lived until 1152.

5. The precise dates of Herman's visits to Rome are uncertain. Most scholars
agree on 1140 and 1142: see *Hist. litt.* (cited n. 1) 12:281; *GC*, 3:211E-
212C; Waitz, 'Hermann' (cited n. 1) 432–433, and *MGH, Scriptores* in

Saint Martin at Tournai, which he continued until at least
1146, and perhaps later, if he survived the crusade.[6] The
text history is complicated. It consists of several parts,
which may have originated separately, and an anonymous
continuation, in which Herman is referred to in the third
person,[7] but it is a work of high authority and considerable
historical importance. Presumably on one of his visits

---

fol., 12:267; and McCormick, *Index* (cited n. 3) 3:1, 128; but Niemeyer,
'Miracula' (cited n. 1) 147–151, proposed 1142 and 1143. It depends on
the date of Innocent II's order to the canons of Tournai to choose a bishop
and have him consecrated by the archbishop of Rheims, presuming that this
is the privilege Herman was said to have obtained allowing the election of a
bishop of Tournai (PL 180:125C-126C, and *MGH, Scriptores* in fol., 14:326):
Samuel Loewenfeld, *Epistolae pontificum Romanorum ineditae* (Leipzig, 1885)
pp. 93- 94, no. 184 (dated 30 December 1138–1142). It is dated 1141 in
JL, no. 8165; *PU in Frankreich*, N.F., 7: *Nördliche Ile-de-France und Vermandois*,
ed. Dietrich Lohrmann, Abhandlungen der Akademie der Wissenschaften in
Göttingen: Phil.-hist. Kl., 3 F., 95 (Göttingen, 1976) p. 97; cf. *PU in den
Niederlanden*, I: *Archivberichte*, ed. Johannes Ramackers, Abhandlungen der
Akademie der Wissenschaften in Göttingen: Phil.-hist. Kl., 3 F., 8 (Berlin,
1934) pp. 24–25, but 1142 by Niemeyer, 'Miracula' (cited n. 1) 151. Abbot
Anselm of Saint Vincent of Laon, with whom Herman stayed in Rome, was
in Rome on 12 December 1142, when he received a privilege from Innocent
II: *PU in Frankreich*, N.F., 4: *Picardie*, ed. Johannes Ramackers, Abhandlungen
der Akademie der Wissenschaften in Göttingen, Phil.-hist. Kl., 3 F., 27
(Göttingen, 1942) pp. 119–120, no. 33; cf. 138–140, no. 45, showing that
Anselm was still abbot on 28 February 1146 (o.s.), and 212–213, no. 97, for
abbot Walter in 1164. On Herman and the reestablishment of the bishopric of
Tournai, see Albert d'Haenens, 'Moines et clercs à Tournai au début du XIIe
siècle', in *La vita comune del clero nei secoli XI e XII. Atti della Settimana di studio:
Mendola, settembre 1959*, Pubblicazioni dell'Università cattolica del S. Cuore:
3 S., Scienze storiche, 2–3. Miscellanea del Centro di studi medioevali, 3
(Milan, 1962) 2: 99, with references in n. 130, and Constant Mews, 'The
Council of Sens (1141): Abelard, Bernard, and the Fear of Social Upheaval'
(forthcoming in *Speculum*).
6. PL 180:39–130, and (better) *MGH, Scriptores* in fol., 14:274–327; tr.
(through chapter 90, i.e. without the Continuation, of which the authorship
is doubtful) by Lynn Nelson, *The Restoration of the Monastery of Saint Martin
of Tournai*, Medieval Texts in Translation (Washington, D.C., 1996). See
McCormick, *Index* (cited n.3) 3:2, 129–130.
7. These sections were published together by Waitz, and studied by him,
under the title *Monumenta historiae Tornacensis*, in *MGH, Scriptores* in fol., 14,
but their precise origins and relation are uncertain.

to Rome Herman stayed in Vienne, where he met the
archbishop, Stephen, to whom he dedicated his treatise
On the Incarnation of Christ.[8] In the introductory letter he
thanked Stephen for his hospitality and gave some valuable
information about his own history and family.

Herman's *Miracles of Mary of Laon* and *Life of Saint
Ildefonsus of Toledo* were written at the request of Bishop
Bartholomew of Laon, who had gone to Spain, as Herman
explained in the introductory letter, to visit his cousin
King Alfonso of Aragon and Navarre.[9] The king had
promised Bartholomew

> that if you returned to see him a second time he
> would give you the body of the blessed deacon and
> martyr Vincent and also his most precious chasuble,
> which the blessed mother of God had given to Saint
> Ildefonsus, the archbishop of the city of Toledo,
> in return for the three little books he had written
> concerning her virginity.

Herman had 'by chance (*forte*)' seen these works at
Châlons-sur-Marne, and Bartholomew sent him back to
make a copy. 'I therefore first wrote a life of the said

8. PL 180:9–38, and (for the prefatory letter) *MGH, Scriptores* in fol., 14:268–269. See McCormick, *Index* (cited n. 3) 3.2, 127–128.

9. For editions of the *Vita* of Ildefonsus and the *Miracula Mariae*, see McCormick, *Index* (cited n. 3) 3.1, 84–85 and 106–107; *BHL* 3920 and 5398. The *Miracula* is of importance for the history of the arthurian legend: see J. S. P. Tatlock, 'The English Journey of the Laon Canons', *Speculum*, 8 (1933) 454–465, where it is attributed to Herman of Laon (see n. 1 above). On Bartholomew of Ver, who was bishop of Laon from 1113 until 1150/1, when he resigned to become a cistercian monk, see *Hist.litt.*, 12 (cited n. 1) 524–527; *GC*, 9:528E–532E; and Baudouin de Gaiffier, 'Relations religieuses de l'Espagne avec le nord de la France. Transferts de reliques', in his *Recherches d'hagiographie latine,* Subsidia hagiographica, 52 (Brussels, 1971) p. 13 (with references in n. 4), who also discussed (p. 15, n. 7) the manuscripts of Ildefonsus's *De virginitate*. Bartholomew was a nephew of Felicia of Roucy, the second wife of Alfonso I, king of Aragon and Navarre from 1104 to 1134, on whose family see José Maria Lacarra, *Vida de Alfonso el Batallador* (Saragossa, 1971) pp. 15–16.

Ildefonsus and afterwards I added his aforesaid little books.' He then composed a history—written in the name of the canons of Laon, he said, not his own—of the miracles performed in France and England by Mary's relics at Laon. To this he added an account of the ten premonstratensian and cistercian monasteries founded through the efforts of Bartholomew. Finally he expressed the hope, if he lived, to add 'other things that have happened or will happen in your days'.[10]

This information helps to explain the background of the *Letter about the body of Saint Vincent*, with which this article is concerned.[11] It is addressed to Anselm, abbot of Saint Vincent at Laon from 1129 until 1146, when he became first bishop of the reestablished see of Tournai, and to his brother Walter, who succeeded Anselm's successor William (d. 1156) as abbot of Saint Vincent and served until 1179.[12] When Herman was in Rome 'the previous year (*praeterito anno*)', he wrote, he had stayed with Anselm and Walter, who treated him with great courtesy. He had promised to send them the passion of some saints he had found in Saragossa, including Saint Vincent, the patron of their monastery. In Saragossa, the brother of Bishop Bertran, the archdeacon William, had received him and, when Herman expressed

10. PL 156:961B-964A, and *MGH, Scriptores* in fol., 14:268.
11. 'Epistola . . . de corpore s. Vincentii', *Analecta Bollandiana*, 2 (1883) 243–246; *BHL* 8649; McCormick, *Index* (cited n. 3) 3.1, 148. It is printed from a twelfth-century ms Brussels, BR, 9119, where it is associated with the Passion of Saint Vincent: see *Catalogus codicum hagiographicorum Bibliothecae regiae Bruxellensis* (Brussels, 1886–1889) 2:269. The text is also printed in Leopoldo Peñarroja Torrejón, *Cristianos bajo el Islam. Los Mozárabes hasta la reconquista de Valencia*, Monografías históricas, 4 (Madrid, 1993) pp. 321–325. A translation is appended to this article, with notes on points not covered in the text.
12. *GC*, 3:212BE, and 9:577C-578E (on Anselm) and 579BD (on Walter); René Poupardin, 'Cartulaire de Saint-Vincent de Laon', *Mémoires de la Société de l'histoire de Paris et de l'Ile-de-France*, 29 (1902) 257 (on Ansellus/Anselinus/Anselm) and 260 (on Walter), and the references in *PU in Frankreich*, N.F. 4 (cited n. 5).

his desire to visit Saint Vincent's shrine in Valencia, had summoned two monks from the so-called monastery 'of the Crow' of Saint Vincent. In reply to a number of questions about their monastery, where they had lived for thirty years, they told Herman that the only safe way to get there was, not by the direct route, which took six days, but by way of Compostela, where he could join a merchant caravan under safeguard from the king.[13] They themselves, they said, could not return to their monastery because it had been destroyed by the Muslims after the attack on Valencia by King Alfonso, who had brought the monks to the province of Saragossa and established them by pairs in various churches. Herman therefore abandoned his plan to go to Valencia, but before leaving Saragossa he visited the church of the Holy Martyrs, by implication to get some relics, though he did not say so.[14] He burst into tears at the sight of so many martyrs, and immediately (*statim*) wrote an account of their passion,

13. This route, they said, would take five weeks. See Thomas Glick, *Islamic and Christian Spain in the Early Middle Ages* (Princeton, 1979) p. 26, and Olivia R. Constable, *Trade and Traders in Muslim Spain,* Cambridge Studies in Medieval Life and Thought, 4 S., 24 (Cambridge, 1994) p. 45, both mentioning this letter.

14. The church *ad sanctas Massas* still exists in Saragossa under the church of Santa Engracia: see Rosa Guerreiro, 'Le rayonnement de l'hagiographie hispanique en Gaule pendant le haut Moyen Age: circulation et diffusion des *Passions* hispaniques', in *L'Europe héritière de l'Espagne wisigothique. Colloque international du C.N.R.S. tenu à la Fondation Singer-Polignac (Paris, 14–16 mai 1990)*, ed. Jacques Fontaine and Christine Pellistrandi (Madrid, 1992) p. 152 and n. 70, with further references. The term *massas* is explained in *AASS*, Nov. I:639A, as coming 'from the conglomeration (or mass) of ashes' of the compressed bodies. In the twelfth century the church, which was presumably a center of pilgrimage (and therefore a source of revenue), was the subject of dispute between the bishop of Saragossa and the bishop of Huesca: *PU in Spanien*, 2: *Navarra und Aragon*, ed. Paul Kehr, Abhandlungen der Gesellschaft der Wissenschaften zu Göttingen, Phil.-hist. Kl., N.F., 22 (Berlin, 1928) 2:328–329, no. 36 (19 April 1139) and 331–332, no. 39 (2 April 1141). See also *Documentos*, 1:471, 523, and 538, and 2:591, nos. 1, 65, 86, and 203, with several references to baths apparently associated with the church.

presumably the work he sent to Anselm and Walter in Rome.[15]

The visit to Rome which Herman mentioned in this letter probably occurred in 1142, when Anselm is known to have been there. Since Herman said that he was in Rome 'the previous year', his letter can be dated 1143 or perhaps 1144, depending on the style of dating and precise time of the visit. With regard to the visit to Spain, the only clue is the reference to Bishop Bertran of Saragossa and his brother William, who came from Narbonne. This bishop is otherwise unknown, unless his name is a corruption of Bernard, which seems unlikely given Herman's personal knowledge and the general accuracy of the manuscript.[16] Niemeyer suggested that Bertran came between Garcia, who was bishop until 1136, and Bernard, to whom the first sure reference is in 1139.[17] The picture is unclear, however, since Bernard appears on a document apparently dated January 1136, a Bishop William appears in 1134 and 1136, and there were several bishops (of other dioceses) named Bertran who may have been in Saragossa, though Herman specifically said *Bertranni ejusdem civitatis episcopi*.[18] Be this as it may, he

15. This work is lost or unindentified. *AASS*, Nov., I:643–649, printed two versions of a Passion of the Innumerable Martyrs, one of which is found in the same manuscript as Herman's letter: see *Cat. cod. Brux.* (cited n. 11) 2:271, no. 44. *Esp. sag.*, 30:286, referred to a manuscript of a 'Passio SS. Martyrum Innumerabilium' in the library of the Cistercians of Toledo (in 1775). Cf. de Gaiffier, 'Relations' (cited n. 9) p. 15, n. 5.

16. *Documentos*, 1:562, and 2:690, where Bishop Garcia is dated 1130–1136 and Bernard 1136–1152. See also *PU in Spanien* (cited n. 14) 1:222–223, the documents in *PU* cited in n. 14 above, and 2:354–355, no. 52 (19 May 1145/6) and 367–369, no. 63 (1151/2), where Bernard said that he had been to Rome five times during the pontificates of popes Innocent II and Eugene III.

17. Niemeyer, 'Miracula' (cited n. 1) 153–154. She also cited a reference to an archdeacon William of Saragossa in 1166. There are numerous references to Provost William of Saragossa (who may have been an archdeacon) between 1132 and 1142 (*Documentos*, 1:528, 531, and 540, and 2:571, 575, 591, 599, 606, and 607, nos. 73, 78, 87, 177, 181, 203, 217, and 225–227).

18. *Documentos*, 1:543, no. 90 (Bernard in 1136); 533, and 2:586, nos. 80 and 196 (William in 1134 and 1136); 1:500, no. 32 (Bertran of Huesca

probably visited Spain soon after his resignation as abbot in 1136/7. The passion was written at this time, Herman said, and copied 'in the same quire (*in hoc quaternione*)' as the letter, which was later reworked and personalized, as it were, for Anselm and Walter.

It seems reasonable to associate Herman's visit to Spain with the promise of King Alfonso I, who died in 1134, to give Bishop Bartholomew of Laon the body and chasuble of Saint Vincent. Herman may have been at loose ends after he resigned as abbot, and Bartholomew used him to get from Châlons-sur-Marne copies of the three books on the virginity of Mary by Ildefonsus of Toledo. He may also have sent Herman to Spain in order to obtain the relics promised him by the late king.

Vincent was among the most popular of christian saints, and his cult was observed in churches and monasteries all over Europe and in parts of the Greek East.[19] Already a century after his martyrdom at Valencia in 304, Prudentius sang Vincent's praises in the *Peristephanon*,[20] and a few years later Augustine, who wrote several sermons in his honor, asked 'What region today, or what province to which either the roman empire or the christian name extends, does not rejoice to celebrate the birthday of Vincent?'[21] A full account of the distribution of his

in 1123); 2:526, no. 124 (Bertran of Barzas in 1125); and 3:553, no. 330 (Bertran of Osma in 1132).

19. On the cult of Saint Vincent, see Louis de Lacger, 'Saint Vincent de Saragosse', *Revue d'histoire de l'église de France*, 13 (1927) 307–358, esp. 330–351; *Vies des saints et des bienheureux* (Paris, 1935–1959) 1:433–435; Carmen García Rodriguez, *El culto de los santos en la España romana y visigoda*, Consejo superior de investigaciones científicas: Monografias de historia eclesiastica, 1 (Madrid, 1966) pp. 257–278; and other references in my forthcoming article on 'The Crow of St Vincent', cited below, n. 38.

20. Prudentius, *Peristephanon*, IV. 77–108, and V in Corpus Christianorum: Series latina, 126:288–289 and 294–314.

21. Augustine, *Sermo* 276, in PL 38:1257. On Augustine's sermons on Saint Vincent, all of which date from the 410s, see Baudouin de Gaiffier, 'Sermons latins en l'honneur de S. Vincent antérieurs au Xe siècle', *Analecta Bollandiana*, 67 (1949 = Mélanges Paul Peeters, 1) 267–278 (272–274 on the attribution

relics would make an interesting chapter in the history of hagiography.[22] In principle he was buried in the monastery dedicated to him outside the walls of Valencia, but there were many other claimants to his body, or parts of it, and to vestments associated with him, such as the stole or tunic brought back from Spain by King Childeric I and given by him to the monastery of Saint Vincent at Paris, which later took the name of Saint-Germain-des-Prés.[23]

The muslim conquest of Spain led to a period of more or less open season for the relics of Spanish saints, including Vincent, whose bones were allegedly translated many times. They were said to have been taken in the second half of the eighth century to Algarve, later known as Cape St Vincent or the Sacred Cape, the most south-westerly point of the Spanish peninsula.[24] There is no

of *Sermo* 276), and Victor Saxer, 'La Passion de S. Vincent diacre dans la première moitiée du Ve siècle', *Revue des études Augustiniennes*, 35 (1989) 379–383. A seventh has recently been added to the six previously known sermons: François Dolbeau, 'Nouveaux sermons de saint Augustin pour les fêtes de martyrs', *Analecta Bollandiana*, 110 (1992) 265–266.

22. In addition to the works cited in n. 19, see *AASS*, Jan. 3:7–10; Paul Peeters, 'Une invention des SS. Valère, Vincent et Eulalie dans le Péloponèse', *Analecta Bollandiana*, 30 (1911) 296–306 (an account in Arabic from before the tenth century of the translation of Vincent's relics from Barcelona to Monemvasia); Manuel Sanchis Guarner, *La ciutat de València*, 2nd ed. (Valencia, 1976) p. 30; Arcadi Garcia, 'L'enigma històric de sant Vicent de la Roqueta', *L'Espill*, 17–18 (1983=Homenage al professor M. Sanchis Guarner, 1911–1981) 119; Eric Palazzo, 'L'iconographie des fresques de Berzé-la-Ville dans le contexte de la réforme grégorienne et de la liturgie clunisienne', *Les cahiers de Saint-Michel de Cuxa*, 19 (1988) 179; Patrick Geary, *Furta Sacra: Thefts of Relics in the Central Middle Ages*, 2nd ed. (Princeton, 1990) pp. 61–62, 122, and 135–138; and Peñarroja Torrejón, *Cristianos* (cited n. 11) pp. 103–105 and 315–317.

23. Gregory of Tours, *Historia Francorum*, III. 29, in *MGH, Scriptores rerum Merovingicarum*, 1.1, 133–134.

24. Stephen of Lisbon, *Miracula s. Vincentii*, intro., in *AASS*, Jan. 3:21 (*BHL* 8654–8655), and the excerpts from later historians, including Resende and Mariana, *ibid.*, 19–21. Aires Augusto Nascimento and Saul António Gomes, *S. Vicente de Lisboa e seus milagres medievais* (Lisbon, 1988), includes an edition and translation of the *Miracula*, dating the *Miracula* by Stephen before 1185 and the other *Miracula* between 1203 and 1248 (pp. 24–27). Cf. *Esp. sag.*, 8:187–

contemporary evidence for this. The muslim geographer
al-Idrīsī, writing about 1150, described a flourishing
church of the crow seven miles from the cape of Algarve
and said that it had not changed since the time of christian
rule, but he did not mention Saint Vincent.[25] There are

188 (dating the translation 788) and Joaquín (Jaime from vol. 6) Villanueva,
Viage literario á las iglesias de España (Madrid and Valencia, 1803–1852), 4:9
(citing *Esp. sag.*). This translation is mentioned by various modern scholars,
including Robert I. Burns, *The Crusader Kingdom of Valencia* (Cambridge, Mass.,
1967) 1:283; García Rodriguez, *Culto* (cited n. 19) p. 264; Victor Saxer, 'Le
culte de s. Vincent dans la peninsule hispanique avant l'an mil', in *IV Reunió
d'arqueologia cristiana hispànica. Lisboa, 28–30 de setembre / 1–2 d'octubre de 1992,*
Monografies de la Secció Històrico —Arqueològica, 4 (Barcelona, 1995) pp.
145–147, esp. 147, n. 35, on the *Translatio*; and Ann Christys, 'St-Germain
des-Prés, St Vincent and the martyrs of Cordoba', *Early Medieval Europe*, 7
(1998) 213 (dating the translation 759). See also de Lacger, 'Vincent' (cited
n. 14) 345–348, who dated the *Translatio* by Stephen in the thirteenth century,
or later, and discounted its historical value.
25. Edrîsî (al-Idrīsī), *Description de l'Afrique et de l'Espagne*, ed. and tr. Reinhart
Dozy and M. J. de Goeje (Leiden, 1866) pp. 218–219, locating it seven
miles from cape Algarve (Al-Gharb), which was twelve miles from Sagres;
cf. p. 207, with another reference to 'the church of the crow'. See also the
Géographie d'Aboulfeda (Abū al-Fīda, d. 1331), tr. Joseph Reinaud (Paris, 1848)
2.1:241, and the *Crónica del Moro Rasis*, ed. Diego Catalán and M. Soledad
de Andres, Fuentes cronístas de la historia de España, 3 (Madrid, 1974) p.
xxxviii, n. 81. This al- Rāzī, according to Saxer, 'Culte' (cited n. 24) 146, was
not one of the ninth-tenth century doctors named al-Rāzī, but an eleventh-
century traveller. The references to the church of Saint Vincent in Algarve
seem to be interpolations into later vernacular translations of his chronicle :
see Mário Martins, *Peregrinações e Livros de Milagres na nossa Idade Média*, 2nd
ed. (Lisbon, 1957) pp. 43–45, citing C. Michaelis de Vasconcelos, *André de
Resende e a Crónica do Mouro Rasis* (Lisbon, 1922), and Garcia Rodriguez, *Culto*
(cited n. 19) p. 264. It does not appear in E. Lévi-Provencal, 'La "Description
de l'Espagne" d'Ahmad al-Razi. Essai de reconstitution de l'original arabe et
traduction française', *Al-Andalus*, 18 (1953) 51–108, esp. 71–72 on Valencia
and 91 on Silves and Algarve. On the later capture of Silves near the alleged
site of the monastery of Saint Vincent, see Charles W. David, ed., 'Narratio de
itinere navali peregrinorum Hierosolymam tendentium et Silviam capientium
A.D. 1189', *Proceedings of the American Philosophical Society*, 81 (1939) 647–
662. See Francesco J. Simonet, *Historia de los Mozárabes de España*, Memorias
de la Real Academia de la Historia, 13 (Madrid, 1903) pp. 255–257; Antonio
Linage Conde, 'San Vicente mártir lazo peninsular del Mediterráneo al
Atlántico', in *Actas das II Jornadas Luso-Espanholas de História medieval* (Oporto,
1989) pp. 1–15, who discussed the traditions concerning the transfer of

some resemblances between the communities described in Herman's letter and by al-Idrīsī, but the matter remains a puzzle, and unless further evidence comes to light the so-called church of Saint Vincent in Algarve must be considered a ghost of later writers.

In the middle of the ninth century, according to Aimoin of Saint-Germain-des-Prés in his *History of the Translation of Saint Vincent*, a monk named Audaldus went to Valencia and obtained the relics of Saint Vincent, which he brought back to Castres, where they were suitably buried and became a focus of pilgrimage.[26] Aimoin also wrote an account of the efforts of the celebrated martyrologist Usuard to obtain the relics of Saint Vincent, but he was

the relics of Saint Vincent to Algarve and Lisbon; and Christophe Picard, 'Sanctuaires et pèlerinages chrétiens en terre musulmane: l'Occident de l'Andalus (Xe-XIIe siècle)', in *Pèlerinages et Croisades*, Actes du 118e congrès national annuel des sociétés historiques et scientifiques: Pau, octobre 1993 (Paris, 1995) pp. 238- 239 and 241, who cited al-Idrīsī and stressed the importance of pilgrimages but gave no firm evidence from before the twelfth century. There is no reference to this house in Laurent Cottineau, *Repertoire topo-bibliographique des abbayes et prieurés* (Mâcon, 1939–1970); Justo Pérez de Urbel, *Los monjes españoles en la edad media* (Madrid, 1933–1934; 2nd ed., 1945); Antonio Linage Conde, *Los orígines del monacato benedictino en la peninsula iberica,* Fuentes y estudios de historia leonesa, 9–11 (Leon, 1973), of which volume three includes a comprehensive 'Monasticon hispanum' up to 1109, with a section (pp. 741–746) on Portugal; or José Mattoso, 'A cultura monástica em Portugal (875–1200)', repr. in his *Religião e cultura na Idade Média portuguesa* (Lisbon, 1982) pp. 355–392.

26. Aimoin of Saint-Germain-des-Prés, *Historia translationis s. Vincentii*, in PL 126:1011–1024, and (better) Villanueva, *Viage* (cited n. 24) 4:167–206; *BHL* 8644. See de Lacger, 'Vincent' (cited n. 19) 307–308; *Vies des saints* (cited n. 19) 1:435; de Gaiffier, 'Relations' (cited n. 9) p. 13, n. 3; *Repertorium fontium historiae Medii Aevi*, 2 (Rome, 1967) 159 (dating it after 869); Geary, *Furta* (cited n. 22) pp. 61–62 (dating it 855) and 135–138 (dating it 869); and Christys, 'St- Germain' (cited n. 24) 212–214, who studied this text in comparison with Aimoin's *Translatio Georgii, Aurelii et Nathaliae* (cited n. 27 below). Castres rapidly became an established center for the cult of Saint Vincent, whose presence there was recognized by Pope Clement VII (see Villanueva, *Viage* [cited n. 24] 4:9): see Bernard Gui, *De fundatione et prioribus conventuum provinciarum Tolosanae et Provinciae ordinis Praedicatorum*, ed. P. A. Amargier, Monumenta ordinis Fratrum Praedicatorum historica, 24 (Rome, 1961) pp. 143–148.

unsuccessful and returned with some other relics.[27] The principal rival to Castres was Lisbon, where the relics of Vincent were brought in 1173/5 at the behest of King Alfonso Henriques of Portugal and installed in the cathedral there. The author of one account of this translation said that the body had rested in the basilica at Valencia for eight hundred years 'up to the times of King Alfonso of Portugal'.[28]

This statement must be taken with a grain of salt, since the author wanted to stress that Vincent's body had not left Valencia before being taken to Lisbon. This view was shared, according to the introductory letter to the *Miracles of Mary of Laon*, by King Alfonso I of Aragon, who offered the body of Saint Vincent to Bishop Bartholomew of Laon, and by the monks and clerics whom Herman met in Saragossa and who raised no question about the location of Vincent's body. Nothing definite is known about the shrine during the period of muslim rule, aside from an enigmatic reference to 'the church of the crows of Saint Vincent' in the so-called Pseudo-Isidorian history, which was written in Spain, probably by a writer of hispanic-arabic culture, in the tenth or eleventh century.[29] It remained a place of

27. Aimoin, *Translatio Georgii, Aurelii et Nathaliae*, in PL 115:939–960; *BHL* 3409. See Villanueva, *Viage* (cited n. 24) 4:9; de Lacger, 'Vincent' (cited n. 19) 351–354; Baudouin de Gaiffier, 'Les notices hispaniques dans le martyrologue d'Usuard', *Analecta Bollandiana*, 55 (1937) 268–283 (dating Usuard's visit to Spain in 858); idem, 'Relations' (cited n. 9) p. 13; and Christys, 'St-Germain' (cited n. 24) 199–216.
28. *Translatio s. Vincentii*, in *Analecta Bollandiana*, 1 (1882) 270–278, and *Cat. cod. Brux.* (cited n.11) 2:466–471, and Stephen of Lisbon, *Translatio et miracula* (cited n. 24); *BHL* 8653–8655. See Simonet, *Historia* (cited n. 25), pp. 257–258 and 768, and de Lacger, 'Vincent' (cited n. 19) 348–351, who regarded the anonymous *Translatio* as a later forgery designed to strengthen the claims of Lisbon to the body of Saint Vincent.
29. *Historia Pseudo-Isidoriana*, in *MGH, Auctores antiquissimi*, 11 (= Cronica minora, 2) 382, where the barbarians entering Spain at the time of Constantine were said to have occupied *iuxta Cartaginem, a Cartagine usque ad ecclesiam Corvorum sancti Vincentii*. See *Repertorium*, 5 (cited n. 1) 538, with a

pilgrimage, however, and was honored by Muslims as well
as Christians. Aimoin in the mid-ninth century referred
to the tombs as 'still intact' and the marble container
of the relics as 'of wonderful beauty', and relic hunters
like Audaldus and Usuard seem to have had access to the
shrine, even though one of them was allegedly successful
and the other unsuccessful in securing the relics.[30] The

bibliography on the disputed question of the sources of this chronicle. The
editors of the *Crónica del Moro Rasis* (cited n. 25) p. xxxviii (who thought that
the church in question was on Cape Saint Vincent, whereas it was apparently
on the eastern side of the Iberian peninsula) said that the reference showed
that the *Historia* drew on arabic sources, which mention 'the church of the
crow'. The reverse is probably true, since the association of Saint Vincent
with crows antedated the muslim conquest. On the pre-muslim history of
the shrine, see Enric A. Llobregat, *La primitiva Cristiandat Valenciana. Segles IV
al VIII,* Sèrie Taronja, 17 (Valencia, 1977) p. 102, who raised some question
regarding the existence of the monastery of Saint Vincent at la Roqueta in
the early Middle Ages (cf. Linage Conde, 'San Vicente' [cited n. 25] pp. 14–
15); Victor Saxer, 'La version brève BHL 8638 de la passion de S. Vincent',
Hispania sacra, 43 (1991) 698–700; Peñarroja Torrejón, *Cristianos* (cited n.
11) pp. 47–48 and 55; and Saxer, 'Culte' (cited n. 24) 141–143, citing
recent archaeological evidence. It appears that there were three stages to its
'monumentalization': (1) the primitive tomb and *memoria martyris* close to the
sea (4th century), (2) a basilica outside the city, perhaps in its present location
(5th century?), and (3) the cathedral (6th century?). See also: Rafaela Soriano
Sanchez, 'L'édifice cultique de la prison de saint Vincent à Valence / Espagne',
in *Akten des XII. internationalen Kongresses für christliche Archäologie. Bonn, 22–28
September 1991,* Jahrbuch für Antike und Christentum: Ergänzungsband, 20
(Münster, 1995) 2:1193–1201, who presents, however, no firm evidence
associating the archaeological remains with Saint Vincent.
30. Simonet, *Historia* (cited n. 25) pp. 253 and 256–257; R. Menéndez Pidal,
La España del Cid, 7th ed. (Madrid, 1969) 2:547, saying that the church of
Saint Vincent was the center for Mozarabs in Valencia in the eleventh century;
Burns, *Crusader Kingdom* (cited n. 24) 1:283: 'His [Vincent's] place of burial
remained as a tangible relic to be cherished by native Christians through
the dark night of Moslem rule;' Sanchis Guarner, *Ciutat de València* (cited
n. 22) p. 30; and Antonio Linage Conde, 'Algunas particularidades de la
implantación mendicante en la Peninsula Ibérica', *Arquivo histórico Dominicano
Português,* 3.2, =Actas do II Encontro sobre história dominicana (Porto, 1986)
14 (of offprint). On the disputed question of the Mozarabs in Valencia, see
Isidro de Las Cagigas, *Los Mozarabes* (Madrid, 1947–1948) 1:464; Glick,
Islamic and Christian Spain (cited n. 13) p. 115; Peñarroja Torrejón, *Cristianos*
(cited n. 11) *passim;* and Thomas Glick, *From Muslim Fortress to Christian Castle*

evidence of Herman's letter shows that in addition to the monastery there was a church on the beach near the sea, to which pilgrims were guided by the crows. The monastery was large and prosperous in the early twelfth century, when the two monks whom Herman met in Saragossa joined the community. According to their account, which includes various interesting details about the monastery, there were forty monks living under an abbot and following the Rule of Benedict, though there is no indication of when it was adopted.[31] It may have been during the period from 1094 until 1098, when Rodrigo Diaz, the Cid, controlled Valencia, before its recovery by the Almoravids in 1102.[32]

All this changed, the monks said, after the attack on Valencia by King Alfonso. This must refer to the expedition of Alfonso I of Aragón in the summer of 1129, when he besieged Valencia and defeated the Muslims at Cullera.[33] He came, the monks said, 'with pagans who

---

(Manchester and New York, 1995) p. 54; cf. Christys, 'St-Germain' (cited n. 24) 201, n. 11.

31. See also the hymn to Saint Vincent written by Garnier of Rebais in the first half of the twelfth century, in *Cat. cod. Brux.* (cited n. 11) 2:590–594, which shows some knowledge of the monastery (see n. 43 below). On the introduction of the Rule of Benedict into the Iberian peninsula, where it replaced various native monastic rules, see above all volume two of Linage Conde, *Orígenes* (cited n. 29), and, at Valencia, Peñarroja Torrejón, *Cristianos* (cited n. 11) pp. 109, 117, and 224. Garcia, 'L'enigma' (cited n. 22) pp. 118–119, suggested that before adopting the Rule of Benedict the 'monks' may have been canons.

32. Reinhart Dozy, *Recherches sur l'histoire politique et littéraire de l'Espagne pendant le moyen âge*, 1 (Leiden, 1849) p. 571 (citing arabic sources); Joseph F. O'Callaghan, *A History of Medieval Spain* (Ithaca and London, 1975) pp. 209–212; Sanchis Guarner, *Ciutat de València* (cited n. 22) pp. 58–60; Glick, *Islamic and Christian Spain* (cited n. 13) p. 47; Peñarroja Torrejón, *Cristianos* (cited n. 11) pp. 87–121; and Hugh Kennedy, *Muslim Spain and Portugal* (Harlow, 1996) pp. 165–166.

33. *Documentos*, 2:555, no.157, issued 5 May 1129 'Quando rex Adefonsus senior obsedit Valentiam'. See Lacarro, *Vida* (cited n. 9) pp. 96–99, and Bernard Reilly, *The Contest of Christian and Muslim Spain, 1031–1157* (Cambridge, Mass., and Oxford, 1992) p. 170. On Alfonso's expedition

had been expelled from the city', presumably enemies
of the Almoravids, who believed that the monks of Saint
Vincent had stirred up the king against them. This would
explain the ill-will born by the Muslims of Valencia against
the monastery, and its destruction and the expulsion of
the monks, and also the danger of travelling directly from
Saragossa to Valencia. It may have been safer, though far
longer, to go by way of Santiago, with a safe-conduct
from Alfonso VII, because the Muslims at Valencia were
on better terms with the king of León than the king of
Aragón.[34]

The church was rebuilt, about four thousand feet
south-west of the city in the suburb of Rayosa, after the
attack on Valencia by Alfonso II of Aragón in 1172,[35]
and it enjoyed a measure of protection and autonomy
even before the final conquest of Valencia by James I in
1238.[36] A hospital was added, and it was described as
'the central shrine of the new kingdom' of Aragón and
'the symbol and center of Valencian spiritual life'. In the
thirteenth century it was granted successively to Lagrasse,

into Andalusia in 1125–1126 and the accompanying Mozarab defections, see
Ordericus Vitalis, *Historia ecclesiastica*, XIII.6, ed. Marjorie Chibnall, Oxford
Historical Texts (Oxford, 1969–1980) 6:404–407.

34. On 10 October 1129 Alfonso of Aragón forbade any Muslim to go from
his lands to Valencia without his permission: *Documentos*, 1:522, no. 63.

35. Villanueva, *Viage* (cited n. 24) 4:9–10; Sanchis Guarner, *Ciutat de València*
(cited n. 22) p. 67; Burns, *Crusader Kingdom* (cited n. 24) 1:283–284; and
Peñarroja Torrejón, *Cristianos* (cited n. 11) pp. 276–279.

36. Linage Conde, 'Algunas particularidades' (cited n. 30) 14, mentioned a
grant to the shrine of Saint Vincent by Alfonso VIII of Castile and its cession
by the muslim king of Valencia to Alfonso II of Aragón and, later, to San Juan
de la Peña. See Peñarroja Torrejón, *Cristianos* (cited n. 11) pp. 175–177, and
Garcia, 'L'enigma' (cited n. 22) 115, who dated the grant by Alfonso III in
1167/8. On the conquest of Valencia by James I, see O'Callaghan, *History*
(cited n. 32) p. 247; Kennedy, *Muslim Spain* (cited n. 32) pp. 269–71; and
Robert Burns, 'The Many Crusades of Valencia's Conquest (1225–1280): An
Historiographical Labyrinth', in *On the Social Origins of Medieval Institutions:
Essays in Honor of Joseph F. O'Callaghan*, ed. Donald Kagay and Theresa M. Vann,
The Medieval Mediterranean, 19 (Leiden, Boston, and Cologne, 1998) pp.
167–177, esp. 172–177.

Saint Victorian, the Mercedarians, and, in 1286, the Cistercians of Poblet.[37]

Herman's letter also added a significant detail to the development of the ancient legend of the crow (or, in some accounts, crows) who was said to have protected Vincent's body when it was exposed after his martyrdom.[38] Various sources show the persistance throughout the Middle Ages, among both Christians and Muslims, of the association of crows with Vincent and his monastery, which was known as the monastery of the crow or of the crows, as the monks whom Herman met in Saragossa called it. In reply to Herman's question they said that owing to the monastery's position near the sea the way there was obscured every night by the sand blown by the wind. Two crows, descendants of the crow that protected Vincent's body, lived in the church and flew out to guide pilgrims.[39] This, plus the information about the miraculous daily catch of fish sufficient for any number of guests, suggests that pilgrims continued to visit the monastery in the period before its destruction after Alfonso's attack on Valencia in 1129. To what extent this corresponded to reality, and whether or not the body of Saint Vincent was still there, is another question.[40]

APPENDIX

TO HIS LORD, lord A[nselm], by the grace of God abbot of Saint Vincent of Laon, and to the most sacred lord Walter, his brother not only in the

37. Burns, *Crusader Kingdom* (cited n. 24) 1:215, 285, and 289, cf. 47 and the bibliography in 2:502, n.3.
38. See my article on 'The Crow of St Vincent', forthcoming in the Festschrift in honor of Alexander Murray.
39. In ch. 14 of the *Translatio s. Vincentii* (cited n. 28) the crows were said to have announced visitors by flying ahead of them.
40. See de Lacger, 'Vincent' (cited n. 19) 351–356, on the dispute among historians since the sixteenth century over the location of Vincent's relics.

flesh by also in spirit, brother Her[man], the poor little
servant of both, to be in glory eternally with Christ, from
Christ, through Christ, [and] in Christ.

No word of mouth is enough for me to give thanks
for your kindnesses. My lord the lord abbot deigned to
receive me with him in his own house last year when I
came to Rome and did not know where to lodge, and as
long as he stayed there he wanted never to eat without me,
but even when the meal was ready and served he waited
for me like some great man, and he was accustomed, as a
very polite man, never to address me except as his lord.
I can neither enumerate nor remunerate the good things
that he did for me both in Rome and on my return, but
I pray that God may reward him for me. Lord Walter his
brother, from the time he first knew me, clung to me
with the same affection that Jonathan the son of the king
still showed for the hitherto poor man David. And may
the Lord therefore reward him for me.

I promised to each of you separately that I would send
you the passion of certain martyrs that I found, and wrote
down what was found, in the city of Saragossa, where
your patron Saint Vincent was archdeacon. When I first
came from there, God permitting, I celebrated mass at the
altar of the same Saint Vincent, [and] the lord archdeacon
William, the brother of Bishop Bertran of the same city,
but originally from the city of Narbonne, received me
most graciously in the hospice there. Both in face and feeling the man seemed to me very like lord Walter. Talking
with him in a familiar manner, I said that I wanted to go to
Valencia, where Saint Vincent reposed, and I asked his advice concerning this. He replied that he was roused by the
same desire, but for fear of the gentiles who lived there-
abouts he could not fulfil his desire. He spoke and at once
summoned a boy and ordered him to bring to him two
monks of Saint Vincent who were staying in the same city.

I saluted them when they came and after a kiss asked
them where they came from, and they replied that they

were monks of Saint Vincent of the Crow.[41] 'And where',
I ask, 'is that place?' 'Next to Valencia', they answer, 'is
a certain abbey of monks built in honor of Saint Vincent,
whose body is concealed there in the high altar.' 'And
why', I ask, 'is it called Saint Vincent of the Crow?' 'Because', they reply, 'there are two crows who guide the
pilgrims coming to Saint Vincent, since without their
guidance no one could arrive there. For the church is
built on the shore of the sea; for a certain wind coming
naturally every night from the sea so moves the whole sand
of the shore that, if today an army of ten thousand ran
fighting on the shore of the sea, on the following morning
it would be impossible to find a trace of a single man, since
the sands are removed by the wind and scattered here and
there. But the crows which live in the church fly out to
meet pilgrims and lead them to the church by gradually
flying back in front of them; they also are said to be from
the progeny of that crow which preserved the body of the
blessed Vincent, [after it was] thrown outside Valencia at
the order of Dacian,[42] unharmed by wild beasts.'

Then I say: 'And how many monks are in your monastery?' 'There could', they reply, 'be forty.' 'Do you
have', I say, 'an abbot?' 'We have,' they say. 'What', I say,
'rule do you keep in your monastery?' 'The rule', they
say, 'of Saint Benedict'. 'Do you', I say, 'eat meat?' 'We
do not', they say, 'eat the meat of quadrupeds, since Saint
Benedict forbids it, but we eat the meat of birds, since it is

41. The tenses in the dialogue follow those of the Latin.
42. On the *praetor* or *praeses* Dacian and the location of Vincent's martyrdom
see Baudouin de Gaiffier, 'Sub Daciano praeside. Étude de quelques passions
espagnoles', *Analecta Bollandiana*, 72 (1954) 378–396, who said that he
became 'un personage de premier plan dans l'hagiographie hispanique'
(395) and that according to Augustine he was converted to Christianity,
and Saxer, 'Passion' (cited n. 21) 290–291. Sebastian Lenain de Tillemont
said in his *Mémoires pour servir à l'histoire ecclésiastique des six premiers siècles*
(Paris, 1693–1712) 5:677, that the name Dacian became notorious owing
to Vincent's martyrdom and was applied to other persecutors whose names
were unknown.

not prohibited by him. But we also rarely eat it, because we have a much greater supply of fish than birds. For every day early in the morning our fishermen enter the sea and bring back as many fish [which] they have caught as we have brothers in the house and so large that his [fish] is sufficient for each brother to be fully satisfied. And if we see the number of brothers to be exceeded by the number of fish, we know that guests are going to come there, since although we have lived in this monastery now for thirty years, we have never seen the fish to be less or more than the eaters, but there will be as many eaters that day as there are fish brought by the fishermen in the morning.'[43]

Then I say: 'How great a trip do you think it is to Valencia?' 'He who in view of (*propter*) the fear of the pagans', they say, 'can go by the direct road, will arrive there in six days. But no one dares to go there by the direct way.' 'And what', I say, 'advice do give me to go there? For I desire greatly to pray at the body of Saint Vincent.' 'If', they say, 'you wish to go there, go first to Saint James, and join the merchants who go safely by the safe conduct of the king after the customary tribute has been given, and thus you can go.' 'And in how many', I say, 'days can I then arrive there?' 'Truly, brother', they say, 'it is fitting for you to spend five weeks on the journey'. 'And when', I say 'do you think that you will go to your monastery, so that I can go with you?' 'Truly, brother', they say 'we have no hope of going there any more. For King Alfonso with the pagans expelled from this city laid siege to Valencia with an army in order that he might likewise expel the pagans from this city. The pagans, saying that he came against them by our counsel and request, invaded our monastery in the middle of the

43. Garnier of Rebais in his hymn to Saint Vincent, in *Cat. cod. Brux.* (cited n. 11) 1:594, also commented on the miraculous number of fish caught each day: 'They do not receive more or less . . . than fits those who are coming.'

night, and after all our goods had been plundered they expelled all of us with our abbot, and thus they destroyed our place entirely. But the king took us with him into this province and placed us two by two in different churches.'

When I heard these things, I entirely despaired of making the voyage that I had wished to make and dismissed them to go. The archdeacon, however, led me to a certain church which is called *ad Sanctas Massas*, in which the bones of more than forty thousand martyrs are said to be hidden. When I entered such a sweetness suddenly settled in my breast from the presence, I believe, of the saints that the archdeacon himself was amazed that I could in no way stem the flow of tears that burst forth. I therefore at once wrote their passion in this quire and have sent it to you and all those who wish to read it. Be well. That King Alfonso was the son of King Sancho, born from the cousin of lord Bishop Bartholomew of Laon.[44]

44. This post-script, as it were, may have been added in order to explain the reason for Herman's visit to Spain, since Anselm and Walter would have known of Bartholomew's interest in Saint Vincent and perhaps also of the king's offer to give him some relics.

H. E. J. Cowdrey

Saint Edmund Hall, Oxford

Some Reflections upon Stephen Harding's Letter to the Abbot and Monks of Sherborne

MY OWN INDEBTEDNESS to Father Chryso-gonus Waddell does not arise primarily from the work on medieval music and liturgy by which he has made so outstanding a contribution; it has to do, rather, with the illumination that he has cast upon the thought and writings of Stephen Harding, the English-man who became abbot of Cîteaux from 1109 to 1133 and who died in 1134. Of particular value has been his edition of and commentary upon the letter which, towards the end of his life, Stephen wrote to the abbot and monks of Sherborne in Dorset, and which survives only in a late twelfth-century copy in Cambridge, Jesus College, MS 34 (Q.B. 17), fo. 108ᵛ.[1] It would be vain to seek to add anything save minor details to Fr Chrysogonus's full and excellent commentary. But it may be worthwhile to reflect a little about the wider significance of Stephen's letter, both in its monastic context and in the light of other pieces of evidence for Stephen's monastic aspirations to which Fr Chrysogonus has drawn attention.

---

1. C. Waddell, 'Notes Towards the Exegesis of a Letter by Saint Stephen Harding', in: E. Rozanne Elder (ed.), *Noble Piety and Reformed Monasticism,* Studies in Medieval Cistercian History 7 (Kalamazoo, 1981) 10–39, with text at p. 16 and photograph as frontispiece to the volume; repr. E. Rozanne Elder (ed.), *The New Monastery: Texts and Studies on the Early Cistercians* (Kalamazoo and Spencer, 1998) 88–123.

In general terms, Stephen's letter to Abbot Thurstan and the congregation of monks at Sherborne evokes two ways in which leading abbots might offer edification and encouragement in the religious life to other communities as well as to their own monks. First, Stephen opened the main body of his letter with the significant pronouncement that 'The task of letters is to address those who are absent as if they were present, and to join together by the fellowship of charity those whom the intervals of places separate from one another' (lines 4–6).[2] It should be recalled that, by the conventions of Stephen's time, abbots might address themselves not only to their own monastic houses and subjects but to other communities; as honoured guests, they might preside in chapter and discharge there some or all of the abbatial duties which included the edification of the community which they were visiting. The privilege of so doing might be part of confraternity agreements or it might be exercised on a less formal basis; references to it are sufficiently few in number to suggest that a special honour was involved. Thus, it was to his 'most dear' lord Odo, the venerable abbot of Saint-Remi at Rheims (1118–51) that Abbot Peter the Venerable of Cluny granted that he might hold chapter at Cluny or its dependencies 'like abbots professed by us'.[3] Stephen's letter was written with a comparable note

2. References, including line references, to Stephen's letter and page references to Fr Waddell's articles are to the original version in *Noble Piety* (as n. 1)
3. For the text of the relevant confraternity agreement, see C. H. Talbot, 'Odo of Saint-Remy: a Friend of Peter the Venerable', in: G. Constable and J. Kritzeck (ed.), *Petrus Venerabilis, 1156–1956: Studies and Texts Commemorating the Eighth Centenary of his Death,* Studia Anselmiana 40 (Rome, 1956) 21–37, at pp. 21–22. (I have corrected *nostri* to *nobis* from the MS.) For a similar grant of *c.* 1107 by Abbot Hugh of Cluny to Abbot Godfrey of Vendôme, see C Metais (ed.), *Cartulaire de l'abbaye cardinale de la Trinité, Vendôme,* 4 vols. (Paris, 1892–1900) 2:179–180, no. 416. For the custom within the Cistercian Order when the abbot of a daughter house came to the New Monastery, see *Carta caritatis prior,* cap. 6, in C. Waddell (ed.), *Narrative and Legislative Texts from Early Cîteaux* (Brecht: Commentarii Cistercienses, 1999) 277–278, 446.

of privileged intimacy and was to be heard as though he were amongst them, with the fellowship of charity (*caritatis contubernium*) implying his presence. By this means, Stephen suggested that he had a special standing with the hearers of his letter.

Second, Stephen was concerned to offer edification and encouragement to his former community because he was writing to them in prospect of his own death: 'I am entering prosperous upon the way of all flesh' (*viam universe carnis letus ingredior*) (line 14). As a gift in some measure to be shared with them, his prosperity at the end of his life afforded another reason for the note of privileged intimacy in which he addressed them. It is reminiscent of the tone and content of the final dispositions of other leading figures in the contemporary monastic order which they made over a period of time as death approached. For this time was one of especial solemnity; it had its own conventions and accepted themes of speaking and writing. Again, cluniac sources are particularly suggestive, and especially the last statements of the great Abbot Hugh of Semur (1049–1109) which are preserved at length.[4]

Major differences, to be sure, spring to the eye between the lengthy statements which Abbot Hugh made at the very end of his life to his own family of monks and Abbot Stephen's brief letter addressed to an abbot and congregation who were not his subjects. Yet there are significant points in common. Both great men, who were powerful to support those less strong than themselves, made their statements not in reply to the approaches of others but on their own initiative and as seemed right to them in their last days. Such is the implication, not only of Hugh's fatherly words, but also of Stephen's

4. See H. E. J. Cowdrey (ed.), 'Memorials of Abbot Hugh of Cluny (1049–1109)', in *Two Studies in Cluniac History 1049–1126,* Studi Gregoriani 11 (Rome, 1978), esp. Gilo, *Vita sancti Hugonis abbatis,* 2.6–13, pp. 96–103, and *Miscellanea,* 8–9, pp. 170–175.

reference to the good report of the monks of Sherborne that had percolated to him (*bonam famam que de vobis ad nos usque manavit*) (lines 16–17). Both men identified closely with their hearers. Hugh did so as their abbot, addressing his most beloved and most dear brothers, sons, and daughters, present and absent.[5] Since the monks of Sherborne were not his subjects nor was he now of their congregation, Stephen was the more at pains to identify himself with them: they were his bone and flesh (line 6); God, the living fountain, had filled him, the empty vessel, in order that they might hold strongly to monastic religion and be bold concerning the Lord (*ut vos . . . religionem fortiter tenere, et de Domino presumere auderetis*) (lines 10–13).[6]

Both abbots recalled that they had greatly extended the monastic families that they had undertaken to rule. Hugh did so factually: he had enlarged Cluny with monks and possessions not only in Burgundy but throughout southern and western Europe.[7] Stephen was more reflective on the point. Having left his own land alone and poor (*pauper*), he approached his death rich (*dives*) with forty companies. For this reason, he could write of himself as he approached death as being 'prosperous' (*letus*); for the context surely requires that the adjective should be so translated, rather than as 'glad'. Stephen could thus express a confidence, not rooted in inadmissible presumption on his part but in the palpable and objective blessing of God, that in return for his work as abbot of Cîteaux he could confidently expect the penny promised by God to faithful workers in the vineyard (lines 13–16). Hugh had much more to say about his own shortcomings as abbot, but he, too, could reflect that, such as he was, through

5. *Imprecatio, Misc.* 9 (as n. 4) p. 172.
6. For the translation of the last four words, Fr Chrysogonus rightly points to the Vulgate text of Judith 6: 15: 'Notes' (as n. 1), pp. 24–25.
7. *Imprecatio, Misc.* 9 (as n. 4) p. 173.

the prayers of his monks he had discharged the heavy obedience of being abbot for sixty years or more.[8] Each, in his different way, sought the increase of his audience in their vocation to the gaining of eternal life. For Hugh, eternal life was the divinely given end in which at last he and his monks and nuns would mutually rejoice perpetually on each other's account.[9] For Stephen, the monks of Sherborne were to progress until death in virtue and true religion so that they might deserve to see the God of gods (lines 16–21).

In general, Stephen's letter, short though it is, thus evokes the words of exhortation that monastic figures gave both during their lifetimes to favoured communities and in anticipation of their imminent death to those whom they felt an especial obligation to address.

Stephen's letter to the monks of Sherborne may next be considered in its place as the final text in the short but significant series of letters and pronouncements that stand in his name. The first such item, and by far the most difficult to consider, purports to originate from the time before Stephen left Molesme for Cîteaux. Writing *c.* 1125, the english historian William of Malmesbury devoted an excursus in his *Gesta regum* to a eulogistic account of the origin of the Cistercian Order and to Stephen's place in it. His account includes a defence by Stephen, given in direct speech, of a strict observance of the Rule of Saint Benedict in face of the accretions that were current at Molesme.[10] Stephen's reported words are striking and novel. They have attracted surprisingly little discussion, although Fr Chrysogonus has pertinently

8. Ibid.
9. *Imprecatio, Misc.* 9 (as n. 4) p. 175.
10. For the excursus, see R. A. B. Mynors, R. M. Thomson, and M. Winterbottom (ed.), *William of Malmesbury, Gesta regum Anglorum*, 4.334–7, vol. 1 (Oxford, 1998) 576–585; for Stephen's speech, see cap. 334.3–5, pp. 578–581.

drawn attention to them,[11] while Giles Constable has given them passing but trenchant consideration.[12] There can, of course, be no question of a verbatim record of Stephen's actual words, and the possibility lies open that Stephen's speech was wholly concocted by William. But a middle position is also arguable: that William wrote up in his own way a debate at Molesme of which he had received an authentic report. In favour of such a position, it can be argued that Stephen's speech cannot easily be paralleled in form or substance elsewhere in William's writings; although there is much vagueness in William's account of Cistercian origins and of Stephen's career, there is also a basis of otherwise attested circumstantial information; William's warm and generous admiration of the Cistercians, who in many ways challenged his own black-monk way of life, demonstrates that he was familiar enough with their history and aspirations to form an educated opinion. Stephen's set-piece speech may well arise from William's familiarity with arguments that Stephen had actually used.

It is certainly powerfully and distinctively argued. Its keynote is the cardinal place of reason (*ratio*) in cosmology, human motivation, and man's apprehension of proper authority. In a speech of one hundred sixty-four words, the noun *ratio* occurs fifteen times. *Ratio* did not signify a human faculty of reason in anything like the modern sense; indeed, in some respects its meaning is better captured by the modern word 'order'. In macrocosm, it was by his ordering *ratio* that God made, rules, and governs the universe. The macrocosm has its microcosm in man. As such, human nature, too, should subsist by

11. C. Waddell, 'The Reform of the Liturgy from a Renaissance Perspective', in: R. L. Benson and G. Constable (ed.), *Renaissance and Renewal in the Twelfth Century* (Oxford, 1982) 88–109, at pp. 104–107.
12. G. Constable, 'Renewal and Reform in Religious Life: Concepts and Realities', in: Benson and Constable (as n. 11) pp. 37–67, at pp. 61–62; id., *The Reformation of the Twelfth Century* (Cambridge, 1996) 142–145.

reason and balance (*ratione et aequilibritate*). But by sluggishness (*desidia*) human nature often falls from reason. To
restore matters, many laws have been laid down—after
all else (*novissime*) by the Rule of Saint Benedict, which
recalled to reason the looseness of nature (*fluxum naturae*).
In this connection reason and authority are one and the
same; the Rule embodied the reason without which God
had created and recreated nothing, and it supplied the
criterion by which the monastic life should be directed
and corrected.

The sources of this argument remain largely unexplored, but one possibility may be noticed here. Con-
gruity of thought suggests that a cue for this argument
about *ratio* may have been provided by the opening lines
of a passage in Boethius's *De consolatione Philosophiae* which
was widely and pertinently commented upon by earlier
medieval writers and again in the twelfth century: it is
Boethius's superb poetic version of the first part of Plato's
Timaeus which begins:

O qui perpetua mundum ratione gubernas
Terrarum caelique sator qui tempus ab aevo
Ire iubes stablisque manens das cuncta moveri . . .
O you who govern the world by perpetual reason,
Planter of earth and heaven who command time for
    ever to glide,
And remaining steadfast yourself cause all things to be
    moved . . .

It concludes with an expression of lifelong human aspira-
tion for the eternal:

Da pater augustam menti conscendere sedem, . . .
Dissice terrenae nebulas et pondera molis
Atque tua splendore mica! Tu namque serenum,
Tu requies tranquilla piis, te cernere finis,
Principium, vector, dux, semita, terminus idem.
Grant, father, to the mind to ascend the august
    seat, . . .

Cut away the clouds and burdens of earthly weight
And shine in your splendour! For you are brightness,
You are tranquil rest for the faithful; to see you is the
    end—
You, the beginnning, the vehicle, the guide, the path,
    the farthest bound.[13]

Perhaps significantly for Stephen, Boethius introduced
this *metrica* by a *prosa* which ends with this dialogue with
Philosophy:

> 'But since,' she said, 'as Plato has it in the *Timaeus,*
> also in the least of matters divine aid should be
> besought, what do you think should now be done that
> we may deserve to discover the seat of that highest
> good?' 'The father of all things,' I said, 'should
> be invoked; for if this has been left undone, no
> beginning is rightly established (*nullum rite fundatur
> exordium*).'[14]

In debates about the direction of what were seen as
the 'new monasteries' of Molesme and Cîteaux,[15] the
poem *O qui perpetua* may have presented Stephen with
a context of ideas within which to set his insistence
upon the authority and sufficiency of the Rule of Saint
Benedict. While nothing is known for certain or in detail
about Stephen's reading, some of the many discussions of
O qui perpetua may have assisted him in this. It was, of
course, widely acknowledged that the poem, like much

13. *De consolatione Philosophiae,* 3, metrica 9, in H. F. Stewart and E. K. Rand (ed. and trans.), *Boethius: The Theological Treatises and The Consolation of Philosophy* (London and Cambridge Mass., 1918) 262–267. For the study of the *De cons. Phil.* in the middle ages, see P. Courcelle, *La Consolation de Philosophie dans la tradition littéraire: antécédents et posterité de Boèce* (Paris, 1968). For three examples of tenth- and early eleventh-century commentaries, see R. B. C. Huygens, 'Mittelalterliche Kommentare zum *O qui perpetua . . .* herausgegeben', *Sacris erudiri,* 6 (1954) 373–427.
14. *De cons. Phil.* 3, *prosa* 9 (as n. 13) pp. 262–263.
15. Molesme: William of Malmesbury, *Gesta regum,* 4.334.3, (as n. 10) pp. 578–579; Cîteaux: regularly called the New Monastery until *c.* 1119.

else in the *De consolatione Philosophiae*, exhibited platonist ideas that seemed contrary to the catholic faith.[16] But commentators also showed that a christian interpretation could be placed upon it. Thus, Boethius saw that the world was ruled by perpetual reason because he understood it to be made and governed through the Wisdom of God who is his Son.[17] And so the cosmological ideas of *O qui perpetua* were expounded and drawn upon in a christian sense;[18] by Abbo of Fleury they were developed into a widely ranging philosophy of time, number, and form.[19] As part of the christian gloss, the last line of the *metrica* could be related to the christian scheme of faith and conduct: it spoke of God as *principium* through creation, *semita* through law, *dux* through the prophets, and *terminus* through redemption or through the final judgement.[20] Close and demonstrable parallels between *O qui perpetua* as commented upon by earlier medieval writers and the speech attributed to Stephen cannot be claimed.[21] But both in its seizing upon *ratio* as a key to understanding the universe and in its insistence upon law based upon *ratio* as expressing the divine being and purpose, the speech is so illuminated by *O qui perpetua* that it is hard not to suspect a direct influence.

However this may be, the part assigned by the speech to the Rule of Saint Benedict in recalling human nature

16. See, e.g., the commentary of the early tenth-century Abbot Bovo of Corvey, cap. 3, Huygens (as n. 13) p. 384.

17. So the commentary of Bishop Adalbold of Utrecht (1010–26), ed. Huygens (as n. 12) p. 420.

18. Ibid.

19. For an illuminating discussion, see E.-M. Engelen, *Zeit, Zahl und Bild. Studien zur Verbindung von Philosophie und Wissenschaft bei Abbo von Fleury* (Berlin and New York, 1993), esp. pp. 28, 43–53.

20. Commentary of Bishop Adalbold of Utrecht, ed. Huygens (as n. 13) p. 426.

21. Although an admirable illustration of what the speech may mean by *aequilibritas* is provided by the description of the four elements in *O qui perpetua*, lines 4–12; Huygens (as n. 13) pp. 264–265.

from its sluggishness to *ratio* is both clear and remarkable. The Rule stood supreme amongst the many laws formerly given when 'after all else from blessed Benedict a Rule came forth from God (*novissime per beatum Benedictum regula divinitus processit*)'. Its purpose was to recall human nature to the reason that was God; when human reason could not understand it must acquiesce in its authority. For reason and the authority of divine writers (*auctoritas divinorum scriptorum*)—the reference is not only to biblical authors, for the echoing in the adjective *divinorum* of the adverb *divinitus* as applied to Benedict makes it clear that he was mainly intended—were one and the same. Whatever such holy fathers as Benedict said that went beyond the grasp of reason must accepted by authority; nothing that exceeded reason or authority as enshrined in the Rule should be accepted. All monastic practice must be founded on the Rule that is so grounded. To justify it, examples must be forthcoming from the Rule; if the monks of Molesme went beyond this, they protested in vain the prerogative of him (Benedict) whose teaching they spurned to follow.

Such being the place that the speech distinctively assigns to the authority of the Rule as the embodiment of reason, it is difficult to envisage it as having been a free composition of the conventionally minded black monk William of Malmesbury. It appears more probably to reflect, and to a considerable degree to embody, the personal conviction of Stephen, who when a Cistercian would take his stand upon *regula ad apicem literae*. It has to be conceded that, in default of fresh evidence, the mystery that surrounds the speech is unlikely to be resolved. Nevertheless, it can further be argued that some aspects of Stephen's surviving letters are strongly compatible with its theme, particularly his concern to establish such authentic texts warranted by authority and reason as would be proper for use by those who lived strictly by the Rule, and his uniquely expressed conception of the finality of the Rule of Saint Benedict as a guide to the monastic life.

Stephen's concern for an authentic text is illustrated by two letters which seem to date from soon after he became abbot of Cîteaux in 1109. In the first, he described the process by which the Cistercians had sought to establish and to safeguard the correct text of the Bible, especially where there were variant readings.[22] The first step which was taken in copying the historical books, where variants were an especial problem, was to assemble many texts from various churches so that the one, truest text might be followed (*ut veraciorem sequeremur*). In fact, one text so procured seemed to stand out from the rest as being fuller, and so it was followed. But when the histories had been copied, the dissonance (*dissonantia*) of texts remained disquieting; for (Stephen wrote) manifest reason teaches (*plena edocet ratio*) that what a single translator, Saint Jerome, whose version the Cistercians' own forbears (*nostrates*) had come decisively to accept in preference to other translators, had drawn from the one fount of Hebrew truth should itself be consonant (*unum debeat sonare*). A further complication was that there were some Old Testament books that the one translator, Jerome, had translated, because the Jews before him had so allowed, from two languages: Hebrew and Chaldean; two-language books were accepted at Cîteaux along with the rest because they were read according to Jerome's translation.

Surprise nevertheless persisted at the discordance of books which came from the one translator. Recourse was had to Jews skilled in the Scriptures, who resolved the problem of the plurality of texts by showing that

---

22. For the text of Stephen's biblical *Monitum*, see J. Marilier (ed.), *Textes et documents concernant l'abbaye de Cîteaux* (Rome, 1961) no. 32, p. 56. The text is preserved in the so-called Bible of Stephen Harding, Dijon, Bibliothèque municipale, MS 13 (no. 1), fo. 150v.

their scrolls confirmed the shorter readings of the many texts that had been assembled; these were now adopted at Cîteaux in one, authoritative text. And the Jews resolved the problem of the duality of language by showing that for them, too, the Scriptures comprised chaldean as well as hebrew truth in tongues that were throughout concordant. With unity thus safeguarded, the superfluous passages from the aberrant text were entirely erased from the Bible of Cîteaux. The purpose of Stephen's letter was to prohibit for all time their being copied back again into the Bible of Cîteaux so that the one authentic text might be preserved.

It may be suggested that the letter has overtones which convey something of Stephen's deeper thoughts and which, although they do not coincide with those of his supposed speech at Molesme, are nevertheless similar to them. The letter throughout shows him as being concerned to emphasize oneness and to exclude diversity. Jerome stood out as the one translator who drew upon one fount of hebrew verity. Duality of languages (Hebrew and Chaldean) and plurality of latin texts were alike suspect.[23] It was necessary for jewish scholars to provide assurance that there was indeed a single hebrew and chaldean truth. At first, Stephen and his associates had mistakenly (as the Jews established) opted for one, corrupt text; consultation with the Jews showed that, rather, the one authentic text was that of the many witnesses; thus, it alone was henceforth to be accepted at Cîteaux.

Stephen's preoccupation with the one is in conformity with the presentation of all-pervading reason or order as a unifying force in his alleged speech at Molesme. Consistently with this presentation, in his letter he regarded internal consonance as a necessary mark of unity. The

---

23. Cf. the concern for unity and concordance in the early chapters of the *Carta caritatis prior*: caps. 1–3 (as n. 3) pp. 275–276, 443–444.

dissonance of biblical texts was disquieting, for what one translator, Jerome, drew from one hebrew truth should 'have one sound' (*unum debeat sonare*). Such a requirement of harmonious unity agrees well with the speech, with its insistence that human nature should subsist by reason and balance (*ratione et aequilibritate*).

Perhaps most of all, Stephen's letter is compatible with what the Molesme speech has to say about reason and authority. According to the speech, as embodied in sacred writers, who included biblical writers, they were one and the same, even if they seemed to be dissonant (*quamvis dissonare videantur*). Where they seemed to differ, reason might rightly be insisted upon until authority came into line and was proved to be consistent with it: 'because God created and recreated nothing without reason, who can make me believe that the holy fathers . . . say anything besides reason, as if we should give faith to authority alone?'[24] The step described in Stephen's letter of having resource to Jewish scholars in order to resolve not only textual difficulties but also that of Jerome's having translated from a duality of languages was a conspicuous example of the exercise of reason in order clearly to establish authority. The anomaly presented by the apparent discord of the books that had been received from the one translator Jerome was resolved in a manner that satisfied and reconciled authority and reason. In thus arguing for unity and consonance and for an order of things resting on them, Stephen wrote in terms not far removed from those of his alleged speech at Molesme.

The second of Stephen's letters that illustrates his concern for an authentic text is his charge to his successors as abbot about cistercian observance as regards hymns.[25] Fr Chrysogonus has shown that the probable date of the

24. William of Malmesbury, *Gesta regum*, 4.334.4; Mynors *et. al.* (as n. 10) pp. 578–579.
25. For the letter, see Marilier (ed.) (as n. 22) no. 31, p. 55.

letter is not later than 1112. In the letter, Stephen prescribed that the hymns to be used as Cîteaux were those
that had been found to be sung in Milan, the church of
Saint Ambrose (its bishop from 373/4–397). (In a similar
way, Stephen sought what were deemed to be authentic
mass and office chants from Metz, although no further
letter of Stephen's survives.)[26] Stephen justified Milan as
a source for the cistercian hymnal because in the Rule
Saint Benedict himself, 'our blessed father and master',
had set forward these ambrosian hymns (*hos ambrosianos*)
to be sung. Benedict did, indeed, four times enjoin that
an ambrosian hymn (*ambrosianum*) should be sung in the
divine office.[27] For Stephen, the integrity of the holy Rule
should never be changed or breached; as lovers, follow-
ers, and proponents of Benedict, succeeding abbots of
Cîteaux should inviolably hold to such hymns and to them
alone (*hos hymnos inviolabiliter teneatis*). While it cannot
be claimed that the authority of the Rule as cited in this
letter is proposed in the same terms as in Stephen's speech
according to William of Malmesbury, there is none the
less a compatibility with its distinctive presentation of the
Rule as the culmination of such lawgiving, to the authority
of which complete deference was due.

Although Stephen did not refer to the Rule of Saint
Benedict in the letter that he sent to the abbot and
congregation at Sherborne not long before his death,
nor indeed did he directly cite it, Fr Chrysogonus in
his commentary has noted how impregnated the letter is
with the substance and spirit of the Rule.[28] One further

26. The cistercian reform of the hymns and of the chant has been com-
prehensively studied by C. Waddell, *The Twelfth-Century Cistercian Hymnal*, 2
vols. (Gethsemani Abbey [Cistercian Publications], 1984); for an excerpt, see
Elder (ed.), *The New Monastery* (as n. 1) pp. 78–86.
27. *Regula sancti Benedicti,* 9.4, 12.4, 13.11, 17.8, in A. de Vogüé and others
(ed.), *La Règle de saint Benoît*, 6 vols., Sources Chrétiennes 181–186 (Paris,
1971–2), 2.510–511, 518–519, 520–521, 528–529.
28. See esp. 'Notes Towards the Exegesis' (as n. 1) pp. 15, 31–2.

echo may be added which is of especial significance in a letter addressed by an external abbot (or ex-abbot) to a monastic congregation. Stephen encouraged the monks to direct the good report in which they were held to their own progress in the virtues (*bonam famam . . . profectui virtutum applicare*) (lines 17–18). This surely recalls a phrase from Saint Benedict's chapter on the qualities of an abbot (*Qualis debeat esse abbas*) in which an abbot is to beseech monks who are obedient, mild, and patient to make progress for the better (*ut in melius proficiant*).[29]

No doubt such an exhortation in itself might have been made by any devout benedictine abbot. But in two respects it may be suggested that, in the light of what is known of Stephen's career, the letter to Sherborne indicates a distinctive monastic experience on his part; taken together, the two respects tend to confirm his view of the finality and uniqueness of the Rule of Saint Benedict as the Rule is highlighted in William of Malmesbury's report of his speech of years ago at Molesme.[30] First, as a monk at Cîteaux, Stephen achieved a remarkable synthesis of two features of the monastic life that contemporaries did not always find it easy to combine: on the one hand, the renunciation of the world and the spiritual and physical distancing of oneself from its ties, and on the other hand, the striking of deep roots through stability of place. Writing to the monks at Sherborne, Stephen referred to his having crossed the sea from his native land, poor and alone, ultimately to seek the reward of faithful workers in the vineyard, with its implication of stability (lines 7–8, 13–16). Stephen's letter is here reminiscent of the chapter of the Rule about the reception due to stranger, or voyaging, monks, *De monachis peregrinis, qualiter suscipi-*

29. *Regula sancti Benedicti*, 2.25; Vogüé (as n. 27) 1.446–447; cf. *Regula*, 62.4, vol. 2:640–643.

30. For a fuller treatment of the points made in this paragraph, see H. E. J. Cowdrey, 'Stephen Harding and Cistercian Monasticism', *Cîteaux: Commentarii Cistercienses*, 49 (1998) 209–220.

untur. If found well disposed, such a monk was to be urged to settle (*verum etiam suadeatur ut stet*), for in every place the one Lord is served, the one king is followed.[31] The Rule was the ultimate guide to such service and following. Thus, second, for Stephen, life according to the Rule was in itself sufficient to meet the aspirations for progress of both individuals and communities; there was no pointing on to an anchoretic or eremitical life that lay beyond and above it. Such a view was consistent with the last sentence of the Rule:

> Whoever you are, therefore, who are hastening to the heavenly country, fulfil (*perfice*) with Christ's help this least Rule for beginners, . . . and only then will you attain, under God's protection, to the higher peaks of the teaching and of the virtues that we have set out above.[32]

It is implicit in Stephen's final words to the monks of Sherborne that they should continue to the end in the virtues that they had learnt, as men progressing from good to better and firmly cleaving to true religion (lines 18–21). Stephen's presentation of the entire sufficiency of the Rule of Saint Benedict is reminiscent of and consistent with his proclaiming of the finality of the Rule according to William of Malmesbury, even though it cannot be definitively claimed to be derived from it. Indeed, all three of Stephen's surviving monastic letters show evidences of a decisively and individually formed mental outlook which lend credibility to the distinctive ideas of the speech at Molesme as ones that Stephen may, indeed, have voiced.

However this may be, the letter to Sherborne is of the utmost value as indicating that, in the person of Stephen, the beginnings of Cîteaux should not be understood as

---

31. *Regula sancti Benedicti,* 61.1–10; Vogüé (as n. 27) 2:436–439.
32. *Regula sancti Benedicti,* 73.8–9; Vogüé (as n. 27) 2:674–675.

representing too radical a departure from the older black monasticism. So long after he had set out from Sherborne, Stephen felt that its monks were his bone and flesh (line 6), and that he shared with them the fruits of his own lifelong labour (lines 10–13); their capacity to progress in the monastic life according to their way of living it was undoubted (lines 16–21). This fascinating letter is a warning that the supposed early twelfth-century *crise de monachisme* should not be overstated. It underlines the gratitude that is due to Fr Chrysogonus for insisting that it is far from being the valueless piece of evidence for cistercian history that others had suggested and for explaining its interest so helpfully.

Unanimity First, Uniformity Second

I N JANUARY 1983, by a lucky accident, I was able to gatecrash the first of many workshops given by Fr Chrysogonus on the primitive cistercian documents. For me, as for many others, it was something of an eye-opener. I feel astonished, in retrospect, that these wonderful texts had been allowed to lie fallow for so long. What those who participated in Fr Chrysogonus' program in the ensuing years discovered was the need to study these ancient treasures more closely, particularly by a close reading of the texts themselves, with a sharp lookout for the background against which they need to be assessed. What Fr Chrysogonus has done, almost single-handedly, is to rescue these formative documents from the confusion of academic controversy and make it possible for us to read them more acutely aware of their monastic and spiritual significance. In the volume which he completed some fifteen years after this initial foray, he has given us a solid base from which future investigation of the primitive texts can leap forth into ever more brilliant conclusions.[1] Given the complexity of the question that is, in itself, an outstanding achievement.

One of the interesting consequences of Fr Chrysogonus' work has been the renewed attention paid to this phase of cistercian history—notably at the time of the

---

1. Chrysogonus Waddell, *Narrative and Legislative Texts from Early Cîteaux* (Studia et Documenta IX), *Cîteaux:Commentarii cistercienses*, 1999.

ninth centenary of the founding of Cîteaux. A fruit of this more recent research has been the questioning of many of the placid stereotypes imposed on medieval Cistercianism by a reading of texts that was insufficiently sophisticated. The particularities that emerge from a close study of the text in the context of varied local histories soon put an end to the easy generalisations beloved by undergraduates and producers of television documentaries. The complexity and variety of cistercian life is too often overlooked. Conditions changed from one generation of Cistercians to the next. Even within a general context of compatibility, there were different approaches to spirituality,[2] to issues of daily life, liturgy, ecclesiastical politics, architecture, and economic management. To assert otherwise is to impute to the creative men of these times a degree of rigidity and even stupidity that accords ill with what we know of their common sense and their impact on the world around them. Dynamic growth sits ill with inflexible structures.[3]

With this in mind, I would like to return to the topic of *unanimitas*. My general conclusion will be that unanimity is not to be swiftly identified with uniformity, even though the two concepts cover some of the same ground, just as the two realities to which they refer are in a state of constant interaction. Beliefs and values that are not expressed in and regenerated by external practices are dubious—but the inner realities are not identified with the practices, nor are they interchangeable. That

2. '[A]lthough there were indeed essential areas of overlap between all the Cistercian writers, their own personalities, interests, talents, capacities, regions, and dates inevitably made for different approaches to the same goal.' David N. Bell, 'Is There Such a Thing as "Cistercian Spirituality"?' *CSQ* 33.4 (1998) 471. In an article which recaps much of the foregoing the same author repeats, '[A]t least from the time of Bernard there was never one unique Cistercian spirituality, but a variety of Cistercian spiritualities.'- 'From Molesme to Cîteaux: The Earliest "Cistercian" Spirituality', *CSQ* 34.4 (1999) 481.

3. For a parallel consideration, see M. Casey, 'The Dynamic Unfolding of the Benedictine Charism,' ABR 51:2 (2000) 149–167.

uniformity was a means to the goal of unanimity and was, as such, more tangible, does not mean that uniformity was an end itself. To illustrate this assertion it is worth returning to the beginning.

On Sunday, 18 May 1113, a group of monks from the New Monastery began living the cistercian life at La Ferté-sur-Grosne—a day's journey from the mother-house and in the same diocese. The foundation charter sets the scene.

> As the number of brothers at Cîteaux has become very large, there was no longer the possibility of providing the things necessary for their subsistence, nor was there room for them to live in. It pleased the abbot of that place, Stephen by name, and the brothers, to seek another place in which part of them could serve God devoutly and according to rule—separate in body, but not in soul.[4]

'Separate in body, but not in soul.'[5] The offshoot was intended to reproduce the pattern of living of the parent branch. Even though physical distance separated the two communities, no separate spiritual identity was envisaged. The monks of La Ferté lived the 'cistercian' life in a different place, but in the two communities there was a single soul. The *unanimitas* appropriate to a cenobitic community is now declared to be the determining factor in the relations between *self-governing and financially independent* communities.

A worthy sentiment—whose practical implementation was, no doubt, facilitated by the fact that the foundation

---

4. Translated from J. Marilier, *Chartes et documents concernant l'Abbaye de Cîteaux: 1098–1182.* Bibliotheca Cisterciensis 1 (Rome: Editiones Cistercienses, 1961) Text 42, pp. 65–66.
5. The phrase so well represented the ideal that it found developed expression in CC1, Prologue 3: *qua caritate monachi eorum per abbatias in diversis mundi partibus corporibus divisi animis indissolubiliter conglutinarentur.* The question being faced concerned the means by which this ideal could be attained.

was near enough to the mother-house to permit close supervision. The next three foundations, at more than twice the distance, could not be reached by a single day's journey. Moreover, they were located in different dioceses, under the eyes of different bishops. This situation necessitated a different means of maintaining the reformed observance. And so we read in the foundation charter of Pontigny in 1114 that Stephen responded by composing a *Charter of Charity and Unanimity* defining the relation between second-generation 'cistercian' abbeys and the New Monastery, and by having this agreement ratified by the local bishop.[6]

It is probable that this primitive document is reflected in the three first chapters of the *Charter of Charity*, written in the first-person plural in a style redolent of the Bible and the Rule. These chapters require that a founding abbey not exact any material advantage from its foundation, that the Rule be understood and kept by all in one manner, and that all monasteries have the same liturgical books and customs. 'Charity' is practised by the mother-house in not deriving financial benefit from foundations; the offshoot is not merely a grange or a dependent priory intended to feed back its wealth to its mother-house. It is an abbey of theoretically equal dignity, whose abbot is a co-abbot with the abbot of the founding monastery. In complementary fashion, 'unanimity' is expressed by the foundations in accepting the 'cistercian' interpretation of the Rule of Benedict and in having the same usages and liturgical books, keeping in mind that a break has been made and that the new implantation in different soil will inevitably produce fruit that reflects the changed conditions.

Does this unanimity, by defining the details of regular observance, demand an absolute uniformity at the level of daily life, such as Benedict of Aniane seems to have

6. Text 43 in Marilier (as note 4), p. 66.

attempted?[7] As we ponder this, we must never forget that medieval writers, especially reformers, had far less inhibition about using hyperbole than we do. And it seems that medieval readers were less inclined to simplistic literalism in their interpretation of text, particularly if it had practical consequences. So we should not be surprised that the *Summa Carta Caritatis* re-expresses the phrase of CC 3.2 (*similibusque vivamus moribus*) in this strong sense.

> So that an indissoluble unity between the abbeys will last for ever, it is established first that the Rule of Blessed Benedict will be understood in a single [sense] without the slightest hint of deviation. Hence there will be exactly the same books used for the Divine Office, the same clothing, and finally, the same lifestyle (*mores*) and customs are to be found. (SCC 9.6–7)

A similarly strict interpretation, embodied in the adverb *uniformiter*, was adopted by Eugene III in his *Act of Confirmation* in 1152.[8] At first glance, it seems also to be reflected in many of the decisions of the General Chapter during the first century of the Order's existence.[9] Such

7. See Bede Lackner, *The Eleventh-Century Background of Cîteaux* (CS 8; Washington, Cistercian Publications, 1972) 21–24 and 35–39.

8. 'The purpose of that decree was that the Rule of Blessed Benedict will, for all time, be observed in all the monasteries of your Order in the same manner as it is observed in the church of Cîteaux. Also, in the reading of this Rule, no member of your Order may bring any other meaning beyond the simple and common understanding [of the text]. Rather, just as those things that have been defined are recognised, let [the Rule] be understood by all, and inviolably observed in uniformity (*uniformiter*). You are entirely to maintain all the same observances (*easdemque penitus observantias*), the same chant and the same liturgical books in all the churches of your Order. No church or person of your Order may dare to ask from anyone a privilege against the common institutes of this Order or to retain one if acquired through any means whatever.' PL 180:1542ab.

9. See, with some reservations, R. Taylor-Vaisey, 'The First Century of Cistercian Legislation: Some Preliminary Investigation,' *Cîteaux* 27 (1976) 203–225. It is important to remember that repeated prohibitions usually

affirmations, taken at their face value, lead some to the conclusion that 'Uniformity was an integral feature of the Cistercian programme itself'.[10] At the same time, it needs to be remembered that the response of the General Chapter to many of the abuses that came to its notice was not an automatic reflex; the usual solution was to commission one or two local or particularly skilled co-abbots to look more fully into the situation and to prescribe appropriate solutions. More often than not—in the absence of complementary documentation—we have to attempt to read between the lines to appreciate both the difficulty and the General Chapter's response to it.

TO WHAT EXTENT IS AN IDEAL OF UNIFORMITY REFLECTIVE OF THE REALITY OF CISTERCIAN LIFE IN THE TWELFTH CENTURY?

First of all, we have to dissociate the rhetoric of unanimity from practical uniformity. Then we have to distinguish historical approximation from monastic politics and the sort of hyperbole often associated with moral exhortation. If we believe that the early Cistercians consciously gave priority to law in the ordering of their daily lives, then we will end up imagining a form of monasticism inflexible to the point of stupidity. If, in defiance of the topographical, archeological and anecdotal evidence, we continue to embrace the concept of cistercian uniformity in its most materialist sense, we will certainly be at a loss to explain how the Order expanded so rapidly, and why all those with whose careers we are acquainted lived lives that seem to be atypical.

It is, perhaps, important to begin by seeing *unanimitas* as a spiritual rather than a juridical concept: firstly it

indicate persistent deviance rather than universal acceptance of the norms in question.
10. W. Eugene Goodrich, '*Caritas* and Cistercian Uniformity: An Ideological Connection?' *CSQ* 20 (1985) 32–43, at p. 38.

operates primarily in the interior sphere of attitude and affectivity more than in the arena of observable behaviour and, secondly, it represents an ideal maximum rather than an enforceable minimum. The theme of *unanimitas* was deliberately chosen to place the emphasis on personal dispositions and not on external observance.[11] I would like to present some pointers to this conclusion by looking at the pedigree of the word.

We know as a matter of fact that, besides the Rule of Benedict, the founders of the New Monastery cherished Gregory the Great's *Moralia* and his *Life* of Benedict (EP 15.4). If we expand our field of investigation to include all the writings of Gregory plus those of his two principal mentors in spirituality, Augustine and John Cassian, and then add to this the Vulgate Scriptures, we are likely to arrive at a more finely-nuanced appreciation of the semantic content of this singular term.

In the Latin Bible I count ten uses of the adjective *unanimis* and eight of the adverb *unanimiter*; the abstract noun does not appear. In four occurrences unanimity signifies agreement among many, including two instances of concerted hostility.[12] In eight cases the term qualifies common prayer.[13] Three times it indicates the closeness of friendship.[14] Three times the christian community is described as *unanimis*.

11. See M. Jean Vuong-Dinh-Lam, 'Le monastère: foyer de vie spirituelle d'après Gilbert de Hoyland,' COCR 26 (1964) 5–21, especially 14–19. He speaks of unanimity in terms of a compenetration of spirit (p. 15). Yet, for Gilbert, within the context of a common search for God (*Tractatus Asceticus* 2.1; PL 184:259a) the uniqueness of each remains (SC 32.6; 169c 37.3; 193d). See also 10.2 (59a), 35.7 (187bcd), 36.2 (189a).

12. Psalm 82:6; Acts 7:56, 8:6, 12:20.

13. Judith 4:10, 6:14, 7:4; Acts 1:14, 2:46, 4:24, 5:12; Romans 15:6. The two occurrences of the term in the *Rule of the Master* follow this usage; they are not taken over in the Rule of Benedict: with one soul the community is to pray for its delinquents. Cf. 14.25 and 15.25.

14. Psalm 54:14; Ecclesiasticus 6:12; Philippians 2:20. In addition, the *Vetus Latina* rendering of Psalm 67:7 has *Deus qui inhabitare fecit unanimes in domo*, where the Vulgate has *unius moris*. Augustine often cites this text according

Philippians 1:27—You stand in one spirit, unanimous, working together in the faith of the Gospel.

Philippians 2:2—Fill up my joy by being concerned (*sapere*) for the same thing, having the same charity, unanimous, being of the same mind (*sentientes*).

1 Peter 3:8—Finally let all be unanimous, compassionate, lovers of the brotherhood (*fraternitatis amatores*), merciful, modest, humble . . . .

The key image around which all these texts revolve is that of the primitive Jerusalem community drawn by Luke in Acts 4:32—the company of believers were of one heart and one soul. The first Christians were not only together (*pariter*: Acts 2:43), rid of the divisive force of private ownership, but they were inwardly united: *cor unum et anima una*.

The writings of John Cassian are said to mark an important stage in the process of seeing the primitive Jerusalem community as the model of monastic life.[15] Yet the text of Acts 4:32 is quoted only three times in the *Conferences* and twice in the *Institutes*. When Philippians 2:2 is quoted in full with its use of *unanimes*,[16] it is introduced to support an argument in favour not of affective community but of humility, based on non-assertion of self. Moreover, Psalm 132:1 about the *fratres in unum* is quoted only twice—to describe the state of perfect chastity,[17] when the vices have been expelled and self-will neutralised.[18] Unanimity among brothers is said to incur the devil's displeasure,[19] so it must be a good thing. The term is used once in parallel

to the Vetus Latina, but in his commentary he follows the variant *unius modi*; *In Ps* 67.7; CCh 39, p. 872.

15. See Adalbert de Vogüé, 'Monasticism and the Church in Cassian', *Monastic Studies* 3 (1965) 19–52.
16. *Conl* 16.11; SCh 54:232.
17. *Conl* 12,11; Sch 54:138.
18. *Conl* 16.3; SCh 54:226.
19. *Conl* 16.8; SCh 54:230.

to *concordia*, [20] and once in a citation of Psalm 54:14 with reference to Judas.[21] In the entire *corpus* of Cassian there are only four occurrences, all of them in *Conference* 16. Despite this paucity of evidence, Abba Joseph appreciates the value of the unity that reigns between friends, where there is no attachment to material goods or to individual opinions. 'Love can last without disruption only among those in whom there abides a single commitment (*propositum*) and a single will, who will one thing and reject one thing (*unum velle ac nolle*)'.[22] 'The grace of full and perfect friendship is not possible except for those who have the same will and a single commitment (*propositum*) and who never or rarely think (*sentire*) differently or are in disagreement in what pertains to spiritual progress.'[23] We have to conclude, however, that affective sense of community associated with the term 'unanimity' was not a high priority in Cassian's thought.[24]

With Augustine, the other stream of influence within the benedictine and gregorian tradition, there is a much greater reliance on the myth of the Jerusalem community and, consequently, more interest in the value of unanimity.[25] The first injunction his Rule lays on the monastic community expresses this: 'First, because you have been gathered as one flock (*in unum estis congregati*), in order that you may live unanimously in the house, let there be one soul and one heart among you, [directed] towards God.'[26]

20. *Conl* 16.12; SCh 54:232.
21. *Conl* 16.18; SCh 54:239.
22. *Conl* 16.3; SCh 54:225–226.
23. *Conl* 16.5; SCh 54:226.
24. It scarcely rates a mention in Julien Leroy, 'Le cénobitisme chez Cassien', RAM 43.2 (1967), pp. 121–158.
25. This treatment depends on Luc Verheijen, 'Spiritualité et vie monastique chez saint Augustin,' in *Nouvelle Approche de la Règle de saint Augustin* (Vie Monastique 8; Bégrolles en Mauges: Éd. de Bellefontaine, 1980) 93–123.
26. *Praeceptum* 1,2. Luc Verheijen, *La Règle de saint Augustin: I. Tradition Manuscrite* (Paris, Études Augustiniennes, 1967) p. 417 = Ep 211.5; PL

The younger Augustine had originally interpreted the
cor unum of Acts as an individual's undivided heart, not
in communitarian terms.[27] This meaning came only later,
perhaps at the instigation of Paulinus of Nola.[28] From his
frequent addition of the phrase *in Deum*, we may conclude
that it is from a common orientation towards God that
unanimity derives. Augustine's commentary on Ps 132:1
dates from 407; its whole flavour is monastic. This is
where he introduces his curious etymology of *monachus*
as signifying that 'monks are those who live together in
such a way that they form a single person, so that what
was written is true of them: "They have one soul and one
heart". There are many bodies but not many souls. There
are many bodies but not many hearts. Rightly is *monos*
applied to them for they are "one alone".'[29] In his letter to
Laetus, Augustine reveals the theological undergirding of
his thought. 'Your soul is not yours alone; it belongs to all
your brothers, just as their souls belong to you, or rather
their souls and yours are not souls in the plural, but they
are one soul, the single soul of Christ.'[30] Unanimity for
Augustine is not a canonical concept, it is christological

33:960a. The phrase 'one soul and one heart among you, [directed] towards
God' recurs in *Contra Faustum* 5.9; PL 42:225, with the addition *caritatis igne
conflantes*.

27. *Enarr in Ps* 4.10: CCh 38:19.

28. See Augustine's reply, Ep 31.2; PL 33:122d, and his later letter to
Paulinus Ep 186.7; PL 33:824–825.

29. *In Ps* 132.6; CCh 40:1931. I have discussed this interpretation in 'The
Dialectic of Solitude and Communion in Cistercian Communities', *CSQ* 23
(1988) 273–309, at pp. 279–280. See also Jean Leclercq, *Études sur le vocab-
ulaire monastique du moyen âge*. Studia Anselmiana 46 (Rome: Herder,1961)
p. 9, note 10. Idung of Prüfening will later quote the text of Augustine
in support of his teaching on unanimity. See *Dialogue* II,36, translated by
Jeremiah O'Sullivan, *Cistercians and Cluniacs*, CF 33 (Kalamazoo, Cistercian
Publications, 1977) p. 84.

30. Ep 243.4; PL 33:1056c. For Augustine's Trinitarian theology and the
idea of divine adoption as the basis of unity among human beings see Ep.
238.13; PL 33:1043ab.

('Unanimous means being one thing in Christ'[31]) and therefore ecclesiological.

Examining his specific usage with the help of a concordance, we find that his fifty-seven instances of terms associated with *unanimitas* are often biblical. Apart from the connection with Acts 4:32, we perceive a semantic field defined by such themes as fraternity, peace, concord, collaboration, having one spirit and the same charity, thinking the same, united in prayer, joined in firm and inseparable charity, consensual joining together in community. His exhortation to communities is simple: 'All live together in unanimity and concord.'[32]

The emphasis is continued by Gregory the Great, although he was more aware that unanimity exists not only among the good but also among the wicked, such as the monks of Vicovaro[33] and sundry enemies of the Church.[34] On the other hand, Gregory has a clear vision of christian unanimity. 'One is our Lord and Redeemer. Even here below he binds together the hearts of his chosen ones in unanimity, and by inward desires continually stimulates a heavenly love.'[35] He recognises that because we are different persons involved in different tasks, we should try to ensure that our acts do not lead to discord, but keep intact a certain unity of mind with others, 'so that we may, as far as is justly possible, preserve unanimity with those among whom we live, not by leaving aside the things we do, but by taking precautions to avoid the evil of discord that we fear.'[36] 'Even though what they do is dissimilar, nevertheless by having one and the same

---

31. *In Ps* 142.4; CCh 40:2063.
32. *Praeceptum* 1,8; Verheijen (as note 26), p. 420. = Ep 211.6; PL 33:960c.
33. *Dial* 2.3.5; SCh 260:144, line 42. Also 2.3.10; p. 148, line 91.
34. *Reg Past* 3.23 (bis); PL 77:93b. *Mor* 13.10.12; CCh 143a:675, line 15; 17,10,12; p. 859, line 12.
35. *Ezek* 2.9.3; CCh 142:260, 106.
36. *Ezek* 2.9.14; CCh 142:367, 422.

orientation (*sensus*) they associate themselves with the words and virtues of the saints . . . . (Despite different vocations) they are joined to each other in unanimity by their confession of voice and virtue.'[37]

Gregory's favoured image of unanimity is that of a clod of earth, 'dust made into a lump by moisture',[38] and thus more closely related both to God and to the neighbour.[39] By the grace of the Holy Spirit believers

> came together in such close concord of unanimity . . . that there was in them but one heart and one soul . . . . Thus the Lord, preserving the sacrament of unity, combines in the Church faithful peoples who rightly have different ways of living (*mores*) and languages . . . Just as from one earth there are different and distinct forms of clod, so in one faith and one charity are manifested the different merits of those engaged in good works.[40]

Far from being a move in the direction of uniformity, Gregory's teaching on unanimity is built upon his profound respect for diversity. We have only to recall the 36 admonitions in the *Pastoral Rule* prescribing different remedies for different characters. This was the Pope who recommended inculturation at the level of *consuetudo* to Augustine of Canterbury: "Things are not to be loved because of places, but places are to be loved for their good things."[41] When he preaches unanimity it is in the awareness that those whom he addresses express their common faith by a plurality of external forms.

37. *Mor* 29.31.71; CCh 143b:1483, 77–84.
38. *Mor* 30.6.22; CCh 143b:1506, 11.
39. *Mor* 18.33; CCh 143a:921, 58.
40. *Mor* 30.6.22–23, CCh 143b:1506, 15–33: *in illa pacatissima unanimitatis concordia convenerunt.*
41. Ep 11.64; PL 77:1187a. A variant of the letter is given by Bede in his *History of the English Church and People*, 1.27.

Whatever may have been the attitude of other popes, Saint Gregory the Great emerges from his writings as the one who, in a particular way, cherished the theme of 'diversity within unity' in the Church. Diversity he believed to be present at all levels, not excluding that of liturgical ritual: what made this diversity into a unity was the bond of one Faith and one Charity.[42]

Leaping ahead to the middle ages at this point, we have to assert that the use by the cistercian founders of the relatively unusual term 'unanimity' (and other related words) followed this tradition. It was more indicative of a concern for an interior bonding than mere external uniformity. Throughout the primitive documents there is a proliferation of words with the prefix *con*, indicating joint action. That is why there are three 'Holy Founders' and not one. Charity was not only the goal, but the means to it. No wonder that the next generation developed an ethos of the *schola caritatis*.

The context of unanimity within the Order was the grace of communion among autonomous monasteries. The Order was seen as the community of communities— separate in body, but not in soul. Just as in a single community unanimity occurs in some middle region between regimentation and fragmentation, so at the level of the Order. Just as a community that has 'one heart and one soul' is able to contain a certain measure of adaptation 'according to need', so it would be daft to assume that the early Cistercians were unaware that in somewhat different circumstances the same goal is achieved by using somewhat different means. There was nothing indefinite about cistercian discipline, and the Chapter of

42. Paul Meyvaert, 'Diversity within Unity, A Gregorian Theme,' *Heythrop Journal* 4 (1963), 141–162; reprinted in *Benedict Gregory and Others* (London: Variorum Reprints, 1977) 162.

Faults was used to enforce it, both at the local level and at the General Chapter. Of course abuses—both real and symbolic—occurred and required intervention, but this did not amount to a program of total prescriptiveness. Over-regulation usually becomes rampant in times of backsliding or confusion. The first half-century of cistercian existence was neither.

By way of verification we may examine the writings of Bernard of Clairvaux, a key player for forty years in the affairs of the first cistercian half-century. Bernard testifies to the acceptance of a plurality of customs in his work *On Precept and Dispensation*, written between 1141 and 1144. Although the work is generally concerned with differences in observance between Black Monks and Cistercians, the following passage clearly shows that Bernard took for granted that in many trivial instances, local customs were generated locally, with the result that different usages obtained.

> Concerning whether clothing should be changed and washed because of nocturnal illusions, my advice is brief. I suggest that you follow the practice of the house in such matters. It is obvious that these things are done differently in different monasteries (*quae diversis modis diversis in monasteriis certum est observari*) . . . I will pass over those other matters of canon law which you ask about, because such things do not concern us, since we are monks. [43]

He comments elsewhere that 'In every monastery can be verified those four kinds of monks which Saint Benedict described'[44] and even develops a spirituality to correspond with this reality. 'We do not all run in the same way.'[45] His notion of unity, so extensively developed

43. Pre 57; SBOp 3:291, lines3–6, 8–10.
44. Sent 3.31; SBOp 6b:84, 20.
45. SC 22.9; SBOp 1:135, 9.

in *De consideratione,* is not the reductionist elimination of multiplicity, but a comprehensive, proactive and all-inclusive reality.

The monastery is truly a paradise, a region fortified with the rampart of discipline. It is a glorious thing to have men living together in the same house, *following the same way of life.* How good and pleasant it is when brothers live in unity. You will see one of them weeping for his sins, another rejoicing in the praise of God, another tending the needs of all, and another giving instruction to the rest. Here is one who is at prayer, another at reading. Here is one who is compassionate and another who inflicts penalties for sins. This one is aflame with love and that one is valiant in humility. This one remains humble when everything goes well and the other one does not lose his nerve in difficulties. This one works very hard in active tasks while the other finds quiet in the practice of contemplation.[46]

Bernard quotes Acts 4:32 eighteen times and there are fifty-two instances of *unanimitas* words. Not a single example refers to uniformity of observance. All occur within the line of Augustine and Gregory described above. Unanimity cannot be externally imposed; it is a unity that is the result of consent, freely given and the operation of charity.[47] This 'joyful and social unanimity'[48] is a matter of peace, concord and mutual charity is often referred to in the context of the prayer of the Apostolic Church. Christ is its source.[49] Unanimity is an appropriate object of striving, especially at the time of elections, for the devil and other troublemakers have in mind to destroy

46. Div 42.4; SBOp 6a:258, 16–23.
47. Csi 5.18; SBOp 3:483, 1–2.
48. *Dominica VI post Pentecosten* 1.4; SBOp 5:209,1. He is referring to bread made by many grains and leavened by the divine wisdom.
49. SC 54.8; SBOp 2.108.7. See the variant of Mich 2.1; SBOp 5.300.21.

it. This moral aspect of unanimity is close to Merton's interpretation of *voluntas communis* as distinct from *voluntas propria*.[50] We might also note that Bernard's text *sed concordes et unanimiter viventes in domo Domini* seems reminiscent of the sentence from the Rule of Augustine already quoted, *Omnes enim unanimiter et concorditer vivite*.[51]

Perhaps the clearest text, for our purposes, comes from the second sermon for Septuagesima:

> Meanwhile the Spirit of wisdom is not only single but also manifold compacting interior realities into unity, but in judgement making distinction among exterior things. Both are recommended to you in the primitive Church when 'the multitude of believers had one heart and one soul' (that is, the birds were not divided) and 'distribution was made to everyone according as each had need' (the animals were divided). So should there be a unity of souls among us, beloved. Hearts should be united by loving one thing, seeking one thing, adhering to one thing, and among ourselves being of the same mind. Thus external division will involve no danger and produce no scandal. Each will have his own field of tolerance and sometimes his own opinion about what is to be done in earthly matters. Furthermore there will even be different gifts of grace, and not all members will appear to follow the same course of action. Nevertheless interior unity and unanimity will gather and bind together this very

50. See *Thomas Merton on Saint Bernard* CS 9; (Kalamazoo: Cistercian Publications, 1980), 139. By way of commentary on this see, M. Casey, 'Merton's Teaching on the 'Common Will' and What the Journals Tell Us', *The Merton Annual* 12 (1999) 62–84.
51. Bernard's text is in a variant of Parable 1, published in ASOC 18 (1962) 55; line 101. Augustine's text is from *Praeceptum* 1,8; 420. = Ep 211.6; PL 33:960c.

multiplicity with the glue of charity and the bond of peace.[52]

If we need any further confirmation it can be found in the *Ecclesiastica Officia* when harvesting is discussed. The following qualification is added to the standard regulations:

For this and for all the other things appropriate to this time [of harvesting], each monastery [*ecclesia*] is to act according to its location and the arrangements made by the abbot and prior, since it is not possible to observe these things equally in all places.[53] (EO 84.32)

The first Cistercians, despite their protestations to the contrary, were eclectic in their fidelity to the Rule of Benedict.[54] They were unlikely to have abandoned common sense through enslavement to an abstract concept of uniformity. Like Saint Benedict they were aware that part of the reality of community life is the diversity that comes from different characters (*multorum servire moribus*—RB 2.31) and different graces (*alius sic, alius vero sic*—RB

---

52. Sept 2.3; SBOp 4:352,2–14. The allusion to animals and birds refers to Genesis 15:9–10, where Abraham is said to have divided the sacrificial animals, but not the birds.

53. EO 84.32. Danièle Choisselet and Placide Vernet [ed.], *Les* Ecclesiastica Officia *cisterciens du XIIème siècle*, Documentation Cistercienne 22 (Reiningue: Abbaye d'Oelenberg, 198) 244.

54. '[T]he founders of Cîteaux assumed a peculiarly ambivalent attitude toward the Rule of Saint Benedict. They declared their utter devotion to it, but in fact they used that venerable document with remarkable liberality. They invoked it and applied it when it suited their purpose, ignored or even contradicted it when they thought they had better ideas . . . If the founders of Cîteaux were indeed as much devoted to the Rule as they proclaimed [themselves] to be, their adherence to it was certainly more to its spirit than to its letter.' Louis J. Lekai, 'Ideals and Reality in Early Cistercian Life and Legislation', in John R. Sommerfeldt [ed.], *Cistercian Ideals and Reality* CS 60 (Kalamazoo: Cistercian Publications, 1978) 4–30 at pp. 5–6. See *id.*, 'The Rule and the Early Cistercians,' *CSQ* 5 (1970) 243–251.

40.1). As at the level of community, so at the level of the Order. Unity of persons was an incontestable ideal. On the other hand, although disunity at the level of practice was to be minimised, absolute uniformity was neither directly sought nor achieved.

John R. Sommerfeldt

The University of Dallas

Bernard of Clairvaux and the Trivial Arts: A Contemplative's Thoughts on Literature and Philosophy

ALTHOUGH CHRYSOGONUS WADDELL is re-
nowned as a master of one of the quadrivial
arts, music, his encyclopedic erudition makes it
appropriate to honor him with an article on the trivial
arts. Father Chrysogonus has been a dear friend to four
generations of Sommerfeldts, who have delighted in his
simplicity, openness, and generous good will as they have
visited him or been visited by him. We know him as a
splendid scholar and deeply dedicated monk—and, above
all, as a good, a holy man. With sincere affection, I offer
him this article on another holy man and *his* use of the
trivial arts.

The prevailing scholarly measure of Bernard's attitude toward the *trivium* concentrates almost exclusively
on the stance he took toward the third of the trivial
arts—dialectic, most often viewed in light of his much
misunderstood controversy with Peter Abelard.[1] When
Bernard's position on the other two trivial arts, grammar

---

1. The vast literature on this question defies citation or even enumeration. I
have tried to ascertain Bernard's attitude toward the dialectic of the schools
in 'Abelard and Bernard of Clairvaux', *Papers of the Michigan Academy of
Science, Arts, and Letters* 46 (1961) 493–501. See also my 'The Intellectual
Life According to Saint Bernard', *Cîteaux: Commentarii cistercienses* 25 (1974)
249–56.

and rhetoric, is considered, it is most commonly examined through studies of Bernard's own literary genius and command of the latin language.[2] I should like to suggest that an additional insight into Bernard's thought on the question can be gained through viewing his comments, direct or implicit, on the cultivation of literature and rational investigation in the light of his ecclesiology—more particularly his position on the ecclesial role of bishops and others dedicated to pastoral ministry in the world.

For Bernard, the Church is not merely an institution or a corporation; she is the sum total of all those pursuing, however feebly, the path to perfection.[3] Bernard's images of the clergy who minister to that people and Church are rich and diverse: they are the Noahs who steer the

2. Among the many studies of Bernard's use of rhetorical devices—and of his style and method of composition in general—are: Elizabeth T. Kennan, 'Antithesis and Argument in the *De consideratione*', in [M. Basil Pennington (ed.)], *Bernard of Clairvaux: Studies Presented to Dom Jean Leclercq*, CS 23 (Washington, D.C.: Cistercian Publications, 1973) 91–109; Kennan, 'Rhetoric and Style in the *De consideratione*', in John R. Sommerfeldt (ed.), *Studies in Medieval Cistercian History 2*, CS 24 (Kalamazoo, Michigan: Cistercian Publications, 1976) 40–48; Jean Leclercq, 'L'art de la composition dans les sermons de s. Bernard', in his *Recueil d'études sur saint Bernard et ses écrits* 3 (Rome: Edizioni de storia e letteratura, 1969) 105–162 (reprinted from *Revue Bénédictine* 76 [1966] 87–115); Leclercq, 'Sur le caractère litteraire des sermons de s. Bernard', in *Recueil* 3:163–210 (reprinted from *Studi medievali* 7 [1966] 701–744); Christine Mohrmann, 'Le style de saint Bernard', in *S. Bernardo: Pubblicazione commemorativa nell'VIII centenario della sua morte*, Pubblicazione dell'Università Cattolica del S. Cuore, nuova serie 46 (Milan: Società Editrice 'Vita e Pensiero', [1954]) 166–84; Dorette Sabersky, 'The Compositional Structure of Bernard's Eighty-fifth Sermon on the Song of Songs', in E. Rozanne Elder (ed.), *Goad and Nail: Studies in Medieval Cistercian History 10*, CS 84 (Kalamazoo, Michigan: Cistercian Publications, 1985) 86–108; Sabersky, '*Nam iteratio, affectionis expressio est*: Zum Stil Bernhards von Clairvaux', *Cîteaux: Commentarii cistercienses* 36 (1985) 5–20; and Emero Stiegman, 'The Literary Genre of Bernard of Clairvaux's *Sermones super Cantica canticorum*', in John R. Sommerfeldt (ed.), *Simplicity and Ordinariness: Studies in Medieval Cistercian History 4*, CS 61 (Kalamazoo, Michigan: Cistercian Publications, 1980) 68–93.

3. See SC 25.2 (SBOp 1:164), SC 57.3 (SBOp 2:120–21), SC 68.2 (SBOp 2:197), and SC 78.3 (SBOp 2:268). The translations throughout this article are mine.

ark,[4] physicians who care for ailing souls,[5] mothers who suckle their children,[6] friends of the Bridegroom,[7] public fountains and reservoirs from which all may drink,[8] bridges over which their folk walk to God,[9] shepherds who feed their flocks,[10] and gardeners who cultivate and water God's garden.[11] They are sweating farmers hoeing the Lord's fields,[12] the beams and panels which hold together God's house,[13] and watchmen guarding the city of God.[14]

To fulfill the obligations implicit in the use of these images, Bernard believes that the clergy must be both virtuous and learned. He writes:

> If I am not mistaken, to guard the city [which is the Church] is the work of a strong, spiritual, and loyal man. He must be strong to repulse all violence to it; he must be spiritual to detect any ambush which threatens it; he must be loyal so as not to seek his own interest [see 1 Cor 13:5]. . . . [Likewise,] how can an uneducated shepherd lead the Lord's flock into the pasture of divine eloquence? But, if he were learned and not good, I fear he would not suckle his people with the breasts of his teaching but harm them by the barrenness of his life.[15]

Bernard cites the book of Malachi to refute anyone who might question his joining of learning to virtue as

4. See Abb 6; SBOp 5:292.
5. See SC 25.2; SBOp 1:163–64.
6. See SC 23.2 (SBOp 1:140), SC 85.13 (SBOp 2:315), and SC 9.8 and 9 (SBOp 1:47).
7. See Ep 238.2; SBOp 8:116–17.
8. See Csi 1.5.6 (SBOp 3:400) and SC 18.3 (SBOp 1:104).
9. See Mor 10–11; SBOp 7:108–109.
10. See, for example, Csi 2.6.13 (SBOp 3:420) and Csi 4.2.3 (SBOp 3:451).
11. See SC 77.5; SBOp 2:264.
12. See Csi 2.6.9; SBOp 3:416–17.
13. See SC 46.2; SBOp 2:56–57.
14. See SC 77.3; SBOp 2:263.
15. SC 76.10; SBOp 2:260–61.

a qualification for pastoral leadership: 'If you should say:
"what is this to me?" [Mt 27:4], then this sentence would
censure you: "The lips of the priest shall guard knowledge,
and they shall seek the law from his mouth; for he is the
messenger of the Lord" '[16] [Mal 2:7]. Underscoring his
insistence on the coupling of clerical virtue and learning,
Bernard complains, not without hyperbole: 'Who would
give me learned and holy men as pastors presiding in
God's churches—if not in all, certainly in many, at least
in some?'[17] Bernard's insistence on clerical virtue is easily
understood, but why should the clergy be learned?

Bernard's answer is that learning is necessary if clerics
are to fulfill their function in society and Church. The
clergy must serve the people of God, the Church, be she
seen through the image of city, bride, or sheepfold.[18]
Clerics are to nourish their people with the milk of
doctrine,[19] instruction in both faith and holiness.[20] Bernard's clergy must labor to bring about christian justice
in the world—in *this* world.[21] This task necessitates the
clergy's continuing efforts to preserve the Church's freedom, the freedom to promote justice.[22] Justice requires
peace as well as freedom, and Bernard sees the clergy as
preeminent peacemakers.[23] The peace and justice which
Bernard would have the clergy foster is internal as well as
external; they must correct the evil actions of individuals
as well as reform society and Church.[24] Pastors must likewise be paternal in their care for the poor, those suffering
from want of physical necessities[25] or from want of the

16. Ep 200.2; SBOp 8:58.
17. Ep 250.2; SBOp 8:146.
18. See SC 76.9; SBOp 2:259–60.
19. See SC 41.6; SBOp 2:32.
20. See SC 76.7; SBOp 2:258.
21. See Csi 4.4.12; SBOp 3:458.
22. See Ep 348.3 (SBOp 8:293) and Ep 180 (SBOp 7:402).
23. See Ep 358 (SBOp 8:303) and Conv (SBOp 4:107–108).
24. See Csi 4.7.23 (SBOp 3:466) and VMal 8.16 (SBOp 3:325–26).
25. See Ep 257.2 (SBOp 8:166) and Ep 95 (SBOp 7:245).

true faith.[26] Clerics must do battle with heresy by their preaching;[27] but, Bernard insists, those found in heresy must be taught, not fought with force.[28]

This manifold ministry demands heroic virtue and devotion to duty. But, as Bernard sees it, it also requires considerable sophistication—a sophistication provided, in large part, by the clerics' learning. To fulfill their function, then, the clergy must possess, as Bernard puts it, '. . . the ornaments of knowledge and erudition. . . .'[29]

Sometimes Bernard can seem to disparage clerical learning in defense of clerical virtue. But he is well aware of his own hyperbole in so doing, as he reports in his *Thirty-sixth Sermon on the Song of Songs*:

> Perhaps you think I have gone too far in scorning knowledge, as if to censure the learned and condemn the study of letters. God forbid! I am not ignorant of how much the Church's learned have benefitted her, whether by refuting her opponents or by instructing the ignorant. For I have read: 'Because you have rejected knowledge, I have rejected you, that you may not function as priest for me' [Hos 4:6]. I have read: 'These who are learned shall shine as the vault of heaven, and those who have instructed many in justice as stars for all eternity' [Dn 12:3].[30]

Bernard's clergy must be learned to fulfill their function of preaching sound doctrine, instructing their folk in the truths they must know to pursue the path to perfection.

To successfully carry out his ministry of teaching and preaching, the cleric must know that which he would impart to others.[31] Love for the flock is not enough; the

26. See Ep 189.5 (SBOp 8:16) and Par 6 (SBOp 6/2:294).
27. See Par 6 (SBOp 6/2:287) and SC 65.1 (SBOp 2:172).
28. See SC 64.8; SBOp 2:170.
29. Ep 104.1; SBOp 7:261.
30. SC 36.2; SBOp 2:4.
31. See SC 18.3; SBOp 1:104.

knowledge which comes from a thorough course of study must fill the cleric as well. For errant, ignorant, or unwise sheep must be, as Bernard puts it, '. . . persuaded by pleas and convinced by reason. . . .'[32] Zealous love for those who have strayed from the faith is necessary but insufficient. Learning is the buttress of the preaching which may win heretics back to true belief. Bernard declares: '. . . Heretics are to be caught rather than driven away. They are to be caught, I repeat, not by force of arms but by arguments by which their errors may be refuted. . . .'[33] Bernard insists: 'Faith should be a matter of persuasion, not of imposition';[34] hence heretics '. . . must be convinced by invincible reasoning. . . .'[35]

Bernard's insistence on the necessity of clerical learning extends even to liturgical matters. Writing to the canons of Lyons, in reaction to their institution of a liturgical celebration of Mary's conception, Bernard declares:

> . . . I am amazed that some of you might wish to change your finest color [see Lm 4:11] by introducing at this time a new celebration. This is a rite which the Church does not know, which reason does not demonstrate, and which the ancient traditions do not commend. Are we more learned or more devout than the Fathers? We presume at our peril something which they in such prudence passed over.[36]

All this presupposes a knowledge of the Church's tradition, a thorough acquaintance with the Church Fathers, and an ability to reason correctly—in short, learning.[37]

32. Ep 6.2; SBOp 7:30.
33. SC 64.8; SBOp 2:170.
34. SC 66.12; SBOp 2:186–87.
35. Csi 3.1.3; SBOp 3:433.
36. Ep 174.1; SBOp 7:388.
37. See Thomas Renna, 'St. Bernard and the Pagan Classics: An Historical View', in E. Rozanne Elder and John R. Sommerfeldt (eds.), *The Chimaera of His Age: Studies on Bernard of Clairvaux*; *Studies in Medieval Cistercian History 5*, CS 63 (Kalamazoo, Michigan: Cistercian Publications Inc., 1980) 125–26.

The need for learning in the clerical ministry leads Bernard to befriend the learned clergy of his time.[38] William of Champeaux, Abelard's former master at Paris; Alberich, the noted master of the cathedral school at Reims; and Hugh of Saint Victor, master at his Paris house's famed school, are all friends of Bernard's. To Master Geoffrey of Loreto, Bernard writes: 'You have the favor of God and the people alike [see Lk 2:52]; you have knowledge [see 1 Cor 8:1]; you have the spirit of liberty; you have the living and effective word [see Heb 4:12], a speech seasoned with salt [see Col 4:6]. . . .'[39] In another cordial letter Bernard praises the virtue and learning of Master Gilbert, now bishop of London:

> Such progress [in virtue] gives witness to the clarity of your own philosophy; this great clarity is the fulfillment of your study. . . . He is wise who, taking his pleasure in all the letters and studies of the wise of this world, has also studied all the Scriptures. . . . [40]

Erudition is praiseworthy in Bernard's eyes when coupled with virtue—especially praiseworthy in one who has undertaken the ministry of bishop.

And Bernard goes beyond recognizing the utility of learning in those who have it to encourage the education of young men destined for the clerical life. Among Bernard's famous protégés are Peter Lombard[41] and John

38. An extended treatment of the material in the following two paragraphs may be found in my 'Bernard of Clairvaux and Scholasticism', *Papers of the Michigan Academy of Science, Arts, and Letters* 48 (1963) 266–70. See also Erich Kleineidam, 'Wissen, Wissenschaft, Theologie bei Bernhard von Clairvaux', in Joseph Lortz (ed.), *Bernhard von Clairvaux, Mönch und Mystiker: Internationaler Bernhardkongress, Mainz 1953*, Veröffentlichungen des Instituts für europäische Geschichte Mainz 6 (Wiesbaden: Franz Steiner Verlag GmbH, 1955) 128–31; and Nikolaus Häring, 'Saint Bernard and the *Litterati* of His Day', *Cîteaux: Commentarii cistercienses* 25 (1974) 199–222.
39. Ep 125.1; SBOp 7:307–308.
40. Ep 24; SBOp 7:76–77.
41. See Ep 410; SBOp 8:391.

of Salisbury,[42] who would fulfill Bernard's educational program for the clergy by being elected bishops, Peter of Paris and John of Chartres. In supporting the academic pursuits of Robert Pullan, Bernard praises the program of studies at Paris by writing to Robert's bishop at Rochester:

> If I have advised Master Robert Pullan to spend some time at Paris, for the sake of the sound teaching which is known to be imparted there, [it was because] I thought it necessary—and I still do. If I have asked you to allow this, I would ask the same even now—except that I have sensed your indignation at my prior request. . . . By the witness of my conscience, I dare still to present my request as well as my counsel, that, with your full support, Master Robert might stay for some time at Paris.[43]

It has been argued that Bernard's support for Robert and many other scholars is given in spite of Bernard's distance from their intellectual culture. This support has been seen merely as a sign of Bernard's liberality and broadmindedness.[44] The letter Bernard writes to Robert—by this time a cardinal—on the occasion of Eugenius III's election as pope, reveals an entirely different sentiment:

> Blessed be God, who, according to his mercy [see 1 Pt 1:3] to our—or, rather, his—Eugenius, has gone before him with blessings of sweetness [see Ps 20:4], to prepare a lamp for his anointed [see Ps 131:17], sending in advance a faithful man [see Prv 28:20] for his help and my great consolation as well. . . . Be concerned, dear friend, for him for whom God has appointed you consoler and counselor. Watch over

42. See Ep 361; SBOp 8:307–308.
43. Ep 205; SBOp 8:64.
44. Kleineidam, 'Wissen', 131.

him carefully, according to the wisdom given you
[see 2 Pt 3:15], so that, amid the tumult of manifold
affairs, he will not be beset by the deceit of the
wicked and snatched away by their words—all of
which would be unworthy of Eugenius' apostolate.[45]

Eugenius is a Cistercian and was at one time a monk at
Clairvaux; he is thus Bernard's spiritual son. Yet Bernard
entrusts the care of one schooled in the monastery to one
whose education was in the schools. The reason seems
to me quite clear: Eugenius has embarked on a ministry
to the folk of the world, a ministry which requires the
counsel of one whose education suits the task.

The educational program which properly prepares
prospective clergy for their ministry, Bernard believes,
is the curriculum offered in the contemporary schools,
the basis of which is study of the *artes litterarum*. The
first step in this curriculum is, of course, study of the
latin literature of antiquity, under the traditional head-
ings 'grammar' and 'rhetoric'. This was Bernard's own
educational experience. William of Saint Thierry reports
that Bernard's mother, 'as soon as she could, handed him
over to the teachers of letters at the church of Châtillon
for his education.'[46]

Bernard did not later reject his literary education.
Throughout his writings one discovers citations from
classical authors: Cicero, Horace, Juvenal, Ovid, Perseus,
Seneca, Statius, Tacitus, Terrence, and Vergil.[47] Much
more frequent and obvious is his use of the vast array
of rhetorical techniques and devices learned from the
ancients studied in his youth. Bernard writes: 'I do not
say that we should despise the knowledge of letters, which

45. Ep 362.2; SBOp 8:309–310.
46. *Vita prima* 1.1.3; PL 185:228.
47. See Bernard Jacqueline, 'Repertoire des citations d'auteurs profanes dans
les oeuvres de saint Bernard', in *Bernard de Clairvaux*, Commission d'histoire
de l'Order de Cîteaux 3 (Paris: Editions Alsatia, [1953]) 549–54.

adorn and refine the soul and make it possible to instruct others.'[48] Instructing others in the truth is, of course, one of the primary functions of the clergy.

William of Saint Thierry tells us that, as a boy, Bernard ' . . . so submitted himself to the pursuit of letters that he soon learned to discover God in the Scriptures'.[49] To preach the truth, one must discover it—primarily by searching through that vast body of literature which is the Bible, a search immeasurably assisted by a sophisticated understanding of the many literary forms found there. Communicating the truths thus discovered is also immeasurably aided by a knowledge of those rhetorical devices learned through a classical education. The effort and literary sophistication necessary to communicate the truth Bernard underscores in writing to Oger, a canon regular whose vocation requires facility in teaching:

> How much tumult is there in the mind which is composing, where a multitude of words resound, a variety of phrases and a diversity of meanings join in battle. Where often the word that occurs must be rejected, the word one needs escapes one's grasp. Where what gives a more beautiful literary effect, what conveys the meaning more suitably, what is more accurately understood, what is more useful to the conscience, what then should be placed after or before what, must all be strictly scrutinized. And many other things must be assiduously observed by those learned in such matters.[50]

To those clerics whose style reflects this effort and erudition Bernard offers high praise, as to Hildebert, the archbishop of Tours: 'In your writings, others can be exceedingly pleased with the learning shown, the sweet

48. SC 37.2; SBOp 2:9.
49. *Vita prima* 1.1.3; PL 185:228.
50. Ep 89.1; SBOp 7:235.

and pure language, the rich eloquence, the welcome and praiseworthy brevity. . . .'[51] All this requires learning—learning in the classical literary arts, a learning to be had only in the schools.

Beauty of expression is also essential, Bernard believes, in the liturgy, which is for him a powerful means of conveying divine wisdom. Asked by Abbot Guy and the brethren of Montiéramey to compose a liturgical office in honor of Saint Victor, Bernard writes of the goal of his efforts:

> The unmistakable sense [of the words] should shine with truth, resound with justice, incite humility, teach moderation. The words should offer light to the mind, shape to behavior, the cross to vices, devotion to the affections, discipline to the senses.[52]

Those whose office requires instructing others, whether through preaching or the liturgy, must be learned in the literary and rhetorical skills.[53]

But what of the third of the trivial arts: dialectic? What is the role of reason, what the role of philosophy in Bernard's educational program for the clergy? Bernard's response is an enthusiastic endorsement of philosophical studies. Bernard's enthusiasm is based on three fundamental assumptions: the rational order of the universe, the accessibility of that ordered universe to the human mind through the senses, and the ability of that mind, structured according to the same rational patterns as the universe, to analyze and synthesize sense data properly.

For Bernard, God has created an ordered universe, a universe ordered by his wisdom and power. Bernard writes, in one of his sermons on Pentecost:

51. Ep 123; SBOp 7:304. See Ep 408 (SBOp 8:389) where Bernard recommends a young man for entrance into a community of regular canons because he is ' . . . learned in letters. . . .'
52. Ep 398.2: SBOp 8:378.
53. See Ep 398.1; SBOp 8:377.

We must ponder three things about the great work
which this world is, namely, what it is, how it exists, and for what purpose it is established. Ines-
timable power is shown even in the existence of
things, for they are created so many, so marvelous,
so diverse, and so splendid. Clearly, a unique wisdom is apparent in the manner [of creation], for
some things are placed higher, some lower, and some
in between—all this in a most orderly fashion. If
you reflect on the purpose for which [the world]
was made, there appears a beneficence so beneficial, a benefit so beneficent, that it could overwhelm
even the most ungrateful by the multitude of its
benefits. Indeed, all things were created with perfect power; they were created beautiful with perfect
wisdom; they were created beneficial with perfect
beneficence.[54]

Thus, the universe Bernard inhabits is beautiful in its
order and friendly to those who live within that order.

This beautiful order, Bernard affirms, is the product
of a Creator 'in whom there is no inconsistency, . . .
in whose decisions there is likewise no inconsistency'.[55]
Thus it is possible for all rational beings to attain knowledge of the author of creation by studying that creation.
Bernard writes:

. . . This immense variety of forms and multitude
of kinds in the created universe, what are they but
rays of the divine nature, showing that he from whom
they come truly is, but not defining precisely what he
is? . . . [Thus] means are not denied the seeker [for
God's existence] and ignorance not excused those
who ignore the means. Truly, this sort of seeing
is . . . available to all using their reason. . . . [56]

54. Pent 3.3; SBOp 5:172.
55. I Nov 2.3; SBOp 5:309.
56. SC 31.3; SBOp 1:221. See also SC 22.6; SBOp 1:132–33.

As the order of creation is a source of knowledge about the Creator, Bernard is also sure that that order is a means of knowing those actions which will promote one's own well-being. For there is, he believes, an order in the universe, a natural law, which both drives the behavior of things and can inform humans about their proper behavior. Even without a revelation of God's benevolent mandates, human beings can know fundamental ethical principles. Bernard is sure that knowledge of natural law makes available to all people principles such as the 'golden rule'. 'Natural precepts' such as these can be 'discovered by reason', for they are implicit 'in nature'.[57]

Access to the rationally ordered universe, Bernard is certain, comes through the agency of the human body. He writes, in his fifth sermon on the *Song*:

> That which God has made—that is, all corporeal beings which are thus visible—comes to our attention only through the instrumentality of our bodily senses. Therefore, the spiritual creatures which we are must have a body. Without it we can by no means attain to that knowledge which we perceive is the only basis for knowing those things essential to our happiness.[58]

Thus, he continues, ' . . . that spirit which is clothed in flesh and dwells on earth strives to acquire knowledge—in a step by step, gradual way—by progressing in the consideration of sensible things. . . .'[59]

Sensation is, for Bernard, ' . . . a vital activity of the body, alert to that which is external.'[60] The data provided by the senses are essential in knowing the created world;

57. Bapt 1.2; SBOp 7:186.
58. SC 5.1; SBOp 1:21–22.
59. SC 5.4; SBOp 1:23. The body also serves as a means of communicating the truths acquired through it. See SC 5.5; SBOp 1:23.
60. Gra 3; SBOp 3:167.

knowledge does not come directly to the mind through the agency of angels or any other spiritual entities:

> Know this: no created spirit can of itself act directly on our minds. It is evident that, without the mediation of our or its bodily equipment, it cannot interact with us or infuse our minds so that by its [merely spiritual] activity we may be made learned or more learned, made good or still better.[61]

Human knowledge, and thus human life, is both constrained and immeasurably assisted by the corporeal nature of humans. Thus, the spiritual component of the human being requires the invaluable support of the senses in the search for truth. Bernard writes:

> . . . In this life the bodily senses exert themselves freely and powerfully, but the spiritual eye is shrouded in a perplexing darkness. What wonder, then, if the stranger [the soul] stands in need of the natives [the senses]? Happy is the traveler in this time who can turn to his or her service the kindness of these citizens—without whom he or she cannot continue the journey. . . . Great is the traveler who is content to consider the use of the senses as the treasure of these citizens, dispensing well that wealth for his or her own benefit and that of many others.[62]

Bernard calls this quest for knowledge based on sense data dispensative consideration: 'Consideration is dispensative when it uses the senses and sensible things in an ordering and synthetic way. . . .'[63] Thus the senses are the firm bases of the naturally acquired knowledge needed by all in their quest for happiness.

61. SC 5.8; SBOp 1:24–25.
62. Csi 5.1.2–2.3; SBOp 3:468.
63. Csi 5.2.4; SBOp 3:469.

Though sense data are the bases of the knowing process, they require, Bernard says, 'an ordering and synthetic' method to attain true knowledge. That method is reason or logic,[64] mastered by the study of the principles of dialectics.

Bernard defines the human being as a 'rational animal' and considers this a 'dignity'.[65] As evidence of this dignity, Bernard offers the example of the incarnate Second Person of the Trinity. He writes: 'Surely, the Son of God, manifestly the Word and wisdom of the Father, actually assumed the first of our soul's powers, which is called reason. . . .'[66] Likewise, humans ' . . . share with angels the best natural gift, and it is reason. . . .'[67]

The ability to reason is a gift of God. Bernard writes: ' . . . The light of reason, as a little spark, has been given to us by [God's] insuperable mercy.'[68] Just as God has bestowed on the human body the power of sensation, so he has given the human soul a rational power; these two gifts enable humans to ' . . . discern between what is proper and what is improper, between good and bad, between truth and falsity'.[69] Logic applied to sense data can thus lead humans to knowledge of what is, the truth, and what to do, the good. Even 'wood and stone', Bernard says, could attain such knowledge if likewise endowed with the powers of sensation and reason.[70] This

---

64. Bernard distinguishes the faculty of reason (the intellect) and the method reason (logic). Here the discussion is primarily of the method; the faculty is discussed more fully in my *The Spiritual Teachings of Bernard of Clairvaux, An Intellectual History of the Early Cistercian Order* [1], CS 125 (Kalamazoo, Michigan: Cistercian Publications, 1991) 8–9.

65. Csi 2.4.7; SBOp 3:415.

66. Hum 21; SBOp 3:32

67. Csi 5.3.5; SBOp 3:470.

68. V Nat 3.2; SBOp 4:212.

69. V Nat 3.8; SBOp 4:217.

70. See Ded 1.6; SBOp 5:374. See Luke Anderson, 'Wisdom and Eloquence in St. Bernard's *In dedicatione ecclesiae sermo primus*', in John R. Sommerfeldt

sort of knowledge is the result of what Bernard calls 'scientific consideration'.[71]

Thus, for Bernard, philosophy attains 'understanding' of reality.[72] Like faith, this understanding achieves certainty,[73] but understanding possesses an epistemological efficacy which faith does not. While faith's knowledge is 'hidden and obscure', that of understanding is 'naked and manifest'.[74] Consequently, Bernard is sure that rational investigation and analysis and synthesis of sense data results in true knowledge, in knowledge of the truth. Clearly, philosophical conclusions and all other knowledge obtained and transmitted by 'rational disputation'[75] are of immense importance to the clergy whom Bernard would have master dialectic in the schools of his time.

Logic has its limits, to be sure, as do the philosophy and theology which employ it. This is especially true, Bernard believes, in pursuing knowledge of God's nature.[76] God's love too is only inadequately understood by the human mind.[77] Even God's actions in the world and time are sometimes only incompletely comprehended. Bernard writes of the Incarnation: 'Who can grasp with understanding and discern with reason how the inaccessible splendor could pour itself out into a virginal womb?'[78]

(ed.), *Erudition at God's Service; Studies in Medieval Cistercian History 11*, CS 98 ([Kalamazoo, Michigan]: Cistercian Publications Inc., 1987) 126.

71. Csi 5.2.4; SBOp 3:469.
72. Csi 5.3.5; SBOp 3:470.
73. Csi 5.3.6; SBOp 3:471. On the certainty attained by faith, see my 'Bernard of Clairvaux on the Truth Accessible Through Faith', in E. Rozanne Elder (ed.), *The Joy of Learning and the Love of God: Studies in Honor of Jean Leclerq*, CS 160 (Kalamazoo, Michigan; Spencer, Massachusetts: Cistercian Publications, [1995]) 239–51.
74. Csi 5.3.6; SBOp 3:471.
75. SC 66.12; SBOp 2:186.
76. OS 4.4; SBOp 5:358.
77. Dil 8.17; SBOp 3:133.
78. Miss 4.4; SBOp 4:50.

But, clearly, to see the limits of logic is not to deny its efficacy.

Rational investigation has other limitations, as Bernard sees them: ' . . . reason can ignore truth . . .';[79] the method can be inappropriately used[80] or used not at all. In addition, prudence must be used in its application. Bernard writes that

> Paul said: 'By the grace of God given to me, I say to all among you not to be wiser than you ought to be, but be wise soberly [Rom 12:3].' He does not forbid being wise but being wiser than one ought. But what does it mean to be wise soberly? It means to observe most vigilantly what one ought to know more and first. For the time is short [see 1 Cor 7:29]. To be sure, all knowledge is good in itself—provided it be founded on truth. But you, who hasten to work out your salvation in fear and trembling [see Phil 2:12] because of the brevity of time, should take care to know more and first what you feel is more bound up with your happiness.[81]

To prioritize the objects of rational inquiry is not, of course, to deny validity to that inquiry. Rather, Bernard's admonition clearly carries the conviction that logic properly and prudently applied to sense data results in truths of fundamental importance to the happiness of the cleric whom he would have study philosophy—and to the happiness of the flock to which that cleric would one day minister.

Thus all three trivial arts—grammar, rhetoric, and dialectic—receive Bernard's enthusiastic endorsement. Clerics must command these arts to fulfill their function

79. Csi 5.12.26; SBOp 3:489. See Sent 1.25; SBOp 6/2:16.
80. This is one of Bernard's objections to Peter Abelard's work. See my 'Abelard and Bernard of Clairvaux', 495.
81. SC 36.2; SBOp 2:5.

in the Church. Of course, the study prerequisite to such learning in not independent, Bernard thinks, of moral considerations. He writes:

> If, for example, someone decides he or she must pursue the truth—and this solely out of love for the truth—is this not obviously honorable both in matter and in motive? . . . But if that person's desire is less for the truth than for empty glory [see Gal 5:26, Phil 2:3], or if that person intends to obtain, through the truth, another end or any sort to temporal favor, . . . you would not hesitate, I think, to consider that person partially deformed, . . . disfigured by a shameful motive.[82]

Study must be motivated by an unadulterated and unswerving desire for truth.

Learning should be sought for its own sake—but also for the sake of others who will benefit from it:

> Paul says: 'If any one thinks he or she knows something, that one does not yet know as he or she ought to know [1 Cor 8:2]'. . . . What . . . does he say this manner of knowing is? What, except that you know what order, what effort, and what end are necessary when investigating anything? As for the order: you should prefer that which is more useful for salvation. As for effort: you should pursue more eagerly that which is more powerful in promoting love. As for the end: your purpose should not be empty glory or [mere] curiosity or anything like that, but wholly directed toward your own welfare or the welfare of your neighbors.[83]

82. SC 40.2; SBOp 2:25. See Agustín M. Altisent, 'Inteligencia y cultura en la vida espiritual, segun los "Sermones super Cantica" de S. Bernardo', in *Los monjes y los estudios: IV semana de estudios monasticos, Poblet 1961* ([Poblet]: Abadía de Poblet, 1963) 147–62, especially pp. 154–156.
83. SC 36.3; SBOp 2:5.

Knowledge of the trivial arts is indeed useful in promoting one's own welfare and that of others, but literary and philosophical study must be preceded by awareness of God and of one's true self to attain meaning and utility.[84]

Always the student must recognize that, in the end, knowledge of the liberal arts, while useful, is not necessary to humankind's ultimate goal:

> Even lacking knowledge of all those arts called liberal—as much as those studies may be quite honorably and usefully taught and practiced—how many more people have been saved by their lives and deeds? How many does the apostle enumerate in his letter to the Hebrews [11], those made dear [to God] not by their knowledge of letters but by their pure conscience and by their genuine faith [see 1 Tm 1:15]? All pleased God by their lives, lives of merit not of knowledge. Peter and Andrew and the sons of Zebedee, and all the other disciples, were not chosen from the schools of rhetoric or philosophy; yet through them the Savior made his salvation effective throughout the world [see Ps 73:12].[85]

---

84. See SC 37.2; SBOp 2:9–10.
85. SC 36.1; SBOp 2:3–4.

Marsha L. Dutton

Ohio University

The Learned Monk of Gilbert of Hoyland: Sweet Wisdom in Cells of Doctrine[1]

*W*HEN GILBERT OF HOYLAND *wrote in his fifth sermon on the Song of Songs that 'joy itself is a certain divine eagerness of mind' he might have been thinking of Fr Chrysogonus Waddell, a man in whom eagerness of mind and joy coinhere. He is in anyone's book a truly learned monk.*

'Not that I disparage erudition in the arts, a quick memory in liberal studies and a clear intelligence, in all of which consists the integrity of knowledge [*scientie*]', writes Gilbert of Hoyland. 'For acquaintance with these arts is good, but only if one properly uses them, as a kind of step and track, not where one remains and clings, but on which one relies to advance to higher, holier, and more intimate mysteries of wisdom [*sapientie*], to those hidden sweet retreats and that light inaccessible which God inhabits.'[2] Throughout his works Gilbert emphasizes this relationship between worldly learning and divine wisdom, always showing learning as incomplete unless fulfilled by wisdom and identifying the monastery as the place where wisdom gives herself most freely. In his sermons he warns against the false allure of learning, contrasting its hard labor and poor fruit with wisdom's

---

1. I thank Philip F. O'Mara and John R. Sommerfeldt for their assistance.
2. Epistle 2.2; PL 184:291.

generosity. But in the second of his twelve surviving epistles, Gilbert urges a learned man named Adam to enter
monastic life by emphasizing the rich intellectual opportunity awaiting him there. He not only promises that as a
monk Adam can go on learning and teaching but also says
that in the monastery wisdom will complete his learning,
transforming him into a new Adam and so making him
one with Christ.

Gilbert, perhaps originally a monk of Clairvaux or
Rievaulx, became abbot of the Lincolnshire abbey of
Swineshead sometime after 1147, when it—with all
other savigniac houses—became cistercian. Best known
for his Sermons on the Song of Songs, he also wrote
twelve epistles, three fragmentary sermons, and other
uncertainly identified works before dying in 1172.[3] In
all of these he repeatedly explored the relationship of
learning and wisdom, revealing a deep ambivalence about
learning—attraction to it combined with anxiety about
its distractions and dangers—reinforcing Étienne Gilson's
comment about the early Cistercians: 'each and all of
these hardy ascetics carried in his bosom a humanist who
by no means wanted to die.'[4]

Gilbert always insists that wisdom, not learning, is
the goal of the monk and that Christ is the exemplar.
Monks, he writes, must not explore the stony streets of
philosophy but emulate Christ, filling the honeycomb of
doctrine with the honey of wisdom and offering to others

3. Still the best survey of Gilbert's life and works is that of Edmond Mikkers,
'De vita et operibus Gilberti de Hoylandia', Cîteaux 14 (1963) 33–43, 265–
279. Gilbert's works appear in J.-P. Migne's Patrologia Latina 184:11–298;
Ep 2 in cols. 291–293. My critical edition of Gilbert's works will appear in
Corpus Christianorum, Continuatio Mediaevalis. The english translation is
that of Lawrence C. Braceland, trans., Gilbert of Hoyland I–IV, CF 14, 20,
26, 34 (Kalamazoo: Cistercian Publications, 1978–81); Ep 2 is in vol. 4, CF
34:93–98. All translations below are mine, Ep. 2 from Oxford MS Bodley
24 and sermon passages from Laon MS 59.
4. The Mystical Theology of Saint Bernard, trans. A. H. C. Downes (London:
Sheed & Ward, 1940; Kalamazoo: Cistercian Publications, 1990) 63.

the overflow of its abundance. Such integration of learning and wisdom, with its natural outcome in teaching, sets the learned monk apart from the philosopher.

But Gilbert shapes his comments on the nature and value of learning to his audience. Although he warns monks against being enticed from the monastic paradise into the world, when he urges the teacher-scholar Adam to leave that world for the monastery, he acclaims the capacity Adam's learning gives him for wisdom and notes its value for the community. In monastic life, says Gilbert, Adam will not abandon but fulfill his learning, by following, approaching, and becoming one with Christ.

THE INVITATION TO ADAM

Medieval letters from monks encouraging friends and relatives to enter monastic life provide a window into the self-understanding of the writers, revealing, as Jean Leclercq writes, 'what they think of their monastic life'.[5] In his discussion of such letters he catalogues the elements they commonly share: the certainty of death, Old Testament antecedents, an invitation to follow Christ in personal poverty, and a warning against learning. Above all, Leclercq says, whatever other elements are present or absent, one above all is treated 'as decisive and sufficient, . . . a concern [souci] for personal salvation. It is never a question of doing good to others, even through prayer. It is always only a matter of seeking God and replying to his appeal' (197). That Cistercians, following the example of Saint Bernard, were the most frequent writers of such letters, he says, 'indicates their fervor, but also explains, in a certain measure, their astonishing recruitment' (172).

Although Leclercq mentions Gilbert's letter to Adam as one instance of the vocational letter genre, it differs

5. 'Lettres de vocation à la vie monastique', *Analecta Monastica* 37 (1955) 169.

markedly from the usual pattern. It says nothing of the certainty of death, of Old Testament antecedents, of denying oneself to follow Christ in poverty, or indeed of personal salvation or a reply to God's call. Gilbert focuses on the good Adam can do for others, Gilbert himself among them, and far from warning against learning, a point on which Leclercq insists,[6] Gilbert promises that the learning Adam already has will in monastic life find opportunity for expression and fulfillment in wisdom.

Indeed, the whole emphasis of Gilbert's invitation to Adam is his promise of intellectual growth rather than ascetic or spiritual benefit, an assurance that becoming a monk does not require abandonment of learning and teaching. Not now as in the sermons disparaging worldly learning, 'the traditions of the Jews and the dogmas of the philosophers' (S 5.2), Gilbert emphasizes the value of Adam's erudition. And when he contrasts knowledge and wisdom he categorizes them not as bad and good but as route and goal, explaining that Adam's learning outside the monastery has prepared him to find wisdom inside.[7]

Gilbert begins his argument with what Adam's conversion will offer others, assuring him that even in his new life he may continue to guide and teach. Conscious of Adam's popularity among students—an important element in a twelfth-century professor's success—and of the pleasure Adam receives from the influence he exercises, Gilbert declares that they as well as others who are already monks will follow Adam's lead in seeking wisdom and perhaps, in the case of the students, a *conversio morum* as well: 'How

6. Leclercq comments: 'One of the principal obstacles to [monastic] vocation appears to have been the frequenting of the urban schools, where one prepared for ecclesiastical careers: the perspective of the honors and advantages that they promised seems to have been one of the temptations that candidates for the cloister had to surmount' (197).
7. Cf. Augustine's *De doctrina christiana* [Ddc] 2.7, which identifies knowledge as the third of seven steps on the ascent to wisdom, the vision of God's face.

wide an open window you will offer for emulation, you who are soon to become an example for others and—if I may here mention us as well—how wide a door on the road to virtue' (§1). He expects Adam to derive satisfaction from turning his students from their current empty path to that of life and salvation: 'Happy indeed and twice happy are you if you make your conversion an occasion of salvation for others, if you draw towards life and truth those who now run after you—in a kind of vanity, I wanted to say' (§2). In so leading others, Gilbert suggests, Adam is already like Christ the bridegroom: 'I seem to hear that verse of the Canticle being sung about you: "draw us after you; we shall run in the fragrance of your perfumes"' (§1).

While Adam may continue to do good to others by his conversion, Gilbert says, the monastery will offer to him rich intellectual opportunity as his love of learning guides him to wisdom. Gilbert assumes that Adam seeks wisdom not for academic success, fame, or the chance to teach, but for the joy it brings and its power to fill and change him. As a monk he will be able to go beyond the simulacra of wisdom he has so far known to their source: 'Of all the arts, I would call it *the* art, and the law, the form, the norm, the principle, and the universal, uniform, invariable model. As we are not able to advance beyond it, so we ought not to stop short of it' (§2). Finally Adam will attain to the origin of all wisdom, Christ, and become united with him, 'reaching even into the understanding of Christ, in whom are hidden all the treasures of the wisdom of God' (§4).

The real value of all learning is thus the preparation it gives to receive wisdom, Gilbert says. If regarded as a means rather than an end, it may serve as a foothold on the way to wisdom or, alternatively, as a scaffolding for wisdom. But if valued for itself, it is empty and even dangerous in the ease with which it distracts from the pursuit of truth:

> Next to it [*sapientie*] all other wisdom [*omnis alia . . .
> sapientia*], of whatever kind or extent, is vain if in-
> commensurate to it and even perverse if not directed
> to it. If it so invites and entices our study that it de-
> tains and distracts our delight to itself, finally the
> mind, content, rests, accepting the repulse that pre-
> vents it from moving on to hidden things; it feeds
> on emptiness and painted platters, never hungering
> and never tasting how sweet the Lord is. For what is
> sweet except the Lord? (§2)

The danger of learning, then, lies not in learning itself
but in the temptation to stop there, to be so pleased with
the journey as not to continue to the end. The similar-
ities between learning and wisdom provide much of the
seductive appeal of learning, allowing learning to coun-
terfeit the reality, mimicking the form but denying the
substance. Glancing askance at Adam's 'study of empty
literature', Gilbert warns against 'depriving yourself of
the light by following a shadow, lest led astray by Aristotle's subtleties you object to our silence and simplicity'
(§4). Adam has not, however, gone far astray, for all along
he has followed the lead of wisdom, the source of all
knowledge:

> The narrow and untrustworthy idea of natures and
> reasons, to which one barely arrives even by a long
> and circuitous course and bending curves, violently
> delights you, seizing and pulling your soul and love
> to itself. What therefore of the one who instituted
> all things so that they might exist and brought them
> to light so that they might be known, wisdom the
> creator? (§2)[8]

8. Augustine writes: 'If the pleasures of the journey and the movement of the
vehicles delighted us, and we began to enjoy those things that we ought to use,
we would not wish to reach the end of the way quickly. So we would become
alienated from our homeland, whose sweetness would make us happy' (Ddc
1.4.4). Gilbert makes this image more explicit in S 36.7 (PL S 37:7).

Thus while learning, as a flawed child of wisdom, may mislead because of its likeness to its parent, Gilbert says, that likeness may finally lead to wisdom. As Adam has misled those who followed him 'in a kind of vanity' but may now draw them 'to life and truth' (§2), so wisdom may lead him back from false understanding to truth, for she is the prototype, solid food rather than a painted feast, light rather than shadow. As Adam has loved her creation, he has already loved and sought her and will continue to do so, and she who led him to search for her in her counterfeits will by giving herself fully to him lead him still further onward:

> Will your awareness of her not commend her to you more energetically? Will she not pour her sweetness more caressingly into your enlightened affections, with unaccustomed emotion stimulating insatiable desire? Indeed she says 'those who eat me will still hunger, for my spirit is sweeter than honey.' (§2)[9]

Adam's learning has prepared him for wisdom not only by leading him toward her but also by making him able to receive and hold her treasures. Instead of filling him, it has given him the capacity to be filled, creating cells for the Lord's sweetness, a honeycomb for the honey of wisdom:

> You have some large receptacles, my friend, for storing this honey; I mean a sharp and practiced understanding, a knowledge of many and subtle things. I think of these as cells of a honeycomb, capacious but still empty. Come then to be filled up so that your cells may be full, that they may overflow and run over and spill on us, who will justly praise

9. Cf. Braceland: 'Will the winning of Wisdom not coax you to court her much more earnestly?' (CF 34:95) (*Nonne multo ambitiosius eius se tibi commendabit perceptio?*).

you with words of the Canticle: 'your lips are a dripping honeycomb.' (§3)[10]

Gilbert also speaks to Adam of the new method by which he must seek wisdom. Although in the sermons he warns monks of the labor required for worldly learning, citing the first Adam's digging in barren ground for only thorns and thistles (e.g., S 34), he says little to this twelfth-century Adam about the labor of learning or the ease of obtaining wisdom. He, after all, has already dug in the soil outside the monastery and found it not so barren; he has produced not thorns but a honeycomb. And because he has found satisfaction in both the effort and its fruit, Gilbert offers him more of the same. Anticipating that he will continue to seek wisdom, Gilbert suggests that a new method, silence and simplicity, may replace the old with its circuitous research, uncertainties of investigation, and toil of writing. Adam must give up any disdain he may have for the monastic method as unproductive, recognizing it as the direct route to God and so to wisdom:

> Does our leisure seem to you a sterile silence? Therein is communicated and exercised a certain art of advancing toward God by a direct route, to be transformed and changed into the new man, the new Adam, and to reach into the understanding of Christ, in whom are hidden all the treasures of the wisdom and knowledge of God. (§4)

This method, says Gilbert, is easier and more productive than the one Adam is used to. And while it still requires a certain labor, it offers rewards rich and sure: 'At all times almost manifest are the veins of this shining metal, if only one chooses to dig in the depths rather than to beg outside' (§4).

---

10. For other instances of Gilbert's use of this image see Lawrence C. Braceland, 'The Honeycomb in Gilbert of Hoyland,' CSQ 17 (1982) 233–243.

The true reward of such digging, of course, is Christ himself. Although Gilbert is less explicit in identifying Christ with wisdom here than in his sermons, he promises that in monastic life by approaching Christ Adam will become transformed into Christ and so be filled with wisdom to share. As Adam will in coming to the monastery be like Christ in drawing others after him, he will once there rise to 'more interior mysteries of wisdom . . . to the very light inaccessible which God inhabits' (§2). And when wisdom completes his learning, he will, like Christ, find that it overflows for the benefit of others: 'your lips are a dripping honeycomb' (§3; Sg 4.11). Finally through applying himself to the monastic method he will find in the mind of Christ all that was heretofore hidden from him.

The wisdom that will fill Adam will come not from study but from monastic life as it engages his mind and understanding. Monks, Gilbert explains, receive the gifts of wisdom at all times and in all places. In silence they perceive the vision of God's glory and are 'transformed into the same image from splendor to splendor' (§4), and in choir they chant God's teaching: 'you will discover that the laws of the Lord are our songs even in this place of pilgrimage' (§5). Thus far from denying Adam intellectual opportunity, monastic life will welcome and reward his thirst.

In this letter Gilbert explicitly refrains from the usual appeals to prospective monks, emphasizing not 'the healing hurts of the present time' and 'the future punishments . . . the glory to come' (§5) but rather the particular pleasures that await Adam in the monastery now, its intellectual rewards: 'I aim to persuade by painting only the present reward, not the future, the first-fruits rather than the full harvest' (§5). But as the honeycomb waits for honey and as learning leads toward wisdom, Gilbert says, these monastic first fruits anticipate and ensure the fullness of beatitude: 'the future harvests at the end of the age are sown in these early joys' (§5).

This image of wisdom as honey in the honeycomb of learning runs throughout Gilbert's sermons, exemplified by both Christ and Aelred of Rievaulx. Gilbert shows Christ as at once wisdom and its source and Aelred as the learned monk, filled with wisdom and so one with Christ. In this life, Gilbert explains, Christ offers himself to human understanding in his humanity rather than his divinity, as wisdom incarnate and knowable rather than as its essence. The wisdom Christ offers in his Incarnation is a foretaste, Gilbert says, an anticipation of beatific knowledge of him face to face, no longer *in enigmate*: 'Both are yours, good Jesus, the honey you give and the honey you are. But in this place the honey which you are presents itself more readily to our understanding' (S 39.8).

Gilbert also uses this image to explain the two natures of Christ and human knowledge of him during his Incarnation. In the Incarnation, he says, the honey of Christ's divinity was poured into the comb of humanity. But now, before the last days, his divinity obscures his humanity:

> Before being conceived by the holy Virgin, he was like honey alone, without a honeycomb, the divinity not yet incarnate. Afterwards the honey was in the honeycomb, God in man. Now, however, the honeycomb is in the honey, man clothed in deity. (S 39.8–9)

In the following sermon Gilbert moves to the moral plane, still with the same image. After praising the primitive church, when 'bees were building the honeycombs of a more perfect and mystic doctrine' (S 40.1), and bewailing his own distance from those patristic bees, he eulogizes the learning and wisdom of a Cistercian of his own time, Aelred of Rievaulx: 'How great a honeycomb, how vast, how fruitful, has been taken in these days to the celestial banquet. . . . His word was the comb, filled with the honey of knowledge [*scientiam*]' (S 40.4). Aelred's wisdom, moreover, spilled over in his teaching: 'This honeycomb of ours . . . abounded with interior liquid. He was full of cells, dripping sweetness on every side. An assiduous laborer, he fashioned honeycombs of the divine word' (S 40.6).

Gilbert's use of the image of honey overflowing from the honeycomb for both Christ and Aelred shows Aelred's oneness with Christ in wisdom. Thomas J. Heffernan explains the doctrine that underlies this identification:

> in a theological system which presumed the indivisibility of divine truth, one whose most profound truths sanctioned the possibility of transcendence through an enactment of the life of Christ, those mortals who achieved this sanctity came into full possession of this divine truth and became in turn possessed by it, one with it.[11]

As in the sermons Gilbert shows Christ and Aelred as exemplars for human wisdom and for teaching, in his epistle to Adam he writes that as a monk Adam too will become so full of wisdom that it will spill over on others, filling those less able to learn, either because inherently weaker intellectually or untaught, those with no cells of learning in which to store wisdom. But whatever the state of the students, the nature of the wisdom Adam is bound to obtain in monastic life will necessitate his sharing it with others. Such teaching is in Gilbert's view a natural and indeed inevitable result of becoming wise.[12] Far from suggesting that in ascetic self-denial Adam should leave behind his intellectual gifts and the pleasure he takes in sharing them, Gilbert invites him to come where he

---

11. *Sacred Biography: Saints and their Biographers in the Middle Ages* (New York: Oxford University Press, 1988) 136. In chapter 3 Heffernan examines Walter Daniel's *Vita Aelredi* as exemplification of the medieval understanding of the saint's life as *imitatio Christi*.

12. I have discussed the cistercian emphasis on service and spiritual teaching as an result of intimacy with Christ in 'Intimacy and Imitation: The Humanity of Christ in Cistercian Spirituality', *Erudition at God's Service, Studies in Medieval Cistercian History, XI*, ed. John R. Sommerfeldt, CS 98 (Kalamazoo: Cistercian, 1987) 33–70, esp. 62.

can use them more satisfyingly, emphasizing the rich opportunity offered by the monastery: 'Nowhere else is it possible for anyone, however eager and erudite, to be employed more abundantly and fruitfully' (§3).

Gilbert here offers a second image of wisdom's abundance. Now portraying the teacher as a fountain, drawing up wisdom from the depths and distributing its excess to students (cf. SS 34.4–5, 36.5), he declares his longing to hear Adam teach: 'I would gladly hear you prophesying of these things and, when as a diligent seeker you have immersed yourself in the great profundity of that sea, sprinkling the sweet dew of life-giving water on those who are not fit for that abundance' (§3; cf. S 34).

Although all the abbey's monks will benefit from Adam's learning, Gilbert suggests that he will himself find most pleasure in it. Nowhere in this epistle does he write more lyrically than when he describes the subjects on which he hopes to hear Adam lecture. Explaining the intellectual benefits of monastic life for Adam, he also reveals his own passion for theological exposition and his longing for a teacher and preacher at Swineshead worth listening to and, presumably, talking with:

> O, if I might sometimes hear you discoursing in the house of the Lord, expounding secret and sacred sentences, touching and subtly distilling on us some drops of the majesty of the divine essence, its eternity, immensity, and simplicity. There nothing is insignificant because it is simple, and nothing is multiple because it is immense, but all is infinite. . . .
> (§3)

Promising Adam the chance to teach in all areas of christian faith and life, Gilbert lists the areas he is particularly eager to hear explained:

> about what you think about pardon, grace, and glory, about what the Lord has given, given back, or

added, and about all he endured for us and conferred
on us; your telling of Christ's past sufferings and
future glories, of patience in tribulation, of the
expectation of reward, and of the elements of faith
and laws of morality; and your listing each of the
degrees of renewal and the stages of progress toward
perfection. (§3)

Gilbert's approach indicates not only his own love of
learning but his desire to improve the intellectual environment of Swineshead. His eagerness to hear Adam
'distilling on us some drops' of understanding, and his
list of topics on which Adam will lecture show his concern for the education of the community and his eagerness to recruit those able to raise its intellectual level.
Though Gilson, writing of 'Bernard's anti-philosophism',
has characterized Gilbert as the Cistercian who 'most
fully developed it' (229 n. 75), Gilbert reveals himself
here as fully appreciative of the values of non-monastic
learning and aware of its benefits for the monastery.

Gilbert's apparent concern with the lack of learning
at Swineshead and the need for learned men to become
monks there corroborates Philip F. O'Mara's recent suggestion that savigniac houses made little effort to attract
learned men. Gilbert may have been surprised when he
arrived at Swineshead to find a scarcity of intellectually
active or trained monks, especially in comparison with
Clairvaux or Rievaulx. What his letter to Adam implies
about conditions there bears out O'Mara's statement of
the state of savigniac learning: 'Men who joined Savigny
and its dependencies . . . would work, but not hard; it
seems that they would scarcely study at all, since certainly
they have left almost no evidence of study.'[13] This letter
with its evidence of a desire to have another learned man

---

13. Philip F. O'Mara, 'A Fairly Honorable Defeat: Why Clairvaux Had to
Absorb the Monastic Congregation of Savigny', a paper presented at the 1999
Cistercian Studies Congress, Kalamazoo, MI.

at Swineshead is probably only one instance of Gilbert's effort to attract theologians and teachers.

Gilbert's invitation thus appeals almost entirely to Adam's intellectual gifts and joy in learning. Rather than arguing that Adam's learning is without value or use, he declares its value for the monastery and its continuing use to Adam as he perseveres in following Christ. Through a seasoned love of truth, a continuing search for wisdom, and even a willingness to dig in the depths and follow circuitous routes toward understanding rather than receiving gifts from others' labor, he has come this far and should continue to the end. Gilbert does not disparage who Adam is or what he has done but praises his preparation for further growth.

Gilbert's epistle to Adam is highly personal and specific, directed to a man full of the love of learning. Whereas elsewhere Gilbert warns monks against seeking vain learning, here he only hints at that concern. But as in the sermons he shapes his message to his audience. Monks must not allow a desire for learning to lure them from the monastic life, for that would be exile, a step away from wisdom. So the sermons laud the ease and joy of wisdom while attacking the fruitlessness of worldly learning. But this new Adam, still outside the monastic paradise, needs not a warning against such learning but rather encouragement to persist in following it as a clue and path to its origin, source, and end. It has, after all, already drawn him to the next level, to the desire for a life that will benefit from his learning and renew him, fill his cells of doctrine with the sweetness of wisdom, admit him to all the mysteries of light inaccessible, and make him one with Christ.

Daniel M. LaCorte

Saint Ambrose University

Aelred of Rievaulx's Doctrine of *Grace* and its Role in the *Reformatio* of the Soul[1]

CHRYSOGONUS WADDELL was the first person to whom I was introduced at the International Medieval Studies Congress in Kalamazoo. From that first meeting to the present day, Father Chrysogonus has taught me about the monastic life and the meaning of compassion, and has been a powerful example of a loving friend. I should like to thank him for: his scholarly work, from which I continue to learn, and for his humor, which endears him to so many; and for his clement and loving counsel during my first visit to Gethsemani. To him I offer this study of another Cistercian's thought.

1. Abbreviations Used for the Works of Aelred of Rievaulx

Adv	*Sermo in adventu Domini*
Anima	*De anima*
Ann M	*Sermo in annuntiatione beate Maria*
Asspt	*Sermo in assumptione sanctae Mariae*
In st incl	*De institutione inclusarum*
Nat Ben	*Sermo in natali sancti Benedicti*
Nat M	*Sermo in nativitate sanctae Mariae*
Nat PP	*Sermo in natali sanctorum apostolorum Petri et Pauli*
Oner	*Sermo de oneribus*
OS	*Sermo in festivitate omnium sanctorum; sermo in festo sanctorum omnium*
Pent	*Sermo in die pentecosten; sermo in die pentecostes*
Pur	*Sermo in purificatione sanctae Mariae*
Spec car	*Speculum caritatis*
Spir amic	*De spirituali amicitia*
Vir	*Sermo beate Virginis*
YP	*Sermo in ypapanti Domini de diversis moribus*

Many twelfth century spiritual writers developed the theme of the *reformatio* of the *imago dei*,[2] the topic that Gerhart Ladner identifies as the central issue to the spirituality of twelfth-century monasticism.[3] In France, Cistercians such as Bernard of Clairvaux, William of Saint Thierry, and Isaac of Stella produced texts on the soul's re-formation, and in England Aelred of Rievaulx devoted his last years to exploring this topic in what was to be his final work, *On the Soul*.[4] Adopting an augustinian model of the tripartite soul, Aelred argued that the soul's faculties—*ratio, voluntas, memoria*—reflected the *imago dei* but had been damaged by sin and needed restoration, and he also called particular attention to the way in which monastic life, as established by Saint Benedict in his *Rule*, efficiently facilitated that reform.[5] Aelred insists, however, that in

2. I am grateful to Professor Marsha Dutton for her assistance with this study. See Gerhart B. Ladner, 'Terms and Ideas of Renewal', in *Renaissance and Renewal in the Twelfth Century*, ed. Robert Benson, Giles Constable, and Carol Lanham (reprint, Toronto, 1991) 14–15. See also Marie-Dominique Chenu, *Nature, Man and Society in the Twelfth Century*, ed. and trans. Jerome Taylor and Lester K. Little (Chicago, 1968) 30–37, 46–55.

3. Writers such as John Scotus Erigenus, Hugh of Saint Victor, Anselm of Canterbury, Anselm of Havelberg, and Hildegard of Bingen each wrote on the idea of the reformation of soul's *imago dei*. Ladner, 'Terms and Ideas of Renewal', 13–15.

4. Aelred of Rievaulx, *Dialogue on the Soul*, trans. C. H. Talbot (Cistercian Fathers series 22) [hereafter CF]; Kalamazoo, 1981.

5. For Augustine's tripartite image in humans: see *De Trinitate* 10.17; PL 42:983. See Elizabeth Connor, 'Saint Bernard's Three Steps of Truth and Saint Aelred of Rievaulx's Three Loves', in John R. Sommerfeldt, ed., *Bernardus Magister*, CS 135 (Kalamazoo, 1992) 227 and n. 6. For the idea of *reformatio* of the soul, see Gerhart B. Ladner, *The Idea of Reform: Its Impact on Christian Thought and Action in the Age of the Fathers* (Cambridge, Massachusetts: Harvard University Press, 1959) 153–283. The tripartite model of the soul is found throughout Aelred's *De anima* as well as in *Speculum caritatis* 1.3.9; CCCM 1:16; CF 17:92: 'Tria haec memoriam dico, scientiam, amorem siue uoluntatem'. See also *Pent*; SI 107–109; *Pur* 34.8; CCCM 2A:280; and *Vir*; SI 137. See Elizabeth Connor, 'The Doctrine of Charity in Book One of Aelred of Rievaulx's *Mirror of Charity*' *Cistercian Studies Quarterly* 29 (1994) 61–82; Charles Dumont, 'Fraternal Love in the Monastic Doctrine of Aelred of Rievaulx', *Cistercian Studies Quarterly* 32 (1997) 25–35. See also

the end it is not human action but the grace of God that accomplishes the *refomatio* of the *imago Dei* in the monk.

Scholarly attention to the augustinian grounding of the cistercian understanding of the *imago Dei* and its *reformatio* has, for the most part, focused on the great french writers of the cistercian golden age, Bernard, William and Isaac. Étienne Gilson's *The Mystical Theology of Saint Bernard* calls particular attention to Bernard's insistence on the subsistence of the *imago* after the Fall,[6] and John R. Sommerfeldt's chapter on Bernard's anthropology in *The Spiritual Teachings of Bernard of Clairvaux* includes two sections devoted to the effects of the Fall and the restoration of the soul.[7] David N. Bell's exploration of the augustinian spirituality of William of Saint Thierry, *Image and Likeness*, identifies the ways in which William's anthropology depends on and departs from the augustinian understanding of the faculties of the soul and its restoration by grace. The different kinds of grace, creative grace, and 'the grace by which we actualize that potential for participating in God, by which we restore the likeness of the image . . .', Bell identifies as illuminating grace in William's thought.[8] In *Three Treatises on Man: A Cistercian Anthropology,* which contains anthropological treatises by Bernard, William, and Isaac, Bernard McGinn emphasizes in his thorough Introduction the influence exercised by Augustine on cis-

---

my 'Reformation of the Intellect in the Thought of Aelred of Rievaulx', in *Reform and Renewal in the Middle Ages and the Renaissance: Studies in Honor of Louis Pascoe, SJ.,* Thomas Izbicki and Christopher M. Bellitto eds. (Leiden: Brill, 2000) 35–49; and Ladner, 'Terms and Ideas of Renewal', *The Idea of Reform*, 13–15.

6. Étienne Gilson, *The Mystical Theology of Saint Bernard*, trans. A.H.C. Downes, (London 1940; rpt. Kalamazoo: Cistercian Publications, 1990) 45–51.

7. John R. Sommerfeldt, *The Spiritual Teachings of Bernard of Clairvaux* (Cistercian Studies series [hereafter CS] 125; Kalamazoo, 1991) 21–31.

8. David N. Bell, *Image and Likeness: The Augustinian Spirituality of William of Saint Thierry* CS 78 (Kalamazoo, Michigan: Cistercian Publications, 1984) 131–132.

tercian understandings of the soul, the effects of the Fall, and God's role in restoring the *imago* within it:

> Augustine's thought on the nature of man and of the soul was to be a rich mine for the twelfth-century theorists. In questions of the origin of the soul, its immateriality and immortality, the manner of its presence in the body, and the nature of the soul as the image of God, his authority was of central weight.[9]

Little attention has so far been given to Aelred's anthropology, however, especially among English-speaking scholars, perhaps because of the incomplete ending of *On the Soul*. Anselme Hoste, in his 1962 *Bibliotheca Aelrediana*, lists only four studies of the work, none of them in English. Pierre-André Burton lists only one in his 1997 *Bibliotheca Aelrediana II*, the 1971–72 italian article of M. K. Otani, drawn from his 1956 Milan thesis. In fact the work appears to have been little known or valued even in the Middle Ages. David N. Bell has located only two medieval library catalogues in Britain that list it.[10] And, although Aelred also deals with the *reformatio* of the soul in works which have received a great deal of scholarly attention, such as *Mirror of Charity*, no one has dealt specifically with the role of grace in Aelred's anthrolpological teaching. Amédée Hallier identifies the creation of humankind in God's image as 'the fundamental concept and the dogmatic-psychological foundation of Aelred's doctrine', concluding that 'accurate knowledge of the nature of man cannot be obtained without considering

9. Bernard McGinn, Introduction to *Three Treatises on Man: A Cistercian Anthropology*, CF 24 (Kalamazoo, Michigan: Cistercian Publications, 1977) p. 7.
10. David N. Bell, *An Index of Cistercian Authors and Works in Medieval Library Catalogues in Great Britain,* CS 132 (Kalamazoo, Michigan: Cistercian Publications, 1994).

the mystery of God'.[11] But while he writes of the divine
visitations that lead the soul toward God, he, like most
others who write on the subject, concentrates on the role
of charity as that faculty which renders humans 'capable
of union with God',[12] and on spiritual friendship, which
he claims Aelred identifies with God.[13] He thus focuses
on the human response to God's invitation rather than
on God's role in reforming the fallen soul. Although in
*Ancient and Medieval Memories: Studies in Reconstruction of
the Past*, Janet Coleman studies the augustinian character
of Aelred's anthropology, especially as expressed in *On the
Soul*, she concentrates, naturally, on his view of the memory's role in receiving God.[14] Charles Dumont comes
closest to the matter in his introduction to the 1990 English translation of *The Mirror of Charity*, when he writes:

> This experience of love is not simply that of the
> soul's efforts in its struggle against the passions. It is
> at the same time the experience of grace. . . . Love
> of self and love of neighbor represent a purification,
> a catharsis, of the heart by which it frees itself from
> tensions and divisions and recovers its unity.[15]

Yet for Aelred it is always God who is the primary
worker in reforming the fallen soul, drawing it to himself,
educating it once it has responded to that initial impulse,
and finally accomplishing its reformation. While he insists
on the assistance provided to the monk by the regular
monastic life, which 'contains the divesting of the old
man, the renewal of his mind, and the re-forming of

11. Amedee Hallier, *The Monastic Theology of Aelred of Rievaulx*, CS 2, (Cistercian Publications, Inc., 1969) 25.
12. *Ibid.*, 32.
13. *Ibid.*, 36
14. Janet Coleman, *Ancient and Medieval Memories: Studies in the Reconstruction
of the Past* (Cambridge: Cambridge University Press, 1992) 208–227, esp. 21.
15. Charles Dumont, Introduction to *The Mirror of Charity*, trans. Elizabeth
Connor, CF 17 (Kalamazoo, Michigan: Cistercian Publications, 1990) 36–37.

the divine image',[16] Aelred was no pelagian, nor was he a semi-pelagian.[17] Desiring the soul's *reformatio* and participating in the monastic life are both in themselves gifts from God, and it is God who initiates, assists, and restores the soul.

GOD'S IMAGE, SIN AND GOD'S GIFT

Aelred, like his cistercian brethren across the Channel, followed Augustine in beginning his discussion of the soul with its creation in God's image, clothed in the splendor, dignity, and beauty bestowed on our first parents, which was the likeness of God, but lost in the Fall by original sin.[18] That sin cloaks the *imago* and must be removed if the soul's faculties are to be revealed and released to the exercise of their proper functions.[19] When humans clothed themselves with the concerns of the brute animals, Aelred says, they sullied the soul's beauty, ceasing to resemble God and banishing themselves from Paradise: 'the soul thus lost its likeness to God, and cast itself into a land of unlikeness, the *regio disimilitudinis*'.[20] Even so the image of God remained.[21] That image persists in the descendants

16. *Spec car* 1.8.24; CCCM 1:22; CF 17:100: *Ideo saluberrime nobis indicitur istius unius praecepti compendium, in quo et ueteris hominis exspoliatio, et mentis renouatio, et diuinae imaginis consistit reformatio.*

17. I have borrowed this line from John R. Sommerfeldt's lectures and presentation on Bernard and Aelred. I am indebted to Professor Sommerfeldt for his insights and continual assistance with my work on Aelred.

18. *Pent*; SI 108–109.

19. 'Homo in honore positus non intellexit, comparatus est iumentis insipientibus et similis factus est illis, et, amissa dei similitudine, similis factus est illis. . . ." *Pent*; SI 108–109.

20. ' . . . et qui per rapinam Dei usurpat similitudinem, merito iumentorum induit dissimilitudinem." *Spec car* 1.4.11; CCCM 1:17; CF 17:93. For further study of the term *regio dissimilitudinis,* see Hallier, *Monastic Theology*, 12–16; A. E. Taylor, 'Regio dissimilitudinis," *Archives d'histoire doctrinale et litteraire du moyen age*, 9 (1934):305–306; and Etienne Gilson, 'Regio dissimilitudinis de Platon à Saint Bernard de Clairvaux," *Mediaeval Studies*, 9 (1947):108–130.

21. ' . . . etsi non imagine, diuina tamen similitudine. . . .' *Spec car* 1.2.6; CCCM 1:15; CF 17:90 and *Pent* (SI 108–109). The tripartite model of the soul

of those first parents; the problem in all ages is how to restore the likeness to God that has been lost. Aelred insists that such restoration is possible: 'they were still able to return to their pristine form, re-formed by him who had formed them. . . .'[22] The renewal of the soul, he goes on, takes place through 'an attachment of charity'.[23] Perfect charity, he explains, restores the image, unveiling the faculties of the soul and restoring their original power and beauty: 'if the mind assumes this charity perfectly, the other two, the memory and the knowledge . . . will most assuredly be reformed.'[24]

Throughout his works, Aelred emphasizes the role of charity in the soul's reformation. But, he notes, 'assuming charity perfectly', has inherent difficulties grounded in the conflict between self-interest and charity. That conflict makes divine aid necessary in enabling humankind to will what is good, for humans cannot ascend from the land of unlikeness without assistance.[25] That aid is God's gift of charity, poured into the human soul to pull it from its sinful self-interest and so to reform the soul: 'between this concupiscence, correctly called self-centeredness, and that spirit which we properly call charity, which surely is not a spirit of ours but from God; for the charity of God is diffused in our hearts by the

---

is found throughout Aelred's *De anima* as well as in *Spec car* 1.3.9; CCCM 1:16; CF 17:92: 'Tria haec memoriam dico, scientiam, amorem siue uoluntatem." See also *Pent*; SI 107–109; *Pur* 34.8; CCCM 2A:280; and *Vir*; SI 137.

22. ' . . . nec tamen desiit esse et vivere: qui posset ad pristinam formam, eo qui formaverat reformante, redire. Ipsa autem forma, sapientia est; via vero, per quam ad ipsam formam redeatur, eruditio." *Oner* 2; PL 195:363C.

23. 'Quod ex caritatis affectu homo in Dei imaginem reformetur.' Title to *Spec car* 1.8.24; CCCM 1:22; CF 17: 100.

24. ' . . . hanc caritatem si mens perfecte induerit, profecto duo illa . . . memoriam scilicet et scientiam, ipsa reformabit.' *Spec car* 1.8.24; CCCM 1:22; CF 17: 100.

25. *Spec car* 1.10.28; CCCM 1:23; CF 17; 102. See Amedee Hallier, *The Monastic Theology of Aelred of Rievaulx*, CS 2, (Cistercian Publications, Inc., 1969), 3–24.

Holy Spirt who is given to us' [Rm 5:5].[26] For Aelred, therefore, charity is God's grace, given to humankind for the soul's reformation.

God bestows several types of grace on his creatures, according to Aelred. The first of these, prevenient grace[27] works to bring them to salvation as it 'draws, entices, attracts' them.[28] Yet, while God grants this grace, its efficacy is 'accomplished in or through us',[29] Aelred explains, because God

> inclines our will so that we might consent to it. Thus, thanks to his grace, the reward becomes ours. If I do the work willingly, I also receive the reward. But, so that I might be willing to do the good work, it is God who causes even my willing. [see Rm 9:16][30]

God thus begins the process of reformation of the soul through his love for humankind, providing the initial impulse to the will to seek its happiness. That initial impulse is charity.

A second type of grace enables one to respond to the initial, prevenient grace. What is more, Aelred explains, the corrective curriculum that God provides as the second gift is Wisdom, which informs the essence of monastic

---

26. *Spec car* 1. 10.28; CCCM 1:23–24; CF 17:102: ' . . . concupiscentiam quae cupiditas congruentissime appellatur, et illam spirtus quam caritatem non immerito dicimus, quae utique spiritus est, non nostri, sed Dei; caritas enim Dei diffusa est in cordibus nostris, per Spirtum sanctum, qui datus est nobis. . . .'

27. See Elizabeth Connor's article on Aelred's understanding of prevenient grace in, 'Monastic Profession According to Aelred of Rievaulx', in Francis R. Swietek and John R. Sommerfeldt (edd.), *Studiosorum Speculum: Studies in Honor of Louis J. Lekai, O.Cist.*, CS 141 (Kalamazoo, Michigan: Cistercian Publications, 1993) 59.

28. *Spec car* 2.19.57: CCCM 1:93: CF 17:203.

29. *Spec car* 1.11.31: CCCM 1:25: CF 17:104.

30. *Spec car* 1.11.31: CCCM 1:25: CF 17:104: ' . . . inclinat uoluntatem ut consentiamus; sicque ex eius gratia, merces fit nostra. Si enim uolens id facio, mercedem accipio; ut autem sim uolens in bono opere, Deus est qui operatur et uelle.'

life: ' . . . this formation is wisdom; truly, and the road along which we are brought back, is education'.[31] Education in Wisdom requires a formation and a study of God, the very things that are, not coincidentally, the foundation for the monastic curriculum of reform. Each faculty of the soul or is formed by this curriculum and by the healing benefits of encountering God. For example, Aelred says that the intellect touched by Wisdom distinguishes ' . . . between truth and falsehood, justice and injustice, and, since the intellect has the capacity for wisdom, it is through reason that knowledge of God is attained'.[32] The memory's encounter with the grace of Wisdom provides it with the corrective it requires, the will also benefits, becoming able once again to turn itself toward that which can give it happiness, which is love: 'The teaching of Holy Scripture rectifies the memory; the mystery of faith restores the intellect; continually growing love reforms the will.'[33]

As the faculties come to know the Creator, they increasingly take on the central characteristic of God, love. The intellect knows what to love, the memory recalls love, and the will can choose to love perfectly because it has been reformed by love himself.[34]

GRACE AS CONSOLATION AND VISITATIONS

While explaining the types of grace God gives to reform the deformed *imago Dei,* Aelred considers three ways in

31. *Oner* 2; PL 195:363C: 'Ipsa autem forma, sapientia est; via vero, per quam ad ipsam formam redeatur, eruditio.'
32. *Anima* 2.18; CCCM 1:713; CF 22:80: 'Ratione distinguimus inter uerum et falsum, inter iustum et iniustum, quae cum capax sit sapientiae, per ipsam ad Dei notitiam peruenitur.'
33. *Spec car* 1.5.14; CCCM 1:18; CF 17:94: 'reparatur tandem memoria per sacrae Scripturae documentum, intellectus per fidei sacramentum, amor per caritatis quotidianum incrementum.' See also *Adv*; SI 34.
34. See again *Spec car* 1.8.24; CCCM 1:22; CF 17:100: ' . . . hanc caritatem si mens perfecte induerit, profecto duo illa . . . memoriam scilicet et scientiam, ipsa reformabit.'

which the monk receives and understands grace, describing them in terms of God's consolations and visitations. The first of these is the at first frightening power of a grace-filled encounter with the Holy Spirit:

> *The love of God is poured out into our hearts by the Holy Spirit who has been given to us* [Rm 5:5]. Surely the Holy Spirit has been bestowed at the Jordan, but he was given in groans, in tears, in compunction, in fear, in the renunciation of worldliness . . . to those tired and wearied by many temptations, so that they might be consoled and refreshed. . . . In these places the Spirit is given. . . . He is kind to those who seek, generous to those making progress, glorious to those standing at the summit of perfection.[35]

This visitation of the Holy Spirit, Aelred says, empowers and assists the monk in the daily living of the *Rule*.

One's first encounter with this gift of grace, Aelred warns, effects not so much consolation as a sense of fear,[36] a starting point through which the monk may begin to consider himself and his relationship with God in a more truthful way.[37] God's grace, he explains, is a means to

> wake people up. . . . To wake up those who are sleeping. . . . [Grace] first frightens the scornful or coaxes on the fearful. . . . It is accorded to the elect for advancement, and to the reprobate for judgement.[38]

---

35. *Pent; SI* 111. ' . . . caritas dei diffusa est in cordibus nostris per spiritum sanctum qui datus est nobis. Datur certe spiritus sanctus in Iordane sed datur in gemitu, in lacrimis, in compunctione, in timore, in mundi abrenuntiatione, . . . ut consolentur, ut refrigerentur, . . . spiritus portio datur. . . . Benignus petenti, beneficus proficienti, gloriosus in perfectionis culmine consistenti.'
36. See *Spec car* 2.12.29; CCCM 1:79; CF 17:182.
37. *Adv*; SI 35: ' . . . invenit homo diligenda, se, proximum, deum.'
38. *Spec car* 2.8.20; CCCM 1:75; CF 17:176: 'Fit enim aliquando ad excitationem. . . . Ad excitationem dormientibus . . . Prima terret contemnen-

Awakened by the awe elicited from this initial encounter with God's love, the soul responds to its Creator with compunction.[39] But it is compunction not for ' . . . judgement but for advancement'.[40] Yet fear and compunction, Aelred explains, must not be the monk's permanent response to the encounter with God. The recipient of such grace must move beyond fear of hell to perfect charity and to joy:

> . . . a servile fear of hell makes this way narrow; perfect charity broadens it. As long as anyone fears, he suffers difficulty in the way of God, and experiences hardship. When, however, he comes to that love (*caritas*) which perfectly casts out fear [cf 1 Jn 4:18], then he cries out with unmingled joy with the Apostle: 'I have fought the good fight; I have finished the race; I have kept the faith' [2 Tm 4:7]. . . . [41]

As a final result of this first visitation of God's grace, then, the monk may leave his fear behind, replacing it with the freeing and broad path of true love, rejecting the sinful actions and attachments of his past life.

This rejection of the sin of the past involves not only private but public repentance; the monk confesses and does penance. Repentance is itself, Aelred explains, a result of love; and yet ' . . . the soul moves with love (*caritas*), so that by confession and satisfaction we avoid

---

tem, uel illicit timentem. . . . Fit enim electis ad profectum, reprobis ad iudicium.'

39. *Spec car* 2.11.26; CCCM 1:77–78; CF 17:180.

40. *Spec car* 2.9.23; CCCM 1:76; CF 17:178: 'huiusmodi compunctione excitantur non ad iudicium, sed ad profectum. . . .'

41. *Nat Ben* 12–13; CCCM 2A:63: 'Hanc uiam timor gehennalis, qui et seruilis dicitur, angustat, *caritas perfecta* dilatat. Quamdiu enim quis *timet*, in uia Dei difficultatem patitur et sentit asperitatem. Quando autem ad caritatem peruenit, quae *perfecta foras mittit timorem,* tunc cum ingenti gaudio illud Apostolicum proclamat: *Bonum certamen certaui, cursum consummaui, fidem seruaui.*'

the chains of sin'.[42] The penitential practices of the monk
manifest themselves in both physical exercises[43] and their
concomitant virtues: abstinence, poverty, humility, and
restraint of the will.[44] These external physical exercises
become a vehicle by which the monks receives the healing
benefits of grace.

While God's first visitation of grace both consoles the
monk and prompts him to repent and make satisfaction, a
second visitation—which Aelred calls *pietas* in the Mirror
of Charity—assists him in his daily labors.[45] Portraying
the monks as toiling, groaning under the weight of manual
labor, and fasting—characteristic features of the austere
cistercian approach to the Rule—he assures his monks
that the Lord's consolation helps strengthen them to bear
the weight:

> Those who have abruptly shaken off their torpor to
> undertake sweat and struggles for Christ are singled
> out by him for that more excellent kind of compunc-
> tion, which heals the infirm, strengthens the weak,
> and encourages the hopeless. It is consolation for
> those who sigh, pause for those who toil, protection
> for those who are tempted, and food for those who
> are on their way.[46]

What is more, Aelred continues, the monk will receive these gifts of encouragement, healing, assistance,
strength, and nourishment through additional encounters

42. *Adv*; SI 35: 'Animam nostram movet caritas, ut per confessionem et
satisfactionem vitiorum laqueo devitemus. . . .'
43. *Nat M* 22.7; CCCM 2A:178: 'Ergo qui uult ut dissipentur et destruantur
peccata sua, quae sine dubio sunt quasi murus inter nos et Deum, necesse
habet ut se operibus paenitentiae tradat.'
44. See *Nat M* 8; CCCM 2A:178.
45. See *Spec car* 2.11.26; CCCM 1:77; CF 17:180.
46. *Spec car* 2.10.24; CCCM 1:77; CF 17:179: 'Qui exusso tepore statim ut
sudores et agones pro Christo susceperint, ab illo excellentiori compunctionis
genere excipiuntur, quae infirmos sanat, debiles roborat, alleuat desperatos.
Ipsa est consolatio gementibus, pausatio laborantibus, tentatis protectio,
uiaticum itinerantibus.'

with the consoling effects of grace.[47] Consolation of this sort does not come but once but is provided throughout the monk's life. As Aelred puts it, it comes like ' . . . milk from the breasts of his [God's] consolation to those progressing. . . .'[48]

The third and highest form of consolation that God gives the monk, according to Aelred, involves an encounter with True Love. This encounter presupposes, and is conditioned by, the purifying effects of the first two forms: first, compunction and repentance and then, the on-going daily struggle with labor and pain. This third form of divine consolation, the all-embracing experience of True Love, Aelred teaches, anticipates beatitude itself:

> . . . the mind, accustomed to the countless incentives of heavenly attachments, is moved along little by little to that most sublime kind of visitation experienced by the very few. There it begins to have some foretaste of the first-fruits of its future reward.[49]

Unlike the first two sorts of visitation, this third experience of grace comes not at all through the activity of the monk but requires instead a certain passivity; this is reflected in Aelred's use of the word *raptus* [having been caught up] in describing it. He identifies the monk who receives this grace with Paul himself, who ' . . . whether in his body or outside his body was rapt to the third heaven [2 Co 12:2]. . . .'[50] This experience not only prefigures

---

47. Aelred uses terms of protection for those tempted, as for example, *Spec car* 2.10.25; CCCM 1:77; CF 17:179. 'Prouenit enim aliquando tentatis, ne corruant, aliquando tentandis ut leuius ferant.'
48. *Spec car* 2.12.30; CCCM 1:79; CF 17:183: 'Proficientibus lac ab uberibus consolationis eius. . . .'
49. *Spec car* 2.11.28; CCCM 1:78; CF 17:181: 'In hoc statu innumerabilibus caelestium affectuum incentiuis assuefacta mens, paulatim in illud sublimissimum ac perpaucis expertum uisitationis genus prouehitur, ubi quasdam futurae suae remunerationis primitias incipiat praegustare. . . .'
50. *Asspt*; SI 162: 'Et sive in corpore sive extra corpus raptus fuerit ad tertium celum. . . .' See also *Nat PP* 15.14 (CCCM 2A:285) and *Pur* 34.26 (CCCM

188 Daniel M. LaCorte

the joy to come, but even now brings to the monk 'perfect happiness'.[51]

The effects of God's repeated visitations and consolations to the monk who responds with compunction to God's initial visitation and who then courageously perseveres are manifold, in this life and in the life to come. Though life's labors, trials, and temptations are many, Aelred says, the rewards of this encounter with God's love are also many and enduring, a great consolation indeed:

> Indeed, when he has been carried away to the upper room by the most sublime love to continue in tranquility of the mind, . . . fear will be expelled, his toil will be changed to peace, sadness to joy, it will surely be accomplished that neither death, nor life . . . will separate him from the love of God [see Rm 8:39].[52]

Despite the burdens of the present day, then, Aelred declares, divine consolation soothes and gives hope to the monk who struggles with the restorative exercises of the monastic life:

> Whenever someone is so inflamed by the love of God, and so instilled with the love of Jesus Christ . . . that he will doubtlessly be carried off [rapt] in such security that he sees himself secure and that he will

---

2A:285); John R. Sommerfeldt, 'The Vocabulary of Contemplation in Aelred of Rievaulx's, *On Jesus at the Age of Twelve, A Rule of Life for a Recluse*, and *On Spiritual Friendship*,' in E. Rozanne Elder, ed., *Heaven on Earth,* Studies in Medieval Cistercian History 9, CS 68 (Kalamazoo, Michigan: Cistercian Publications, 1983) 72–89.

51. See *Spec car* 2.13.31; CCCM 1:81; CF 17:184.

52. *Pent*; SI 111: 'Verum, cum in caritatis [sic] sublimissimum translata cenaculum ad continuam mentis tranquillitatem, . . . timor expellitur, labor in requiem, dolor in gaudium commutatur, efficitur certa, quod *neque mors neque vita . . . separabunt eam a caritate dei*.'

not be damned and indeed without any doubt will be saved.[53]

Finally, Aelred states that the monk who has been visited by God's grace of consolation experiences an attachment so great that he prefers nothing to this experience of God. Here, at last, Aelred identifies grace explicitly with the love of Jesus, and the monk's knowledge and experience of him he calls *affectus*. *Affectus,* he writes, 'is a kind of spontaneous, pleasant inclination of the spirit towards someone.'[54] 'Spiritual attachment', he goes on to say, 'can be understood in two ways. The spirit is stirred by this attachment [*affectus*][55] when, touched by a hidden and—we might say—unforeseen visitation of the Holy Spirit, it is opened either to the sweetness of divine love or to the pleasantness of fraternal and true charity.'[56] This experience of divine love and true charity powerfully and profoundly re-focusses the monk's desires.

> Like an abyss, indeed, my Lord Jesus ought to be absorbed in the *affectus*, thus adhering to that taste of delightful and pious love, so that there is no desire other than Jesus; there is no desire to know anyone but Jesus. Thus, without a doubt, the attachment of

---

53. 'Quicumque aliquando ita arsit in amore Dei, in quodam dulci affectu Iesu Christi . . . sit raptus in qualem talem securitatem ut videretur sibi quasi securus et certus esse quod non debeat damnari sed sine ulla ambiguitate saluari. . . .' *Pur* 34.26; CCCM 2A:285.

54. 'Est igitur affectus spontanea quaedam ac dulcis ipsius animi ad aliquem inclinatio.' *Spec car* 3.11.31; CCCM 1:119; CF 17:241.

55. On Aelred's use of the term *affectus* see Elizabeth Connor, in 'Translator's Preface' to *The Mirror of Charity*, 10 and *idem*, 'Saint Bernard's Three Steps of Truth and Saint Aelred of Rievaulx's Three Loves,' *Bernardus Magister* (see above, n. 5) 227.

56. 'Nam spirituali quidem affectu animus excitatur, cum occulta et quasi improuisa Spiritus sancti uisitatione in diuinae dilectionis dulcedinem, uel fraternae caritatis suauitatem mens compuncta resoluitur.' *Spec car* 3.11.31; CCCM 1:119; CF 17:241.

the mind presumes to embrace this One, by whom he senses himself to be embraced.[57]

In Aelred's sermon on the temple, as described in Ezekiel, he discusses the effects of this experience of Jesus on the *affectus*. Aelred descibes an encounter :

> Indeed, Brothers, when the Lord has come into our bed-chamber, passing into our *affectus*, so that our entire *affectus* is possessed, . . . what kind of embraces will there be, what sort of kisses? . . . Nothing is impure with his love, no blemish, no vice. . . . Wherever love is pure, wherever love is holy, wherever love is not seeking earthly but celestial things, there love is good. There is a love directed to the Son of the Virgin. . . . [58]

Aelred's teaching on the reformation of the monk's soul required a perfect 'attachment of charity,'[59] in which the purity of love sensed in the *affectus* restores and perfects the faculty. Moreover, the encounter with True love affects the entire soul, reforming to it the *imago Dei* in which it/she was created. Aelred speaks of the process as one of deification:

> You alone experience the delights of him when, in a spiritual kiss, created and uncreated spirits join and are merged so that two become one. I do indeed say

57. *YP*; SI 5: 'Sed quasi abysso quodam imo domini mei Ihesu absorbeatur affectu, ita adherens illi glutino dulcis et pii amoris, ut nichil extra ipsum, nichil preter ipsum saltem cogitare dignetur, sic nimirum affecta mens ab ipso se presumat amplecti, quem se quoque senserit amplexari. . . .'

58. *Pur* 32.27–28; CCCM 2A:265:'Eia, fratres, cum intrauerit thalamum nostrum Dominus noster, transiens in affectum nostrum, ut totum affectum nostrum ipse possideat . . . quales ibi amplexus, qualia erunt oscula? Nulla impuritas in amore eius, nulla macula, nullum vitium. . . . Ubicumque amor castus est, amor sanctus, amor non quaerens terrena sed caelestia, ibi amor bonus, amor pertines ad Filium Virginis. . . .'

59. See above, note 23.

'one,' as justifying and justified, as sanctifying and sanctified, as deifying and deified.[60]

COMMUNAL GIFT

However necessary Aelred considers personal reformation and perseverance, no soul, and no monk, is alone on the difficult path to re-formation; the communal nature of monastic life provides a necessary assistance in the restoration and perfection of the soul.[61] In explaining the manner in which life in community can foster the reformation process, Aelred builds on his understanding of the social nature of humanity.[62] Further, and more specifically, he teaches his monks that life in community fosters humility, love, and unity. If a monk lacks some skill or some ability, his reliance on another promotes virtue, because 'each needs the other, and what anyone does not find in himself, he has in the other. Thus, humility is preserved, love increased, and communal unity realized.'[63] If a monk is struggling, he can take heart in another's progress; support comes from one's fellows who share in the same difficulties.[64] Thus each monk contributes his particular talent and unique strength in constructing an environment that fosters love: 'One can offer more

60. *YP*; 51: ' . . . Que sola cuius sit dulcedinis experiris, quando in osculo spirituali sibi obviant sibique miscentur spiritus creatus et increatus, ut sint duo in uno, immo dico unum, sicut iustificans et iustificatus, et sanctificatus sicut sanctificans, sicut deificans et deificatus.'
61. See Charles Dumont, 'Personalism in Community According to Aelred of Rievaulx,' *CSQ* 12 (1977) 250–271; and Dumont's excellent article on, 'Seeking God in Community according to St. Aelred,' in M. Basil Pennington, ed., *Contemplative Community: An Interdisciplinary Symposium*, CS 21 (Washington, D.C.: Cistercian Publications, 1972) 115–150.
62. See *Spir amic* 1.57; CCCM 1:299; CF 5:63.
63. *Nat Ben* 10; CCCM 2A:67: 'Ut unusquisque alio indigeat et quod in se non habet, hoc in altero habet, ut sic seruetur humilitas, augeatur caritas, unitas cognoscatur.'
64. See *Spir amic* 3.79; CCCM 1:333.

work; another, more vigils; another, more fasting. . . .'[65] By offering his particular gift to build up the dwelling place of the Lord, the monk offers all his virtues to all.[66] Charles Dumont has demonstrated that Aelred depended on the phrase *Singula sunt omnium, omnia singulorum*[67] (what belongs to each individually, belongs to all, and what belongs to all, belongs to each individually) to communicate his belief that the members of the community at Rievaulx should be encouraged to share all their struggles, weaknesses, duties, and aspirations. Aelred compares this communal unity of the monastic family to a harp, each string of which produces a unique and single note, yet all of the notes blend together to make a chorus of harmoniously pleasing sound.[68] Another example of unity offered to the monastic community is that which exists among the angels: 'Through unity and concord, whatever belongs to the one, belongs to all, and whatever belongs to all belongs to one.'[69] Consideration and implementation of this angelic unity helps the members of the entire monastic community share in the difficult and sometimes frustrating routine of the cistercian life.

For Aelred, communal unity has as its exemplar the oneness of God:

All these things should bring you back to unity. . . . And this one thing can only be found in the One, near the One, with the One, in whom there is no

---

65. *Nat Ben* 8.7; CCCM 2A:66. See also *Spec car* 1.3.6; CCCM 1:108; CF 17:90.

66. See also *Pent*; SI 112.

67. Dumont, 'Personalism in Community' [cited n. 59], 255–259. Dumont cites several instances where Aelred uses this phrase, for example, *OS* 26.45; CCCM 2A:220.

68. *Oner* 21; PL 195:496D.

69. *OS* 26.45; CCCM 2A:220:' per unitatem et concordiam, quidquid est singulorum, hoc est omnium, et quidquid est omnium, hoc est singulorum.'

change or shadow of change; he who cleaves to him is made one spirit with him.[70]

The more nearly the monastic community approaches the unity within God and among his angels, the more freely love can flow among the monks and the more deeply can each participate in perfect charity. The goal of the entire community must be for each member to extend a perfect, selfless love to his brothers.

Moreover life in community allows the monk to encounter Christ in another monk. As the persons in community grow in love, their souls become re-formed; they begin to radiate the love of God to each other. The monastery becomes a community united in love, and this love is reenforced in a variety of ways: through shared physical and spiritual exercises, through God's visitations, and through love for one another. The progress made by each individual contributes to building the spirit of love in the community or peace, which Aelred describes as paradise: 'The peace of the cloister is paradise. A paradise even more beautiful, it seems to me, than that in which Adam was placed.'[71]

Finally, Aelred's view of the monastic community had a profound effect on his doctrine of the necessity of friendship and therefore shaped the environment at Rievaulx.[72]

---

70. *Inst incl* 2.26; CCCM 1:659; CF 2:74:'His enim omnibus ad unum necesse est ut conscendas, quoniam unum est necessarium. Illud est unum quod non inuenitur nisi in uno, apud unum, cum uno, apud quem non est transmutatio, nec uicissitudinis obumbratio. Qui adhaeret ei unus cum eo spiritus efficitur, transiens in illud unum quod semper idem est, et cuius anni non deficiunt.'

71. *Ann M*; SI 88:'Paradisus corporalis est quies claustralis. Et quidem pulchrior, ut michi videtur, illo paradiso, in quo positus est Adam, non inferior.'

72. Charles Dumont, 'L'amour fraternel dans la doctrine monastique d' Aelred de Rievaulx,' *Collectanea Cisterciensia* 51 (1989) 79–88; Brendan Callaghan, 'Friendship and Love in Aelred's Theology,' *The Month* 14 (1986) 133–136; Marsha L Dutton, 'Aelred of Rievaulx on Friendship, Chastity, and Sex: The Sources,' *CSQ* 29.2 (1994) 121–196. On the topic of monastic

Aelred begins his teaching on friendship by discussing the effects of the fall on human relations, and goes on to identify the love with which we love friends—the attachment humans have for friends—as identical with their ideal attachment to God.[73] Aelred, aware that human relationships advance the process of love by which the soul follows its path to the Lord, insists people progress from human friendship to that love which leads us to love and to accept being loved by Christ.[74] Human friendship not only imitates Christ's friendship for us but allows for an encounter of Christ himself: 'From the love we have as friends, inspired as it is by Christ, there can be an ascent to Christ himself, who gives himself to us as our friend.'[75] Aelred writes eloquently about the encounter of Christ through another person:

> And, therefore, a friend cleaving to his friend in the spirit of Christ, is made one heart and one mind with his friend and, through this love, rises to friendship with Christ and is made one with him. . . . [76]

friendship, see Jean Leclercq, 'Friendship and Friends in the Monastic Life,' *CSQ* 24.4 (1989) 293–300; Michael Casey, 'The Virtue of Friendship in the Monastic Tradition,' *Tjurunga* 25 (1983) 21–35; Brian Patrick McGuire, *Friendship and Community: The Monastic Experience 350–1250*, CS 95 (Kalamazoo: Cistercian Publications, 1988).
73. *Spir amic* 1.70; CCCM 1:301; CF 5:66: 'Quod tamen sequitur de caritate, amicitiae profecto dare non dubito: *Qui manet in amicitia in Deo manet, et Deus in eo.*'
74. *Spir amic* 2.20; CCCM 1:306; CF 5:74: 'Quae omnia a Christo inchoantur, per Christum promouentur, in Christo perficiuntur.'
75. *Spir amic* 2.20; CCCM 1:306; CF 5:74: 'Non igitur uidetur nimium grauis uel innaturalis ascensus, de Christo amorem inspirante quo amicum diligimus, ad Christum semetipsum amicum nobis praebentem, quem diligamus. . . .'See also *Spir amic* 3:134; CCCM 1: 349; CF 5:131: ' . . . quo amplectitur Christum.'
76. *Spir amic* 2.21; CCCM 1:306; CF 5:74: 'Itaque amicus in spiritu Christi adhaerens amico, efficitur cum eo *cor unum et anima una*; et sic per amoris gradus ad Christi conscendens amicitiam, unus cum eo spiritu efficitur in osculo uno.'

Encountering Christ through a friend is itself a kind of grace which bestows spiritual benefits to both individual and community: 'This friendship . . . will be outpoured upon all and by all outpoured upon God, and God shall be all in all [1 Cor 15:28].'[77]

As abbot, Aelred knew he must balance the physical and spiritual exercises found in the Rule which, when properly performed, assist in the soul's reform. Life according to the Rule, a life of balance and moderation, was central to Aelred's teaching. He teaches that the monastic life is, as we would say, a holistic method of reform which aids the healing of body and soul and transforms relationships between people by properly ordering them toward God and one another through a continual re-education in Wisdom and Grace. In response to the outpouring of loving desire—itself initiated by God—God gives the monk the power to respond to his merciful divine love.

Aelred knows well the power of grace in the heart of the monk. He insists that, through God's loving gifts of grace, the monk will sense a movement in his soul, a sense of love itself being poured into his soul, and that this will give him the strength and the courage to continue his quest to live the monastic life. Through an encounter with the spirit of Christ—Love himself—in his service to his fellows, and through an abundance of loving consolations given in grace, each monk can become an expression of God's inexhaustible and merciful love to his people. Aelred stresses the importance of these human relationships based and focused on the love of Christ and he insists that the more frequently monk encounters Love through grace, in consolations and visitations, or by encountering a Christ-like example in a friend, the

77. *Spir amic* 3.134; CCCM 1:350; CF 5:74: 'Cum haec amicitia . . . transfundetur in omnes, et ab omnibus refundetur in Deum, cum *Deus* fuerit *omnia in omnibus.*'

more he is re-formed to the likeness of God. Aelred fostered a community in which love was the goal of each member. The community at Rievaulx won its reputation for virtue by expressing Aelred's understanding of re-formation through love, and, as such, the monastery could be properly called a School of Love.

Charlotte Ziegler

Stift Zwettl

Tendencies in Cultural Criticism after 1100 and around 1900: A Comparison

W HEN WE ATTEMPT, in this essay,[1] to link the mentality and art of such widely disparate eras, as the twelfth and the thirteenth centuries, we are following the methodology of the most eminent representative of the early Viennese School of Art History, Max Dvořák. Prominent in his concept, put forth in his *Kunstgeschichte als Geisteswissenschaft* [Art History as a Discipline of the Humanities],[2] was the importance he placed upon the integration of the disciplines of Art History and the History of Ideas. Let us begin by focusing upon the time just after the turn of the century (i.e., the early twentieth century), which—in Vienna—was a period marked by revolutionary developments in the fields of Art and Humanities.

This article aims to address the question and the significance of the absence of ornamentation in residential architecture at the turn of two centuries, the periods after 1100 and 1900. It will compare the sacred residential complex, the *domus monachi* or more precisely, the monastic architecture of the Cistercian Order in the first half of the twelfth century, with the residential architecture

---

1. This essay is based on a paper given at the Cistercian Studies Conference of the 30th International Congress on Medieval Studies at Western Michigan University in Kalamazoo, Michigan on May 4, 1995.
2. Vienna 1924.

after 1900, primarily as defined by the architect Adolf Loos.

Of interest in both periods is the very specific attitude manifested in the design of the buildings, namely, the inherent cultural criticism that led to the virtual exclusion of architectural ornamentation. In both periods, radical processes of reform can be observed opposing the lavish adornment of architecture, especially with costly materials.

Our reflections were not initially inspired by any formal art-historical criteria. The main stimulus came, rather, from certain passages in William Bartley's *Wittgenstein* (1973), in which the author characterizes the philosopher's lifestyle. On page three, for example, he records: '[he] seriously contemplated entering monastic life himself'.[3]

The renunciation of his material wealth, which Ludwig Wittgenstein gave to his sisters, and the conversion to an ascetic way of life that at times resembled that of a monkish recluse, formed the basic foundation for his philosophical work. But we shall address this specific topic later.

Not only Bartley, but various other authors on Wittgenstein, as well as Wittgenstein himself,[4] repeatedly

3. William W. Bartley III, *Wittgenstein* (London, [1973] 1977) 3.
4. Michael Nedo, M. Ranchetti, *Ludwig Wittgenstein—Sein Leben in Bildern und Texten* (Frankfurt am Main, 1983); idem, *Ludwig Wittgenstein—Wiener Ausgabe*, 'Einführung' (Vienna, New York, 1993); Allan Janik, Stephan Toulmin, *Wittgensteins Wien* (Munich, 1987); G.H. v. Wright, *Wittgenstein* (Oxford, 1982, german edition Frankfurt am Main, 1990); B. McGuiness, *Wittgensteins frühe Jahre* (London, 1988, german edition Frankfurt am Main, 1992); R. F. Kaspar, *Wittgensteins Ästhetik—Eine Studie* (Vienna, Zurich, 1992); R. Fleck, *Was gezeigt werden kann, kann nicht gesagt werden. Wittgensteins Mädchenkopf* (Klagenfurt, 1993); Ludwig Wittgenstein, 'Tractatus logico philosophicus. Logisch-philosophische Abhandlung'. *Werkausgabe* 1 (1984); 'Über Gewißheit'. *Werkausgabe* 8 (1984); 'Vermischte Bemerkungen'. *Werkausgabe* 8 (1984); 'Bemerkungen über Farben'. *Werkausgabe* 8 (1984); *Vorlesungen 1930–1935*, D. Lee, A. Ambrose, eds. (Oxford, 1980,

mention the intense kinship between Wittgenstein, the man and the philosopher, and other contemporary representatives of the arts. Those frequenting Wittgenstein's house at Alleegasse 16 around the year 1900, and others with whom Wittgenstein came into contact later, included the architect Adolf Loos, the composer and musician Arnold Schönberg, the authors Hugo von Hoffmansthal and Karl Kraus, and the painter Oskar Kokoschka—to name only the most distinguished. They were the forces behind the radical renewal of intellectual and cultural life in Austria in the first third of the twentieth century.

Of special interest to us here is one intellectual viewpoint characteristic of this group—in particular of Ludwig Wittgenstein, Arnold Schönberg, and Adolf Loos. This viewpoint is characterized by a proclivity for clear, simple, 'truthful' forms of expression in language, thought, music, and architecture. We are especially interested in the opinions Adolf Loos expresses in his polemical works on the rejection of architectural ornamentation. Loos also influenced Wittgenstein in this respect,[5] as the following passage, quoted from *Wittgenstein's Vienna* by Allan Janik and Stephan Toulmin, illustrates:

> With regard to Wittgenstein's contemporaries, we know that he influenced Weiniger, Kraus and Loos. In particular, Wittgenstein was friends with the architect Adolf Loos, whose contempt of ornamentation and the decorative arts exactly corresponded to Wittgenstein's own ideas and whose 'functionalist' concepts shed significant light on Wittgenstein's later excursions in the field of architecture.[6]

---

german edition Frankfurt am Main, 1984); Ch. Mann, *Wovon man schweigen muß. Wittgenstein über die Grundlagen von Logik und Mathematik* (Vienna, 1994).

5. Wittgenstein, 'Vermischte Bemerkungen', 476; McGuiness, *Frühe Jahre*, 145.

6. Janik, Toulmin, *Wittgensteins Wien*, 238–239.

In his works *Meine Bauschule* [My Architectural School] (1907), *Ornament und Verbrechen* [Ornament and Crime] (1908), and *Architektur* [Architecture] (1909), Adolf Loos discusses the tangibility of the use of fine raw materials, the dexterous skill with which a craftsman works the raw materials, aiming for the pure effect of the material, skillfully shaped into an architectural form with total negation of ornament. He considered the use of ornament in architecture superfluous embellishment which impaired the clear aesthetic effect of the architectural form, failed to attain any artistic effect, was too expensive, and expended too many valuable working hours.

The 'New Spirit' in modern architecture Loos defined as follows:

> The architects are there to fathom the depth of life, to think necessity through to the ultimate consequences, to help the weaker members of society, to supply the greatest possible number of households with perfect implements. The 'new form'?—how uninteresting that is for the creative human being. It is the New Spirit that matters.[7]

The following quotation from W. Schütte's article 'Adolf Loos und die Moderne Architektur' [Adolf Loos and Modern Architecture] further illustrate this point:

> It is no coincidence that he was the first to deal with the subject of applied arts. In the following years, he repeatedly reexamined the relationship between art and craftsmanship, and the amateurish meddling of architects and decorators intent on their fantastic forms—the 'artists'—in the work of the master craftsman, who is shaped by function and material.

---

7. W. Schütte, 'Adolf Loos und die Moderne Architektur'. *Alle Architekten sind Verbrecher;—Adolf Loos und die Folgen—Eine Spurensicherung*, Adolf Opel und Marino Valdez, eds. (Vienna, 1990) 119–120.

From an early age, he acquired an affinity for the craft, a sense of the authenticity of craftsmanship.

One cannot imagine any better educational background for the assignment given me by the world than that which was granted me. On the great workplace that was the site of my childhood, almost every kind of trade save the textile industry could be found; sculptors, stonemasons, grinders, sign painters, painters, varnishers, gilders, bricklayers, cement pourers, blacksmiths worked there. Therefore, I had already in my childhood absorbed the spirit of all the trades.

Loos was the son of a stone sculptor in Brünn, Moravia. He learned bricklaying after studying architecture for three years at the Dresden Technical College, and he later stressed how much he profited from actually having practised his trade.[8] He viewed his life work as an ongoing struggle for culture, and his contribution to the development of culture was the 'battle against the ornament'. For, 'The path of culture is a path leading from ornamentation towards the total lack it. The evolution of culture is tantamount to the removal of the ornament from the utilitarian object.'[9] Loos claimed furthermore that, 'Only there, where it has disappeared by dint of time, can it never again be replaced',[10] and concluded, 'The absence of ornamentation has elevated the remaining arts to undreamt-of heights'.[11] In the same breath Loos remarked, 'Beethoven's symphonies would never have been written by a man who had to prance about in silk, velvet, and lace'.[12]

Loos defined the New Spirit's function as follows: 'The

8. Ibid, 121–122.
9. Ibid, 123.
10. Ibid.
11. Ibid.
12. Ibid.

New Spirit—that is, design according to a new order, new
needs, accomplished by new means—is the framework
for authentic life, freed of everything superfluous, every
single thing set in its own place, with no silly antics.'[13]
According to Schütte 'Loos once wrote:

> You shrinks, why don't you go and analyze how birth
> and death occur, how the cries of pain of an injured
> son, how the death rattle of a dying mother, how the
> last thoughts of a daughter preparing to commit sui-
> cide sound in a bedroom designed by Olbrich![14] . . .
> Contemporary architecture needs consciously to ex-
> amine the essential manifestations of our time, of
> society, of technology, and of the economy. While
> pondering this question, we must clarify where the
> problems lie, in order that those lasting guidelines
> and preconditions may be singled out, that will
> bring about an architectural unity appropriate to
> our times.[15]

Loos called the architect ' . . . a bricklayer who has
learned Latin.'[16]

To our mind, this observation is also applicable to the
early Cistercians' perception of architecture. Going back
in history more than eight hundred years before Adolf
Loos, we find a similarly radical and critical reform endeavor in the formation and development of the Cistercian Order. The perniciousness, the excess, and immod-
eration, of artwork in church buildings, the overindulgent
lifestyle, the aristocracy's great influence and their presence in monastic life, as manifested by Cluny towards the
end of the eleventh century, drove one group of monks to

13. Ibid, 125.
14. Ibid.
15. Ibid, 125–126.
16. Adolf Loos, 'Sätze von Adolf Loos 1946'. *Alle Architekten sind Verbrecher*, 172.

renounce their previous monastic life completely in order to return to the fundamental principles of a humane and monastic lifestyle based upon a strict observance of the Rule of Saint Benedict. These monks withdrew to the backwoods of Burgundy to live together in isolation and renunciation true to the Rule of Saint Benedict. Concurrently with this new interpretation of the Benedictine Rule, a new era in culture and art was inaugurated, albeit unconsciously and unintentionally.

Before the monks could begin their mutual praise of God, their daily *officium*, in complete seclusion, before they could seek to come close to God through meditation, they needed to erect the *domus monachi*. In accordance with their new monastic ideals, by means of strenuous manual work, they cleared the site—the forest and brushwood—with their own hands. Timber, stone, and a nearby source of water were the fundamental prerequisites for the practical and functional realization of the monastic complex for the *opus Dei*. This meant that the architecture needed to be purely functional in character. Monastic architecture served the basic necessities of the communal life of the monks; it was functionally oriented towards spiritual meditation. The house of God and the *domus monachi* were not to be outward demonstrations of the power of an Order. Instead, within the plain structure, the individual monk was to perceive his own nearness to God and achieve oneness with Him, in the sense of the Rule of Saint Benedict. The Cistercians developed an 'ideal plan' for the architecture of cloister and church, giving outward expression to the monk's asceticism and poverty in the plain forms of its masonry and timber structure.

Architectural sculpture was rejected, ornamentation consciously and resolutely eliminated from architecture. Anselme Dimier writes in *Cistercian Art*:

Adornment is scorned, therefore architectural sculpture is denied the right to exist in cistercian art. Capital, too remain, for the most part, unadorned, limited to plain geometric, often stereotype, forms. . . . The spirit that pervades in these buildings however, seems to the last detail totally new. It is characterized by a voluntary and deliberate renunciation, an entirely modest lifestyle that had seldom before been taken to such extremes.[17]

Here we can detect certain analogies to Loos's understanding of architecture. The workrooms and outbuildings hardly differ from the rooms for the monks' *officium*. In his *Art of the Cistercians,* Georges Duby emphasizes the sociological element in the evolution of the Order:

> No distinction should be made between singing in the choir and working in the field, clearing the land, guarding the herds, felling timber, weaving, forging. Why should the psalms not have been sung on the construction site, if time ran short, and why should one not have shortened the psalmody, if necessity so dictated?[18]

The outward appearance of a cistercian granary resembles a small church, and the house of God an enormous factory building with elevated nave. Similarly, the structure of interior spaces serving utilitarian purposes visually resembles sacred interior space, and vice versa. This is the case, for instance, in the late-romanesque architecture of the abbey of Zwettl: here the lower room, with its single central support, dating from c. 1141–1145, differs, structurally, hardly at all from the chapter room of the monks (built around 1150–1159). The nearly square layout of this lower room, presumably the oldest surviving room of the earliest monastic complex of Zwettl Abbey

17. Anselme Dimier, *Die Kunst der Zisterzienser* (german edition Würzburg, 1986) 14. Originally published as *L'Art Cistercien* (Paris: Lodiaque, 1982).
18. Georges Duby, *Die Kunst der Zisterzienser* (German edition Stuttgart, 1993) 68. *L'Art Cistercien* (Paris, 1989).

(founded in 1138), suggests its multi-purpose function during the abbey's construction.[19] In the beginning, this room, located next to the latrines, served simultaneously as chapter room, chapel, and dormitory. Once the chapter room and the dormitory—located above the chapter room and the monks' dayroom—had been completed, this room was used exclusively as a workroom.

The simplicity and clarity of the masonry, the hewn stone, the timber roof construction, were meant to radiate beauty and advance the spiritual edification of the monks. The strength and intensity of the light streaming through the rose window and the clerestory between the thick walls enhances the aesthetic effect of the raw materials wood and stone, at times making them appear dematerialized. When the sun reaches its zenith, the garden in the center of the cloister garth is bathed in light. If one gazes through the rounded arches of the chapter room towards the garden, a halo of light appears, and the masonry opposite it seems immaterial, while the interior of the chapter room seems very dark. This gradual progression from the dark-earthly to the light-heavenly is symbolic of the purification of soul the monk is meant to experience during his meditations in the chapter room and the cloister. One can perceive from this example alone how well thought-out cistercian architecture is, and how this dialogue between the plain, unadorned linear architectural structure and the fall of light can bring about wondrous images.

In the cistercians' architectural concept, the source of light held a mystical, divinely transfigured quality; for Loos the light source merely served the enhancement and improvement of the pure architectural materials.[20]

19. Charlotte Ziegler, 'Zisterzienserstift Zwettel—Katalog der Handschriften des Mittelalters, Teil III, Codes 20–300', *Scriptorium Ordinis Cisterciensium Monasterii BMV in Zwettl, 3* (Zwettl, 1989/1990) XI, note 8.
20. 'Loos's aesthetics derive, as does his technical flair, from the building materials that he utilizes. Steel and glass are not the substance of his creativity,

Bernard of Clairvaux is the first personality in the Cistercian Order to campaign—in various polemical treatises and statements—against the excessive ornamentation in architecture. The social aspect in particular plays a major role in his arguments: the wealth, the splendor, the excess, the slackness of monastic life in Cluny, propagated by its abbots. In the *Apologia* to William of Saint Thierry, Bernard ardently criticizes the deplorable state of affairs: 'Tell me, o poor men—if you really are poor men—why is there gold in the holy place?'[21] Elsewhere Saint Bernard remarks, 'Oh, vanity of vanities, whose vanity is rivalled only by its insanity! The walls of the church are aglow, but the poor of the church go hungry'.[22] And in yet another passage elsewhere, one reads: 'I say it for the simpleminded, who are unable to distinguish the color from the form: the form is fundamental to being'.[23] Architecture needed to be released from the thicket of ornamentation distracting the monk from his meditation and his quest for self-fulfillment in union with God. This was equally true of the calligraphy and the illuminations in the Bible manuscripts and liturgical texts used in the monks' offices; they needed to be purged of ornamentation and grotesqueries as well.

Both Bernard of Clairvaux and Adolf Loos saw in the ornamental elaboration of architecture an unnecessary expenditure of time, labor, and money. Loos: 'Ornament is wasted labor and therefore wasted health. That's how

---

but the pier and light are. Where the pier cannot be perceived it is made visible, even if making it visible merely serves its perceptibility and not its capacity to support a load.' B. Rukschio, 'Ornament und Mythos'. *Ornament und Askese im Zeitgeist des Wien der Jahrhundertwende* (Vienna, 1985) 64.

21. Apo 12.28; *Cistercians and Cluniacs. Saint Bernard's Apologia to Abbot William*, translated by Michael Casey (Kalamazoo, 1970) 64.

22. Ibid. (Casey, 65).

23. Bernard, Apologia (cited from Georges Duby, *Der heilige Bernhard und die Kunst der Zisterzienser*, [German edition Stuttgart, 1981] 125, lines 7–8).

it's always been. Today, however, it also means wasted materials, and both mean wasted capital.[24]

In the *Apologia* to William of Saint Thierry, Bernard gives an apt analysis of the consequences of wealth and splendor:

> Let me speak plainly. Cupidity, which is a form of idolatry, is the cause of all this. It is for no useful purpose that we do it, but to attract gifts. You want to know how? Listen to the marvels of it all. It is possible to spend much money in such a way that it increases; it is an investment which grows, and pouring it out only brings in more. The very sight of such sumptuous and exquisite baubles is sufficient to inspire men to make offerings, though not to say their prayers. In this way, riches attract riches, and money produces more money. For some unknown reason, the richer a place appears, the more freely do offerings pour in. Gold-cased relics catch the gaze and open the purses. If you show someone a beautiful picture of a saint, he comes to the conclusion that the saint is as holy as the picture is brightly colored. When people rush up to kiss them, they are asked to donate. Beauty they admire, but they do no reverence to holiness. This is the reason that churches are decked out, not merely with a jewelled crown, but with a huge jewelled wheel, where circles of lamps compete in radiance with precious stones. Instead of candle-sticks we see tree-like structures, made of much metal and with exquisite workmanship, where candles and gems sparkle equally. Do you think such appurtenances are meant to stir penitents to compunction, or rather to make sight-seers agog? Oh, vanity of vanities, whose

---

24. Adolf Loos, 'Ornament und Verbrechen', 1908. *Trotzdem 1900–1930*, reprint of the original edition 1931, Adolf Opel, ed. (Vienna, 1988) 83–84.

vanity is rivalled only by its insanity! The walls of
the church are aglow, but the poor of the church go
hungry. The stones of the church are covered with
gold, while its children are left naked. The food of
the poor is taken to feed the eyes of the rich, and
amusement is provided for the curious, while the
needy have not even the necessities of life.[25]

With great derision and contempt, Bernard of Clairvaux condemns the ostentatious lifestyle, the extravagant
meals of his brothers at Cluny: 'Jokes and laughter and
chatter are all we hear. At table, while the mouth is filled
with food the ears are nourished with gossip so absorb-
ing that all moderation in eating is forgotten.'[26] Bernard
denounced the way vital practices had been exalted to
elaborate ceremonies. His biting satirical intention could
just as well have come from Karl Kraus.

In comparison, Adolph Loos, eight hundred years later,
spoke disapprovingly of utilitarian objects having elaborate design: in dining culture, for instance, such things as
silverware, tableware, glassware, and fine apparel. That
is, he denounced ennobling of these objects into objects
of art.[27] Loos drew a sharp distinction between art and
craftsmanship. The products of the Wiener Werkstätte,
as far as Loos was concerned, cannot be classified as works
of art.[28]

In his treatise 'Ornament und Mythos' [Ornament
and Myth], B. Rukschio writes of Loos: 'We have here
the insurrection of the creator of space, of a three-
dimensionally creative Loos, against the planar 'deco-
ration-mania', as he called it . . . . It is the aesthetics of

25. Apo 12.28–29 (Casey, 65–66).
26. Apo 9.20 (Casey, 55).
27. Loos, 'Kulturentartung', 1908. *Trotzdem*, 75.
28. Loos, 'Ornament und Verbrechen', 79–81.

materials and the aesthetics of function, opposed to the aestheticizing ornament'.[29] Further:

> Steel and glass are not the substance of his creativity, but the pier and light are. Where the pier cannot be perceived it is made visible, even if making it visible merely serves its perceptibility and not its capacity to support a load. It is the emotional side of a person he is addressing, not the intellectual. His houses are cave, not transparent protective foil. Because 'superfluously large windows are ornaments, equivalent to turrets and gables'.[30]

The outward anonymity of a building which denies any view of the interior design unfolding within is characteristic of Adolph Loos in the early twentieth century and of the architectural concept of the Cistercians in the early twelfth century.

The 'ideal plan' of a cistercian monastery encloses the monastic complex, separating it from the outside world like a 'fortress', enveloping the church much like the chapel of a royal court.[31] The *ecclesia* is a sacred space, not for the masses, the populace, but primarily a sacrosanct space for the offices of the monks in the *oratorium*; the nave is reserved for the lay brothers, so they may listen. For this reason, a monumental central portal, through which the general public may flock into the *ecclesia*, is not a feature of the church's western facade. Instead, two small side entrances suffice to provide access to the lay brothers and other lay persons associated with the cistercian abbey.

Primarily rectangular, but also square, forms prevail in the architectural concept of interior space in a monastery. Construction progresses from the lowest

29. Ruschkio, 'Ornament und Mythos', 63.
30. Ibid, 64–65.
31. Duby, *Kunst*, 144.

point in the terrain upward (as at Zwettl, for example). Each room is the logical prerequisite and complement of the next room; construction progresses towards the cloister, which is regarded as the center of meditation for the entire monastic complex. All rooms essential to the monks' daily life and prayer are accessible from the cloister through relatively narrow, arched portals. A staircase directly connects the church interior with the monks' dormitory, which lies above the chapter room and the monks' dayroom. For this reason the chapter room is vaulted, to support the main load of the dormitory.

The domed vault of the chapter room is also symbolic of the 'vault of heaven', from which, through the Holy Spirit, the abbot and the monks hope to receive inspiration. The column or pier that supports heaven's vault is the life-root or life-source of the monks, *radix vitae, fons vitae*. Through these symbolic channels the monks receive the influence of God's power over their own actions. By regarding the back view of the chapter room, that—combined with the dormitory and rectangular sanctuary of the church—originally constituted the eastern end of the cistercian abbey, i.e. the *domus monachi*, the viewer can perceive—as in the example of Zwettl—the energy and aesthetic effect of the sturdy masonry. The observer is left completely unaware of the two-story structure behind the smooth, solid masonry (chapter room and dormitory). The structure of the interior space is given an anonymous external design (see above). The sacred areas and the working quarters, with their spiritual-symbolic content on the one hand, and the socio-economic on the other, are indiscriminately concealed behind the same wall. By means of this divergence of appearance between exterior and interior in the architecture of a cistercian monastery, expression is given to the essence and meaning of the *vita monachorum* within the monastery.

An analogous concept of inner and outer appearance of residential buildings can be discerned eight hundred years later from a private home designed by Adolf Loos, although under completely different social preconditions and without symbolic religious significance.

C. Schorske, in his essay 'Abschied von der Öffentlichkeit—Kulturkritik und Modernismus in der Wiener Architektur' [Taking Leave of the Public—Cultural Criticism and Modernism in Viennese Architecture], states:

> The exteriors of Loos' dwellings have no face, they convey no message, they symbolize nothing, they are inconspicuous. 'The house', wrote Loos, 'should be outwardly discreet, whereas the interior should reveal its whole wealth.' This leads to the following conclusion, regarding the differentiation between the public and the private: that which is expressive does not belong on the outside, in the public sphere, but rather on the inside, in the private. The exterior proclaims nothing, receives nothing from the public environment, it does not transmit anything to the interior, it merely divides the public and the private. It is a wall, a mask, that portrays nothing, distorts nothing, that doesn't participate, but separates'.[32]
> . . . A house designed by Loos was a rational container.[33]

Loos made several revolutionary contributions to the field of commercial and residential architecture for the middle class and for the socially needy in the early twentieth century. Because of his overall rejection of ornamentation and his accentuation of the linear form in architectural structure, he belonged to the vanguard of twentieth century architecture not only in Austria, but beyond its borders as well. Loos himself was greatly influenced by the classical architecture of Antiquity, especially the social

32. C. E. Schorske, 'Abschied von der . . . Öffentlichkeit—Kulturkritik und Modernismus in der Wiener Architektur'. *Ornament und Askese im Zeitgeist des Wien der Jahrhundertwende* (Vienna, 1985) 56.
33. Ibid.

Charlotte Ziegler

architectural style of the Romans, as he states in his essay 'Meine Bauschule' [My Architectural School] (1907): 'From the Romans we have inherited our social awareness and the discipline of the soul'.[34]

Let us now return to the starting point of our reflections, the philosopher and 'monk' Ludwig Wittgenstein. In our opinion, legitimate parallels may be drawn between the religious life led by a christian monk and Wittgenstein's lifestyle, from which his philosophy and his aesthetic appreciation of architecture arose. In 1949, two years prior to his death, Wittgenstein remarked: 'Culture is a monastic rule, or at least presupposes a monastic rule'.[35]

The monk retreats from the circumstances of the world, as they are, into seclusion, in order to cast off the Old Man and don the garment of the New Man. The monk of christian western culture reveals to us, however, how God's world, into which one is born, is actually a frontier, a threshold to heaven. To cross over, one must withdraw from the worldly environment, so that one may, by means of *contemplatio* in solitude, through prayer, through silence, draw nearer to heaven, to God. Let us examine, for example, the monastic lifestyle of the Cistercians of the early twelfth century, who reformed the benedictine way of life by returning to the original fundamental values of the Rule of Saint Benedict.

The basic principles of their reform included: (1) living in harmony with nature, in voluntary seclusion, seeing the affairs of the world for what they were. The retreat to the rough wilds of the country was simultaneously a retreat to the purity of nature, a nature the cistercian monks were forced to clear with their own hands before being able to cultivate it to support their modest lifestyle. A forest, a quarry, and a stream sufficed, and with this 'roof

34. Loos, 'Ornament und Verbrechen', 65.
35. Nedo, Ranchetti, *Wittgenstein—Sein Leben*, 152.

over their heads', the Cistercians proceeded to search for the path that would lead them from their bounded temporal world to God's heavenly sphere. This leads us to the second essential principle. (2) the pure forms of the world that surrounded them were a limited whole. The true significance of this world lies beyond it. (3) The monks' rule of silence is more than just an ascetic element of their rule; it is a form of concentration in preparation for *contemplatio* and finding union with God. Silence also signifies the simultaneous renunciation of worldly life and orientation towards a supernal sphere which cannot be verbalized, except in silent or communal prayer and in chant.

The Cistercian Bernard of Clairvaux came from a very wealthy background. When he entered the Cistercian Order at Cîteaux in 1112, he renounced everything he owned. He was a brilliant rhetorician, a linguistic genius in his day, an eminent representative of mysticism; and he launched the second great liturgical reform of the daily cistercian *officium* in 1134, completing it in 1147; he aided the needy.

Asceticism, solitude, manual work, charitable endeavors also became Wittgenstein's lifelong fundamental 'monastic' rule. Wittgenstein, too, came from a wealthy background. He supported such penniless artists, such as Oskar Kokoschka, Georg Trakl, and Adolf Loos, and finally gave all his personal property to his sisters. He lived like a 'hermit', occasionally like a 'monk'. At times this advocate of pure logic would tend toward mysticism. Wittgenstein, a linguistic and mathematical genius, once, briefly, studied sculpture and architecture. He also explored religion intensively. Wittgenstein was familiar with the works of Saint Augustine. He analysed the religious content in the works of Leo Tolstoy and Fyodor Dostoyevsky. He read Tolstoy's *Kurze Darlegung des Evangeliums* [A Short Explanation of the Gospel] repeatedly, and carried a copy of it into battle with him in the First World War, earning himself the nickname 'The One with the Gospel'.[36] Wittgenstein was further influenced by Tolstoy in that, 'He adopted Tolstoy's viewpoint, that only work that was 'beneficial to people'—especially manual work—possessed true value and dignity'.[37] Wittgenstein's paramount architectural principal was, 'The significance is the use'.[38] 'But priority is given to purity of form, which manifests the clarity of function'.[39] And, 'Architecture immortalizes and glorifies something. Therefore, there can be no architecture where there is nothing to glorify.'[40] According to R. F. Kaspar, this last sentence exemplifies the hidden aesthetics of the later Wittgenstein.[41] He vehemently advised his students against pursuing an academic career in philosophy.[42] Wittgenstein, as we have already mentioned, held skilled manual work in high esteem, because craftsmanship, which requires working with the pure material, intends and determines the original, true function and appearance of an object.

Simplex sigillum veri [Simplicity is the sign of truth]. Wittgenstein included this interpretation of William of Ockham in his main work, 'Tractatus logico philosophicus'.[43] Ludwig Wittgenstein employed this maxim on principle in the design and construction of a house for his sister, Margaretha Stonborough, in the Kundmanngasse in Vienna. Wittgenstein even supervised the construction down to the smallest detail (November 1925 and 1926),

36. McGuiness, *Wittgensteins frühe Jahre*, 344.
37. Janik, Toulmin, *Wittgensteins Wien*, 276.
38. Ibid, 279.
39. Kaspar, *Wittgensteins Ästetik*, 84.
40. Ibid, 93.
41. Ibid, 76.
42. Janik, Toulmin, *Wittgensteins Wien*, 277.
43. Paul Wijdeveld, *Ludwig Wittgenstein. Architekt*, (German edition Wiese Verlag, 1994) 183, 186.

after having taken over and completed the planning begun by the architect Paul Engelmann.[44]

The 'functional aesthetics' and the 'language' of the undecorated, fine materials of the interior design of the house are a consequence of Wittgenstein's philosophic-ascetic lifestyle. 'The ascetic Wittgenstein never understood the worldly Loos', says B. Rukschio.[45] Wittgenstein's concept of architecture, stylistically in the same category as Loos, cannot be interpreted solely on the basis of his philosophical perspective. Both his artistic and his philosophical positions were decisively influenced by his monastic-ascetic lifestyle. Compared to the lifestyle of the first cistercian monks which we have looked at above, we can conclude that this form of 'monkish' lifestyle played a major role, consciously and unconsciously, in Wittgenstein's view of life. To this day, this essential comparison of perspectives has been more or less neglected by the scholars of Wittgenstein. Some research has been done on the question of Wittgenstein's 'religiousness', but only very recently, in the work of Norman Malcom edited by Peter Winch.[46]

Social life in *fin de scièle* Vienna was an impediment to his philosophical way of thinking. Wittgenstein claimed that he was able to develop his philosophy of logic only in seclusion. In Cambridge, where he studied, he indulged in long evening discussions with his teacher Bertrand Russell, after which Wittgenstein would withdraw into the solitude of the surrounding countryside, convinced

44. Nedo, Ranchetti, *Wittgenstein Đ Sein Leben*, 206–207, 220–221, 355; Nedo, *Wittgenstein—Wiener Ausgabe*, 27; Janik, Toulmi, *Wittgensteins Wien*, 279.
45. Rukschio, 'Ornament und Mythos', 64.
46. Norman Malcom, '*Wittgenstein—A Religious Point of View*', edited with a response by Peter Winch (Ithaca, New York, 1995). The author was unaware of this work until after the presentation of this paper at Kalamazoo on May 4, 1995, but was able to purchase a copy at the congress book fair the next day.

he could think philosophically only in complete solitude. In 1913/1914 Wittgenstein also retreated to the isolation of the norwegian fjord region of Sognefjord, to Skjolden. Technically and mathematically talented since youth, he built himself a simple house of wood in the rough, wild terrain: 'I am now building a small house in the solitude', he wrote to Bertrand Russell in April-June 1914.[47] In 1931 Wittgenstein wrote: '. . . it seems to me as if I had borne new movements of thought within myself back then'.[48]

Twice Wittgenstein worked in a monastery—once as an assistant gardener at Klosterneuburg Abbey (August 1920), and once as a gardener for the 'Barmherzige Brüder' (Brothers of Mercy) in Hütteldorf (May 1926)— in an attempt to find a way out of his depression by doing regular manual labor. At one time Wittgenstein even seriously contemplated becoming a monk himself.[49]

Solitude, asceticism, modesty, faith, the fear of God are fundamental principles and basic requirements that characterize the life of a monk, as has been stressed above. For Wittgenstein, silence was an essential condition for clarifying the concept of truth in philosophical logic. The word 'clarify'[50] becomes a fundamental term in Wittgenstein's philosophy, in the sense of 'gaining clarity about something' or 'making something clear', cleansing it of all unnecessary ballast, in order to explain better the original truth-oriented function of speech, object, subject, and the world as a basic existential principle. Wittgenstein wrote:

> The meaning of the world must lie beyond it. In the world, all is as it occurs; it has no value. . . . If a

47. Nedo, Ranchetti, *Wittgenstein—Sein Leben*, 353; Wijdeveld, *Wittgenstein. Architekt*, 30, including an illustration of the wood house.
48. Nedo, *Wittgenstein—Wiener Ausgabe*, 19.
49. Ibid, 23, 27.
50. Cf. Fleck, *Was gezeigt werden kann*, 12–13.

value exists that is of value, then it must lie beyond all occurrence and so-being. For all occurrence and so-being is coincidental. That which does not occur coincidentally cannot be of the world, otherwise it would again be coincidental. It must lie beyond the world. That is why there can be no sentences in ethics. Sentences cannot express higher things.

. . . Moral philosophy is transcendental. Ethics and aesthetics are one and the same.[51] The subject is not of the world, but rather a boundary of the world.[52] The inexpressible, however, does exist. This shows itself; it is the mystical. The contemplation of the world *sub specie aeterni* is contemplation of a limited whole. The sense of the world as a limited whole is the mystical.[53]

The inexpressible, which according to Wittgenstein equals the mystical, is derived from the greek word for 'keeping silent'. As Wittgenstein said: 'Things we cannot speak of, we must remain silent about'.[54]

Bernard of Clairvaux, Adolf Loos, and Ludwig Wittgenstein all had one thing in common: the battle against the ornamental, especially in architecture. Neither Loos nor Wittgenstein, however, was aware of the architectural ideals against ornamentation of the early Cistercians around the year 1100, that found their emphatic verbal expression around 1125 in Bernard of Clairvaux. To our mind, the early Cistercians from Cîteaux and Clairvaux were important precursors of cultural criticism and of

51. Wittgenstein, 'Tractatus', 82–83, nos. 6.41–6.421; Mann, *Wovon man schweigen muß*, 117–118.
52. Wittgenstein, 'Tractatus', 57–58, no. 5.632; Mann, *Wovon man schweigen muß*, 106.
53. Wittgenstein, 'Tractatus', 85, no. 6.522, 84, no. 6.45; Mann, *Wovon man schweigen muß*, 120, 121; Kaspar, *Wittgensteins Ästhetik*, 18, 51.
54. Wittgenstein, 'Tractatus', 7; McGuiness, *Wittgensteins frühe Jahre*, 479; Mann, *Wovon man schweigen muß*, 126.

new conceptions in architecture, such as those of Loos and Wittgenstein.

Incidentally, in both eras parallel reforms and innovations can also be observed in the field of music. These occurred, however, on two separate levels: in vocal music, in the cistercian liturgy in the first half of the twelfth century, and in instrumental music, in the compositions of Arnold Schönberg in the early twentieth century.

Currently, in the contemporary architectural scene in the Viennese area, we can observe among architects and prominent artists a resurgence of the campaign against a plethora of ornamentation in architecture.

Translated by Cornelia Oefelein

Xavier Frisque ocso

Abbaye N.-D. d'Orval

L'Ange et le Lys : la Sagesse des Sens

'Pensée du Fils plus vraiment homme qu'aucun homme
Puisqu'il est vraiment Dieu fibre à fibre enduré
Amour de Dieu pour l'homme accompli par un homme
Gouffre d'être, insondable et pourtant incarné!
La gloire de Jacob est de sentir ce gouffre
Cet orage d'amour contre lui prendre corps:
Dieu de tout son désir mesure en résistant!
Par la blessure de béante ressemblance
L'âme écoute Dieu devenir un coeur battant.'[1]

TU ES BEAU, le plus beau des enfants des hommes, et la grâce est répandue sur tes lèvres, aussi tu es béni du Seigneur à jamais' (Ps 44:3). L'éclat de la beauté serait-il du même ordre que la révélation de l'amour? La relation personnelle au Dieu vivant passerait-elle par l'expérience du beau? Le rapprochement des expériences pourrait induire une propédeutique esthétique et une poétique du discours mystique. Toutefois réduire à un dénominateur commun entre ces deux voies conduirait dans une impasse, soit en restreignant l'esthétique à une iconographie explicitement chrétienne produite par un artiste confessant, soit en cherchant à départager d'une mystique agnostique ambiante, un art soi-disant sacré. La réponse ne viendra pas uniquement à la suite d'une critique sur l'authenticité des deux expériences, mais de la traversée de deux situations concrètes: le témoignage auroral de Guillaume de

---

1. P. Emmanuel, *Jacob* (Paris: Seuil, 1970) 143.

Delacroix, Eugène (1798–1863)
Jacob Wrestling With the Angel
St. Sulpice, Paris, France.
Detail.

Saint-Thierry devant l'éclosion du lys et celui d'Eugène
Delacroix (1798–1863), devant Jacob blessé et béni. Le
mystère d'alliance dans une vie dialogale avec Dieu, Père,
Fils et Esprit indiquera que le sens du beau n'est jamais
immédiat, ni exclusivement transcendant. L'esthétique
comme la mystique édifient une sensation charnelle qui
s'expose à la beauté de l'oeuvre sainte. La clarification
commencera par une délimitation des domaines puis
s'exercera dans l'imbrications des expériences avant de
retrouver le sens du beau en face de la croix et du saint.
Comment le mystique rend-il compte du beau et jusqu'où
l'artiste vit-il la kénose de l'incarnation? Les expériences
se rapprochent-elles ou plutôt s'interpénètrent-elles,
voire s'équilibrent-elles réciproquement?

POROSITÉ DES LANGAGES ET DES ATTITUDES

Le statut de l'oeuvre autant que celui du discours mystique sont redevables de leur époque. La cathédrale, chef-
d'oeuvre de foi et expression artistique totale, est englou-
tie. Seul subsiste un frémissement dans un monde saturé
d'images plates. L'artiste s'effaçait au Moyen Age, s'idéal-
isait à la Renaissance ou se projetait au romantisme. Aujourd'hui, il se justifie abondamment. On connaît les
scrupules d'Augustin devant les charmes de la beauté
musicale ou la diatribe de Bernard contre les grotesques
sculptés qui ornaient les cloîtres.[2] La vraie beauté serait-
elle seulement ailleurs, toute spirituelle? Le vrai mystique
serait-il condamné à abandonner toute médiation sensible?

---

2. 'Lorsque le chant m'enchante plus que les paroles, je confesse avoir
commis un péché qui mérite répréhension, et j'aimerais mieux ne pas
entendre chanter.' Augustin, *Confessions* 10. 33. 50, trad. E. Trehorel et
G. Buissou, coll. Bibliothèque augustinienne, n°14 (Bruges: Desclée de
Brouwer, 1962) 229. 'Que viennent faire dans les cloîtres, sous les yeux
des frères lisant, cette monstruosité risible, ces semblants de belles formes
difformes et cette difformité si bien formée?' Bernard, *Apologie à Guillaume*,
12.19, dans OEuvres complètes, trad. M. Charpentier (Paris: Vivès, 1866)
t. 2: 306.

Dialogue de l'esthète et de l'ascète

La confrontation des extrêmes, l'esthète et l'ascète, met en garde contre un rapprochement simpliste des expériences. Les chemins du beau en christianisme côtoient l'ordonnance et les proportions, le naturalisme ou l'abstraction, l'analogie ou l'épiphanie, l'émotion, l'harmonie ou le sublime. Toute religion de l'art appelle à juste titre un iconoclasme et tout angélisme fondra à l'épreuve de la patience. Aucune expérience n'est une voie assurée, car autant l'apparence captive l'esthète que l'orgueil détourne le spirituel. Le pathos esthétisant et l'excessif hagiographique s'éloignent de l'amour chrétien qui vit l'admiration dans l'engagement et la contemplation dans la fidélité. L'expérience artistique autant que mystique se pervertissent facilement en cette mise en scène qui fait soi-même son salut par la consommation de sacré et d'abandon.

Deux extrêmes se rejoignent: la quête spirituelle d'une beauté hypostasiée et le culte du génie artistique.[3] L'assignation transcendantale du beau au vrai laisse vacante la particularité de l'oeuvre qui requiert tant le spectateur que le créateur. L'expérience artistique semble prolonger la création divine, à partir de l'imitation de la nature jusqu'à une créativité humaine libre de tout: musique concrète, installations éphémères, art conceptuel. L'artiste bénéficierait-il de plus de liberté pour faire venir l'invisible à la représentation? Revendiquer ce prophétisme est une attitude séparatrice par elle-même qui confine à l'élitisme ou à la complaisance. N'importe qui a sa place dans le monde de l'expérience, le maudit comme l'ange, le pécheur comme le saint. La sagesse des sens spirituels témoigne de l'incarnation du Christ en notre

---

3. 'Beauté qui ne réside pas dans un être différent d'elle-même, mais qui existe absolument et éternellement par elle-même et en elle-même ; dans laquelle participent toutes les autres beauté.' Platon, *Le banquet* 221 c, trad. L. Robin, dans Oeuvres complètes (Paris: Les belles lettres, 1929) t. 4:70.

monde. Il n'y aurait pas d'extase sans le support d'un corps et pas d'émerveillement concret sans une sortie de soi.

Loin de toute effusion passive, la démarche artistique passe par un enfantement de l'oeuvre et la vulnérabilité de la donation. La joie profonde d'une production tient du secret et d'une tâche qui s'impose dans l'impératif d'un appel. Cette beauté-là de l'oeuvre éclate et rayonne, car elle réconcilie l'homme avec la Vie, 'tant le désir du Beau qui entraîne à cette ascension ne cesse jamais de s'étendre à mesure qu'on avance dans la course vers le Beau'.[4] Serait-ce autre chose la Bonne Nouvelle?

GOÛTEZ ET VOYEZ

Une connaissance de Dieu qui laisserait le coeur et les sens en l'état, une composition artistique qui serait purement cérébrale, seraient chacune en contradiction avec la vérité humaine. Aussi la référence à la jouissance est-elle continue, plus affirmée encore chez les mystiques que chez les artistes. Une rencontre intense dans le monde déclenche pour eux une recherche infinie. Cette jouissance se vit autant avec le goût du beau qu'avec celle de l'amour divin, autant dans l'épiphanie du saint que dans une création toujours nouvelle. L'apparence en retour est dépassée dans un mouvement qui va vers le fond par une concentration de l'être et touche à l'expérience nocturne de l'abîme. A chaque fois, l'itinéraire esthétique et mystique ne s'arrête pas à l'événement de l'expérience, mais se poursuit dans une communication partagée. La production n'est pas l'apanage artistique et la réceptivité réservée à la seule disposition mystique. Il y a un charisme du style chez Ruysbroeck, Jean de la Croix, ou François de Sales. Un écrit spirituel se reflétera dans une certaine

---

4. Grégoire de Nysse, *La Vie de Moïse*, 238, trad. J. Danielou, coll. Sources chrétiennes n°1 ter (Paris: Cerf, 1968) 271.

justesse d'expression qui reflue littérairement. Il y a
un sens spirituel chez Fra Angelico, Rouault ou Olivier
Messiaen.

L'expérience mystique parle du désir et configure le
corps. L'expérience esthétique parle de l'inspiration et
trace une quête. L'éventail des expressions rappelle de
part et d'autre la mise en présence, l'excès et le don. Si
le mystique éprouve la blessure de l'absence, l'artiste vit
l'errance dans la production jamais achevée. Les deux
vivent la vigilance d'une relation jamais sans "toi" et
ouvre un dialogue dans la matière des mots, des sons, des
couleurs. Les deux expériences parlent de reconnaissance
offerte et jamais de plaisir intéressé.

Comment dire l'expérience, quelles images utiliser,
quel sens donner aux étapes mystiques? La tension entre
l'éloignement de la transcendance et la proximité d'une
présence vécue caractérise chaque langage. Trouver et
vérifier un style spirituel passe par l'expression et la confession. La saisie correspond au moment où l'expérience
s'impose comme conscience de la réalité de Dieu. Cette
présence effective d'une grâce divine reçoit une évidence
sensible, une mise-en-perception.[5] A ce stade le langage
de l'expérience devient productif. Le texte mystique
n'est pas simple compte-rendu, mais ouvre à une restruc-
turation de la conscience croyante. Sans cesse les fruits
de l'action divine sont discernés dans l'âme et le corps.
L'expérience est affermie par la nouvelle cohérence des
images symboliques. L'expression verbale prolonge les
qualités vécues dans la relation à Dieu et débouche sur le
témoignage. Dire l'expérience possède un retentissement
par sa force créatrice.

---

5. La mise en perception rencontre les formes artistiques. 'Les contemplatifs
écoutent les orgues mystiques et perçoivent le concert des harpes (Apoc
14:2–3). Dans un repos plein de délices, toujours accompagnés de cithare
et de cymbale, ils s'attardent profondément en cette mélodie et jamais ne
s'écartent d'un service doux comme miel.' Richard Rolle, Le chant d'amour,
44, 136, trad. moniales de Wisques, coll. Sources chrétiennes n°169 (Paris:
Cerf, 1971) t. 2: 115.

La rencontre de l'oeuvre d'art tient elle aussi d'une saisie, d'une effectuation et d'un témoignage. Le beau n'est pas un jeu purement formel, mais il porte une relation symbolique, une modalité nouvelle dans l'habitation commune qui provoque une liberté à naître et à inventer un monde. Cette joie créatrice échappe à toute dénomination et reste en dernière analyse indicible. L'esthétique suscite les sensations qui forgent à leur tour les sens spirituels pour la qualité délectable d'une présence divine, goûtée dans l'affectivité du coeur humain. En chacun, l'oeuvre d'art surgit de l'esprit aveugle vers la lumière. L'intensité symbolique de l'existence n'implique-t-elle pas cette médiation esthétique?

L'ouverture de la sensibilité dans l'esthétique ou la mystique côtoie soit la libération, soit l'aliénation. La rencontre peut devenir séductrice, dotée d'un pouvoir de fascination qui aveugle le jugement comme lorsque David s'éprend de Bethsabée (1 Ch 11:2). La beauté rayonne aussi d'une présence habitée: 'Ainsi, lorsque l'esprit de Dieu assaillait Saül, David prenait la cithare et il en jouait. Alors Saül se calmait, se sentait mieux et l'esprit mauvais se retirait de lui' (1 Sam 16:23). Contempler toutes les manifestations de la vie, humbles ou sublimes, demande aussi un regard épris d'amour pour la façon dont le mystère se tient, grâce à elles, en proximité sensible. Ni l'expérience esthétique ne se limitera au musée, ni l'expérience mystique au sanctuaire! Comment s'initier à la perception de la beauté dans le provisoire? Que voit le regard et qu'écoute l'oreille qui les tiennent en proximité de joie? La beauté désigne un lieu de vocation où l'homme est saisi et ravi.[6] Cette expérience fréquente l'oeuvre en sa

---

6. 'Bien tard, je t'ai aimée, ô beauté si ancienne et si neuve, bien tard, je t'ai aimée! Mais quoi, tu étais au dedans de moi, et j'étais, moi, au dehors de moi même, et c'est au dehors que je te cherchais. Je me ruais dans ma laideur, sur la grâce de tes créatures. Tu étais avec moi, je n'étais pas avec toi, retenu loin de toi par des choses qui ne seraient point si elles n'étaient en toi. Tu m'as appelé, et ton cri a forcé ma surdité. Tu as brillé et ton éclat a chassé

découverte toujours nouvelle, comme la joie de retrouver un ami. c

IMBRICATION DES EXPÉRIENCES

Une beauté produite par l'homme ne risque-t-elle pas de fournir l'alibi du pharisien (Lc 18:11), dont il dispose? Tendre à l'absolu dans l'élément sensible du fini ne détourne-t-il pas la liberté de l'Esprit? Quelle beauté peut-on espérer voir, écouter ou toucher: Dieu chantable, Dieu représentable?

CONVERTIR À L'AMOUR PAR LA BEAUTÉ

L'interprétation de l'expérience ne juge pas à partir de catégories extrinsèques mais suppose une connivence et une familiarité. L'attitude esthétique envers le lys de Guillaume de Saint-Thierry, relève bien d'une expérience intégrale et authentique de la beauté, d'un exercice d'admiration avec tous ses sens qui contraste avec une approche spéculative.[7] L'appel à prêter attention s'attarde à l'exercice du regard, de l'odorat et du toucher qui forment l'expression intuitive de son expérience mystique. Le spirituel ne reste pas sur la rive de la profondeur charnelle mais il la traverse après une lutte sans prise. L'expérience des sens se relie au monde et contredit une extase mystique qui voudrait s'en détacher. En même temps, la stérilité de la plus belle des fleurs éloigne toute attitude qui considérerait 'la manifestation de la grâce

---

ma cécité. Tu as exhalé ton parfum et je l'ai respiré. Et voici que pour toi je soupire. Je t'ai écouté et j'ai faim de toi, soif de toi. Tu m'as touché et j'ai brûlé d'ardeur, pour la Paix que tu me donnes.' Augustin, *Confessions*, 10. 27. 38: (vide supra, n. 2) t. 14: 209.

7. 'Si le beau est aimé, tu es la beauté de tout ce qui est beau. Si c'est le bien, tu es le bien de tout bien. Si c'est l'utile, tout homme, même celui qui hait, se sert de toi.' Guillaume de Saint-Thierry, *Commentaire sur le Cantique des cantiques* 45, trad. M.-M. Davy (Paris: Vrin, 1958) 73.

illuminante' comme la réponse de Dieu à l'effort de l'homme. La perception sera transfigurée par la lumière pour être reconnue de 'l'intelligence et de la sagesse'. Toutes les expressions sensibles restent ordonnées à un connaître dans la 'grâce créatrice': 'Grâces soient à Dieu qui, dans le Christ, nous emmène dans son triomphe et qui, par nous, répand en tous lieux le parfum de sa connaissance' (2 Co 2: 14).

L'abbé cistercien critique une expérience esthétique qui se refermerait sur elle-même. Il n'y aura pas de blancheur sans la foi, de parfum sans le Christ, ni d'adoucissement sans la patience. L'expérience dépasse l'asservissement des sortilèges ténébreux du moi pour s'offrir à la clarté du Verbe créateur. Guillaume doute que le beau sauve le monde.[8] Mais il ne doute pas que par delà les ambiguïtés de l'*aisthésis*, l'homme puisse résoudre les tensions de l'extérieur et de l'intérieur. La 'grâce illuminante' loin de reléguer la sensibilité esthétique en révèle toute la fécondité pour 'l'intelligence', la 'volonté' et la 'sagesse' chrétiennes. La vie spirituelle ne se déploie pas dans un univers à part, mais dans cet univers habité dont l'attention spirituelle perçoit le 'secret'. Guillaume n'exhorte pas à renoncer aux sens, mais à les épanouir dans un 'sourire' en fleur qui serve l'ordinaire humain.

Prisonnier de la nuit, l'homme passe souvent à côté du lys, affairé, sans même soupçonner l'existence de ce qui, près de lui, porte l'éclosion de la présence divine. Par chacun de ses sens, il s'ouvre au définitif qui se redresse dans la beauté cachée et intime d'une corolle. L'intensité de

---

8. La lettre aux artistes utilise la formule 'La beauté sauvera le monde', reprise à Dostoïevski dans L'Idiot, non sans quelque relent apologétique. L'art tout comme la philosophie est une donnée à part entière de l'homme et aurait à souffrir tout autant qu'elle de tentatives d'annexion totalisante. 'On a dit avec une intuition profonde que «la beauté sauvera le monde». La beauté est la clé du mystère et elle renvoie à la transcendance. Elle est une invitation à savourer la vie et à rêver de l'avenir.' *Lettre de Jean Paul II aux artistes,* n°16 (Paris: Téqui, 1999) p. 40.

cet émerveillement sensible met à nu l'essentiel, là même
où l'apparence semble médiatiser le plus précairement
ce qui la dépasse infiniment. L'expérience esthétique en
christianisme ne vise pas une quelconque hiérophanie naturelle qui absolutiserait la manifestation sensible, mais
s'attache à cette connivence profonde entre le sensible
et le spirituel. Ce que Jésus montre à celui qu'il appelle
est une réalité en 'fragrance'. Désormais chaque fleur
deviendra en Christ le signe de la gratuité de l'amour
divin: 'Observez les lis des champs, comme ils poussent:
ils ne peinent ni ne filent' (Mt. 6:28). Ne convient-il pas
de se laisser interpeller par l'esthétique en s'initiant à un
regard attentif et de plaider la cause d'une spiritualité qui
fasse croître en l'homme son don de sentir?

La beauté transcendantale qui irradie ne peut être
attribuée à Dieu sans équivoque, sorte d'objectivité qui
contraindrait à déduire la foi d'une admiration. Le coeur
s'ouvre plutôt à l'altérité de l'oeuvre concrète. Cet
abandon confiant demeure sans cesse en excès par rapport
à sa propre sensibilité pour se dresser vers l'horizon
du 'plein midi'. Guillaume recueille cette proximité de
l'invisible qui perce déjà au-dehors. Si la mystique trouve
un sol et des racines dans l'expérience esthétique, elle
n'en est pas moins suscitée par un appel qui vient de plus
loin que le sensible. Le corps expressif conduit au-delà
de toute *aisthésis* en répondant à une parole de Dieu. Le
sceau du Créateur permet de vivre les polarités esprit et
chair pour donner voix divine à toutes réalités humaines.

Blessé et béni

Eugène Delacroix n'hésite pas à peindre cet invisible,
en proximité charnelle: 'Je ne te lâcherai pas que tu
ne m'aies béni'.[9] Dans la longue nuit contre l'inconnu,

9. 'Quelqu'un lutta avec lui jusqu'au lever de l'aurore. Il dit: «Lâche-moi,
car l'aurore est levée», mais Jacob répondit: «Je ne te lâcherai pas, que tu

Jacob combat pour passer sur l'autre rive de la Terre promise. De quelle expérience spirituelle la composition de sa fresque retentit-elle? Le combattant solitaire est vu de dos, dans un corps à corps aveugle et obscur, sans regards échangés. L'ampleur de la nature attire par deux trouées, l'une vers la montagne et le ciel au-dessus de l'ange et l'autre vers l'écoulement laiteux des troupeaux qui se hâtent. A l'angle, s'entasse une nature morte. Carquois mortifère et gourde de la soif sont délaissés. C'est un combat sans brutalité, sans coups où le geste du peintre s'échappe comme éclate l'oxymoron mystique. La passivité angélique vers laquelle Jacob se cambre, change le monde autour de lui. Le récit biblique apprend que si la rencontre de la nuit a transformé Jacob, Esaü aussi, d'une façon mystérieuse, d'ennemi acharné qu'il était, se montre le plus tendre des frères (Gn 33:4).

Trois motifs clairs et colorés surgissent donc dans cette immense paysage: le combat, la fuite et les tenues abandonnées. Ils se font mutuellement échos. La lance acérée pointe le bras de l'ange qui agrippe la jambe de Jacob. Elle se dédouble avec la baguette du berger dont le dos nu reproduit exactement la posture arc-boutée de Jacob. Le rouge vif relie les vêtements à terre et ceux du cavalier. La circularité d'un triangle sur pointe est établie comme dans l'icône de la Trinité de Roublev. Le combat touche à sa fin, l'angoisse guerrière (Gn 32:8) est abandonnée et la vie s'écoule. Dans l'échange se clôt la lutte. Le plus fort demande grâce et le blessé impose les conditions de la fin du combat. Ne fallait-il pas que Jacob fût blessé pour qu'Israël fût béni? Jacob et l'Ange se livrent leur secret, ils scellent une alliance, se donnent un nom et une bénédiction.

---

ne m'aies béni.» Il lui demanda: «Quel est ton nom?» «Jacob», répondit-il. Il reprit: «On ne t'appellera plus Jacob, mais Israël, car tu as été fort contre Dieu, et contre les hommes tu l'emporteras.» Jacob donna à cet endroit le nom de Penuel, «car, dit-il, j'ai vu Dieu face à face et j'ai eu la vie sauve.» Au lever du soleil, il avait passé Penuel et il boitait de la hanche' (Gn 32:27–32).

La bénédiction féconde vient d'ailleurs. Les corps enchevêtrés et imbriqués se prolongent par deux mains jointes, tendues vers le ciel. La nature elle-même avec ses arbres semblent épouser le mystérieux combat. L'ange éveillé recule et contient l'ardeur d'un Jacob incliné. Là où Jacob résiste, le messager divin se retire. Trois pieds touchent le sol dans lequel s'enracinent trois troncs noueux, aux branches basses, brunes et recroquevillées. L'eau du Yabboq coule petitement en bas à gauche. Sa force vive est du côté de l'ange pour traverser Jacob et remonter par les troncs épais vers une ramure ample et luxuriante qui s'épanouit dans toute la plénitude de la voûte arrondie en redescendant jusqu'au troupeau. Ce symbolisme rejoint le vitrail de Chartres dans lequel le bois de la croix est vert comme l'arbre de vie.

Delacroix n'est pas seulement l'homme de l'émotion. Il est aussi celui de la mise en forme. L'oeuvre d'art ne naît que si son auteur parvient à donner forme à l'informe, à mettre de l'ordre où ne régnait que le chaos. Alors l'extériorité ne fait plus obstacle à la révélation de l'intériorité, le visible devient manifestation de l'invisible. Cet esthétique implique le recours à une inspiration qui n'est pas celle de la nature en sa pure spontanéité. Quand l'oeuvre recrée le langage mystique, le christianisme doit apprendre un mode nouveau d'expression, se familiariser avec lui, et le fréquenter. Il est bon pour Jacob de peiner, de se cabrer et de se dépenser jusqu'à l'épuisement des énergies trop humaines. Jacob fait l'expérience de Dieu par sa propre chair. Il adhère au messager, il s'enfonce en lui, il en devient comme l'empreinte.

L'expérience esthétique intimement transformée par l'action qu'opère en elle l'oeuvre, s'initie aux manières divines tout en demeurant active et personnelle. Elle tient de ce corps à corps où la sève, les muscles, la tunique de bête sont requis dans une lutte qui inaugure le dialogue. 'Comment un homme peut-il, naître, une fois qu'il est vieux?' (Jn 3:4). Jacob est transformé en profondeur, il change de nom. Son combat est une passion, une agonie jusqu'à la violence extrême dans la passivité de l'Ange. Lorsque le Yabboq sera franchi, chacun laissera sur la rive le vieil homme avec ses armes. Alors la démarche claudiquera et perdra de son aplomb charnel pour s'offrir aux desseins de Dieu. L'assurance et la fidélité dépendront du soutien de sa bénédiction. L'oeuvre dans son principe est cette lutte en acte:

'Toute vie spirituelle en nous est sacramentelle. Parce que nous sommes corps et âme. Des réalités matérielles, images, sons, parfums entrent en nous et y deviennent idées et amour. Cette alchimie de la nature qui se spiritualise en nous est notre mode connaturel d'activité spirituelle.'[10]

VERS UNE BEAUTÉ RESSUSCITÉE

Le spirituel se nourrit d'esthétique et l'artiste trace une rencontre mystique. Ils se soutiennent mutuellement. La connaissance de soi en Dieu passe par une rencontre dans la désappropriation face à toute hiérophanie panthéiste ou idolâtrique. L'oeuvre d'art indique le sens de la médiation sensible face au vertige du rapt ou de la perte de conscience. La mystique rappelle la vulnérabilité et s'oppose à toute maîtrise technique. La purification de la sensibilité ne sera jamais oubli de la matière, du corps ou des autres. Dans l'icône byzantine, le visage n'est beau qu'en ayant rencontré l'ascèse, connu les veilles et les jeûnes de l'iconographe.

LE RÉALISME DE LA CROIX

Le Beau de saint Thomas comme splendeur du Vrai, le thème hégélien de l'épiphanie sensible de l'Idée ou encore la réflexion d'Heidegger sur l'oeuvre d'art dévoilant

---

10. M. A. Couturier, *Se garder libre. Journal* (1947–1954), (Paris: Cerf, 1962) 155.

l'être de l'étant comme fin de la métaphysique de la représentation, achoppent chacun sur la croix. L'art en christianisme ne craint pas de montrer la souffrance, mais le regard croyant qui se pose sur le crucifié, confesse que cette face n'est pas la dernière. Le cri du Christ abandonné rappelle que toute beauté est dans le monde travaillée par une mort. Le désir d'une pure vision et l'attachement à l'harmonie devront l'un et l'autre consentir à l'épreuve de l'absence: 'Ne me retiens pas ainsi' (Jn 20:17).

Le 'Quatuor pour la fin des temps' de Messiaen, composé dans un camp de prisonniers, ne s'avance pas vers la contemplation de l'essence divine, mais rappelle que la Sagesse des sens n'abandonne pas à la perversion. L'art n'est pas affaire de jeu plaisant, mais aptitude à voir et à écouter ce qui traverse. L'humilité de cette expérience est d'interpréter le présent à partir de la promesse à venir alors même qu'elle ne prend en compte que la présence de l'abandon. L'artiste, celui qui s'exprime dans la contingence sensible, n'accumule aucune preuve, ne comble aucune ouverture, mais creuse le mystère. Son langage est celui du *Kairos*. Selon le réalisme esthétique chrétien, les sens ne sont pas à mépriser, mais à guérir. L'éveil de la sensibilité rencontrera la pacification, en se laissant surprendre par cet inespéré dont les mystiques ne cessent de parler. Aujourd'hui, l'abstraction et l'atonalité touchent à cette réalité exigeante. L'oeuvre d'art n'est plus la conformité de la représentation. Celle-ci en fait est d'un autre ordre, non point celui de la ressemblance mais celui de la lieutenance ; ni iconoclasme ravageur, ni dévoilement béat. Une beauté passée par la mort est une beauté constatée comme croyable au bord du Yabboq.

L'oeuvre n'envisagerait pas le kérygme si elle ne se fondait sur l'incarnation de la Parole dans la vie, la mort et la résurrection de Jésus. 'Comment donc le soldat comprit-il la beauté du crucifié et reconnut-il le Fils de

Dieu dans cet homme mis au rang des criminels?'[11] La
présence sans beauté ni éclat de celui qui vient pour sauver
est le premier donné esthétique chrétien (Is 52:14).
La kénose ne montre pas le premier-né d'une création
nouvelle par delà le sensible. L'expérience du beau et de
l'amour se pose à la démesure de l'entrée de Dieu dans
le monde de la perception: 'Tu l'as couronné de gloire et
de beauté' (Ps 8:6).

SORTIR DU FORT AVEC ANTOINE

Toute proximité esthétique est de rencontre. Pour rencontrer, il faut se laisser rencontrer, s'exposer dans le
don précaire de l'événement et de l'avènement. L'espace
de l'oeuvre n'est commun que parce qu'il est mis en
commun, dans le dialogue ou le silence, l'activité ou
l'imagination, le face à face ou le clair obscur. Si vif que
soit l'émerveillement, jamais il ne formera une réponse
adéquate à ce qui réjouit dans l'exposition de notre être à
la beauté. Lorsque la beauté est conçue comme objet de
contemplation, il est possible de la définir comme une fi-
nalité. Mais lorsque l'épreuve du beau fait découvrir que
sa présence adresse une requête, alors le don premier
de la beauté suscite amour et dépouillement: 'Après le
tremblement de terre, il y eut un feu ; le Seigneur n'était
pas dans le feu. Et après le feu, le bruit d'un silence ténu'
(1R 19:12). L'oeuvre elle-même enseigne comment la
comprendre dans le seul dépouillement, car elle donne
d'abord ce dépouillement qui permettra de la reconnaître
comme forme de vie, beauté de Dieu, art spirituel.[12]

---

11. Bernard, SC 28. 4, dans OEuvres mystiques de saint Bernard, trad.
A. Beguin (Paris: Seuil, 1947) 340.
12. Benoît dans sa Règle décrit ainsi les instruments des bonnes oeuvres:
'Voilà quels sont les instruments de l'art spirituel (*artis spiritalis*). Si, jour
et nuit, sans relâche, nous nous en servons, quand, au jour du jugement,
nous les remettrons, le Seigneur nous donnera la récompense qu'il a promise

Comme l'artiste, le spirituel, à travers des limites et
des choix, rencontre une beauté réconciliée fruit de la
contingence, de la liberté et du don gratuit. Chaque vie
personnelle s'édifie à la manière d'une 'oeuvre' dont la
tentation esthétisante n'est pas exclue. La perte du visage
est le sujet réel des angoisses dans la vieillesse, la maladie
ou la mort, où la sainteté de l'homme n'est pas spectacu-
laire. Au terme du chemin, la gloire dira la beauté du lys
comme épiphanie de la sainteté propre à tous chrétiens.
Les beautés intimes de l'expérience spirituelle ne peuvent être dissociées des gestes qui attestent de sa sainteté: 'C'est à leurs fruits que vous les reconnaîtrez' (Mt
7:16). Si le discernement spirituel doit avoir son moment
esthétique, il aura lieu dans cette histoire d'exposition et
de dépouillement du beau. La beauté n'est pas seulement un attribut extérieur: belle peut être aussi une
vie, une histoire, une relation. Beau est alors ce qui
touche le coeur: beauté d'un amour naissant, beauté
d'une fidélité à toute épreuve, beauté du couple vieil-
lissant. L'art manifesterait-il ce réel mieux que le réel
lui-même? Tout art rencontre sur son chemin des réalités
gracieuses pour 'convertir à l'amour par la beauté'.[13]
L'esthétique sainte qui brille sur le visage vient de son
avenir partagé entre croyants:
        'Près de vingt ans Antoine mena en reclus la vie ascét-
ique: il ne sortait pas et on ne le voyait que très rarement.
Après cela, comme beaucoup désiraient et voulaient
imiter son ascèse et comme d'autres de ses familiers
étaient venus, avaient forcé et brisé sa porte et voulaient
le pousser dehors, Antoine sortit comme du fond d'un
sanctuaire où il aurait été initié aux mystères et inspiré

---

lui-même: «ce que l'oeil n'a pas vu, ce que l'oreille n'a pas entendu, ce que
Dieu a préparé pour ceux qui l'aiment (1 Cor 2:9)».' Benoît, *Règle* 4, 75–77,
trad. P. Schmitz (Turnhout: Brepols, 1987) 28–29.
13. *Convertere ad amorem pulchritudine,* Guerric d'Igny, *Sermon 2 pour la Nativité
de Marie,* 2, trad. P. Deseille, coll. Sources chrétiennes, n° 202 (Paris: Cerf,
1973) t. 2:491.

d'un souffle divin. C'est alors que, pour la première fois, il sortit du fort et se fit voir à ceux qui venaient à lui. Quand ils le virent, ils furent dans l'admiration de voir que son corps avait gardé le même état.[. . .]'[14]

Le regard croyant rencontre la liberté divine capable aussi de devenir ce beau visage humain devant tous: 'J'ai vu Dieu face à face et j'ai eu la vie sauve' (Gn 33:31). Toute beauté expérimentée atteste une transfiguration pascale. L'art dit vrai non en visant une immédiateté formelle, mais en manifestant plus de réalité que le réel n'en manifeste tel quel. Le réalisme artistique chrétien remet cette exigence en mémoire, chaque fois qu'une piété rêve d'une eschatologie réalisée. De même nulle expérience des êtres, des lieux et des histoires n'est purement esthétique, car nulle part le beau ne justifiera jamais le cynisme qui détournerait du bien dans le divertissement. L'esthétique et la mystique sont imbriquées: 'Ephata, ouvre-toi! Et ses oreilles s'ouvrirent et aussitôt le lien de sa langue se dénoua et il parlait correctement' (Mc 7:34).

GUILLAUME DE SAINT-THIERRY:
EXPOSÉ SUR LE CANTIQUE DES CANTIQUES

Mon Bien-aimé est à moi, et je suis à lui,
Il paît parmi les lis,
Jusqu'à ce que le jour commence à respirer
Et que les ombres fuient. (Cant 2.15–17)

COMMENT LE LYS REÇOIT LA GRÂCE

'Le lys est la fleur la plus belle entre les fleurs, mais elle est stérile. Se dressant vers les hauteurs à partir de la terre sur une tige droite et verte, elle est d'une couleur

14. Athanase, *Vie d'Antoine* 14. 1–3, trad. G. J. M. Bartelink, coll. Sources chrétiennes, 400 (Paris: Cerf, 1994) 173.

blanche et candide à l'extérieur, mais d'une couleur de
feu à l'intérieur, elle est pleine de grâce pour l'oeil, suave
pour l'odorat, elle a la vertu naturelle d'adoucir ce qui est
dur. Or vois le lys avant le lever du soleil: il semble fuir
la face du froid nocturne et des ténèbres de la nuit et se
cacher à l'intérieur de lui-même en contenant enfermées
en lui ses tendres délices; mais bientôt, quand la face du
soleil naissant a brillé pour lui d'une lumière plus pure,
il semble s'ouvrir à lui tout entier dans un sourire et
reconnaître le sceau de son Créateur dans toute sa gloire.

Tel est exactement l'état d'un esprit que la grâce
créatrice rend bon, mais qui est encore stérile quant aux
fruits de l'intelligence et de la sagesse; il les attend de
la grâce illuminante. Telle est la conscience même d'une
volonté et d'une intention dirigées tout droit vers Dieu,
préférant parmi les hommes la blancheur lumineuse de
la chasteté et des oeuvres extérieures de la foi, envers
Dieu le joug intérieur et la fragrance du désir, répandant
autour de soi la bonne odeur du Christ (2 Co 2:14), en
tout lieu, dans les tribulations et l'oppression, gardant
la vertu de patience pour amollir toute dureté de la
méchanceté humaine, possédant tous ses biens dans le
secret de la grâce créatrice et donatrice jusqu'à ce que
soit produite au-dehors comme la lumière sa justice, avec
le jugement qui l'atteste comme un plein midi (Ps 36:6),
dans la manifestation de la grâce illuminante.'[15]

15. Guillaume de Saint-Thierry, *Exposé sur le Cantique des cantiques* 2, 4, 174,
d'après trad. A. Michel, *Théologiens et mystiques au Moyen Age. La poétique
de Dieu Ve-XVe siècle* (Paris: Gallimard, 1997) 306.

Bernard McGinn

Divinity School, University of Chicago

Does the Trinity Add Up? Transcendental Mathematics and Trinitarian Speculation in the Twelfth and Thirteenth Centuries

THE HIGH MIDDLE AGES, that is the twelfth and thirteenth centuries, was one of the richest periods in the history of christian theology. Modern study of this era, at least until about 1950, concentrated on the study of the scholastic mode of theology that was still in its infancy in 1100, but by 1200 had come to exercise a dominant role. Beginning with the work of Jean Leclercq in the 1950s, however, theologians and medievalists came to recognize the twelfth century, if not the thirteenth, as the Golden Age of western monastic theology. A number of important Benedictines (for example, Rupert of Deutz, Honorius Augustodunensis, Hildegard of Bingen), but especially the great Cistercians, like Bernard of Clairvaux, William of Saint-Thierry, and Aelred of Rievaulx, demonstrate that the twelfth century was an era of remarkable theological achievement among monastics. In the past two decades, we have come to recognize a third broad, if more diffuse, theological tradition of the High Middle Ages, the vernacular theology represented by male and female authors who preached and wrote in the burgeoning vernacular languages, especially after 1200.[1]

1. For a sketch of the three modes of medieval theology, see Bernard McGinn, 'Introduction: Meister Eckhart and the Beguines in the Context of Vernacular

The vibrant theological world of the High Middle
Ages turned its attention to many issues in christian
faith. Among the most important was the doctrine of
the Trinity. Confession that the one God is a Trinity of
Father, Son, and Holy Spirit—however expressed and
understood—had been essential to christian belief and
practice even before the orthodox formulation of the
doctrine in the fourth century. Furthermore, if we take
mysticism as that element within the christian religion
that concerns the preparation for, the attainment of,
and the effects of what is described as an immediately
conscious presence of God, then christian mysticism, like
christian theology, is also fundamentally trinitarian, at
least in the sense that the God sought and attained by the
mystic is the God confessed in the trinitarian formulae
of belief.[2] This was especially the case in the twelfth
and thirteenth centuries, when theology and mysticism
intermingled more productively than perhaps in any other
era of christian history.

To try to survey the many varieties of trinitarian theology of the High Middle Ages, and the ways in which they
interacted with the mystical currents of the time, would
be beyond the scope of a short essay. Even the mystical
trinitarianism of the great cistercian authors—a teaching
most fully developed by William of Saint-Thierry, but
one by no means absent from Bernard, Isaac of Stella,
and other white monks—is too extensive to be easily
surveyed in a single paper.[3] Here I intend to investigate

Theology,' *Meister Eckhart and the Beguine Mystics. Hadewijch of Brabant, Mechthild
of Magdeburg, and Marguerite Porete*, edited by Bernard McGinn (New York:
Continuum, 1994) 1–14.

2. For this view of mysticism, see Bernard McGinn, *The Foundation of
Mysticism. Origins to the Fifth Century* (New York: Crossroasd, 1991) xiii–xx.

3. For a more detailed study of the role of the Trinity in the cistercian mystics,
see Bernard McGinn, *The Growth of Mysticism. Gregory the Great through the
Twelfth Century* (New York: Crossroad, 1994) chapters 5–7. While Bernard of
Clairvaux does not have as much explicit discussion of the role of the Trinity
in mystical transformation as his friend William of Saint Thierry, this is not to

only one minor, but fascinating, aspect of the trinitarian theology of the twelfth and thirteenth centuries. This attempt to present the mystery of the Trinity was most richly developed by a twelfth-century schoolman, a *magister*, who, like a number of other university men of the era, ended his life as a white monk.

Thierry of Chartres is the central figure in the following account.[4] Born in Brittany, and most likely the brother of the noted teacher, Bernard of Chartres, Thierry was the chancellor of the cathedral school at Chartres in the 1140s. In the early 1150s he entered the Cistercian Order, possibly at the abbey of Vaux-de-Cernay. He died sometime not long after 1156.[5] As one of the most creative minds of the mid-twelfth century schools—'*totius Europe philosophorum precipuus,*' as his student Clarembald of Arras called him—Thierry contributed to many areas of thought in the liberal arts, as well as in philosophy and theology. He was a major exponent of the twelfth-century attempts to create what I have elsewhere described as a 'unified field theory that would show the inner harmony not only among the human sciences but also between human *scientia* in general and the divine *sapientia* of theology'.[6] One of the most striking aspects

---

say that there is not rich teaching on the Trinity in his *Sermones super Cantica Canticorum*, as has been shown by Anne Morris, 'The Trinity in Bernard's Sermons on the Song of Songs', *Cistercian Studies Quarterly* 30(1995) 37–57.

4. For an introduction to Thierry, see Peter Dronke, 'Thierry of Chartres', *A History of Twelfth-Century Western Philosophy*, edited by Peter Dronke (Cambridge: Cambridge University Press, 1988) 358–385. Also helpful is Nikolaus Häring, 'Chartres and Paris Revisited', *Essays in Honor of Anton Charles Pegis*, edited by J. R. O'Donnell (Toronto: PIMS, 1974) 279–294; and Édouard Jeauneau, 'Note sur l'école de Chartres', *Studi Medioevali*, 3a serie, 5(1964) 821–39.

5. On Thierry's entry into the Cistercians, see A. Vernet, 'Une épitaphe inédite de Thierry of Chartres', *Mémoires et documents publies par la Societé de l'École des chartes 12: Recueil des travaux offert à M. Clovis Brunel* (Paris: Societé de l'École des chartes, 1955) Vol. 2: 660–70.

6. Bernard McGinn, 'The Role of the *Anima Mundi* as Mediator between the Divine and Created Realms in the Twelfth Century', *Death, Ecstasy, and Other*

of Thierry's thought was his development of what can be
called a speculative mathematics of the Trinity. This relatively unstudied form of trinitarianism was not just a brief
aberration in the history of theology.[7] Deeply tied to ancient pythagorean speculation on the transcendental role
of numbers, as well as neoplatonic traditions about God
as the Absolute One, it had christian roots in Augustine,
Boethius, and Pseudo-Dionysius. Though Thierry was its
main twelfth-century exponent, many other figures of his
age referred to this 'mathematics of the Trinity'. It was
also to be taken up by two of the most important mystical
thinkers of the later Middle Ages—Meister Eckhart and
Nicholas of Cusa. Cusa's development is the richest,[8]
but here I will be able to look only at some twelfth and
thirteenth-century attempts to investigate the mystery
of the Trinity in terms of the mathematics of God as
Absolute Unity.

   In order to understand this form of trinitarian theology we must start with Augustine of Hippo. As everyone
knows, Augustine wrote a big book on the Trinity, one
that has been more decisive than any other in the history
of western theology of the triune God. The notion of
the human person as *imago Trinitatis*, developed with such
subtlety by the bishop of Hippo in this great work, was
combined with the exploration of the dynamics of erotic
love of God through the exegesis of the Song of Songs

Worldly Journeys, edited by John J. Collins and Michael Fishbane (Albany:
SUNY, 1995) 290.

7. The first scholar to draw attention to this aspect of the history of trinitarian
theology was M.-D. Chenu in his article, 'Une définition pythagorienne de
la verité au moyen âge', *Archives d'histoire doctrinale et littéraire du moyen âge*
28(1961) 7–13. Shortly afterwards, a pioneering study of Thierry's use of
the theme was published by Édouard Jeauneau, 'Mathematiques et Trinité
chez Thierry de Chartres', *Die Metaphysik im Mittelalter. Ihr Ursprung und
ihre Bedeutung* (Berlin: De Gruyter, 1963. Miscellanea Mediaevalia, Vol. 2)
289–295.

8. For Cusa's use, see my forthcoming paper, '*Unitrinum seu Triunum*: Nicholas
of Cusa's Trinitarian Mysticism'.

in the twelfth century—especially by William of Saint-
Thierry—to form the fountainhead of one of the major
trajectories of late medieval trinitarian mysticism.[9] This
tradition, enriched by the contribution of women mystics
of the thirteenth century, is found in many later mystical
authors, such as John Ruusbroec in the mid-fourteenth
century. A second form of trinitarian mysticism, also dependent on Augustine's *De Trinitate* (especially book 8),
was initiated by Richard of Saint Victor in the twelfth
century and developed by Bonaventure in the thirteenth
century. There is, however, a third aspect of Augustine's
teaching on the Trinity that also had a role both in trinitarian speculation and in christian mysticism. This third
tradition depends on a relatively early formulation of the
bishop, one that did not make its way into the *De Trinitate*,
and therefore has been somewhat neglected by historians
of theology. Nevertheless, it had a significant impact on
the trinitararian speculations of the twelfth century, and it
was to have a role in the mystical trinitarianism of Eckhart
and Nicholas of Cusa.

At the beginning of his *De doctrina christiana*, written in
396, Augustine sets forth his famous distinction between
signs (*signa*) and things (*res*). Augustine distinguished
three classes of things on the basis of whether the *res*
in question is one to be enjoyed, one to be used, or one
to be both enjoyed and used (*De doctrina* 1.2.4–1.3.7).
Given that 'to enjoy is to inhere by love in something
for its own sake' (1.4.8), Augustine declares that 'the
things that are to be enjoyed are the Father and the
Son and the Holy Spirit, and the same Trinity is one
supreme thing common to all who enjoy it . . .'(1.5.10).
After a brief summary of orthodox trinitarian teaching,
Augustine concludes his discussion with a short reflection

9. For Augustine on the *imago Trinitatis*, see *The Foundations of Mysticism*, 243–
48. On William of Saint-Thierry's 'Spirit-centered' Trinitarian mysticism,
see *The Growth of Mysticism*, chapter 6.

on what the tradition would later describe as common
and proper divine attributes (1.5.12). As he puts it:

> The same eternity, immutability, majesty, and power
> are common to the three. In the Father there is unity,
> in the Son equality, in the Holy Spirit the agreement
> (*concordia*) of unity and equality. And all three are
> one because of the Father, equal because of the Son,
> and connected (*conexa*) because of the Holy Spirit.[10]

Unity or Absolute Oneness, therefore, is the proper
attribute of the Father (1), while the total Equality of
Oneness (1 = 1) is proper to the Son. The Holy Spirit
is the co-equal Bond, Agreement, or Connection (X) of
the two, thus giving the implied formula (1 X 1) as the
mathematical expression of the trinitarian mystery.

Augustine did not end here, however. In the following
lines he paused to reflect on the paradox involved in
claiming that God is ineffable and yet still using names
about him, even the name *ineffabilis*. He concludes:

> For this reason God should not even be said to be
> ineffable, because when this is said a statement is
> made. There results a form of verbal strife in that
> if the ineffable is what cannot be said, then what
> is called ineffable cannot be ineffable. This verbal
> strife is to be avoided by silence rather than resolved

---

10. *De doctrina christiana*, ed. G. M. Green (Corpus Scriptorum Ecclesiasticorum Latinorum LXXX, Sect. VI, Pars VI. Vienna: Holder-Pichler-Tempsky,
1963) 10–11: *Frui est enim amore inherere alicui rei propter se ipsam. . . . Res igitur
quibus fruendum est, pater et filius et spiritus sanctus, eademque trinitas una quaedam
summa res communisque omnibus fruentibus ea. . . . Eadem tribus aeternitas, eadem
incommutabilitas, eadem maiestas, eadem potestas. In patre unitas, in filio aequalitas,
in spiritu sancto unitatis aequalitatisque concordia. Et tria haec unum omnia propter
patrem, aequalia omnia propter filium, conexa omnia propter spiritum sanctum.* While
Augustine does not explicitly say in this passage that the terms are proper to
the Persons, the context certainly suggests this. The later and more detailed
consideration of common, proper and appropriated names in *De Trinitate*,
books 5–7, dropped the triad of *unitas-aequalitas-concordia* completely, either
as proper or appropriated.

by speech. Although nothing can be spoken of God worthily, he still welcomes the homage of the human voice and wishes us to rejoice in praising him in our own words.[11]

Thus, the bishop is keen to remind us that any attempt to name, or to number God—as one or as three—is always an impossible, but necessary, task. Absolute Oneness, its Equality, and Concord/Connection with itself is not a part of our limited ways of knowing.

What led Augustine to this particular form of effable-ineffable trinitarian language? Previous latin trinitarian theology had used *unitas* only as a common term to express the oneness of the Father and the Son.[12] Augustine himself, in his later reflections on *unitas* as a divine attribute in *De Trinitate*, books 6–7, also treated the term as a common not a proper attribute and therefore did not take up the triadic formula of *unitas-aequalitas-concordia* found in the *De doctrina christiana*. In using *aequalitas* as the distinctive property of the second Person, Augustine may well have been inspired by anti-arian intentions, employing the word as a latin equivalent to the *homoousios* of nicene orthodoxy.[13] If this is the case, though, it is significant that Augustine later shied away

---

11. *De doctrina christiana* I.6.13–14: *Ac per hoc ne ineffabilis quidem dicendus est deus, quia et hoc cum dicitur, aliquid dicitur. Et fit nescio qua pugna verborum, quoniam si illud est ineffabile quod dici non potest, non est ineffabile quod vel ineffabile dici potest. Quae pugna verborum silentio cavenda potius quam voce pacanda est. Et tamen deus, cum de illo nihil digne dici possit, admisit humanae vocis obsequium et verbis nostris in laude sua gaudere nos voluit.*

12. E.g., Hilary of Poitiers, *De Trinitate* 3.4, 8.4, 10.5–6, and 12.54. It is possible that Augustine was led to experiment with the trinitarian significance of the term by his early philosophical reflections on *unum*, as seen, for example, in *De ordine* 2.17.48. One early sermon has a formulation distantly related to that found in the *De doctrina christiana*; see Sermo 33.3 (PL 38:208): *Unitas enim divinitatis a Patre habet exordium, inde primum praeceptum de uno Deo maxime loquitur. Admonemur autem secundo praecepto, ne filium Dei creaturam putemus, si eum acceperimus inaequalem Patri.*

13. See 'Aequalitas 3'. (Basil Studer) in the *Augustinus-Lexikon*, General Editor Cornelius Mayer (Basel: Schwabe, 1986–94) Vol. 1:146–49.

from this understanding, since *aequalitas* appears in the *De Trinitate* only as a common name.[14] Finally, *concordia* as a trinitarian term also seems to have been an enthusiasm soon abandoned, since it occurs in only one other early passage,[15] and even there it is not used as a term proper to the Holy Spirit.

Although this section of the *De doctrina christiana* has attracted some interest for its reflections on the problem of speaking about God,[16] the vast body of augustinian scholarship has paid little attention to this discussion of the Trinity as *unitas-aequalitas-concordia/conexio*, thereby missing the significance, if not of a major element in Augustine's own trinitarianism, at least of one aspect of his influence in the later Middle Ages.[17] As taken up by Thierry of Chartres and his successors, the formula had a history that might have surprised Augustine. In order to demonstrate the richness of its later development, it is important to consider the text not as an isolated element in the writing of the early Augustine, but as part of a broad tradition of trinitarian speculation. We must turn to Boethius, a western follower of Augustine, and to the mysterious eastern author known as Pseudo-Dionysius in

14. E.g., *De Trinitate* 6.2.9–10; 15.3.5. There are many similar passages in other works; e.g., *In Iohannis evangelium tractatus* 21.14.
15. The *Augustinus-Lexikon*, Vol. 1:1107, cites *De moribus catholicae* 1.15.25, written about 388, where *concordia* appears as a divine attribute, though clearly a common one: *Sed hunc amorem non cujuslibet, sed Dei esse diximus, id est summi boni, summae sapientiae, summaeque concordiae* (PL 32:1322).
16. See Vladimir Lossky, 'Les éléments de "Théologie négative" dans la pensée de saint Augustin,' *Augustinus Magister*, 3 vols. (Paris: L'Année théologique augustinienne, 1954) 1:575–81; and Peter Van Ness, *Sermo fallibilis: The Problem of Speaking about God in the Augustinian Tradition* (University of Chicago Ph.D Dissertation, 1983).
17. The recent volume of essays devoted to the work, *De doctrina christiana. A Christian Classic*, edited by Duane W.H. Arnold and Pamela Bright (Notre Dame: University of Notre Dame, 1995), has no treatment of its doctrine of the Trinity, though it does contain a useful account of the common divine attributes by Leo Sweeney, 'Divine Attributes in the *De doctrina christiana*: Why Does Augustine Not List "Infinity"? 195–204.

order to understand why this brief text in the *De doctrina* became the center of a complex of themes in later western trinitarianism.

Boethius's *De Trinitate*, written in the early sixth century, begins by expressing its desire to bear fruit from the seeds sown in the works of Augustine.[18] This proto-scholastic investigation of the logic of trinitarian predication is scarcely mystical in nature, but it made a contribution to the doctrinal development of Augustine's *De doctrina* text through its analysis of the role of unity and number in speaking of the Trinity.

The ancient Pythagoreans had found in the study of numbers the key to understanding the universe. Plato was also convinced that no one could become a real philosopher without mastering mathematics. In the *Republic* he said that 'The study of unity (*to hen*) will be one of the studies that guide and convert the soul to the contemplation of true being'.[19] Boethius, one of the last western thinkers for a millennium to have access to much of Plato's writings, also conveyed knowledge of ancient mathematics to the early medieval world. In his *De Trinitate* he took up the deeper issue of the relation between transcendental unity and christian belief in the Trinity of Persons. The fundamentals of Boethius's treatment are set forth in the context of a discussion of the speculative sciences found in *De Trinitate* II.[20] According to Boethius, *mathematica* functions as the knowledge which mediates between *physica*, the science that studies the forms of bodies, and *theologia*, which deals with 'the

18. Boethius. *The Theological Tractates and the Consolation of Philosophy* (Cambridge: Harvard University Press, 1962). *De Trinitate*, prol. (4): . . . *an ex beati Augustini scriptis semina rationum aliquos in nos uenientia fructus extulerint.* For an introduction to Boethius's theological tractates, see Henry Chadwick, *Boethius. The Consolations of Music, Logic, Theology, and Philosophy* (Oxford: Clarendon Press, 1981) chapter IV.

19. Plato, *Republic* 7 (525a).

20. Much has been written on this distinction; see especially Philip Merlan, *From Platonism to Neoplatonism* (The Hague: Nijhoff, 1968, 3rd ed.).

divine substance without matter and motion'.[21] Although mathematics can help lead the mind to God, because it is 'not abstract' (*inabstracta*), it cannot function within the 'abstract and separable' (*abstracta atque separabilis*) domain of *theologia*, at least in the way in which we commonly use numbers. Therefore, in discussing how number is related to the Trinity, Boethius says: 'When we repeat "God" three times, naming Father, Son, and Holy Spirit, the three unities do not make a plurality of number in what they are, if we pay attention to the things we are counting and not to the number we count by'.[22] Boethius bases this exclusion of number from the Trinity on the distinction between the 'number with which we actually count things' (i.e., one, two, three, and the like), and the 'number which is rooted (*constat*) in the things to be numbered'.[23] The point of the distinction is clear: ' . . . threefold predication in God does not entail number'.[24]

Boethius's exclusion of real numeration from the three in the Trinity can be clarified by attending to a key principle of neoplatonic monodology which he cited in chapter two of the *De Trinitate*: 'That is truly one in which there is no number' (*hoc uere unum est in quo nullus numerus*). As explained—for example, in his treatise *De arithmetica*— *unitas-unum*, one (or better, 'the One') is not really a number at all, but rather the principle or source of all

21. De Trinitate II (ed. 8): . . . *theologica, sine motu abstracta atque separabilis (nam dei substantia et materia et motu caret)*. . . .

22. De Trinitate III (ed. 12.5–9): *Nam quod tertio repetitur deus, cum pater ac filius et spiritus sanctus nuncupatur, tres unitates non faciunt pluralitatem numeri in eo quod ipsae sunt, si aduertamus ad res numerabiles ac non ad ipsum numerum*. Augustine had also excluded any real number from the Trinity, e.g., *De Trinitate* 6.2.9.

23. Ibid.: *Numerus enim duplex est, unus quidem quo numeremus, alter uero qui in numerabilibus constat*. On the neoplatonic roots of this distinction in Plotinus and Proclus, see Chadwick, *Boethius*, 215–16.

24. De Trinitate III (ed. 14): *Ergo in numero quo numeramus repetitionem unitatum facit pluralitatem; in rerum uero numero non facit pluralitatem unitatum repetitio*. . . . *Non igitur si de patre ac filio et spiritu sancto tertio praedicatur deus, idcirco trina praedicatio numerum facit*.

numeration.[25] The same teaching appears in other neo-platonic works that were formative for medieval thought, especially Macrobius's *Commentarium in Somnium Scipionis* 1.6.7, and the Proclean *Liber de causis*, propositions 217–19. This insistence on 'the One beyond number', a form of transcendental mathematics, was the foundation of the speculative mathematics of the Trinity developed from Augustine's brief passage in the *De doctrina christiana*.

Foundational as these texts from Augustine and Boethius were, the speculative mathematics of the Trinity cannot be understood apart from a third source, the dialectical negative theology found in the writings of Dionysius.[26] The development of 'hard' apophatic theology (i.e., thoroughgoing insistence that God lies beyond all human language, both positive and negative), was begun in Christianity by Clement of Alexandria in the second century and carried forward by Gregory of Nyssa in the fourth. It attained systematic exposition in the writings of Dionysius. The mysterious Dionysius insisted that *trias*, or Trinity, was the highest of the positive revealed names that manifests *thearchia*, the God who communicates himself in creation.[27] Yet the hymn that begins the *De mystica theologia* opens with the invocation: 'Trinity! Higher than any being, any divinity, any goodness!'[28] The second chapter of the *De divinis nominibus* contains a detailed consideration of the unified and differentiated names of positive, or cataphatic, theology in a form of mini-treatise on the divine Unity

25. Boethius, *De arithmetica* 1.3.
26. For a brief treatment, see *The Foundations of Mysticism*, 157–182, and the literature cited there. Also helpful is Denys Turner, *The Darkness of God. Negativity in Christian Mysticism* (Cambridge: Cambridge University Press, 1995) chapter 2.
27. In *De caelesti hierarchia* 7.4 (PG 3:212C) Dionysius defines *thearchia* as 'a Monad and Tri-hypostatic Unity'.
28. *De mystica theologia* 1.1 (PG 3:997A): *Trias hyperousie, kai hyperthee, kai hyperagathe.* . . . , using the translation of Colm Luibheid, *Pseudo-Dionysius. The Complete Works* (New York: Paulist Press, 1987) 135.

and Trinity. In the thirteenth chapter of the same work Dionysius also provides a lengthy treatment of the One (*to hen*) as the central negative name of God insofar as 'One' signifies the unknown ground of all number and created reality. Dionysius's theory of redoubled negation, or hypernegation, ultimately leads to the position that all names, both positive and negative, do not *really* signify the divine mystery. As he notes toward the conclusion of *De divinis nominibus* 13: 'No unity or trinity, no number or oneness, no fruitfulness, indeed, nothing that is or is known can proclaim that hiddenness beyond every mind and reason of the transcendent Godhead which transcends every being. There is no name for it or expression.'[29] In a characteristic phrase, Dionysius calls it the *anonymon autēn*, the 'Nameless Itself' (DN 1.6 [596A]).

Along with this insistence on the limiting horizon of the absolute *innominabilitas* of God, the dionysian writings contain, as Werner Beierwaltes has shown,[30] the earliest christian attempt to explore the process of trinitarian self-constitution. Dionysius bases his argument on a form of the coincidence of opposites as the most adequate linguistic way to render the praise to the unknown God which is the duty of the christian worshipper.[31] This approach, developed in various ways by thinkers like John Scottus Eriugena, Meister Eckhart, and Nicholas of Cusa, was to remain a lynch-pin of Christian Neoplatonism.

It was not until the twelfth century that the three components described above combined to form a distinctive transcendental mathematics of the Trinity. The crucial figure, as we noted, was Thierry of Chartres. Thierry seems to have to been lecturing on Boethius's theological tractates around 1150. Earlier, probably in the late 1130s, he had

29. DN 13.3 (PG 3:981A). Similar passages of hypernegation can be found, e.g., in DN 2.4 (641A), and MT 1.2 (1000AB), and 5 (1048B).
30. See Werner Beierwaltes, 'Unity and Trinity in East and West', in *Eriugena East and West*, edited by Bernard McGinn and Willemien Otten (Notre Dame: University of Notre Dame, 1994) 214–219.
31. A key text in this connection is found in DN 2.4 (PG 3:641B).

composed an unusual interpretation of the beginning of Genesis, the *Tractatus de sex dierum operibus*, in which he sought to provide a literal and scientific account of the Hexaemeron, along with a sketch of the doctrine of the Trinity.[32] These works show how concerned the chartrian *magister* was to explore new directions in the theology of the Trinity.

Thierry's Genesis commentary marks the earliest reappearance of Augustine's *unitas-aequalitas-concordia / conexio* formula as a key to trinitarian theology. Yet, the way in which the triad appears in the *De sex dierum operibus* is initially surprising. What is a 'mathematical' proof of the Trinity doing in a treatise purporting to give a 'scientific' explanation of creation? The answer, I believe, rests in the early twelfth-century attempt to construct a general field theory that would embrace and unify all knowledge— physical, mathematical, theological.[33] Expanding upon Boethius's observation about the mediating character of *mathematica*, Thierry argued that the whole *quadrivium* could be used to provide proofs leading to the Creator:

> There are four forms of demonstrations that lead humans to knowledge of the Creator: arithmetical proofs, musical, geometrical, and astronomical. We make brief use of these instruments in this theology so that the Creator's skill may appear in things and that there may be a reasonable demonstration of what we are proposing.[34]

---

32. These works are available in Nikolaus Häring, ed., *Commentaries on Boethius by Thierry of Chartres and His School*. I side with Häring (see p. 47) against Dronke ('Thierry of Chartres', 360) on the early dating of the *De sex dierum operibus*. On the role of scripture in Thierry's thought, see Willemien Otten, 'Nature and Scripture: Demise of a Medieval Analogy', *Harvard Theological Review* 88(1995) 257–284.

33. On the integration of all human knowledge as an ideal of Thierry and the 'School of Chartres', see Dronke, 'Thierry of Chartres', 361 and 385.

34. *Tractatus de sex dierum operibus* 30 (ed. Häring, 568): *Adsint igitur quatuor genera rationum que ducunt hominem ad cognitionem creatoris: scilicet arithmetice probationes et musice et geometrice et astronomice. Quibus instrumentis in hac theologia*

Thierry's language here suggests Anselm's *rationes neces-sariae*, especially the abbot's proof for God's existence found in the *Proslogion*. But the differences are striking. The scholastic *magister* procedes on the basis of the *quadrivium* rather than the logical and rhetorical disciplines of the *trivium* used by the monastic author.[35] In other words, he insists that it is on the basis of the study of the natural world, not merely from logic, that necessary proofs for God's existence can be made.[36] Although the status of his *probationes*, like those of Anselm, are ambiguous, they are problematic in a different way from those of Anselm. Briefly put, Anselm continues to intrigue philosophers because of their suspicions that his analytical arguments, however beset with logical problems, may contain the hint of a solution to proving God's existence. Thierry, on the other hand (and after him thinkers like Meister Eckhart and Nicholas of Cusa), remains puzzling because of his conviction that arguments that disregard the usual rules of human logic can nonetheless manifest both *that* God is and that God *necessarily* is one and three— while remaining radically insufficient to reveal what that *unitrinum et triunum* God might be.[37]

---

breuiter utendum est ut et artificium creatoris in rebus appareat et quod proposuimus rationabiliter ostendatur.

35. It is interesting to note that while Thierry develops only a *ratio arithmetica* in the *De sex dierum operibus* and the boethian commentaries, a passage from his unedited *Heptateuchon*, or introduction to the liberal arts, cited by Dronke ('Thierry of Chartres', 381–382) indicates the form in which he may have developed parallel geometrical proofs. Nicholas of Cusa was to be his successor in this endeavor. Thierry evidently agreed with William of Conches, who, in his *Accessus ad Timaeum* claimed: *Et dicitur* [mathesis] *doctrinalis antonomastice, scilicet quia perfectior fit doctrina in quadruvio quam in aliis artibus. In aliis enim enim sola voce fit doctrina, in ista vero et voce et oculis. . . . (Guillaume de Conches. Glosae super Platonem*, ed. Édouard Jeauneau [Paris: Vrin, 1965] 61).

36. This point is well brought out by Jeauneau, 'Mathématiques et Trinité', 291–292.

37. Peter Dronke in 'Thierry of Chartres', 367–368, and 380, explains Thierry's ambiguity by appealing to the notion of literary device of *integumentum* widely used among the chartrian thinkers. Since Thierry never uses

The form that Thierry's necessary proof for the Trinity took remained consistent throughout his works, despite individual variations.[38] In the *De sex dierum operibus* he begins by invoking the contrast between unity and diversity (*alteritas*), and goes on to explain why true Unity must be eternal and divine and therefore also the 'form of existing' (*forma essendi*) in all things. He bases this argument on the boethian axiom, 'Everything that exists does so because it is one'.[39] He then turns to the exploration of the term *equalitas* as proper to the Person of the Son.[40] The One, he argues, can be productive in two ways: 'When it is multiplied through other numbers [e.g., 1 X 2, 1 X 3, and so on] it generates all numbers', that is, the forms of diversity that express created reality. 'From itself and from its own substance, however, it can generate only Equality [i.e., 1 X 1], since other numbers multiplied by themselves produce inequalities. Unity, once and for all, is nothing else but unity.'[41] The consubstantial implications

_____

the term in connection with these *probationes*, however, it is more reasonable, given his subsequent appeal to the masters of apophatic theology, especially Hermes Trismegistus (i.e., the Hermetic *Asclepius*) and Dionysius, to think of his arguments as something closer to Nicholas of Cusa's 'non-precise' demonstrations which point to, but never can logically prove, the triune God. Human logic does not work in the divine realm.

38. The proof appears in the major texts that reflect Thierry's lectures: the *De sex dierum operibus* 30–47 (Häring ed., 568–75); *Commentum super librum Boethii De Trinitate* (often known as the *Librum hunc*) II.30–43 (ed., 77–82); *Lectiones in Boethii librum De Trinitate* V.16 and VII.5–7 (ed., 218, 224–25); *Glosa super Boethii Librum De Trinitate* V.17–23 (ed., 296–98). In addition, three other texts that are based on Thierry's ideas though they may not be products of his pen also contain the mathematical proof: *Tractatus De Trinitate* 12–20 (ed., 306–08); *Abbrevatio Monacensis. De Trinitate* V.16 and VII.5–7 (ed., 391–92, 397–98); and the *Commentarius Victorinus* (Pseudo-Bede) I.81–96 (ed., 498–501).

39. *De sex dierum operibus* 31 (ed., 568–69). For the axiom *omne quod est ideo est quia unum est*, see Boethius, *In Porphyrium* I (PL 64:83B).

40. On Thierry's notion of *equalitas*, see especially Chenu, 'Une définition pythagorienne de la verité au moyen âge'.

41. *De sex dierum operibus* 38 (ed., 571): *Hec igitur duplex generatio circa unitatem potest reperiri. Et quidem per alios numeros multiplicata omnes numeros generat. Ex*

of this Equality are then discussed, as is the necessity
that it include 'every idea of something' (n. 42), that
is, the traditional teaching that the Divine Logos is the
exemplary cause of all things. Thierry's treatment of the
Trinity in his Genesis commentary, however, is truncated.
The treatise ends without any consideration of the *conexio*
which is the Holy Spirit. For this we must turn to the
master's commentaries on Boethius's *De Trinitate*.

In these commentaries Thierry invokes the notion of
three forms of trinitarian language: 'We speak of the
Trinity in three ways—theologically, mathematically, and
ethically. Mathematically speaking, Augustine says that
Unity is in the Father, Equality in the Son, and the
Connexion of unity and equality in the Holy Spirit.'[42] The
most mature development of the proof in the Boethian
works is found in the text known as the *Glosa*. 'Unity
itself', Thierry says here, 'is *ontitas* or being which exists
before all otherness.' When generation takes place by way
of the multiplication of the same nature [i.e., 1 X 1], a
unity is produced which is not other than that from which
it is born, though it is a 'unity *from* unity'. Thierry then
goes on to say that 'because this was from the beginning,

---

se autem et ex sua substantia nichil aliud generare potest nisi equalitatem cum alii
numeri ex se multiplicati inequalitates producant. Unitas enim semel nichil aliud est
quam unitas.
42. *Lectiones* VII.5 (ed., 224): *Tribus enim modis de Trinitate loquimur: theologice*
scilicet mathematice et ethice. Et Augustinus quidem mathematice dicit quod in Patre
est unitas in Filio equalitas in Spiritu sancto unitatis equalitatisque conexio. Similar
texts are found in *Abbreviatio Monacensis De Trinitate* VII.5 (ed., 397–98); and
Commentarius Victorinus I.81 (ed., 498). The most advanced treatment of this
reflection on ways of speaking of the Trinity is found in *Glosa* V.17–23 (ed.,
296–98) which distinguishes: (1) teaching of the Trinity *secundum phisicam*
doctrinam, i.e., the triad of *pondus-mensura-numerus* found in Augustine's *De*
Trin. 8.1 and in Claudianus Mamertus; (2) ethical doctrine based on the triad
of *fides-spes-caritas*; (3) mathematical doctrine; and (4) theological doctrine.
This last seems to be understood as the personal names of *Pater-Filius-Spiritus*
sanctus, though in n. 22 Thierry makes the interesting observation that the
three Persons lie beyond all gender because they are also hinted at in the
feminine 'abelardian' triad of *omnipotentia-sapientia-benignitas*.

that is as much as to say that it was unity as soon as it was like the One which is unity, I call this generation an eternal one'. Both Unity and the Equality of Unity, or *forma essendi*, are eternal. The *conexio*, namely, the third Person of the Trinity, is the further necessary implication of such transcendental Unity and Equality. As he puts it:

> Without beginning there always existed a Bond of Love from Unity toward its Equality by means of which they remained without end or mutable succession, a Bond reciprocated toward the same Unity from its Equality. Unity provided perfectly for the Equality of Being, for it would not exist if it were contemptuous of itself, and likewise the Equality of Unity embraced Unity as Entity perfectly, because it would perish if it underwent separation from it.

The conclusion repeats the augustinian formula: 'Therefore Unity is the Father, the Equality of Unity the Son, the Connection of Unity and Equality the Holy Spirit'.[43]

In the boethian commentaries Thierry advances these mathematical proofs within a broad context that includes not only reflection on the relation between *unum* and numeration, but also lengthy discussions of the superiority of negative over positive theology.[44] These treatises also

43. *Glosa* V.18–21 (ed., 297): *Unitas enim ipsa est* ontitas *atque entitas que ante omnem alteritatem est. . . . Apparet quod unitas de unitate generatur. Sed quia hoc a principio fuit—ex quo enim si dici potest fuit unitas mox fuit similiter unum quod est unitas—ideo hanc generationem eternam appello. . . . Sed sine principio semper ab unitate uersus sui equalitatem quo sine fine et successsionis mutabilitate manerent nexus et amor quidam extitit qui ad eandem reciprocatur ab equalitate unitatis. Unitas enim ualde ornat essendi equalitatem. Aliter enim non esset si se contempneret. Similiter unitatis equalitas ualde amplectitur unitatem quasi entitatem. Periret enim si diuisionem incurreret. . . . Unitas itaque Pater est, Filius unitatis equalitas, Spiritus sanctus unitatis equalitatisque conexio.*
44. For the discussions of negative theology, see *Lectiones* IV.7–37 (ed., 188–198); *Glosa* IV.11–22 (ed., 286–289); *Tractatus* 26–27 (ed., 309–310); *Abbrev. Mon. De Trin.* IV. 10–11 and 28, *De Hebdom.* 34–37, and *Contra Eutychen* I.27 and III.63 (ed., 366–367, 372, 411, 445, 465); *Comment. Victor.* I.99–115 (ed., 501–504).

present a suggestive, if not fully developed, treatment of the *complicatio / explicatio* model of the relation between God and the world, a theology later to be systematized by Nicholas of Cusa.[45] To what extent Thierry may have been dependent on Eriugena in this connection is an issue that cannot delay us here,[46] but it is intriguing to note how the Chartres master appears to have reinvented major eriugenaean themes, especially in his form of *exitus-reditus* view of the relation between God and the world. For example, when Thierry speaks of God as 'the unity enfolding (*complicans*) in himself the universe in simplicity', we catch not only hints of Eriugena, but we can also understand why Cusa praised Thierry so highly. Also revealing is the fact that Thierry, like Eckhart and Cusa, used the terms *complicatio* and *explicatio* to understand the nature of the human intellect's relation to God and to the created world. An example can be found in the *Glosa* where he says:

> The soul is made according to the nature of the universe. Now she unfolds herself as it were, and

45. See especially *Lectiones* II.4–14 (ed., 155–159); and *Abbrev. Mon. De Trin.* II.4–11 (ed., 337–340). For a discussion, see Dronke, 'Thierry of Chatres', 368–374. Nicholas of Cusa read the *Lectiones* (often circulating as anonymous) and praised their author as '*vir facile omnium, quos legerim, ingenio clarissimus.* . . . ' See *Nicolai de Cusa Apologia Doctae Ignorantiae*, edited by Raymond Klibansky (Leipzig: Meiner, 1932) 24.

46. The hunt for demonstrable eriugenean sources for Thierry's thought has thus far turned up a rather meagre catch. See, e.g., the cautious remarks of Édouard Jeauneau, 'Le renouveau érigénean du XIIe siècle', *ERIUGENA REDIVIVUS. Zur Wirkungsgeschichte seines Denkens im Mittelalter und im Übergang zur Neuzeit*, edited by Werner Beierwaltes, (Heidelberg: Winter, 1987) 44–45. See also the discussion of a possible eriugenean influence in Dronke, 'Thierry of Chartres', 376 and 383. For a suggestion concerning the 'reinvention' by both Eriugena and Thierry of similar theoretical complexes out of parallel reworkings of elements from Chalcidius and Boethius, consult Stephen Gersh, 'Platonism—Neoplatonism—Aristotelianism. A Twelfth-Century Metaphysical System and Its Sources', *Renaissance and Renewal in the Twelfth Century*, edited by Robert L. Benson and Giles Constable (Cambridge: Harvard, 1982) 523–524, n.52.

now she gathers herself into a certain simplicity, as when she is intelligibility. When she comes down from intelligibility, she enlarges herself, unfolding (*evolvens*) what she enfolded. Every existing thing is that which is found in four modes, for it is enfolded in that simplicity which is God himself.[47]

In sum, Thierry of Chartres had created a new theology of the Trinity and the dialectical relation between the triune God and the created universe. Nevertheless, the mystical potential of this development from the brief text in Augustine's *De doctrina christiana* was to be realized only by his successors.

The triad *unitas - equalitas - concordia / conexio* became fairly popular in the schools in the second half of the twelfth century, though it was not always used as the basis for mathematical speculative trinitarianism.[48] Clarembald of Arras, Thierry's student, used it in his own *Tractatus super Librum Boetii De Trinitate*.[49] It also appears in the pseudo-Hermetic text known as the *De septem septennis*.[50] The formula was discussed by the canons who taught at the abbey of Saint Victor at Paris. Achard of Saint Victor, abbot of the house between 1155 and 1161, used the triad in his treatise *De Trinitate*, but not in his

---

47. *Glosa* II.12 (ed., 271): *Ipsa facta est ad naturam rei uniuerse. Modo enim quasi se explicat, modo in quandam se colligit simplicitatem: ut cum intelligibilitas est, a qua cum demittitur se ampliat euoluens quod implicuerat. Res autem uniuersa talis est quod quatuor modis est. Est namque in quandam simplicitatem complicata que est ipse deus.* The four modes of the existence of created things (*necessitas absoluta-necessitas complexionis-possibilitas absoluta-possibilitas determinata*), a formulation that influenced Cusa, are discussed in *Lectiones* II.9–14 (ed., 157–159).

48. For some brief comments on these uses, see Ludwig Hödl, *Von der Wirklichkeit und Wirksamkeit des dreieinen Gottes nach der appropriativen Trinitätstheologie des 12. Jahrhunderts* (Munich: Max Heuber, 1965) 46–48.

49. *Tractatus super Librum Boetii De Trinitate* II.33–40, in Nikolaus M. Häring, *Life and Works of Clarembald of Arras* (Toronto: PIMS, 1965) 119–123. On Clarenbald, see John R. Fortin, *Clarembald of Arras as a Boethian Commentator* (Kirksville MO: Thomas Jefferson University, 1995).

50. *De septem septennis* 7 (PL 199:961BC): *Haec est illa trium unitas quam solam adorandam esse docuit Pythagoras.*

mystical sermons.[51] Richard of Saint Victor does not employ it in his own *De Trinitate* (c. 1160), but in his brief treatise entitled *De tribus appropriatis personis in Trinitate* he discusses two well-known but controversial trinitarian formulations of the past decades: the abelardian *potentia-sapientia-bonitas* and Thierry's *unitas-aequalitas-conexio*.[52] What is significant about this treatise is that Richard treats the triad, not as describing attributes proper to the three Persons, as Thierry had,[53] but merely as appropriated names, that is, predications which really belong to the divine essence as such and are only 'fittingly' applied to the Persons by reason a mode of knowing drawn from creatures.[54] This is the way in which the triad was treated by Peter Lombard in his *Libri Sententiarum* (c. 1160),[55] as well as by Simon of Tournai in the *Summa* that he composed not long after 1165.[56] There were, nevertheless, some late-twelfth century exceptions to this trend of seeing the triad as expressing appropriated names, notably by another master of the schools who died a Cistercian, Alan of Lille.[57]

51. The treatise has not been fully edited; see the account by M.-Th. d'Alverny, 'Achard de Saint-Victor. De Trinitate-De unitate et pluralitate creaturarum', *Recherches de théologie médiévale* 21(1954):299–306; and the summary in Jean Ribaillier, *Richard de Saint-Victor. Opuscules Théologiques* (Paris: Vrin, 1967) 177–178. The triad also appears in the Ps.-Hugh of Saint Victor, *Quaestiones in epistulas Pauli*, Rom., q. 283 (PL 175:501C).
52. For an edition and discussion of this work, see Ribaillier, *Opuscules Théologiques*, 167–187.
53. Thierry notes in several places that the terms are predicated of the Persons *pro proprietate*, e.g., *Lectiones* V.16 (ed., 218): *Hic enim persona pro proprietate non pro rationabilis nature substantia indiuidua accipitur.*
54. See *De tribus personis appropriatis* (ed., 182–85). Richard does, however, qualify his position somewhat by speaking of *unitas* as *quasi specialiter attribuiter [Patri]* (183).
55. Peter Lombard, *Libi Sententiarum* I, d. 31.2–6.
56. Simon, however, ascribed the formula to Hilary of Poitiers rather than Augustine. See Michael Schmaus, 'Die Texte der Trinitätslehre in den Sentenzen des Simon von Tournai', *Recherches de théologie anciene et médiévale* 4(1932) 66–67.
57. Alan of Lille, *Regulae theologicae* 1 and 4 (PL 210:623CD and 625BC), and *De fide catholicae* Bk. 3.4 (PL 210:405CD).

In the world of monastic theology (by no means to be sharply divided from the world of the schools) consideration of the augustinian formula was not neglected. About 1163, Eberhard of Bamberg wrote to the seer Hildegard of Bingen about the proper understanding of *eternitas-equalitas-conexio* in relation to the Persons of the Trinity.[58] Hildegard's response in Letter 31r, although not directly involved with speculative mathematics, because of the replacement of *unitas* with *eternitas*, is an original rendition of the motif and one that is important for her theology of the Trinity.[59] Since Thierry of Chartres had died as a Cistercian, it is not surprising to see the triad *unitas-aequalitas-conexio* also being used by a late twelfth-century Cistercian, Helinand of Froidmont (1160–1229).[60] In his Second Sermon for the Nativity, probably delivered in the early thirteenth century, Helinand provides a relatively extensive discussion of the formula, beginning from the exploration of *veritas* (i.e, the Second Person of the Trinity) as the 'equality' between what is said and the reality it represents. 'This equality of the existence of things', he says, 'is nothing else than the equality of unity. Equality, like unity, is the form of existence in everything. It is the

---

58. See Epistola 31 in *Hildegardis Bingensis Epistolarium*, edited by Lieven Van Acker, 2 vols. to date (CCCM 91 and 91A; Turnholt: Brepols, 1991, 1993). Vol. 1, 81–82. The replacement of *unitas* by *eternitas* may be explained in part by the context of the original passage in Augustine's *De doctrina christiana* 1.5, which uses *aeternitas* in the sentence immediately preceeding the formula: *Eadem tribus aeternitas, eadem incommutabilitas, eadem maiestas, eadem potestas. In patre unitas, in filio aequalitas, in spiritu sancto unitatis aequalitatisque concordia.*

59. See Ep. 31r in *Epistolarium* 1:83–88. There is a translation of this letter in *The Letters of Hildegard of Bingen. Volume 1*, translated by Joseph L. Baird and Radd K. Ehrman (New York-Oxford: Oxford University Press, 1994) 95–98. Hildegrard's theology of the Son as *equalitas Patris* (84–85), developed on the basis of texts from Genesis 1 and the Johannine Prologue, should be compared with her commentaries on these biblical passages found in her *Liber Divinorum Operum*, edited by Albert Derolez and Peter Dronke (CCCM 92; Turnholt: Brepols, 1996), 252 and 303.

60. For a survey of Helinand and the sparse literature about him, see *The Verses on Death of Helinand of Froidmont*, by Jenny Lind Porter, with an Introduction by William D. Paden (Kalamazoo: Cistercian Publications, 1999).

Bernard McGinn

cause through which each thing exists.'[61] Helinand's development of the theme, however, is more christological than mathematical, and also lacks any treatment of the Holy Spirit as *concordia/conexio*, thus demonstrating that the richness of Thierry's investigations had dissipated by the end of the twelfth century.

Many thirteenth-century scholastics discussed the augustinian triad in their treatments of the Trinity. Following the lead of Peter Lombard, whose *Libri Sententiarum* had become the standard theological textbook in Paris by the 1220s, *unitas-equalitas-concordia* was treated as one of the inherited triads of appropriated names of the Trinity.[62] Typical of these treatments is that of Thomas Aquinas in the lengthy article 8 of question 39 of the *Prima Pars* of the *Summa theologiae*, where he discusses 'Whether the Sacred Doctors fittingly attribute essential names to the Persons'. Here Aquinas provides an extended argument defending the fittingness of Augustine's ascription of these three terms, common to the divine nature as such, to the individual Persons. None of these scholastic treatments contributed to mathematical trinitarianism as such, let alone to a possible trinitarian mysticism based upon it.

It would not be until the fifteenth century with Nicholas of Cusa that the full mystical possibilities of considering the Trinity as the unfolding of the Father, or 'One', whose production of the 'Equal One' necessarily implied the absolute 'Connection' of the non-numerable Persons would have its full effect. Nevertheless, one mystic and *magister* of the late thirteenth and early fourteenth century,

61. Helinand of Froidmont, *Sermo II in Natali Domini* (PL 212:489D-90A): *Haec autem aequalitas existentiae rerum nil aliud est quam aequalitatis unitatis. Est enim aequalitas, sicut et unitas, singulis rebus forma essendi, et causa, per quam unumquodque subsistit.* On Helinand's use, see Chenu, 'Une définition pythagorienne', 11–13. The triadic formula also appears in Helinand's unedited *Chronicon universale*.
62. For sample treatments, see William of Auxerre, *Summa Aurea*, Lib. I, tr. 8, cap. 8, q. 4; Bonaventure, *In I Sent.* d. 31, p. 2, q. 3; Thomas Aquinas, *In I Sent.* d. 31, q. 3, aa. 1–2.

Meister Eckhart, did contribute to this drawing out of the mystical implications of the mathematics of the Trinity and thus served as a forerunner of the renaissance cardinal.

Unlike Thierry of Chartres and Cusa, Eckhart did not develop quadrivial arguments for the Trinity as such. Still, the german Dominican's mystical appropriation of a dialectical trinitarianism is an important missing link between Thierry and Nicholas. In the case of Eckhart, the three components—the augustinian understanding of the Trinity as the multiplication of unity, the boethian analysis of *unum* as beyond number, and dionysian hypernegation—all come together, but within the context of his explicitly mystical teaching based on the soul's 'grounding' identity with God one-and-three.

Eckhart's mysticism is fundamentally trinitarian.[63] His preaching and writing were always meant to encourage breakthrough to a life lived out of the realization that 'God's ground and the soul's ground is one ground'—a specifically trinitarian ground. Though all creation 'lives and moves and has its being' (Acts 17:28) 'from, through, and in' (Romans 11:36) the three Persons of the Trinity, only the intellectual creature, humanity as the *imago Dei*, has the capacity for conscious appropriation of this inner triunal meaning of reality.[64] This appropriation begins from the effort to find some form of language

63. I will cite Eckhart's works according to the critical edition, *Meister Eckhart. Die deutschen und lateinischen Werke* (Stuttgart and Berlin: Kohlhammer, 1936–), using the abbreviation DW for the German works and LW for the Latin works.

64. A key text for the trinitarian character of Eckhart's mysticism is Sermo IV (LW 4:22–32) in which Eckhart takes the text from Romans 11:36, *omnia ex ipso, per ipsum, et in ipso sunt* as expressing proper divine attributes. On Eckhart's trinitarian mysticism, see Raphael Oechslin, 'Eckhart et la mystique trinitaire', *Lumière et Vie* 30(1956) 99–120; Rainer Haucke, *Trinität und Denken. Die Unterscheidung der Einheit von Gott und Mensch bei Meister Eckhart* (Frankfurt: Peter Lang, 1986); P.L. Reynolds, '*Bullitio* and the God beyond God: Meister Eckhart's Trinitarian Theology', *New Blackfriars* 70(1989) 169–181 and 235–244; Alain De Libera, 'L'Un ou la Trinité?', *Revue des sciences*

for describing the immanent life of the Trinity itself, that is, 'the reflexive turning back of existence into itself and upon itself and its dwelling and remaining fixed in itself, . . . the glowing in itself, and melting and boiling in and into itself', that Eckhart called *bullitio*.[65] This divine 'boiling' is rooted in the Father understood as *unum*, or Absolute Unity.

> The One . . . does not produce something like itself, but what is one and the same as itself . . . This is why the formal emanation of the divine Persons is a kind of boiling, and thus the three Persons are simply and absolutely one. The production of creatures, however, is a creation that takes place not through formal emanation, but efficient emanation and as an end.[66]

Eckhart's main purpose here is to emphasize the difference between the inner-trinitarian dynamism by which the three coequal Persons are produced (i.e., 1 X 1) from all other forms of production (i.e., 1 x 2, and so on), that is, the *ebullitio* involved in creation (*creatio*) and in all making (*factio*).[67] At the same time, he is anxious to maintain

---

religieuses 70(1996) 31–47; and Bernard McGinn, 'Sermo IV. "Ex ipso, per ipsum et in ipso sunt omnia" ', *LECTURA ECKHARDI. Predigten Meister Eckharts von Fachgelehrten gelesen und gedeutet*, edited by Georg Steer and Loris Sturlese (Stuttgart: Kohlhammer, 1998) 289–316.

65. *Expositio Libri Exodi* n. 16 (LW 2:21): . . . *rursus ipsius esse quandam in se ipsum et super se ipsum reflexivam conversionem et in se ipso mansionem sive fixionem; adhuc autem quandam bullitionem sive parturitionem sui—in se fervens et in se ipso et in se ipsum liquescens et bulliens.* . . .

66. *Expositio Evangelii secundum Iohannem* n. 342 (LW 3:291): *Unum.* . . . *proprie non producit simile, sed unum et idem se ipsum.* . . . *Hinc est quod in divinis personis emanatio est formalis quaedam bullitio* [rather than the *ebullitio* of the edition], *et propter hoc tres personae sunt simpliciter unum et absolute. Creaturarum vero productio est per modum non formalis, sed efficientis et finis creatio.*

67. The dialectical character of the relation between God and the world appears throughout Eckhart's works, nowhere more powerfully than in the famous text on God as *unum* in the *Expositio Libri Sapientiae* nn. 144–157 (LW 2:481–494).

the inner connection between these types of production: the formal emanation of the Persons in the Trinity is the ground of every other activity.[68] This is why Eckhart, like Thierry of Chartres, but unlike Thomas Aquinas, does not hesitate to present 'necessary reasons', or *a-priori* demonstrations, of the Trinity.

Eckhart's descriptions of the relation between the divine ground and the inner emanation of the Persons form a series of complex variations on a set of common themes spread across his latin and vernacular works. In the german sermons he often emphasizes the role of the Father as the source or principle of the whole divine life in a way analogous to that found in Bonaventure.[69] This language has parallels in those places in the latin works where his discussion of the processions in the Trinity concentrate on how the Father, to whom we ascribe the term *unitas/unum*, or 'the One', gives rise to the other Persons. 'Thus he who proceeds by a real procession [i.e., the Son] is the very essence of him who brings forth within the One, into the One, and the One himself [i.e., the Father]. He proceeds from him who brings forth insofar as the One who brings forth is one. This is why the saints very aptly attribute Unity to the Father in the deity.'[70] Eckhart's teaching here is a dialectical version of the relationship first hinted at in the augustinian *unitas-aequalitas-conexio*, and subsequently developed by Thierry of Chartres.

68. See, e.g., Sermo XXV n. 258 (LW 4:236). This theme, central to Eckhart's teaching, is often developed on the basis of an exegesis of Ps 61:2; e.g., *Expositio Libri Genesis* n. 7 (LW 1:191); *In Iohannem* n. 73 (LW 3:61).

69. E.g., Pr. 15 (DW 1:252): . . . *der vater ist ain begin der gothait, wan er begriffet sich selber in im selber.* Cf. Pr. 12, 13, 21, 22, 26, 49, 51. For Bonaventure's teaching on the Father as *fontalis plenitudo*, see Ewert Cousins, *Bonaventure and the Coincidence of Opposites* (Chicago: Franciscan Herald Press, 1978) 52–54.

70. *Liber parabolorum Genesis* n. 215 (LW 1:691): . . . *sed sic procedens reali processione est ipsa essentia producentis intra unum, in uno, et ipsum unum procedit enim a producente in quantum producens unum est. Propter quod sancti optime patri in divinis attribuunt unitatem.*

This is not to say that Eckhart was directly influenced
by Thierry. Rather, his treatment of the mathematics of
the Trinity was more dependent on Macrobius, Boethius,
and Proclus. With regard to terms ascribed to the Trinity,
for example, the Dominican's standard procedure is to
attribute *unum* to the Father, *verum* to the Son, and *bonum*
to the Holy Spirit,[71] rather than to use the *De doctrina
christiana* formula itself. But Eckhart also suggests that
the Son can be spoken of as the *aequalitas* of the Father,
and the Holy Spirit as the *concordia*, *conexio*, or *nexus* of
the other two divine Persons. This is evident in a key
passage from the *Expositio Evangelii secundum Iohannem*,
one which is framed in the typically Eckhartian language
of the relation of the just person to Justice:

> We often say, 'The just person insofar as he is just is
> Justice itself, and does the works of Justice'. The
> term 'insofar as' (*in quantum*) is a reduplication.
> Reduplication, as the word testifies, speaks of the
> bond (*nexus*) or ordering of two things. Reduplica-
> tion expresses the folding together of two things,
> a fold or bond of two. Thus the Spirit, the third
> Person in the Trinity, is the bond (*nexus*) of the two,
> the Father and the Son.[72]

In terms of our central theme, we could paraphrase this to
read: 'Unity-Justice insofar as it is the Equality of Unity-

71. According to this pattern, *esse* is applied to the divine essence or ground,
unum to the Father, *verum* to the Son, and *bonum* to the Holy Spirit. See,
e.g., *Par. Gen.* n. 12 (LW 1:483); *In Iohannem* nn. 511–512, 516–518, 562
(LW 3:442–445, 446–448, 489–490). In at least one place, however, *unum*
is ascribed to the essence and *ens-verum-bonum* are attributed to the three
Persons (*In Iohannem* n. 359–360 [LW 3:304–306]).
72. *In Iohannem.* n. 438 (LW 3:376): . . . *dicimus et solemus dicere: iustus, in
quantum iustus, est ipsa iustitia, facit opera iustitiae et similia. Li in quantum autem
reduplicatio est; reduplicatio vero, sicut ipsum vocabulum testatur, dicit nexum et
ordinem duorum; dicitur enim reduplicatio duorum replicatio, plica et nexus duorum.
Sic spiritus, tertia in trinitate persona, nexus est duorum, patris et filii.*

Justice is so by the Absolute Nexus or Connection of Unity-Justice'.[73]

We should note that Eckhart speaks of the transcendental predicates of *esse-unum-verum-bonum* as appropriated terms, in the language of Peter Lombard and Thomas Aquinas. Nevertheless, his understanding of appropriation is not the same as that found in the other scholastic masters. Eckhart's rigorous apophaticism, which allows only distinctions of reason to be ascribed to God,[74] effectively breaks down any real difference between proper and appropriated terms. As he put in his Latin Sermo IV: 'Everything that is said or written about the Holy Trinity is in no way really so or true'.[75] Like Dionysius, Eckhart always insisted on the limitations of even the most paradoxical formulations. 'God is one without Unity, and three without Trinity, just as he is good without quality', as he once put it.[76]

What the endlessly-inventive verbal strategies of the Dominican are meant to convey is that it is only by the exercise of subverting the claims of all language to adequacy through the dialectical fusion of opposites that we can come to the *docta ignorantia* that is the beginning of wisdom about God. A good summary of the trinitarian application of this logic of reduplication can be found in one of his vernacular sermons:

73. The logic of the reduplicating formulae found in Eckhart and later in Cusa is rooted in the *in quantum* principle which Eckhart summarized thus in his Cologne Defense: *li in quantum, reduplicatio scilicet, excludit omne aliud, omne alienum, etiam secundum rationem, a termino* (*Proc. Col.* I, n. 81).

74. As is well known, a passage to this effect from *In Ex.* nn. 58–60 (LW 2:65–66) was included as the 23rd article in the papal bull of condemnation, *In agro dominico*. For a discussion, see Bernard McGinn, 'Meister Eckhart on God as Absolute Unity', *Neoplatonism and Christian Thought*, edited by Dominic J. O'Meara (Albany: SUNY, 1981) 128–139.

75. Sermo IV.2 n. 30 (LW 4:31): *In summa nota quod omne quod de trinitate beata scribitur aut dicitur, nequaquam sic se habet aut verum est.*

76. Sermo XI.2 n.118 (LW 4:112): *Est enim unus sine trinitate, trinus sine unitate, sicut bonus sine qualitate, etc.*

> Once I preached in Latin on Trinity Sunday and
> said: Distinction comes from Absolute Unity, that
> is, the distinction in the Trinity. Absolute Unity is
> the distinction and the distinction is the unity. The
> greater the distinction, the greater the unity, for it is
> the distinction without distinction . . . The soul has
> a intelligible noetic being; therefore, where God is,
> the soul is, and where the soul is, God is.[77]

In passages like this we begin to sense the mystical dimension of formulating the Trinity in terms of transcendental mathematics.

Trinitarian speculation as a foundation for mysticism has had a complex genealogy in the history of Christianity. My intent in this essay has been to cast some light on one of the lesser-known chapters in the story—the speculative mathematical view of the Trinity first mentioned by Augustine and developed in the mid-twelfth century by Thierry of Chartres. Though this particular form of mathematical trinitarianism may seem strange to us today, its impact on the twelfth century, as well as its subsequent history, has much to say about how the mystery of the Three-in-One has served as the foundation for attempts to seek the ground of authentic living, as well as more intellectual endeavors of trying to speak about what is by nature beyond all speaking and knowing.

---

77. Pr. 10 (DW 1:173.1–12): *Ich predigete einest in latîne, und daz was an dem tage der drîvalticheit, dô sprach ich: der underscheit kumet von der einicheit, der underscheit in der drîvalticheit. Diu einicheit ist der underscheit, und der underscheit ist diu einicheit. Ie der underscheit mêr ist, ie diu einicheit mêr ist, wan daz ist underscheit âne underscheit. . . . Diu sêle hât ein vernūnftic bekennelich wesen;dâ von, swâ got ist, dâ ist diu sêle, und swâ diu sêle ist, dâ ist got.* The reference is not an exact fit with any particular passage in the surviving Latin Sermons for Trinity Sunday, but the teaching is close to what we find in Sermo II n.14, and Sermo IV.1 n.24 (LW 4:14 and 25).

Jean Longère

Centre National de la Recherche Scientifique—
Institut de Recherche et d'Histoire des Textes, Paris

Alanvs de Insvlis:
Sermo ad Clavstrales

I. L'AUTEUR. LA PLACE DU SERMON DANS
L'ARS PRAEDICANDI

C'EST PROBABLEMENT lors de son séjour prolongé dans la région de Montpellier qu'Alain de Lille entra en contact avec les cisterciens, chargés, on le sait, de prêcher contre les hérétiques cathares.[1]

Dans le *Contra Waldenses,* deuxième livre du *De fide catholica contra haereticos*, Alain reproche aux Vaudois de prêcher, alors qu'ils sont illettrés et ignorent les Écritures. Il leur oppose ceux qui, comme de nombreux cisterciens, plus saints et plus instruits en science scripturaire, s'abstiennent cependant du ministère de la parole, parce qu'ils n'ont pas été envoyés à cet effet.[2]

Quand un *abbas cisterciensis* doit s'adresser au peuple en langue romane, Alain met ses talents de lettré et de 'rhéteur', à son service, pour traduire en latin son sermon et le transmettre ainsi à la postérité.[3] Peut-être, cet *abbas*

---

1. Voir, entre autres, *Les Cisterciens de Languedoc (XIIIᵉ–XIVᵉ s.),* Cahiers de Fanjeaux, 21 (Toulouse, Privat, 1986) 410 p.
2. *De fide catholica* II.1: PL 210.379C: '*Quomodo etiam praedicabunt illitterati qui Scripturas non intelligunt? . . . Videmus etiam sanctiores iis non praedicare, qui intellectum sacrae Scripturae habent, ut multos Cistercienses, quia nimirum missi non sunt'.*
3. *Sermo quem composuit abbas Cisterciensis, romanis uerbis, apud Montempessulanum in ecclesia beati Firmini, quem postea magister Alanus transtulit in latinum.* Venite et ascendamus in Bethel et edificemus altare Domino (Gen 30:3). *Venite et*

cisterciensis désigne-t-il Arnaud Almaric, abbé de Grand-selve au diocèse de Toulouse en 1198, puis de Cîteaux, fin 1200 ; légat en 1204, il devient archevêque de Narbonne (1212–1225).[4] Est-ce Arnaud Almaric qui orienta Alain vers Cîteaux, où celui-ci devait mourir en 1203?[5]

En tout cas, l'*Ars Praedicandi* paraît avoir été rédigé par Alain de Lille durant son séjour dans le Midi de la France. Le catharisme, le peu de vigilance du clergé local qu'il dénonce souvent, l'auront incité à écrire des oeuvres d'apologétique comme le *De fide catholica*, ou de pastorale comme le *Liber poenitentialis*,[6] l'*Ars praedicandi,*[7] le *Liber sermonum*[8] souvent rattaché au précédent par la tradition manuscrite, et d'autres sermons isolés.[9]

Le sermon 43 de l'*Ars praedicandi* n'est pas particulièrement destiné aux cisterciens. Il est adressé *ad claustrales* en général, ce qui inclut, outre les moines blancs, les moines noirs, et nombre de congrégations canoniales alors en plein développement.

Ce s. 43 se situe dans la dernière partie de l'*Ars praedicandi*, où l'on peut distinguer, après une introduction sur la prédication en général (s.1), trois grands ensembles:

ascendamus in Bethel: ecce uia . . . Dijon BM, f° 73v-95; Paris, B.N. lat. 14859, f° 233–234, N. acq. lat. 547, f° 159 v -161 (anon.). Voir M-Th. d'Alverny, *Alain de Lille. Textes inédits, avec une introduction sur sa vie et ses oeuvres,* Études de philosophie médiévale, 52 (Paris, 1965), 139.

4. Voir É. GRIFFE, 'Amalric (Arnaud)', dans *Catholicisme*, 1 (1948), c 393–394; M-Th. d'Alverny, *Alain de Lille*, 15.

5. M. Lebeau, 'Découverte du tombeau du bienheureux Alain de Lille', *Collectanea OCR* 22 (1961) 254–260.

6. Alain De Lille, *Liber poenitentialis.* T.I. *Introduction doctrinale et littéraire.* T.II. *La tradition longue.* Texte inédit publié et annoté par J. Longère, Analecta Mediaeualia Namurciensia, 17–18 (Louvain–Lille, 1965); J.Longère, 'Alain de Lille '. *Liber poenitentialis.* Les traditions moyenne et courte' dans *AHDLMA*, 32, année 1965 (1966), 169–242.

7. PL 210:109–195D.

8. Liste des vingt-sept sermons du *Liber sermonum*, dans M-Th. d'Alverny, *Alain de Lille,* 125–127.

9. J. Longère, 'Alain de Lille (+1203), prédicateur', *Les sermons au temps de la Renaissance*, Société intern. de rech. interdisciplinaires sur la Renaissance (Paris: Sorbonne, 1999), 125–142.

s. 2–10, s. 26–28: contre les vices; s. 11–25, s. 29–37: les vertus, le sacrement de pénitence; s. 38–47: qui doit prêcher (le *praelatus*, s. 38); à qui: chevaliers, hommes de loi, cloîtrés, prêtres, gens mariés, veuves, vierges.

Appeler 'sermons' les quarante-sept divisions de l'*Ars praedicandi* rend compte du but visé par Alain: fournir aux prédicateurs des matériaux pour leur tâche, mais cela risque de favoriser une interprétation quelque peu faussée de l'oeuvre. Car il s'agit moins de sermons tout faits que de citations bibliques, patristiques, profanes ou de réflexions personnelles d'Alain pouvant aider le prédicateur à bâtir lui-même ses propres exhortations. En somme, une anthologie sommaire, quelque peu commentée, des données de l'Écriture et de la Tradition, où le prédicateur peut puiser idées et références aux autorités. D'ailleurs, les copistes ne se sont guère engagés dans la qualification des subdivisions: si les rubriques *sermo* ou plutôt *inuitatio* peuvent être présentes, la plupart du temps il n'y a pas d'autre indication que celle du thème traité (*contra gulam*, *de prudentia* . . .), ou de l'auditoire visé (*ad milites*, *ad claustrales* . . .).

La *Patrologie latine* parle de *capitula* plutôt que de *sermones*, ce qui finalement rend davantage compte de l'oeuvre considérée dans sa totalité. Mais quand on traite un chapitre en particulier de l'*Ars praedicandi*, comme dans le présent article, le qualifier de *sermo* se justifie et permet un rattachement immédiat à un genre littéraire précis.

Sans remonter à des Pères comme Augustin ou Grégoire, ou à des auteurs tels Raban Maur (+856), Alain s'insère par l'*Ars praedicandi* dans une tradition ancienne et surtout un contexte pastoral proche d'aide aux prédicateurs,[10] comme le manifestent le traité *Quo ordine sermo*

---

10. Voir Marianne G. Briscoe, *Artes praedicandi*, Typologie des sources du Moyen Age occidental, 61 (Turnhout, 1992), 1–76, qui ne dispense pas de recourir à Th-M. Charland, *Artes praedicandi. Contribution à l'histoire de*

debet fieri de Guibert de Nogent (+1124),[11] le *Speculum ecclesiae* d'Honorius Augustodunensis (+ vers 1150),[12] les introductions aux trois parties du recueil inédit de Maurice de Sully (+1196),[13] quelques chapitres du *Verbum abbreuiatum* de Pierre le Chantre (+1197).[14] Mais ces auteurs se limitaient globalement à des considérations morales et spirituelles sur la personne et la fonction du prédicateur, ou à des conseils pratiques sur l'adaptation à l'auditoire, les gestes à faire, la manière de parler.

Avec la dernière partie de l'*Ars praedicandi*, Alain inaugure vraiment le genre sermon *ad status*, aux différents états de vie, qu'illustreront au XIIIe siècle Jacques de Vitry (+1240), par la série de soixante-quatorze *Sermones uulgares*,[15] Guibert de Tournais OFM (+1284), auteur de quatre-vingt-dix *Sermones de diuersis statibus et officiis*, très dépendant du précédent,[16] Humbert de Romans o.p. (+1277), dans la seconde partie du *De eruditione praedicatorum*.[17]

Par rapport à ses successeurs, Alain de Lille fait oeuvre plus courte: ainsi, un chapitre de l'*Ars praedicandi* équivaut, au plus, au dixième d'un sermon de la série *ad*

la rhétorique au Moyen Age, Publications de l'Institut d' études médiévales d'Ottawa, 7 (Paris-Ottawa, 1936), 421p. Sommaire sur les Artes praedicandi des XIIe–XVe siècles, dans J. Longère, La prédication médiévale (Paris, 1983) 195–200.
11. PL 156:21–32.
12. PL 172:807–1108.
13. J.Longère, Les sermons latins de Maurice de Sully, évêque de Paris (+ 1196). Contribution à l'histoire de la tradition manuscrite, Instrumenta patristica, 16 (Steenbrugge-Dordrecht, 1988) 491 p.
14. PL 205:36–44.
15. J. B. Schneyer, Repertorium der lateinischen Sermones des Mittelalters für die Zeit von 1150-1350 (Autoren: I-J), BGPTM 43/3 (Münster W., 1971) 212-221. Liste des sermons ad status édités de Jacques de Vitry, dans Jacques de Vitry, Histoire occidentale. Trad. Gaston Duchet-Suchaux, introduction et notes par J. Longère, Sagesses chrétiennes (Paris, 1997) 24–26.
16. J. B. Schneyer, Repertorium (Autoren E-H), BGPTM 43/2 (Münster W, 1970) 299–307.
17. Voir Bibliotheca maxima Veterum Patrum, 25 (Lyon, 1677) 426–567.

status de Jacques de Vitry. Il embrasse surtout un nombre beaucoup plus restreint d'états de vie: au bref chapitre *ad claustrales* de l'*Ars*, correspondent chez Jacques de Vitry: deux sermons *ad monachos nigros*, deux *ad monachos albos*, deux *ad moniales nigras,* deux *ad moniales albas*, trois *ad canonicos*, deux *ad eremitas*, sans parler des autres catégories de religieux (*fratres minores*, *fratres ordinis militaris*, *hospitales* . . .) absents du traité d'Alain.

Cet arrière-plan oratoire et pastoral doit rester présent à l'esprit pour une bonne interprétation de l'*Ars*, dans son ensemble, et du c. 43 *ad claustrales* en particulier.

II. CONTENU DU SERMON

La première citation scripturaire du thème se termine par *in unum*; la seconde commence par *unam:* tout le sermon va porter sur l'unité (1).

Après une rapide affirmation sur la valeur de l'unité en 'philosophie naturelle', Alain souligne que 'l'unité spirituelle' est nécessaire ici-bas à la vie de grâce, au-delà à la vie glorieuse. Sans elle, tout dépérit: la religion, l'amour fraternel, la foi, l'obéissance. À l'inverse, elle manifeste la consonance et la concorde (2).

Puis Alain distingue trois unités: supercéleste, céleste, subcéleste.

La première, supercéleste, se subdivise elle-même en trois. 'Unité unissante et unie': le saint Esprit qui unit le Père et le Fils. 'Unité unissante non unie': la nature divine, qui unit les trois personnes entre elles, mais qui ne leur est pas unie, car elle n'est pas une personne. 'Unité unie, non unissante': le Père (3).

La deuxième unité, dite céleste, est celle des anges. Unité de nature par leur ministère d'envoyés; unité de grâce et de gloire. Une juxtaposition, par deux, de mots opposés (*concors dissonantia*, *unita pluralitas* . . .) souligne la concorde dans la diversité des offices (4).

La troisième unité, subcéleste, doit exister dans l'Église: foi, charité, obéissance. Plusieurs réminiscences scripturaires soulignent le caractère unique du témoin biblique (5). Mais l'application qu'en fait Alain à la vie de l'Église ne paraît pas s'imposer.

On passe ensuite à l'unité trine, vécue au cloître, et qui doit se manifester dans l'observance religieuse (6), puis le renoncement aux biens propres et à la propriété commune (7), enfin la charité fraternelle (8). On a, là, un enseignement plus direct et pratique, le coeur du sermon, puisqu'il s'agit de vie claustrale, alors que les trilogies précédentes, d'inspiration fortement théologique et se rapportant à la Trinité, aux anges et à l'Église, pourraient figurer dans un grand nombre d'exhortations adressées à des publics diversifiés. Le ton n'est polémique, avec retenue d'ailleurs, que dans les reproches concernant les infractions aux observances vestimentaires et alimentaires, aux vigiles et aux jeûnes, au silence. Alain dénonce tout ce qui traduit les accommodements avec la règle claustrale et le relâchement personnel ou communautaire.

L'exhortation relative à l'unité de la charité est plus positive: Alain encourage à l'attention active envers le frère, qu'il soit pécheur, moins instruit ou malade.

En finale, Alain rapporte à la vie claustrale la triple division faite au début: 'supercéleste, céleste, subcéleste'(2), avec chaque fois une triple application à la vie claustrale.

Comment peut être vécue au cloître la première unité supercéleste (la Trinité). C'est le supérieur (*praelatus*) qui est facteur 'd'unité unissante et unie': unissant ses sujets par son autorité, il est uni à eux par la charité. 'Unité unie non unissante', celle du sujet, du religieux, qui n'est pas structurellement principe d'unité, mais qui est relié aux autres par la charité. 'Unité unissante, non unie', la charité elle-même qui unit les cloîtrés entre eux, sans faire cependant pleinement corps avec chacun ici-bas.

Correspondant à l'unité céleste (des anges), celle de la nature, que les cloîtrés doivent aimer en eux; celle de

la grâce, qu'il leur faut mutuellement partager; celle de
la gloire éternelle, vers laquelle ils tendent d'une même
espérance.

La troisième unité, subcéleste (de l'Église) se vit au
cloître par la foi qui préserve de l'hérésie, la charité qui
empêche le schisme, l'espérance opposée à toute forme
d'obstination (9). Ainsi le moine est-il ici-bas témoin
privilégié de trois unités: celle de la Trinité, des anges et
de l'Église.

Le sermon peut s'achever par une reprise des citations
bibliques initiales, dont la première (*Ecce quam bonum et
quam iucundum habitare fratre in unum*), propose ici une
très brève glose, sans lien strict avec les développements
antérieurs.

Le s.43 *ad claustrales*, est fort bien construit, comme
en témoignent cette forme d'inclusion que constitue, en
finale, la reprise des thèmes scripturaires, et surtout la
structure trinaire (autour de *celestis*) dont chacun des
termes donne lieu à une nouvelle subdivision trinaire.
Certes, une telle construction peut sembler artificielle et
constituer aujourd'hui un obstacle plus qu'une aide à la
lecture. De ce procédé rhétorique, les *Artes praedicandi*
postérieurs et les sermons qu'ils inspireront donneront
maints autres exemples. On n'oubliera pas qu'en lien avec
les phrases rythmées et parfois rimées, la division voulait
favoriser la mémorisation par l'orateur et l'auditeur.

III. LES SOURCES

Les psaumes 132:1 et 26:4 ont inspiré le thème. A la
subdivision 5, on a cinq allusions à des personnages
ou épisodes bibliques, symboles d'unicité ou d'unité.
Ailleurs aussi, il s'agit le plus souvent de réminiscences
plutôt que de citations explicites.

Le Nouveau Testament intervient plus souvent que
l'Ancien: douze références sur dix-sept. Pour l'Ancien
Testament, outre les deux psaumes du thème, Alain

renvoie deux fois à la Genèse (5 et 7), une fois à Job
et à II Samuel (5).

Mathieu, Luc, Jean interviennent chacun trois fois; les
Actes deux fois, Éphésiens et Hébreux une fois chacun.
Mais, là encore, les citations explicites sont rares: à la
limite Jean 17:11, 22:22 (3); plus nettement Mathieu
19:27 et Luc 14:33 (C 7), Éphésiens 4:5–6 (C 5),
Hébreux 1:14 (4).

La liturgie est présente par les premiers versets de
l'hymne de Tierce (3).

Un seul auteur est nommé: Hilaire (3, à la fin); même
si l'on peut trouver chez Hilaire un texte assez proche, la
source est plus sûrement Augustin, *De doctrina christiana*,
à travers quelque florilège.

Bernard de Clairvaux a inspiré l'image du baiser, sym-
bole de l'Esprit et de l'amour que se portent le Père et
le Fils (3).

Cependant, si l'on peut dire, l'auteur à qui Alain se
réfère le plus est lui-même. Ainsi un sermon et les *Regulae
coelestis iuris* proposent la triple division: supercéleste,
céleste, subcéleste. De même, les *Regulae* et l'*Elucidatio
in Cantica canticorum* reprennent l'image du baiser pour
l'Esprit saint. Et l'amour de la nature, recommandé au
moine (9) est un thème cher à l'auteur du *De planctu
naturae*.

La répétition ou mieux l'emprunt à soi-même ne sont
pas l'apanage du seul Alain de Lille. Chaque auteur,
chaque prédicateur, hier et aujourd'hui, a ses thèmes
de prédilection; il est humain et normal d'y revenir et
d'utiliser également un même et fécond ensemble de
sources et de citations. Mais, plus que d'autres, Alain
semble avoir travaillé par 'fiches'; il n'hésite pas à re-
produire, à réinsérer, d'un ouvrage à l'autre, les mêmes
développements, ce qui peut d'ailleurs faciliter la solution
des problèmes d'authenticité.[18]

18. Voir, par exemple, Alain De Lille, *Liber poenitentialis*, 1.I. *Introduction*. . . .
par J. Longère (*supra*, n. 6) 133–160.

Si Alain semble donner parfois l'impression d'une écriture trop rapide, le sermon 43 *ad claustrales* souligne plusieurs aspects de sa personnalité : vigueur et rigueur théologique, formation rhétorique, sens de l'observation, haute estime de la vie cloîtrée et de sa place dans l'Église.

Note sur l'édition de s. 43 *ad claustrales*

Dans le but de publier un jour l'*Ars praedicandi* et le *Liber sermonum* qui l'accompagne, la presque totalité des manuscrits proposant ces deux oeuvres a été photographiée : les microfilms sont à l'IRHT, 40 avenue d'Iéna, 75116 Paris.

La publication provisoire du s. 43 s'appuie sur un groupe de témoins, dont quelques-uns : Città del Vaticano, Reg. Lat. 424; Paris B.N.F., N.a.l. 335; Dijon B.M. 211; München, Clm 4616, reproduisent, selon M-Th. d'Alverny, 'une édition mise au point du vivant de l'auteur de l'*Ars praedicandi* et du *Liber sermonum*, et constituent une base solide pour la publication de l'ensemble'.[19]

Les variantes, nombreuses pour un texte assez court, mettent cependant en valeur la complexité de la tradition textuelle et laissent entrevoir les difficultés d'une édition voulant tenir compte de l'ensemble de la diffusion manuscrite (plus de cent témoins).

∼

---

19. Voir M-Th. d'Alverny, *Alain de Lille*, 113. Description des manuscrits, *ibid.*, pp. 111–119.

ALANVS DE INSVLIS

SERMO AD CLAVSTRALES[a]

V   Città del Vaticano, Bibliotheca Apostolica. Reginenses
    latini 424 (Paris, Sainte-Geneviève?), f° 43r–44r
P   Paris, Bibliothèque nationale de France , Nouvelles
    acquisitions latines 335 (Cluny), f° 73r–75r
D   Dijon, Bibliothèque municipale 211 (Cîteaux), f°
    114r–115v
M   München, Bayerische Staatsbibliothek, Clm 4616
    (Benediktbeuern), f° 78va–80 ra
T   Toulouse, Bibliothèque municipale 195 (Augustins),
    f° 65r–66r
L   London, British Museum 19767 (Ottöbeuren), f°
    46ra–vb
Bg Burgge, Stadsbibliotheek 193 (Ter Doest), f° 129 vb–
    131 rb

Cfr. PL 210, 189B-191 C; PL 217, 671–674B (Ps.
INNOCENTIVS III)

< 1 > Ad claustrales loquens Scriptura ait: ECCE QVAM
BONVM ET QVAM IVCVNDVM HABITARE FRATRES IN VNVM.[a1]
   Et alibi psalmista in persona claustralis ait: VNAM PECII
A DOMINO: HANC[b] REQVIRAM, VT[c] INHABITEM IN DOMO DO-
MINI, OMNIBVS DIEBVS VITE MEE[2].

< 2 > Cum apud naturalem[a] philosophum unitas celeber-
rimis[b] annotetur misteriis,[c] apud teologum non minoribus
subiacet sacramentis.
   Sine[d] unitate, spirituali, nec in presenti gratia[e] habere-

---

1a. (rubrica) sermo ad claustrales (P D, ad claustrales L Bg, om. V M T
1. Ps 132:1.
1b. hanc . . . mee (etc. L
1c. ut . . . mee (etc. Bg
2. Ps 26:4.
2a. naturalem (moralem Bg
2b. celeberrimis (om. prius T sed corr. marg.
2c. misteriis (laudibus Bg
2d. sine (nam praem. Bg
2e. gratia nec in presenti T

tur, nec in futuro gloria conferetur. Sine unitate, omnis exuflatur religio. Sine unitate,[f] languescit fraterna[g] dilectio. Sine unitate,[h] fides[i] perit. Sine unitate,[j] obedientia deficit.

Vnitas in diuinis parit consonantiam, in angelis concordiam, in ecclesiis obedientiam.

Est enim unitas supercelestis, unitas celestis, unitas subcelestis.[3]

De unitate[a]

< 3 > Vnitas supercelestis est unitas in concordia Trinitatis. Ibi[b] est unitas uniens et unita. Et est ibi unitas uniens non[c] unita.[d] Et est ibi unitas non uniens sed unita.[e]

Vnitas uniens et unita est Spiritus sanctus, qui unit Patrem[f] cum Filio. Vnde dicitur:[g] *Vnus Pater[h] cum Filio.*[i][4]

2f. sine unitate (*om. Bg*
2g. fraterna (superna *T Bg*
2h. sine unitate (*om. Bg*
2i. fides (ipsa *add. Bg*
2j. sine unitate (*om. Bg*
3. Cf. Sermo *Rorate coeli desuper, Is* 45:8. Ut sancti Patres testantur, PL 210:216D: 'Prima terra est ad quam uiandum; secunda, per quam uiandum; tertia, iuxta quam uiandum. Prima, supercoelestis; secunda, coelestis; tertia, subcoelestis'; *Regulae coelestis iuris, Reg. II,* PL 210:623D: 'In supercoelesti unitas, in coelesti alteritas, in subcoelesti pluralitas. Supercoeleste est Deus, in quo summa est unitas. Coeleste est angelus in quo primo est alteritas . . . In subcoelesti uero, ut in istis corporeis, dicitur esse plena pluralitas, quia multiplici uarietati est obnoxium'; *Règles de théologie,* suivi de *Sermon sur la sphère intelligible.* Introduction, traduction et notes par Françoise Hudry, Sagesses chrétiennes (Paris, 1995) p. 100 s.
       Les trois termes utilisés par Alain peuvent être compris comme un abrégé de l'oeuvre du Pseudo-Denys, dont il s'inspire ici: *supercelestis* (*Noms divins* et *Théologie mystique*), *celestis* (*Hiérarchie céleste*), *subcelestis* (*Hiérarchie ecclésiastique*).
3a. de unitate (*om. M T L Bg.*
3b. ubi (ibi *Bg*
3c. non (nec *Bg*
3d. et est ibi . . . unita (*M T Bg, om. V P D*
3e. et unita . . . sed unita (sed non unita *L*
3f. patrem unit *M T Bg*
3g. unde dicitur (*om. V L*
3h. unus Pater (unus Patri *T,* unum Patri *Bg*
3i. unde . . . Filio (*om.D*
4. Cf. Ioh 17:11, 21, 22.

Et alibi dicitur esse osculum et amor Patris et Filii.[5] Et est unitas unita, quia unitur Patri cum Filio, mediante diuina natura.[j] Vnitas uniens non unita est[k] diuina natura,[l] que tres personas sibi inuicem unit,[m] sed eis non unitur quia ipsa non est persona.[n] Vnitas unita non uniens est Pater, quia unitur Filio et Spiritu sancto, sed neuter eorum unitur eo. De unitate uniente et unita dicitur:

Nunc sancte nobis Spiritus
Unum Patri cum Filio.[o6]

De uniente[p] non unita dicitur: 'In maiestate unitas'.

De unitate unita non uniente, dicit Hilarius:[q] 'In Patre unitas, in Filio equalitas, in Spiritu sancto unitatis equalitatisque connexio'.[r7]

5. 'Et alibi dicitur esse osculum et amor Patris et Filii': Bernardus Claraevallensis, *Sermones de diuersis*, 89.1; in *Sancti Bernardi opera*, ed. J. Leclercq, H. Rochais, 6/1: 336; PL 183:707B: 'Si igitur se inuicem osculantur Pater et Filius, quid est eorum osculum nisi Spiritus sanctus?' SBOp 1:37; PL 183:811C: 'Nempe si recte Pater osculans, Filius osculatus accipitur, non erit ab re osculum Spiritum sanctum intelligi, utpote qui Patris Filiique imperturbabilis pax sit, gluten firmum, indiuiduus amor, indiuisibilis unitas.' Cfr. Alanus De Insulis, *Elucidatio in Cantica canticorum*, I; PL 210:53D: 'Aliud osculum est Spiritus sancti quo Patrem osculatur Filius, quo Pater Filium diligit, qui Patrem et Filium unit, qui est amborum amor, nexus et osculum'; *Regulae coelestis iuris*, *Reg. III*; PL 210:624D: 'Spiritus sanctus dicitur ardor, amor, osculum et connexio Patris et Filii, quia Pater spiritaler conuenit eum Filio in spirando Spiritum sanctum'; Alain de Lille, *Règles de théologie* . . . trad. F. Hudry, (supra n. 3) pp. 103–104.
3j. natura diuina *T*
3k. diuina natura est *D*
3l. unitas uniens . . . natura (*om. L per hom.*
3m. sibi inuicem unit personas *M*
3n. sed eis . . . persona (*Bg*, sed eis non unitur quia est ipse persona *V P D*, sed ipsa eis non unitur quia persona *T*, et eis non unitur quia ipse est persona *L*
3o. unum . . . Filio (*etc L*
6. Hymnus ad Tertiam.
3p. uniente (unitate *D L Bg*
3q. dicit Hilarius dicitur ab Hilario *L*
3r. in Filio . . . connexio (*M, T* (*non* connexio *sed* communitas, (*om. V P D L Bg*
7. Rectius Augustinus, *De doctrina christiana* 1.5.5, ed. J. Martin, CCSL 32 (1962) 9; PL 34:21: 'In Patre unitas, in Filio aequalitas, in Spiritu sancto

De trina unitate[a]

< 4 > Vnitas uero[b] celestis est in angelis[c] et est in eis[d] trina unitas:[e] unitas nature, unitas gratie, unitas glorie. Vnitas nature, quia *omnes sunt spiritus anministratorii.*[f][8] Vnitas gratie, quia[g] sunt[h] in gratia confirmati. Vnitas glorie, quia omnes sunt in[i] eterna beatitudine glorificati.

In hoc tamen[j] triplici unitate est diuersitas in dignitatum magisteriis, in officiorum ministeriis,[k] in cognoscendis archanorum[l] misteriis.[m] Est ergo ibi[n] concors dissonantia, consonans[o] discordia, diuersa unitas, unita[p] pluralitas,[q] dissensus consentiens, diuersitas uniens.

< 5 > Vnitas[a] uero subcelestis est[b] in Ecclesia et debet

unitatis aequalitatisque concordia, et tria haec unum omnia propter Patrem, aequalia omnia propter Filium, connexa omnia propter Spiritum sanctum'. Cfr. Hilarius, *De Trinitate* 3.4, ed. P. Smulders, CCSL 62 (1979) p. 75: 'Haec in Filio et in Patre unitas, haec uirtus, haec caritas, haec spes, haec fides, haec ueritas uia uita, non calumniari de uirtitubus suis Deo, nec per secretum ac potestatem natiuitatis obtrectare Filio, Patri ingenito nihil conparare, unigenitum ab eo nec tempore nec uirtute discernere, Deum Filium quia ex Deo est confiteri.'

4a. de trina unitate (*om. M T L Bg*
4b. uero (autem *Bg*
4c. angelis (angelorum concordia *M T Bg*
4d. in eis est *L*
4e. unitas . . . trina(unitas celestis est in angelorum concordia et est ibi triplex *M, T (om.*ibi)
4f. amministratorii spiritus *M*
8. Heb 1:14
4g. quia (in qua *L*
4h. sunt (*om. Bg*
4i. in (*om. M T*
4j. tamen (*om. Bg,* tamen hac *P,* hac tamen hic *D*
4k. in officiorum ministeriis (*om T Bg*
4l. archanorum (angelorum *P*
4m. in cognoscendiis . . . misteriis (*om. L*
4n. ergo (enim *T,* etiam *Bg*
4o. consonans (et *praem. T*
4p. unita (*om. P D,* unitas *V,* et *praem. P*
4q. pluralitas (equalitas *M,* diversitas *Bg*
5a. unitas (de unitate subcelesti *rub. marg. D*
5b. est (*om. T*

esse^c trina: unitas fidei, unitas caritatis, unitas obedientie, ut inferiores superioribus^d obediant, superiores inferioribus^e moderata mansuetudine^f condescendant.

Ad insinuandum^g huius spiritualis^h unitatis meritum, unus qui descendit^i in piscinam saluatur,^j[9] unus filius uidue suscitatur,[10] archa in uno cubito consummatur,[11] ad nuntiandum Dauid uictoriam unus mittitur,[12] unus qui^k nuntiat Iob mortem filiorum a periculo^l liberatur.[13]

Omnia que ad ecclesiasticam^m unitatem^n pertinent, amplectitur unitas, omnia informat singularitas. Est enim *unus Deus, una fides, unum baptisma*,[14] una lex, unus rex,^o una gratia, una gloria.

< 6 > Inter claustrales^a autem^b similiter debet esse trina unitas: unitas religionis, unitas possessionis,^c unitas caritatis.^d

Unitas religionis ut sint uniformes in habitu, uniformes^e

5c. debet esse et *M*, esse debet et *Bg*
5d. superioribus inferiores *Bg*
5e. inferioribus (minoribus *M Bg*
5f. mansuetudine (consuetudine *Bg*
5g. insinuandum (ergo *add. Bg*
5h. spiritualis (*om. Bg*
5i. qui descendit (descendens *Bg*
5j. saluatur (sanatur *Bg*
9. Cf. Ioh 5:4–9
10. Cf. Luc 7:11–17
11. Cf. Gen 6:16
12. Cf. 2 Reg 11:22 et 18:24
5k. qui (*post* filiorum *Bg*
5l. a periculo (*om.T*
13. Cf. Iob 1:18–19
5m. ecclesiasticam unitatem (ecclesiasticum statum *Bg*
5n. unitatem (dignitatem *T*
14. Eph 4:5–6
5o. unus rex (una ecclesia *add. Bg*
6a. claustrales (religiosos *Bg*
6b. autem (*om. T*, etiam *L*, itaque *Bg*
6c. possessionis (passionis *V D*
6d. unitas possessionis, unitas caritatis (*om. M per hom.*
6e. uniformes (*om. Bg*

in uictu, uniformes[e] in ieiuniis, uniformes[e] in uigiliis. Sed quidam anomali se a regula huius unitatis excipiunt,[f] cupientes mollioribus accumbere stratis, paucioribus interesse uigiliis, modico uel nullo uti silentio, delicatioribus uti[g] cibariis.[h]

Quidam enim monachi uilem habitum quoquo[i] modo insigniunt, aut pulueris excussione, aut quadam partium eleganti dispositione, quia aut pedes in calceis[j] artius ponunt, aut manicas stringunt,[k] aut capucium super omnes reflectunt.

Cibos[l] pro posse suo delicatiores appetunt et, in quantum possunt, si non materiam saltem[m] mutant formam, quia si unus uult fabas uel alios cibos tenues parari[n] uno modo, alius uult alio.[o]

Quidam silencia[p] frangunt, etsi non uerbis saltem signis; et sic fabulas uerborum redimunt pluralitate signorum.

Quidam uigilias aut intermittunt, aut intercidunt.[q]

< 7 > Vnitas[a] etiam[b] debet esse in possessione, ut omnia eis sint communia.

Nihil enim proprium debet habere monachus, quia nec proprium debet habere in possidendo, nec proprium in uolendo.[c]

6f. excipiunt (se *praem.* P
6g. uti (uesci *M T*
6h. delicatioribus uti cibariis modico uel nullo uti silencio *Bg*
6i. quoquo (quodam *M*
6j. calceis (calceos *M*
6k. aut manicas stringunt *om. M T*
6l. cibos (quoque *add. Bg*
6m. saltem (tamen *L*
6n. parari (sibi *praem. L*
6o. alio (modo *add. M*
6p. silencia (silencium *T Bg*
6q. intercidunt (interscidunt *L*
7a. de proprietate monachi *rub. marg. D*
7b. etiam (quoque *Bg*
7c. debet . . . in uolendo (*om. M per hom.*

Quod autem debeant[d] nichil[e] habere proprium[f] in re, intelligant exemplo Ananie qui ad pedes Petri expirauit, quia[g] proprium[h] retinuit.[16] Ad[i] instructionem claustralium dicit Dominus:[j] *Nisi quis[k] reliquerit omnia[l] que possidet, non potest meus esse discipulus.*[17] Non[m] sufficit propriis abrenuntiare in re, nisi abrenuntietur uoluntate.[n] Unde et Petrus de hac renuntiatione[o] ait: *Ecce nos reliquimus omnia.*[p][18] Claustralis[q] ergo, qui proprium habere desiderat, retro respicit cum uxore Loth,[19] manum ad aratrum mittit sed[r] retrahit.[s][20] Cum Dina filia Iacob ornatus alienigenarum appetit.[21] Qui ergo a communione possessionis aliquid proprium excipit,[t] locum Iude proditoris et furis emit.[u][22]

O claustralis,[v] qui multa[w] reliquisti, noli ad mundum

7d. debeant (*om. T*

7e. nichil debeant *M Bg*

7f. proprium habere *T*

7g. quia (eo quod *Bg*

7h. proprium (partem possessionis *T*

16. Cf. Act 5:2–5

7i. ad (et *praem. M*

7j. de relictis omnibus *rub. marg D*

7k. quis (*om. M*

7l. reliquerit omnia (renunciauerit omnibus *Bg*

17. Luc 14:33

7m. non (nec tamen *Bg*

7n. uoluntate in *praem. M*

7o. renuntiatione (uoluntatis *add. M T*

7p. omnia (et secuti sumus te *add. Bg*

18. Mt 19:27

7q. de claustrali de uxore Loth de Dyna de Iuda *rub. marg. D*

19. Cf. Gen 19:26

7r. mittit sed (*om. M T*

7s. sed retrahit (*om. M T*

20. Cf. Luc 9:62

21. Cf. Gen 34

7t. excipit (recipit *M T*, excipiunt *Bg*

7u. emit (emunt *Bg*

22. Cf. Mt 27:3–9

7v. de claustrali *rub. marg. D*

7w. multa (in mundo *praem. Bg*

redire unius nummi[x] desiderio! Non capiat te[y] unius nummi[z] appetitus, quem non decipit diuiciarum thesaurus. Timeas ne decipula[aa] diaboli capiat te[ab] in minimo que te[ac] non decipit in maximo.

Propriam[ad] etiam[ae] monachus abiciat[af] uoluntatem, ut sicut communitas[ag] in religione ita[ah] in uoluntate; et[ai] non solum omnia eis[aj] sint communia[ak] quantum ad censum, uerum etiam quantum ad sensum,[al] ut omnes conueniant in una uoluntate, omnes consentiant in una caritate, ut de hiis[am] uere possit dicere:[an] *Erat eis cor unum et anima una.*[23]

< 8 > Tenentur[a] etiam claustrales habere unitatem caritatis, ut in proximi[b] profectu suum profectum[c] inueniat, in proximi defectu suum defectum[d] lugeat,[e] sapientior minus peritum instruat, sanus egroto condoleat, incolumis sano congaudeat. Et sic uita claustralis imago sit uite celestis, ut sicut in uita eterna in dispari claritate

7x. nummi (numeri *V*
7y. te capiat *L*
7z. nummi (numeri *V*
7aa. de decipula (*rub. marg. D*
7ab. capiat te (te decipiat *T*
7ac. te (*om. Bg*
7ad. de monacho *rub. marg. D*
7ae. etiam (enim *L*
7af. monachus abiciat (debet claustralis abicere *Bg*
7ag. communitas (est *add. M T Bg*
7ah. ita (sit *add. Bg*
7ai. et (ut *M T Bg*
7aj. eis omnia *T Bg*
7ak. communia (*om. V P D*
7al. sensum (consensum *Bg*
7am. hiis (eis *Bg*
7an. dicere (dici *P M T Bg,* dici possit *L*
23. Cf. Act 4:32
8a. de claustrali *rub.marg. D*
8b. proximi (sui . *M T Bg*
8c. profectum suum *Bg*
8d. defectum (*om. Bg*
8e. inueniat . . . lugeat (inueniant . . . lugeant *M T Bg*

par[f] gaudium, ita in claustro[g] in dispari caritate uicarium amoris uinculum.

< 9 > Ab hac triplici unitate claustralis monachus dicitur[a] quasi unitatis custos. Si primam unitatem non seruat,[b] sit anomalus; si secundam apostata; si terciam scismaticus. Sit in conuentu claustrali[c] unitas uniens et unita,[d] id est prelatus[e] subditos uniens auctoritate, subditis[f] unitus caritate.[g] Sit ibi unitas unita non[h] uniens, id est subditus qui, si[i] alios non uniat, aliis se caritate iungat.[j] Sit ibi unitas uniens non unita,[k] id est caritas[l] que, etsi[m] claustrales uniat, nulli tamen in presenti se[n] firmiter copulat.

Sit in eis unitas nature, ut in se naturam[o] diligant.[24] Sit unitas gratie, ut sibi inuicem gratiam collatam imperciant. Sit unitas glorie, ut una[p] spe ad eterne uite gloriam tendant.

Sit unitas fidei, ne sint heretici. Sit unitas caritatis, ne sint scismatici. Unitas[q] spei, ne sint obstinati.

8f. par (erit *add. Bg*
8g. claustro (claustrali *M,* uita claustrali *T*
9a. dicitur monachus *Bg*
9b. non seruat unitatem *Bg*
9c. claustrali conuentu *L*
9d. de abbate *rub. marg. D*
9e. prelatus (prelatos *V*
9f. subditis (subditus *M*
9g. subditis . . . caritate (*om. L*
9h. unita non (non unitas *T*
9i. si (*om. P D L,* etsi *Bg*
9j. sit ibi unitas . . . iungat (*om. M per hom.*
9k. unitas . . . unita (unitas non uniens sed unita *T*
9l. id est caritas (*post* unitas *in L*
9m. etsi (*om. M*
9n. se in presenti *M*
9o. naturam (eam *Bg*
24. Cf. Alanus de Insulis, *Liber de planctu naturae,* PL 210:429–482; Alan of Lille, *The Plaint of Nature. Translation and Commentary,* by James J. Sheridan, Medieval Sources in Translation 26 (Toronto, 1980).
9p. una (firma *T*
9q. unitas (sit *praem. D M*

Ut de eis specialiter possit dici:[r] ECCE QVAM BONVM, quantum ad opinionem hominum,[s] et QVAM IVCVNDVM, quantum[t] ad mentis delectationem[u] HABITARE FRATRES IN VNVM religionis, IN VNVM possessionis, IN VNVM caritatis,[v] ut ad illam unitatem peruenire ualeant, de qua dicit propheta: VNAM PECII.[w]

9r. specialiter possit dici (posssit dici spiritualiter *M*
9s. hominum (*om. M*, hominum opinionem *T L Bg*
9t. quantum (*om L*
9u. delectationem (deuocionem *Bg*
9v. possessionis (passionis *P D*
9w. pecii (a domino *add. M T*

Brian Patrick McGuire

Roskilde University

In Search of Bernard's Legacy: Jean Gerson and a Lifetime of Devotion

F OR MUCH OF THE SECOND HALF of the twentieth century, and now in the opening of the twenty-first, monk and scholar Chrysogonus Waddell has been an outstanding figure in cistercian studies. Future generations of scholars may come to remember him especially for his edition and commentaries on the early cistercian sources,[1] but for his own contemporaries, Chrysogonus Waddell is also appreciated for the generosity he has manifested in sharing his vast knowledge of the cistercian tradition. I have drawers filled with letters going back to the early 1980s when we started corresponding, and in almost every case, it is the monk who has taught the university professor and not the reverse.

One of the 'subthemes' of this correspondence has been a subtle exhortation from 'Apa Chrysogonus' to make sure that this friend and colleague does not leave the fertile field of cistercian studies for other pursuits. In the early 1990s, when the siren song of carthusian life and especially the writings of Denis the Carthusian began to attract me, Father Chrysogonus told me of a monk who had once tried to read all of Denis' endless tomes, only

---

1. *Narrative and Legislative Texts from Early Cîteaux.* Cîteaux, Commentarii Cistercienses. Studia et Documenta 9 (1999). *Cistercian Lay Brothers. Twelfth-century Usages with Related Texts.* Cîteaux. Studia et Documenta 10 (2000).

to lose interest in his way of life and leave the monastery before he had finished.

Not only was Denis not conducive to at least one monastic vocation, but even I concluded that this great fifteenth century monk and scholar had read everything but digested very little into his own inner life. His works are as dry as dust. I missed the intensity of cistercian affective life, both in its twelfth-century and in its twentieth-century manifestations. Time and again, thanks to Chrysogonus Waddell, I kept returning to the cistercian sources, medieval and contemporary, for intellectual and spiritual sustenance.

Since the late 1980s, I have looked beyond the fertile twelfth-century fields at the later development of the cistercian tradition and its relation to other late medieval thought and experience.[2] I have not always been faithful to the interests of my scholar friend at Gethsemani, but I have by no means left his company. My correspondence continues with this contemporary desert father.

Another scholar also indebted to Chrysogonus Waddell, Giles Constable, has long known that late medieval writers were heavily indebted to their twelfth-century predecessors.[3] And yet since Constable's seminal articles from 1971, few have dug further in this rich soil.[4] The late Middle Ages are constantly being reassessed, but studies of the influence of one author on another have, perhaps momentarily, gone out of style. In what follows, I will look at one hundred thirty-five Bernard citations which

2. My first attempts are contained in *The Difficult Saint: Bernard of Clairvaux and his Tradition* CS 126 (Kalamazoo: Cistercian Publications, 1991).
3. 'Twelfth-Century Spirituality and the Late Middle Ages', *Medieval and Renaissance Studies* 5 (Chapel Hill: University of North Carolina Press, 1971) 27–60; 'The Popularity of Twelfth-Century Spiritual Writers in the Late Middle Ages', *Renaissance Studies in Honor of Hans Baron*, eds. Anthony Molho and John A. Tedeschi (Dekalb: Northern Illinois Press, 1971) 5–28.
4. Except by Constable himself, who in *Three Studies in Medieval Religious and Social Thought* (Cambridge, England: University Press, 1995) follows central religious themes. See especially the section on the late Middle Ages in the essay, "The ideal of the imitation of Christ", pp. 218–48.

I have found in the works of Jean Gerson (1363–1429), in the hope of explaining how one fifteenth-century academic and spiritual writer made use of the insights of a twelfth-century abbot. I undertake this, perhaps pedestrian, task, not to impress the reader with my accumulation of tedious detail, but in the hope of understanding how one intellectual world, epitomized by a representative individual, viewed another, quite different period, and appropriated the insights of one of its outstanding representatives.

Chrysogonus Waddell might wonder how a late medieval scholastic could possibly be of interest to an historian of cistercian spirituality. But then this monk-scholar would add, in genuine humility, that he is 'just a monk' and 'not an historian' and insist that he really does not know enough about the subject. But it is thanks to Father Chrysogonus's knowledge of Bernard, to which I have had recourse, that I can write the following lines about the legacy of Bernard in the late fourteenth and early fifteenth centuries.

In this meeting of twelfth-century affective spirituality and late medieval spiritual and scholastic writings, I have spent many an hour reading Jean Gerson. In the ten volumes of Gerson's writings published, too hastily, by Palemon Glorieux in the 1960s and 70s,[5] I find a deeply troubled and many-layered priest, theologian, and, from 1395 and until his death in 1429, chancellor of the University of Paris.[6] Never a monk himself, Gerson was drawn to the sources of monastic spirituality and

5. *Jean Gerson. Oeuvres Complètes* 1–10 (Paris: Desclée, 1960–73)—hereafter abbreviated GI with volume and page numbers. The Glorieux edition, according to Gilbert Ouy, the dean of Gersonian studies, is full of faults but it remains our best access to Gerson's writings.
6. For references to the following overview of Gerson's life, see the fuller treatment in Brian Patrick McGuire, *Jean Gerson. Early Works*, Classics of Western Spirituality (New York and Mahwah: Paulist Press, 1998) 4–21. I am in the process of writing what I hope will become a new study of Gerson's life and times, provisionally entitled 'A World Reborn: Jean Gerson and the Last Medieval Reformation, 1350–1450'.

knew its literature well. One merely has to glance at the author index in the final volume of the Glorieux edition to see that, together with Aristotle, Pseudo-Dionysius, Augustine, Jerome and Gregory the Great, Bernard is a name that appears frequently in Gerson's writings.[7]

Jean Gerson was born in 1363 as the first child of a farmer and craftsman in a hamlet northeast of Reims. At the age of fourteen, he was sent by his parents to the University of Paris, where he held a scholarship at the prestigious and aristocratic College of Navarre. Here he met some of the outstanding scholars of his time, including Pierre d'Ailly, who became his teacher and mentor. Gerson's intellectual brilliance and good connections gave him access to the french court, where he began preaching at the end of the 1380s. In 1395, when d'Ailly left the position of chancellor to become bishop, he made sure that his successor at the university was Jean Gerson, who had just completed his doctorate in theology.

The sources for Gerson's spiritual and intellectual life in the first years of his chancellorship are sketchy, but in 1399–1400 he went into a self-imposed exile at Bruges. Here his correspondence with his colleagues in Paris provides a scathing portrait of the academic life he had chosen to leave.[8] When, thanks to his friends and the Duke of Burgundy, Gerson returned to Paris, he set out to reform the university and the Church, then in the throes of the Great Schism. Over the next fifteen years, before he left in January 1415 to participate in the Council of Constance, Gerson lectured and preached with amazing energy. He was active in church and university politics and at the same time sought to live a deeply spiritual

7. 'Table des auteurs cités', 631–44 in Glorieux, *Jean Gerson Oeuvres Complètes* 10.
8. I have translated these letters in *Jean Gerson. Early Works* (above, note 6), 160–91.

life. At Constance he was a central figure, gave important sermons, and helped restore a papacy which he intended to limit by the council. Afterwards, because of the burgundian occupation of Paris and their alliance with the English, it was too dangerous for Gerson to return there. After travelling in German-speaking countries, Gerson settled at the end of 1419 in Lyon, where his youngest brother was prior of a celestine monastery. Here Gerson continued his intellectual activities and summarized the concerns of his life. One of his last treatises, on which he worked until three days before his death, was a commentary on the *Song of Songs*, a work that had long fascinated him.[9]

Throughout his busy life Gerson searched for contemplative experience. At the same time, he believed in hard work and spent his life reading, teaching, writing and preaching. In him we find a forerunner of the puritan ethic of work: only by using the gifts God has given us and doing our level best can we hope to attain the vision of God.[10] As a teacher, Gerson felt obliged to be well informed. There could be no question of limiting oneself to contemporary writings and ignoring the heritage of the past.[11] Gerson digested and recycled the late antique and medieval intellectual heritage in meeting the questions and concerns of his own day. From Augustine, Ambrose and Jerome down to William of Auvergne, Bonaventure, and Thomas Aquinas, Gerson had read the great masters of theology and knew how to use them.

9. Gerson's brother provided this information in a postscript to the work which expressed his devotion and admiration and concludes: ' . . . *et dulcibus nunc, ut pie creditur, amplexibus et osculis dilecti sponsi perfruitur de quibus in his ultimis suis Canticis tanta et tam sublimia mira subtilitate et affectus suavitate dulci gutture velut olor parata modulatus est.*' (Gl 8:639).
10. See, for example, Gerson's letter of advice to a bishop recently elected (Gl 2:108–16).
11. Gerson complained in a letter to his colleagues that his own notes were copied without his permission, while his students failed to read old and respected works of theology (Gl 2:42, trans. *Early Works*, 192).

The corpus of Bernard which Gerson consulted was larger than the Bernard at our disposal today. Gerson, like all other scholars from the thirteenth to the early twentieth centuries, believed that the *Letter to the Carthusians of Mont-Dieu* had been written by Bernard.[12] If we remove from our one hundred and thirty-five references the eleven citations connected with this letter, then the 'real Bernard' is named in one hundred twenty-four places by Gerson. A further reference to Bernard recorded by Glorieux in his index also has to be removed (Gl 8:555), for it occurs in a quotation from Bonaventure. Finally, yet two other references to Bernard, as we shall see later, are actually to Gilbert of Hoyland.

Of the remaining one hundred twenty-one specific references to Bernard in Gerson, fifty-six—almost half—come from the *Sermones in Cantica*, Bernard's *Sermons on the Song of Songs* (abbreviated here as SC); ten from *De consideratione* (Csi), Bernard's work of advice to Pope Eugenius III; nine from *De praecepto et dispensatione* (Pre); four from *De gradibus humilitatis et superbiae* (Hum); nine from various bernardine sermons; eight from his letters; fourteen from episodes in Bernard's life, most of them from the *Vita Prima*. Finally, there are two Bernard references I have been unable to locate. They probably belong to the vast pseudo-bernardian literature whose existence is manifested in volume 184 of the *Patrologia Latina*.[13]

---

12. I have dealt with the borrowings from this 'Bernard' in 'La présence de la lettre aux frères de Mont Dieu dans les oeuvres de Jean Gerson', in Nicole Boucher, ed., *Signy l'Abbaye et Guillaume de Saint-Thierry*. Actes du Colloque international d'Études cisterciennes (Signy-L'Abbaye 2000) 565–574.

13. Found in Gerson's Letter 29, to a bishop-elect, Gl 2:114–5: ' . . . *namque, sicut ait Bernardus, duo sunt morituris tandem amarissima: praestiti scilicet perditi temporis, potissime si onus animarum habitum est, recordatio, et quantum vitae supersit ad debita restaurandum dubia exspectatio'; 'Bibamus autem, inquit Bernardus, ludamus, vanos status ampliemus, haeredes magnos agamus, cetera sicut volumus inania procuremus et aeterna negligamus, et nos forte pro caducis marcescemus et proximum offendamus, nihil minus tamen in brevi moriendum est . . .'* Dom

Most frequently, Gerson provides Bernard's name but
not the title of the work from which he has borrowed. In
about one reference out of four, however, Gerson does
identify the work and at times the section. We find sometimes direct quotations, sometimes a few words, sometimes several lines.[14] When borrowing a whole paragraph
from Bernard, Gerson may start out with a quotation
that more or less corresponds to the text in the Leclercq-
Rochais edition of Bernard's works, but within a few lines
he may skip a section in Bernard and then add another or
summarize it.[15] The end of such a long quotation Gerson
may signal to his reader by concluding with the words,
Haec ille (Gl 5:470).

Gerson's use of Bernard is characterized by great
freedom, and often it is difficult to be certain whether
he intended to provide an exact quotation or simply
'remembered' Bernard. Did Gerson rely on his memory
of Bernard and rarely check his recollections of the text?
In the course of my research I came to realize that the
main difficulty lay not so much in Gerson's ignorance of
the 'real Bernard' as in my own lack of close familiarity
with Bernard's works. Time and again I have discovered
that what appears to be a carefree reference is on closer
inspection a very precise quotation.[16] I can now point out
that Glorieux in his Gerson edition provided very limited
help in identifying bernardine borrowings in Gerson. A
great deal of patient checking has needed to be done

Augustine Roberts of Saint Joseph's Abbey, Spencer, Massachusetts has kindly
assured me that these sayings are not to be found in the Bernard corpus.

14. As in the *Mystica theologia practica*, Gl 8:22, from SC 32.9.

15. As in a sermon on the feast of Saint Louis, where Gerson draws on *De
consideratione*, Gl 5:151–2. Also, in a sermon on the feast of the Purification,
also from Csi, Gl 7/2:1055.

16. Here I have been greatly helped by Anthony Perron, Ph.D. student and
Fulbright scholar in Denmark 1999–2000, who has assisted me with his access
to the University of Chicago's library data bank of the *Patrologia Latina*, much
easier to use than the CETEDOC library microfiches.

292   Brian Patrick McGuire

to provide a firm demonstration of how a late medieval writer made use of his predecessors.[17]

Unfortunately, the only work of Gerson to exist in a respectable critical edition is his *Mystical Theology*, which I used in translating some of Gerson's works into English.[18] Many of the references to Bernard in the notes lead nowhere. Careful checking often fails to reveal any direct link between Gerson's text and Bernard's thought.[19]

The analysis which follows represents only the tip of the iceberg. I have deliberately not counted passages that look as though they may come from Bernard but which Gerson does not identify as his.[20] A more comprehensive study of Gerson's dependence on Bernard would doubtless reveal scores of passages where the later author drew from his twelfth century predecessor. Until undertaking this study, however, I had analysed only a single work by Gerson in assessing his dependence on Bernard: Gerson's *Sermon on the Feast of Saint Bernard.*[21] In order to avoid turning an article into a book, I have limited myself here to the passages where Gerson himself chose to signal his dependence on Bernard. There is no consistency in Gerson's way of referring to Bernard: sometimes he simply calls him by name; most of the time he attaches

17. It is interesting to note that many references to Bernard come together with mentions of Augustine, whose *Confessions* seem to have been one of Gerson's favorite works. A study of Gerson's dependence on Augustine would further elucidate the scholastic's uses of Bernard.

18. André Combes, ed., *Ioannis Carlerii de Gerson De mystica theologia* (Lugano: Thesaurus Mundi, 1958).

19. As in *Jean Gerson. Early Works*, 449, note 36.

20. As in *Sermon pour la fête des saints apôtres* (Gl 7.2:737–8), possibly from 1392, where a reference to Saint Paul (Gal 2:20) turns into a latin quotation based on Saint Bernard (Pre 20.60, SBOp 3:292). Gerson wrote: *Verius est anima ubi amat quam ubi animat*, while Bernard's original statement is: *Neque enim praesentior spiritus noster est ubi animat, quam ubi amat.*

21. See my 'Gerson and Bernard: Languishing with Love', *Cîteaux Commentarii Cistercienses* 46 (1995) 127–156. Gerson's frequent references to the name of Bernard in this sermon have not been added to my computation of the instances in which Gerson made use of Bernard.

an adjective, such as *devotus Bernardus* or *beatus Bernardus*. These titles indicate Gerson's respect, but as we shall see, he can at times also distance himself from Bernard. On the whole, however, Bernard's life and writings provided models for Gerson, significant reference points for his own thoughts and conclusions.

GERSON'S GENERAL STATEMENTS ABOUT BERNARD

However difficult a saint Bernard may be in his life and works, he was a natural part of Gerson's intellectual and spiritual heritage, especially when he came to define the contemplative life.[22] In 1426, a few years before he died, Gerson wrote for the benefit of a Carthusian at La Grande Chartreuse a brief summary of the books that a monk should read. Along with Gregory the Great's *Moralia in Job*, writings by Richard and Hugh of Saint Victor, and Bonaventure's spiritual works, such as his *Breviloquium* and the *Itinerarium mentis ad Deum*, he pointed out:

> There are the books of Bernard, the devout man, especially the Letter to the Carthusian brothers of Mont Dieu and the Sermons on the Song of Songs. He spoke in these as one professed in religion and as someone learned, with a great amount of experience.[23]

After summarizing the benefits of these spiritual writings, Gerson went on to reflect on his own experience:

22. The important subject of Bernard's *Nachleben* or reception in the later Middle Ages was already a concern for some of the chapters in McGuire, *The Difficult Saint: Bernard of Clairvaux and his Tradition.* CS 126 (Kalamazoo, 1991). See also Kasper Elm, ed., *Bernhard von Clairvaux. Rezeption und Wirkung im Mittelalter und in der Neuzeit. Wolfenbütteler Mittelalter-Studien* 6 (Wiesbaden: Harrassowitz Verlag, 1994).
23. *De libris legendis a monacho,* Gl 9:612: '*Sunt libri Bernardi, viri devoti, praesertim epistola ad fratres Carthusienses de Monte Dei; Sermones insuper super Cantica canticorum; locutus est in illis professus religionem et tamquam experientia multa doctus.*'

I confess in my inadequacy that for thirty years and more I have desired to familiarize myself with these works. I have often read them, often ruminated over them, often dealing with the words without penetrating their meanings. And so at my age, and with the leisure I have had, I have scarcely been able to reach my goal and have only begun to taste their contents. In returning to them, these works are always made new to me and give me pleasure.[24]

I have translated Gerson's statement freely, for he compresses into a few words the concerns of a lifetime. By using the verb *ruminare*, which originally meant to chew over again as a cow chews her cud, Gerson linked himself to the tradition of monastic reading and meditation.[25]

Elsewhere Gerson also connected Bernard with these other writers on the spiritual life. Concluding a sermon on Saint Louis, Gerson praised pseudo-Dionysius, Augustine, Gregory, and 'the more recent Bernard, Hugh, Richard and after them Bonaventure'. All of these, according to Gerson, had dealt with the necessity of a 'knowledge of consideration' or the examined life.[26] A similar general evaluation of Bernard is found in Gerson's sermon on the feast of the Nativity of Mary, where he had in mind a carthusian audience:

24. *De libris legendis*, Gl 9.613: '*Confitebor autem in insipientia mea quod a triginta annis et amplius familiares habere volui praedictos tractatulos saepe legendo, saepe ruminando, etiam usque ad verba nedum sententias. Et ecce hac aetate, hoc otio, velut ad votum vix perveni usque ad initium gustus eormdem, qui repetiti mihi semper novi fiunt et placent.*' Gerson, in old age still in contact with his classical training at the faculty of arts in Paris, here added a citation from Horace (*Ars poetica* 365): '*juxta illud Flacci de poemate vel imagine compositi eleganter: decies repetita placebit*'.
25. The word *ruminare* occurs at least fourteen times in Bernard's writings, such as *In festivitate omnium sanctorum* 4.6 (SBOp 4:360): '*Nunc enim reficimur panibus istis, cum iucunda meditatione beatam spem ruminamus, donec veniat. . . .*'
26. *In festo S. Ludovici Regis*, whose dating is uncertain, Gl 5:167: '*Scripserunt multa plurimi virorum divinorum et elevatorum super hac re, et divinus Dionysius, Augustinus, Gregorius et recentiores Bernardus, Hugo, Ricardus et post eos Bonaventura et alii. . . .*'

The venerable Richard of Saint Victor in his *On contemplation* and blessed Bernard in many of his works, and especially to your brothers of Mont Dieu, and others moreover who have written of the contemplation of the soul. . . . [27]

Bernard appears again in a list of works helpful to the pilgrim on his way to God:

You can find in the monasteries of the Celestines, the Carthusians and others, both in French as in Latin, works that speak of . . . the mountain of contemplation and of spiritual medicine and of mystical theology, the clock of wisdom, and meditations of the saints Augustine, Anselm, Bernard and others. [28]

Gerson in this passage recommended some of his own works as well as those of Bernard. The term *meditationes*, used elsewhere in referring to Bernard's writings, [29] may have been intended to refer especially to Bernard's *Sermons on the Song of Songs*, which made up so large a part of Gerson's borrowings from the saint.

GERSON'S DEBT TO BERNARD'S
SERMONS ON THE SONG OF SONGS

The earliest work of Gerson in which I can find him citing Bernard's *Sermons on the Song of Songs* is his sermon for the Circumcision, *Postquam consummati*, dated to 1392. The reference is brief but unmistakable: Gerson describes

---

27. *Quae est ista*, Gl 5:485: '*Venerabilis Richardus de Sancto Victore in suo De contemplatione et beatus Bernardus in multis opusculis, tum nominatim ad vestros fratres de Monte Dei, et ceteri praeterea qui de contemplatione animae conscripserunt . . .*'. Gerson was referring to the work of Richard usually called *The Mystical Ark* or *Benjamin Major*.

28. *Canticordium du pelerin*, Gl 7/1:133. For the *Clock of Wisdom*, see *Jean Gerson. Early Works*, 405, n. 76.

29. As in the *Collectorium super Magnificat*, Gl 8:274: ' . . . *sic de meditationibus Anselmi, Bernardi, Augustini, Isidori et similium* . . .', where Gerson was arguing the need to read the authors of the past.

how 'we read that Augustine and Bernard affirm that no writings had any taste for them of eloquence or shone forth with gravity in their assertions, unless they saw the name of Jesus written there'.[30] Here Gerson must have been thinking of the *Confessions* of Saint Augustine (7.21), and of Bernard's *Sermones in Cantica* 15.6, where the abbot had written: 'Every food of the mind is dry if it is not dipped in that oil; it is tasteless if not seasoned by that salt. Write what you will I shall not relish it if you exclude the name of Jesus.'[31]

Bernard's statement was far more epigrammatic and at the same time more sensual in its language than is Gerson's summary, but Gerson did capture the essence of what Bernard (and Augustine) had asserted. At the end of the same sermon, Gerson showed his knowledge of Bernard's *Homilies in Praise of the Virgin Mother*: 'Let us exclaim together with Bernard, *Super missus est . . .*'(Gl 5:470). This is one of the places where Gerson chose to make it quite clear that he was drawing on Bernard, and his long quotation ends with the words, *Haec ille.* The passage concerns our desire to rid ourselves of avarice, price, luxury, and anger by asking Jesus to come and disperse these vices. Gerson here borrowed from one of the few places where Bernard's prose turns into prayer: *Veni interim, Domine Iesu, aufer scandala de regno tuo, quod est anima mea.*[32] In Gerson's version, some of Bernard's statement is summarized. Instead of doing the easy thing and borrowing from Bernard's own sermon on the Circumcision, Gerson made use of a passage in which Bernard reflected on Luke 2:21, which concerns giving the child the name Jesus. Gerson's use of a description of

30. Gl 5:469: '*Augustinum praeterea, Bernardumque legimus de se affirmantes nullas omnino scripturas eis sapere quantumcumque eloquentia aut sententiarum gravitate pollerent, nisi vidissent nomen Jesus ibidem scriptum.*'
31. SBOp 1:86: '*Aridus est omnis animae cibus, si non oleo isto infunditur; inspidus est, si non hoc sale conditur. Si scribas, non sapit mihi, nisi legero ibi Iesum.*' Trans. CF 4:110.
32. *Sermones in Laudibus Virginis Matris*, Homilia 4.2; SBOp 4:48.

the child Jesus found in a sermon on Mary indicates he knew Bernard's writings well enough to be able to draw on them to illustrate the subject at hand.

This sermon is an important one in revealing the development of Gerson's mind, for his exposition of the text included a very personal meditation on the meaning of Christ's life. Gerson asked what Mary and Joseph felt at the Circumcision. Later in life, especially in his magnificent but little-known poem *Josephina*, Gerson followed in even greater detail this meditative device of asking what the participants in Christ's life experienced.[33] Here also he could have been indebted to Bernard, whose sermons, such as those on the *Song of Songs* and in praise of Mary, frequently emphasized the participation of the individual Christian in the story of Jesus. In this sermon, however, Bernard was used in another way: to emphasize how the coming of Christ enables the individual soul to fight its own vices.

It is difficult to date a number of the other sermons in which Gerson referred to Bernard. By the time the university chancellor wrote his *Mountain of Contemplation* while in his retreat at Bruges (1399–1400), he had been strongly influenced by Bernard. Explaining in the opening of the treatise why he was writing in French, Gerson pointed out that a number of 'holy doctors' had written in Latin on the subject of contemplation. Here he named 'Saint Gregory in his Moralities, Saint Bernard on the Song, Richard of Saint Victor and several others' (Gl 7.1:16).

Gerson proposed to deal with this subject in the vernacular, especially for the sake of women who, apparently like his own sisters, did not read Latin. In the treatise Gerson returned several times to Bernard, as he did in

33. The text of the *Josephina*, one of the greatest and least known latin poems of the Middle Ages, is in Gl 4.31–100. See McGuire, 'When Jesus did the Dishes: The Transformation of Late Medieval Spirituality', forthcoming in Mark F. Williams, *The Making of Christian Communities*.

distinguishing between knowledge and wisdom; Bernard, he claimed, had asserted that knowledge is part of the intellect, while wisdom belongs to affectivity.[34] Gerson may have been thinking of Bernard's epigram that teaching makes us learned, while affectivity renders us wise: *instructio doctos reddit, affectio sapientes* (SC 23.14). Refusing to limit his function as a teacher at the faculty of theology, Gerson was not satisfied with knowledge alone and went time and again to Bernard and other writers on the contemplative life to assert the necessity of reaching beyond knowledge for its own sake.

Another specific reference to Bernard occurs when Gerson deals with the need for silence and solitude in making room for the appearance of God's grace: 'My lord Saint Bernard says that the soul's groom, Jesus Christ, is a shy friend who does not willingly come to his friend in the midst of a great multitude but seeks to be alone with her.'[35] This passage is a clear reference to *Sermon on the Song of Songs* 40.4, where Bernard encouraged his monks to reflect on how the soul or bride must flee everyone, even close friends, to be alone with Christ the groom: *An nescis te verecundum habere sponsum, et qui nequaquam suam velit tibi indulgere praesentiam, praesentibus ceteris?*[36]

This theme of the need for solitude provided Gerson with other opportunities to draw on Bernard. In describing Mary in a french sermon on the Annunciation, possibly from 1397, Gerson emphasized how she had been alone, as Saint Bernard had described her: *L'angle trouva nostre dame comme dit Saint Bernard, toute seulette en sa chambre, non mie parlant a Berthe ou a Gaultier* (Gl 7.2:546).

34. Gl 7.1:19: '*Grande différence mettent li saints docteurs, en especial saint Bernard, entre science et sapience; car science appartient principalement et comme seulement a l'entendement, et sapience a l'affection. . . .*'
35. Gl 7.1:38: '*Dist monseigneur saint Bernard que l'espous de l'ame Jhesucrist est un ami honteux, qui ne vient point volentiers a s'anime present grant multitude mais quiert estre seul.*' Trans. McGuire, *Jean Gerson. Early Works* (note 6 above) 103.
36. SBOp 2:26–27.

In Bernard's *Sermons in Praise of the Virgin Mother*, we find the great abbot visualizing Mary as she was when the angel appeared to her: 'Where did he come to her? I think in the secrecy of her chaste chamber, where perhaps she, with the door closed, was praying . . .'.[37] Summarizing this passage in his own words, Gerson colloquialized Bernard's sermon by referring to potential companions 'Birthe' and 'Walter', assumedly common contemporary names. Unlike Bernard, Gerson was addressing not a monastic but a secular audience and he may have added this aside to keep its attention.

That Gerson worried about the effect which reading the *Song* might have on an unprepared lay audience can be seen in the *Mountain of Contemplation*, written at the end of the 1390s, when he was himself deeply involved with Bernard's *Sermons on the Song of Songs*:

Saint Bernard in all the sermons that he made on the Song deals with a type of spiritual marriage between God and the soul. Such a treatment is pursued in a more recent treatise dealing with the marriage of the soul with divine wisdom. The name of this book is *The Clock of Wisdom*. It is true that this topic is perhaps too lofty and rather dangerous to deal with at the beginning of one's conversion to the mystical life, for when one believes one is thinking about spiritual marriage, one easiliy can slide into thoughts about carnal marriage.[38]

We see here how Gerson viewed Bernard's sermons as part of a continuing exegetical tradition on the *Song of Songs*.[39] In writing on contemplative experience for lay

---

37. *Sermones in laudibus virginis matris*, Homilia 3.1; SBOp 4:36: '*Quo ingressus ad eam? Puto in secretarium pudici cubiculi, ubi fortassis illa, clauso super se ostio, orabat Patrem suum in abscondito.*'

38. Gl 7.1:47, trans. *Early Works* 114.

39. See Denys Turner, *Eros and Allegory. Medieval Exegesis of the Song of Songs*, CS 156 (Kalamazoo, 1995).

people and especially for women, Gerson worried that he might be exposing them to subjects—such as spiritual marriage—which could be interpreted in an all too literal manner. But Gerson went ahead, trusting in the value to lay persons with some education of knowing about Bernard's writings.

When Gerson returned to Paris, he continued to draw on the tradition of spiritual interpretation of the *Song of Songs*. Writing in April 1402 to his brother Nicolas, a celestine monk, and to Nicolas's subprior, Gerson reflected on how his own teaching agreed with what he found in Bernard:

> When recently I reread the sermons of the devout Bernard on the Song, beloved father and brother, I came to that place which teaches the ways by which one comes to the spiritual generation of the Word, that is to contemplation of the ark. I rejoiced not a little because it was so much in harmony with the subject of which I had written recently at Bruges in the bed of my illness, the little treatise of which you have a copy.[40]

Gerson had in mind his *Mountain of Contemplation*. In it he had written of the three elements necessary for climbing the ladder of mystical contemplation: bitter contrition, leisure or solitude, and strong perseverance, and had referred to Bernard (Gl 7.1:26). Now, two years later, he rediscovered the connection. The long quotation Gerson here attributed to Bernard we now realize came instead from Gilbert of Hoyland's continuation of Bernard's *Sermons on the Song of Songs*.[41] Gerson must have been using a manuscript in which Gilbert's sermons had been appended to Bernard's without any notation of the

---

40. Gl 2:54, trans. *Early Works* 200–201.
41. Gl 2:54, trans. *Early Works* 201. See Gilbert, *In Canticum sermones* 7; PL 184:43. In the Glorieux text, Gerson refers to Sermon 100, while this is actually Sermon 7 in the Gilbert collection.

change of author. Gilbert's work, like William's *Letter to the Brothers of Mont Dieu*, had been lumped into the bernardine corpus.

During these first years of the fifteenth century, Gerson profited greatly from rereading Bernard's *Sermons on the Song of Songs* as a few examples will show. When in 1401, in *On Distinguishing True from False Revelations*, Gerson considered whether or not one should reveal visions or other apparently divine revelations, he referred to Bernard's experience:

> We have yet another example in Saint Bernard, who so often insisted that a person hide his virtues, even from his dearest and closest friends, rather than acting as others who try to hide their vices. But he did not think it to be pride that he not only openly spoke a great deal of his gifts and graces obtained through contemplation but also wrote of them.[42]

Gerson could have been thinking of a number of different statements in the *Sermons on the Song of Songs*, as when Bernard claimed awareness of the Holy Spirit's coming to him through the movement of his heart (SC 74.5–6). This passage in Bernard was one to which Gerson several times returned.[43]

Later in the same treatise, this time dealing with the necessity of showing humility in receiving revelations, Gerson provided another favorite Bernard reference:

> In conformity, the devout Bernard swears that he had the fullest experience of such matters in his

42. Gl 3:40, trans. *Early Works* 340: '*Quinetiam devotus Bernardus qui totiens jussit ut plus homo virtutes suas abscondat etiam familiarissimis et devotissimis, quam alii vitia sua occultare satagunt; pluries de suis donis et gratiis per contemplationem adeptis palam nedum loqui, sed scribere non esse superbiam arbitratus est.*'
43. As in a Pentecost sermon on 22 May 1401 (Gl 7.2:687), the *De probatione spirituum* written at the Council of Constance in 1415 (Gl 9:184), the *Collectorium super Magnificat* from 1427–28 (Gl 8:443), and the *Tractatus de Canticis* from 1428–9 (Gl 9:565).

fifty-fourth sermon on the Song of Songs. 'In truth', he says, 'I learned that there is nothing equally effective for meriting God's grace or for keeping or recovering it, than to place yourself at all times before God, not in thinking you know his depth but in fearing it.'[44]

Gerson returned several more times in his writings to this passage, which fitted perfectly into his program of preparing his readers and listeners for a personal meeting with God based not on knowledge but on desire.[45]

Dealing with differences between the active and the contemplative lives, Gerson declared on the authority of Bernard that the experience of God 'cannot be expressed, or taught, but is possessed' (*non exprimi, nec doceri potest sed haberi*).[46] Here the university lecturer in theology warned his students that they could attain the knowledge of God, not through their books, but only through their inner lives. In the midst of a scholastic milieu, Gerson hearkened back to the affective language of the twelfth century. This form of 'intellectual affectivity', originally intended for monks and canons, was being extended to university students and devout women.

In the first years after his return from Bruges, Gerson continued to combine intellectual speculation with the interior life. In his *Practical Mystical Theology*, based on a

44. Gl 3:49: '*Conformiter ad hoc jurat devotus Bernardus talium expertissimus super Cantica*, Hom. 54: *In veritate, inquit, didici nihil aeque efficax esse ad gratiam Dei promerendam, retinendam, recuperandam, quam si omni tempore inveniaris coram Deo non altum sapere sed timere.*' This is SC 54.9; SBOp 2:108.
45. As a sermon on prayer given at Constance, 21 April 1415, but here the Bernard reference is slightly altered: . . . *non alta sapere, sed sapere ad sobrietatem* (Gl 5:404). The same change is made in Gerson's *Practical Mystical Theology*, sixth consideration (Gl 8:28). In a sermon for the Monday after Pentecost, 4 June 1403, Gerson simply dropped the ending about fear: '*Et Bernardus: in veritate comperi nihil ita efficax ad gratiam Dei recuperandam, inveniendam et servandam quam si inveniaris non altum sapere*' (Gl 5:257).
46. *De comparatione vitae contemplativae ad activam*, a commentary on Mark 1.5. Gl 3.68. See Bernard SC 74.5–6, but also SC 23.14: '*Instructio doctos reddit, affectio sapientes. . . .*'

series of lectures given to the Paris students, Gerson made
many references to Bernard. Dealing with the requirement of self-knowledge, Gerson turned to Bernard's use
of Isaiah 55:11 'that the word which goes forth from the
mouth of God, does not return to him empty but prospers
and accomplishes all those things for which he sent it.'[47]
Gerson quoted here directly from Bernard (SC 32.7).

Later in the same treatise, Gerson used Bernard, as
well as Richard and Hugh of Saint Victor, when dealing
with the fear of the Lord as the beginning of wisdom (Ps
100:10): 'But since fear can immediately collapse into
despair, we have to associate hope with it.'[48] Gerson was
probably again thinking of Bernard's statement (SC 54.9)
about the need for fear of God in seeking knowledge
and the hope we gain from this process. The very same
passage, slightly altered, is also used as a warning against
curiosity in pursuit of the contemplative life.[49]

The danger of pride in intellectual pursuits was a theme
to which Gerson returned time and again in the brief
treatises based on lectures given to his students between
1401 and 1415. In writing *De sensu litterali S. Scripturae*
(On the literal meaning of Scripture) at the end of his
Paris years (1413–14), Gerson combined Augustine's
Confessions and Bernard's *Sermons* in speaking of how pride
blocks interior vision: *Bernardus super Cantica: Superbo oculo
veritas non videtur, sincero patet.*[50] This precise quotation
(SC 62.8) provides one more example of how Gerson

47. Gl 8:22: '*Videat autem quisque, ut Bernardus, quomodo verbum quod egreditur
de ore Dei non revertetur ad eum vacuum, sed prosperetur et faciet omnia ad quae misit
illud. . . .*' Trans. *Early Works* 294–95.
48. Gl 8:41, trans. *Early Works* 324.
49. Gl 8:28: '*Hoc expertus Bernardus ita testatur: Vere nihil est ita efficax ad gratiam
hanc vel inveniendam vel retinendam vel recuperandam quae vitam meretur aeternam,
quam si semper inveniaris non altum sapere sed sapere ad sobrietatem.*' Gerson has
apparently changed Bernard's ending. See note 45 above.
50. Gl 3:339. Gerson referred to the seventh book of Augustine's *Confessions*:
'*Tumore meo separabar a te, et nimis inflata facies claudebat oculos meos.*' This passage
can be found at the end of chapter 7 in Book 7.

could clinch his point by using a single sentence in Bernard.

Even though certain passages in Bernard's *Sermons on the Song of Songs* are found several times in Gerson's work, a study of his borrowings indicates that he knew Bernard well enough to take advantage of more than a few quotations. He favored statements on the life of contemplation which reflected Bernard's own experiences, while he rarely even mentions Bernard's celebrations of life in community at Clairvaux and his enjoyment of monastic fellowship. As I have shown elsewhere,[51] the university professor was concerned with Bernard, not as abbot and friend in community, but as a mystic and visionary who points the way to a life of contemplation.

This dimension of Bernard formed Gerson's theme in his sermon *Spiritus Domini replevit*, given at the Council of Constance on 7 June 1416. Speaking on the possibilities of contemplation in this life, Gerson turned to Bernard, 'O good death, sighs Bernard, which does not take life away but turns it into something better' (*O bona mors, suspirat Bernardus, quae vitam non aufert sed mutat in melius,* Gl 5:532). In this sentence, taken from SC 52.4, Bernard was describing the symbolic death of the soul as Christ's bride in the ecstasy she experiences in her union with him.[52] Bernard had asked that he might experience this death in order to be spared the temptations of the senses. Gerson expressed the same desire.

Further on in the same sermon, Gerson again drew on Bernard's *Sermons on the Song of Songs*, this time in dealing with the activity of grace:

> I also find the desire of the devout Bernard that he could so pour the grace of preaching or ministry

---

51. 'Languishing with Love', note 21 above.
52. Note, however, that Bernard's verb in SBO II, p. 92 is *transfert*, not *mutat*. Such minor differences may have been due to the manuscript Gerson used, but there remains the possibility that he was recalling to memory a text he thought he knew.

into others, not as a canal which soon is dried out and leaves behind sediment, but as a reservoir that is filled up and flows over, or as a living fountain that gushes out from its perpetual source, which is not easily disturbed and if disturbed can quickly return to its pristine splendor.[53]

These lines summarize in a compact manner Bernard's language expressing the abbot's desire to form his monks. What follows Gerson's interpretation, however, reflects more the fifteenth than the twelfth century:

For what purpose was this saint seeking? So that action would not take away the grace of contemplation. For this is the proof of Bernard to the brothers that in any action they remember the exhortation of the Church: 'Lift up your hearts', to which I wish that the response would be truly and frequently: 'We have done so to the Lord.'[54]

If we look at other *Sermons on the Song*, such as 54 and 59, we discover a Bernard who claimed to be more than willing to leave his own contemplative concerns to be involved in the active life of an abbot obliged to teach and preach to his monks. Gerson, bent on pointing out to the council fathers the importance of maintaining a contemplative dimension in their own lives, fashioned a portrait of Bernard that left out his concern for the spiritual needs of others, especially his monks.

In the business of the Council of Constance Gerson may have felt his own contemplative life threatened.

53. Gl 5.535: '*Invenio praeterea devoti Bernardi desiderium tale quod gratiam praedicationis seu ministrationis sic in alios effunderet, non ut canale quod protinus siccatur feces retinens, sed ut concha plena supperreffluentis, seu fons vivus perpetua vena scaturiens, qui nec facile turbatur et turbatus protinus ad nitorem pristinum redit.*' See Bernard SC 18.3–4.

54. Gl 5.535: '*Ad quid ita quaerebat sanctus iste? Ut nimirum actio contemplationis gratiam non auferret. Hic est ejusdem ad fratres documentum quod in qualibet actione meminerint illius ecclesiasticae cohortationis: sursum corda, cui tam veraciter quam frequenter utinam fieret responsio: habemus ad Dominum.*'

Afterwards, however, he had more than enough time and leisure to read, write and pray, as it was too dangerous to go back to Paris. Unable to function as professor and chancellor of the University and in enforced retirement at Lyon, Gerson began the final stage of his involvement with Bernard and especially with his *Sermons on the Song of Songs*.

In *De sollicitudine ecclesiasticorum*, written perhaps in early 1423, Gerson borrowed from Bernard's exhortation at the end of SC 47 that the brothers sing the divine office with attention to the words without letting themselves be distracted by other thoughts: 'Purely then, so that you think of nothing else when you sing the psalms than of the psalms you are singing'(Gl 9:451). In Gerson's version, this passage is followed by one not found in the standard edition of Bernard's works. In it Bernard is supposed to have given even more specific advice on how to sing the psalms: *Psalmodiam non multum protrahamus, sed rotunda et viva voce cantemus* . . . . According to Chrysogonus Waddell, these lines, in fact, belong to a tiny treatise ascribed to Bernard entitled *De modo psallendi*, a treatise often found together with the passage from the end of Sermon 47.[55] Gerson was clearly aware of the existence of this treatise, for he referred at the opening of his quotation to this very title: *Nutrit hanc sollicitudinem scrupulosam verbum beati Bernardi De modo psallendi*.

We find here one of the rare places in Gerson's writings where he not only made use of Bernard but commented on its meaning almost line by line. Gerson pointed out,

55. Letter of 27 August 1998: 'I'm happy to say that, even without a concordance, I can identify the texts quoted by Gerson. Gerson had a copy of an *opusculum* attributed to Bernard, 'De modo psallendi'. Some ms copies preface it with a quote from Sermo 47.8 of the Song.' See Chrysogonus Waddell, 'A Plea for the *Institutio Sancti Bernardi quomodo cantare et psallere debeamus*', in *Saint Bernard of Clairvaux. Studies Commemorating the Eighth Centenary of his Canonization*, ed. M. Basil Pennington, CS 28 (Kalamazoo, 1977) 180–207.

for example, that Bernard's instructions made up 'an exhortation, not an order'.[56] At the end of his exposition Gerson admitted that he had difficulties with Bernard's insistence on concentrating exclusively on the words of the psalms even when other spiritual thoughts intervened (Gl 9:453). Elsewhere Gerson referred to the same passage from Sermon 47 in dealing with the more general problem of attentiveness in prayer.[57] Gerson could draw out various layers of meaning from a single statement in Bernard, depending on the purpose at hand.

In the same period at Lyon, Gerson again referred to the Song of Songs in his De canticorum originali ratione, which might be translated as 'The original basis of songs'. It deals in a section on the song of the heart ('de canticordo') with the way the Song of Songs had been interpreted through the ages. Gregory and Bede looked upon the dialogue of the Song in terms of the Church and Christ, while Nicolas of Lyra spoke of the synagogue and God, and Bernard had written 'concerning the soul and the Word, and something of how human nature is joined to the Son of God'.[58] Thomas Aquinas had explored yet other possibilities. The text of Origen's commentary Gerson did not have, but he knew of it through Jerome. The one interpretation he had never found, he said, was 'the matrimony of the prelate with the Church his

56. Gl 9:452: '*Confitemur expediens esse propter minus instructos et nimis litterales, aliqua dicere. Et primo quod haec est exhortatio, non praeceptio: "moneo vos", inquit.*'
57. Gl 2:188, Letter 38, from Constance in 1416–17, to Gerson's brother Jean the Celestine: '*Ingerit quippe scrupulum apud nonnullos dictum Bernardi Super Cantica, ubi prohibere videtur attentionem quamlibet ad alia quam ad orationis significata et verba, etiam si salutaria videantur, sicut exemplum dat de recogitatione sermonum suorum.*' This is a precise summary of Bernard SC 47.8. The same passage is used in Gerson's *De directione cordis*, which combines Letters 37 and 38 to Jean the Celestine (Gl 8:104).
58. Gl 9:553: '. . . *apud expositores Canticorum qui de ceteris mysticis plurima disseruerunt: Gregorius et Beda*, De Ecclesia et Christo; *Nicolaus de Lyra*, De synagoga et Deo; *Bernardus*, De anima et Verbo, *et aliqua* De humana natura ad Filii suppositum. . . .'

mistress, which the Holy Spirit impregnates and is its guardian. This is in the type of Joseph with Mary.'

In this fascinating passage summing up the various ways of interpreting the Song, Gerson revealed his own interest in the figure of the chaste Joseph. Gerson was perhaps preparing himself for his own exposition on the *Song of Songs*. Later in the same work, he drew on Bernard's SC 79.1 concerning the tongue of love which, 'as Bernard witnesses, is incomprehensible to those who do not love'.[59] Gerson indicated here, with Bernard's help, that it is impossible to make sense of the meaning of the Song of Songs if one lacks the experience of divine love.[60]

In writing his own *Super Cantica canticorum* between 15 May and 9 July 1429, Gerson seems to have done his best to keep a distance from Bernard and to provide his own analysis of the text. In the seventy-five pages of the Glorieux edition, there are only four references to Bernard's work. Rather than follow Bernard, Gerson concentrated on the Song of Songs in terms of the words of Peter to Jesus, 'Lord, you know that I love you' (Jn 21:16).

In dealing with the rational soul, Gerson named Bernard and Anselm and may have referred obliquely to Bernard's reflections on the freedom of the soul (Gl 8:568; SC 81.7–9). A more precise reference concerns the kiss of the mouth: Gerson described Bernard's treatment of the image (SC 7.3) as 'beautiful': 'Here he is speaking to the soul which seeks the kiss of the mouth from such a great one who looks at the earth and makes it tremble' (Ps 103:32).[61] If we check the original state-

59. *Tractatus de Canticis*, Gl 9:553: ' . . . amoris lingua, Bernardo teste, barbara est non amantibus'.
60. In Gerson's *Notulae super Dionysium*, Gl 3:218, he uses the same image: ' . . . quia linguam amoris non amans non intelligit, secundum Bernardum.'
61. Gl 8:580: '*Pulchra est hoc loco et prolixa devoti Bernardi deductio, apologizantis ad animam quae petit osculum oris ab illo tali et tanto qui respicit terram et facit eam tremere.*'

ment, we find Gerson has been quite precise in capturing Bernard's meaning, without using the latter's interrogative form: 'What then? He looks at the earth and makes it tremble and that soul asks to be kissed by him?'

Such passages indicate that in this, his last work, Gerson remained intimately familiar with Bernard's *Sermons on the Song of Songs* and could draw on them at will. Yet it is not until more than forty pages later in the same text that Gerson again mentions Bernard by name (Gl 8:624). It occurs when Gerson deals with the union of the soul with God through the Holy Spirit:

> Ambrose, Jerome, Augustine, Bernard with similar authors whom we have, as well as secure reason, make clear that from the most worthy indwelling of the groom with the spouse and of the same person through the seed of grace in its fecundity not by another nor from another than from himself, then the bride dares to say in the coming of the Holy Spirit and in the overshadowing of the power of the Most High, 'You are my son; this day I have begotten you (Ps 2:7). In the day of my betrothal and the joy of my heart, what could be more wondrous than this?'[62]

The convolutions of Gerson's sentence recall some of the most obscure passages in Bernard. If Gerson had lived longer, he might well have revised this section. But it is of interest that the line from Psalm 2 which provided Gerson with the climax of his description is one which Bernard himself never used.

Gerson's final reference to Bernard's language on the Song of Songs occurs in a discussion on the necessity of purgative love (Gl 8:633). Gerson found Bernard had

---

62. Gl 8:624: '*Ambrosius, Hieronymus, Augustinus, Bernardus cum similibus quorum scripta patent, et ratio certa convincit ex dignantissima cohabitatione sponsi cum sponsa et ejusdem per gratiae semen foecundatione non ab altero nec de altero quam de seipso, ut audeat dicere sponsa in superadventum Spiritus Sancti, et in obumbratione virtutis Altissimi: filius meus es tu; ego hodie genui te, in die disponsationis meae et laetitiae cordis mei, quid hoc mirabilius?*'

described this experience in speaking about his novitiate, whose sufferings Bernard characterized in terms of placing on his breast a bundle of myrrh: *Ita fatetur Bernardus egisse se in novitiatu super illo: fasciculus myrrhae dilectus meus mihi* (Sg 1.12). Here, as earlier in the *Mountain of Contemplation*, Gerson recalled and summarized a very specific statement in Bernard (SC 43.4).

In spite of the few explicit references to Bernard in Gerson's own exposition of the Song of Songs, Gerson felt a debt to Bernard and was influenced by his language of love and personal experience in seeking God. In dedicating his work to the Carthusians with whom he had corresponded for so many years, Gerson expressed a fear that he could not possibly manage to bring any new understanding to a work on which 'the greatest geniuses' (*summis ingeniis*) had commented (Gl 8:565). But Gerson went ahead. As he pointed out elsewhere, he had spent decades in thinking about images and words on which he had ruminated with the help of Bernard's own meditations on the Song of Songs.[63]

Reshaping Monastic Thought:
On Precept and Dispensation

In writing his 1402 treatise on the spiritual life of the soul, *De vita spirituali animae*, Gerson again drew heavily on Bernard. The second section of Gerson's work concerns the law of God and the necessity of obedience. Here Gerson makes clear that his treatment depended heavily on 'devout Bernard . . . [who] wrote a very fine work *On Precept and Dispensation*, which has provided the foundation for our work'.[64] Gerson returned time and again to Bernard's treatise, but he used it for his own purposes,

---

63. *De libris legendis a monacho*, Gl 9.612. See note 24 above. For other commentaries on the *Song of Songs*, such as the one by Denis the Carthusian, see Denys Turner, *Eros and Allegory* (note 39 above).
64. Gl 3:129: ' . . . *scripsit volumen pulcherrimum de praecepto et dispensatione, qui liber huic operi nostro pro fundamento supponatur.*'

in several cases lifting Bernard's prescriptions out of the monastery and applying them to ethical behavior in the university and society in general.

Gerson made use of Bernard in the question of right judgments in conformity with the divine law. According to 'the devout Bernard', he writes, 'truth does not suffice without right intention nor right intention without truth; otherwise the Apostle would not have blamed those who had zeal but not according to knowledge' (Rm 10:22).[65] Gerson here simplified and reapplied Bernard's statement that there must be both 'charity in the intention and truth in the choice'. For Bernard the question was one of charity; Gerson narrowed the field to intention and truth.

Later in the same discussion, Gerson dealt with the following syllogism: 'Everyone who kills his father is to be hanged; Peter killed his father; therefore he is to be hanged.' Here Gerson's reasoning seems to be very far from that of his spiritual master, and yet Gerson pointed to Bernard as his inspiration in dealing with this kind of reasoning.[66]

Gerson also made use of Bernard in distinguishing between mortal and venial sins. Bernard argued that minor infringements of Rule of Saint Benedict are not mortal sins, unless they are carried out with contempt for the authority of the abbot. Gerson extends this consideration to moral questions in general:

> Blessed Bernard in the forenamed work *On Precept and Dispensation* establishes and appears to resolve this doubt . . . that every sin which is committed

---

65. Gl 3:159: ' . . . *quia nec veritas sine recta intentione nec intentio recta sine veritate sufficunt; alioquin non inculpasset Apostolus quosdam qui habebant zelum non secundum scientiam.*'

66. Gl 3:160: '*Altera est responsio, et forte rationabilior et magis ad intentionem beati Bernardi dicens minorem praecedentis syllogismi aut alterius similis, non esse istam: Petrus est homicida, sed istam: Petrus probatur homicida per testes inconvincibiles de falsitate; et haec vera esset apud eos sicut major. Si igitur conclusio vera sit talium nullus mirabitur.*'

out of contempt is mortal; if however any act is done against a precept and not out of contempt, it is considered to be venial.[67]

This distinction was central for Gerson. In other treatises he tried to convince his readers that they should not be overscrupulous and pessimistic about the gravity of their sins.[68] Here he was being loyal to Bernard, who had made it clear that contempt is always serious, no matter how unimportant the matter, while failure to follow the precepts of the Rule could be a minor sin.[69] As a theologian in the scholastic tradition, however, Gerson was not completely satisfied with Bernard's definition and so added another from the thirteenth-century theologian William of Auxerre.[70]

A further instance of Gerson's care in making use of Bernard while adding other authorites is found in his citation of a famed letter from Peter the Venerable, the abbot of Cluny, to Bernard on the practices of monastic life. 'Dom Peter' had written 'Saint Bernard', according to Gerson, in order to show that 'every regular institution remains inviolate however much it be changed, provided that the law of charity and the Rule are kept in the things done.'[71] Gerson refers to Peter's example: eating meat

---

67. Gl 3:187: '*Beatus Bernardus in libello praellagato De praecepto et dispensatione sititur et prima facie apparet dubitationem hanc absolvere per hoc quod omne peccatum quod fit ex contemptu est mortale; si fiat autem etiam contra praeceptum actus aliquis et non ex contemptu, venialis reputatur.*' See Pre 8.18, SBOp 3:265.

68. For a summary of Gerson's treatment of this subject, see D. Catherine Brown, *Pastor and Laity in the Theology of Jean Gerson* (Cambridge: Cambridge University Press, 1987) 68–72.

69. Pre 8.18: '*Porro contemptus in omni specie mandatorum pari pondere gravis. . . .*'

70. Gl 3:187: '*Quam distinctionem ut ego melius intelligerem, consului summam domini Antisiodorensis ubi loquitur de contemptu et dicit quod contemnere est appretiari rem minus justo. . . .*'

71. Gl 3:194: '. . . *olim dominus Petrus abbas Cluniacensis in epistola missa ad sanctum Bernardum ubi deducit omnem regularem institutionem inviolatam manere quantumcumque mutetur, dum charitatis lex et regula in his quae fiunt custoditur.*'

and wearing furs is acceptable, so long as the rule of charity is not violated.[72]

This fifteenth-century use of a central letter on the monastic life by the twelfth-century abbot of Cluny enables us to see how broad-ranging Gerson could be in his appreciation of monastic theology.[73] But he did not stop here: to Peter's letter Gerson added a further reference to Bernard, to the effect that monks live according to the rule 'when praiseworthy customs are kept according to the time and place'.[74]

In adjusting monastic customs according to different needs, Gerson was not always completely faithful to Bernard's original intention. The abbot had argued that a monk can leave his monastery for another if he chooses a stricter life. Gerson said almost the opposite: the less strict life can itself be praiseworthy, so long as it is lived in a spirit of charity! Gerson here is much closer to Peter the Venerable than to Bernard, but the scholastic apparently did not want to show open disagreement with Bernard. It was important for him to make use of Bernard in driving home his point that a religious can be so rigoristic in his interpretation of the Rule that he violates the law of charity and neglects the needs of the other brothers.

Aware that he might be misunderstood, Gerson insisted that he was not 'relaxing the restraints on lust, gluttony, and obedience'.[75] He tried to combine Peter

72. Gerson was drawing on Letter 28 in the collection edited by Giles Constable, *The Letters of Peter the Venerable* 1 (Cambridge: Harvard University Press, 1967) 52–101. Gerson especially made use of the final sections of the letter.

73. This is, however, the only time in Gerson's work where Peter of Cluny was mentioned by name as an author and authority.

74. Gl 3:194: '*Cujus simile in libello De praecepto et dispensatione dicit Bernardus, quod ubique regulariter vivitur ubi consuetudines laudabiles pro tempore et loco servantur.*' See Pre 16.47, SBOp 3:285–86.

75. Gl 3:195: '*Propterea non dicimus ea quae dicimus, ad laxandum frena luxuriae, gulae et inobedientiae, non ad dissolvendum vigorem regularis disciplinae, non ad habendum velamen malitiae libertatem. . . .*'

the Venerable's tolerance with Bernard's concern for discipline, to consider not only monastic behavior, but also to comment on the university world. Just as the vows of monks could be modified, so too the oaths taken by university scholars had to be interpreted in the context of charity and the needs of others.

Gerson's precise agenda within university politics is not apparent, but his general point is clear: the oaths being demanded of university scholars and professors are not to be seen as necessarily binding them under pain of mortal sin.[76] The same is true of oaths among people in the world. Institutions are necessary, but their rules are mere supplements to God's law, the basis of all human law. At this point Gerson turns again to the question of religious vows, and his exposition becomes an elegant analysis of the limitations that charity imposes both in the monastery and in university politics. He returns to Bernard's point about contempt of one's superiors and repeats his teaching that some precepts in religious life are not binding on all.[77] He concludes that if monks follow the discipline of their Order, they are obliged to observe its institutes and customs. If they break silence or fail to observe other minor precepts, however, monks do not commit grave sin.

At this point Gerson did not repeat the comparision he had made earlier between monastic obedience and university loyalty. Yet his purpose is transparent: to distinguish between what is essential and what is secondary in both monastic and secular life. Authorities cannot turn custom or convenience into an absolute demand. Gerson

76. Gl 3:196: '*Deinde patet quod non omne impositum fieri generaliter per juramentum et sub omni poena, ut fiunt nunc passim convocationes generales Universitatis, obligat semper sic vocatos et juratos ad mortale perjurium dum omittunt.*'

77. Gl 3.199: '*Sic et accipiendum reor, illud Bernardi et aliorum communiter dicentium talia esse criminalia si contemnantur vel si fiant ex contemptu. Carent autem hoc contemptu qui ex fragilitate humana vel quadam levi curiositate frangunt silentium aut alia agunt opposita his quae monita dicit Bernardus factitia. . . .*'

took his point of departure from the teaching of Saint Bernard, just as he had declared at the opening of the treatise. But he modified Bernard's defence of austerity with the law of charity championed by Peter the Venerable. And towards the end of the treatise, Gerson adds a consideration not found in Bernard's *De praecepto* at all: the danger of scandal. If religious people fail to live up to their obligations and scandalize others, they bear a terrible responsibility. Monks are to be an example to others (*exemplar aliorum*): they may in private do things which they cannot do in public.[78] Thus a Carthusian, because of need, may eat meat, but he is to do so alone and not in the presence of others.

Gerson ended this treatise by distinguishing once again between the absolute requirements of divine law and the human law inspired by it. Church prelates and princes are not to consider their laws and institutes to be divine, 'but these are to be received as healthy admonitions and not to be lightly treated'(Gl 3.202). Moving carefully between permissiveness and absolutism, Gerson found in Bernard, modified by Peter the Venerable, a healthy standard not only for monastic life but for human life in general. Here we can see in depth and detail how Gerson could build on a twelfth-century foundation a structure fitted to his own age, environment, and needs.

REFORMING CHURCH AND SOCIETY
WITH THE ADVICE OF THE PAST

So comprehensive was Gerson's knowledge of Bernard's writings that he could make use of both his letters and treatises to plead for the reform of the medieval Church, one of his major concerns. Like Martin Luther a century later, Gerson esteemed Bernard's treatise-letter of advice

78. Gl 3.200: '*Sic in maximis viris, vel ordine vel sanctitate vel gradu sublevatis, tamquam positis in exemplar aliorum, multa quandoque non licent in publico saltem, quae aliunde vel in occulto licerent.*'

for a pope, the *De consideratione*.[79] In his own criticism
of the practices of church prelates, *Super victu et pompa
praelatorum*, Gerson was ostensibly commenting on the
description in Mark 1:6 of John the Baptist, who dressed
in camel's hair and ate locusts. He referred as well to
the Epistle of James (2:2), which criticizes those who
spurn the poor and honor the rich in their jewelry
and fine clothes. Here Gerson added a long quotation
beginning with the notation *Bernardus ad Eugenium, lib.
de Consideratione*. Bernard asked Eugene how he could
dress in gold finery. 'Did Peter do so? Did Paul exhort
him to do so?'[80] Gerson conflated two passages in which
Bernard described the apostles and contrasted them with
the prelates of his own time.

Later in the same treatise, Gerson asserted that prelates
who forget that they only administer church goods and
treat them as if they owned them fail their duty to give
any surplus income as alms to the poor. They are to keep
for themselves only what they need for food and clothing.
'Bernard asserts that any surplus that is kept back is theft;
no, indeed, sacrilege. This is truly a harsh statement
against churchmen and those who collect treasure . . .
giving nothing to the poor.'[81]

The statement too looks as if it comes from *De consideratione* and it is consistent with Bernard's thinking
there, but not with his rhetoric. Gerson borrowed the
adage about theft-sacrilege, in fact, from one of Bernard's

79. See Bernhard Lohse, 'Luther und Bernhard von Clairvaux', *Bernhard
von Clairvaux. Rezeption und Wirkung im Mittelalter und in der Neuzeit* (note 22
above) 271–301, esp. 295–96.
80. Gl 3:100: '*Tu pastor procedis deauratus tam multa circumdatus varietate, oves
quid capiunt. Si auderem dicere, demonum magis quam ovium pascua haec. Sic faciet
Petrus, sic Paulus suadebat? Item Petrus nescitur aliquando processisse vel gemmis
ornatus, vel sericis vel textus auro nec vectus equo albo, nec stipatus milite nec
circumseptus ministris. . . .*' See Csi 4.5 (SBOp 3:452) and Csi 4.6 (SBOp
3:453).
81. Gl 3:101: '*Definit ultra Bernardus quod quicquid ultra retinetur rapina est,
immo sacrilegium. Dura vero sententia contra ecclesiasticos et eos qui thesaurizant et
qui in luxuriis variis et impudicitiis conversantur, nihil dantes pauperibus.*'

letters—a prominent one traditionally placed second in his collection.[82] The assertion was so important for Gerson that he repeated it later in the same treatise while asserting that churchmen who used more of church possessions than they needed for modest consumption were obliged to restore what they had taken.[83] The phrase *rapina est, immo sacrilegium* appears elsewhere in Gerson, as in the sermon *Bonus Pastor,* given to the clergy at Reims in 1408 (Gl 5:135). The same is the case in one of the sermons in the *Poenitimini* series, from 1404 (Gl 5:451).

A less polemical use of *De consideratione* comes in a sermon on the feast of Saint Louis, in which Gerson lists the benefits of consideration or meditation on one's situation. Here we find precise quotation of Bernard with summaries of his language, a procedure popular with Gerson.[84] Similarly, in preaching on the Feast of the Purification, 1 February 1396, Gerson described the soul crushed by its own hardness and despair by referring to *De consideratione* and giving an exact reference to Book 1, chapter 6.[85] Gerson's sermon, probably delivered at court, was given in French, but he cited Saint Bernard in Latin. Gerson provided an exact quotation but skipped a section. This he indicated by the word *sequitur,* thus providing a guide for potential readers of the sermon who might have wanted to check the text of Saint Bernard.

82. Letter 2.11, to Fulk, a youth who had been appointed archdeacon, SBOp 7:21: '*Denique quidquid praeter necessarium victum ac simplicem vestitum de altario retines, tuum non est: rapina est, sacrilegium est.*'
83. Gl 3:101–102: '. . . *si ecclesiasticus dispensans, immo dissipans in usus prodigos et injustos bona ecclesiae suae, teneatur ad restitutionem, praesertim cum dictum sit auctoritate Bernardi, cui Hieronymus consentit, quod quicquid ecclesiastici ultra parcum vestitum et victum retinent, sacrilegium est.*'The word play *dispensans . . . dissipans* comes from Csi 3.18; SBOp 3:445.
84. Gl 5:151–52, with a direct quotation from Csi 1.8 (SBOp 3:404) and then a summary of Csi 1.9–10.
85. Gl 7.2:1055: '*Mal y attendez jamais remede, comme dit saint Bernard in libro de Consideracione ad Eugenium papam, libro primo, capitulo sexto describens cor durum: Solum, inquit, est cor durum quod seipsum non exhorret, quia nec sentit. . . .*' See Csi 1.3, SBOp 3:396.

A much more summary reference to this work is found in one of Gerson's best-known sermons, *Veniat pax*, a plea to end the schism (4 November 1408). Here Gerson, addressing the king and court, described how 'Saint Bernard, in the first book of *De consideratione* had written about being prudent, wise and well-advised in one's deeds'.[86] Another instance in which Gerson provides a very brief reference to this work of Bernard is found in a sermon attacking someone who had preached in defence of the murder of the duke of Orléans.[87]

A final use of *De consideratione* concerns the bestowal of dispensations. In the treatise *De nobilitate*, written at Lyon in August of 1423, Gerson claimed to make use of Bernard's opinion that there can be two causes for dispensations: necessity or public utility: *Doceat te, non ego sed ipse Bernardus, duplicem assignans quam tetigimus causam; una est justa necessitas, altera est publica vel patens utilitas.*[88] If these elements are lacking, then 'if Bernard is to believed, it will be not dispensation but dissipation'.[89] Here, as elsewhere, Gerson picked up Bernard's wordplay and made it into his own.

These above borrowings from *De consideratione* are by no means as comprehensive as Gerson's exposition of *De praecepto et dispensatione*. But his uses of Bernard's language show that the text of the treatise remained in Gerson's mind a possible reference for some of his own ideas in reforming church and society. Also important for Gerson was Bernard's Letter 2, where the abbot had been emphatic about the need for churchmen to live

86. Gl 7.2:1106: ' . . . *comme declare saint Bernart, primo de Consideratione, le fait d'estre prudent, sage et advise en tous ses faits. . . .*'
87. Gl 5:244: '*Respondetur insuper, juxta praedicationem ab uno de magistris nostris in theologia factam alias in civitate Laudunensi, juxta considerationem praeterea notatam a beato Bernardo in suo De consideratione dum de malitia Romanorum loqueretur notans quod uno nomine tota satis exprimitur cum dicitur Romanus est. . . .*'
88. Gl 9:496, which is a summary of Csi 3.18; SBOp 3:445.
89. See note 83 above.

frugal lives. Another letter of Bernard's to which Gerson referred more than once was his missive to the canons of Lyon deploring their observance of the feast of the Immaculate Conception. Gerson, a staunch defender of the doctrine, seems deliberately to have ignored Bernard's theological reasons for not celebrating the feast and merely pointed out that since Bernard's day, the solemnity had spread almost to the whole of the Church. Thus Gerson could reject as outdated Bernard's argument that the Roman Church did not generally observe the feast.[90] Instead of criticizing Bernard for dissenting from the doctrine, Gerson avoided the issue, an indication of his respect for the saint, but also a hint that Gerson, like many of us, could be selective in making use of his sources.

SERMONS BUILDING ON SERMONS

Gerson's lack of specificity in his references to Bernard seems especially to have been the case when the scholastic made use of the abbot's sermons. Of the nine references I have found, some are obscure, while others are easy to find. In *Beati qui lugent*, a sermon for the Feast of All Saints, 1 November 1401 or 1402, Gerson described human sufferings and the consolations found in them: 'But as the blessed Bernard is said to have written: Many people see the crosses we bear but are not aware of our consolations'.[91] This remark sounds like an exact bernardine quotation of the type that Gerson often made. But an exhaustive search of Bernard's writings fails to reveal anything more than passages where he expresses something like this idea, but nowhere does Bernard use the exact phrase Gerson attributed to him. Gerson may have been thinking about the preface to Bernard's

90. Sermon *Tota pulchra es*, Gl 7.2:1077. See Bernard's Letter 174.9; SBOp 7:392.
91. Gl 5.92: '*Quemadmodum dixisse legitur beatus Bernardus: multi vident cruces nostras qui non attendunt consolationes nostras.*'

lenten sermons on the psalm 'He who dwells'. If we share Christ's sufferings, we will come to consolation.[92] Perhaps Gerson was 'remembering' what Bernard had written, but so far as I can tell, the latter does not use the term *cruces* to describe sufferings, while he does employ the term *consolationes*.

In the next sentence of the same sermon, Gerson speaks of those who are taught by anointing and experience (. . . *quos unctio docet, quos experientia erudit*). Here we are very close to the language of Bernard's sermon *On Conversion*, with the key sentence: *Non illud eruditio, sed unctio docet.*[93] The word *experientia* is one of Bernard's key terms. But Gerson did not here mention Bernard by name, and so this 'recollection' cannot be added to our statistic.

A more precise reference to Bernard's text is found in Gerson's 1392 sermon for the Circumcision, *Postquam consummati*. Towards the end, Gerson calls on all his listeners or readers to call upon the name of Christ: 'Let us call out together with Bernard, *Super missus est . . .*' (Gl 5:470). Gerson was referring to Bernard's *Homilies in Praise of the Virgin Mother*, which begin with Luke 1:26–27 on the sending of the angel Gabriel to Mary. The passage which follows is quoted from Bernard's prayer that the Lord take away all sources of scandal from the kingdom which is his soul: *Veni Domine, aufer scandala de regno tuo quod est anima mea.*[94] Bernard lists the various vices which try to take over and describes how he cries out to the Lord for help: *Veni ergo Domine, disperge illos in virtute tua et regnabis in me quia tu es rex meus et Deus meus. Haec ille* (Gl 5:471). The last two words are Gerson's indication that the quotation from Bernard ends here. He made use of one of the few places in Bernard's writings

92. SBO 4:383: '*Quod si abundat tribulatio vestra pro eo, abundabit consolatio vestra per eum. . . .*'
93. *Ad clericos de conversione* 13.25; SBOp 4:99–100.
94. Sermon 4.2 *Missus est*; SBOp 4:48–9.

where the saint's prose turns into a prayer.[95] Gerson, who himself wrote prayers influenced by the affective language of Saint Anselm, revealed his attraction to this dimension of Bernard's spirituality.[96]

In writing his sermons for feasts of the liturgical year, Gerson naturally turned to sermons for the same occasions written by his predecessors. Occasionally he used Bernard as his source of inspiration, as in a Holy Thursday sermon from 27 March 1399, *Si non lavero te*, given shortly before he left Paris for his long stay at Bruges. In considering the events of Holy Week, writes Gerson, 'Bernard says that no heart is so hard that it is not softened if the passion of the Lord is recalled'.[97] If we look at Bernard's own Sermon for Holy Thursday, we discover the source but also the fact that Gerson removed a great deal of the rhetoric and provided only the essence of Bernard's statement: 'Who is so impious that he is not affected? Who is so insolent, that he is not humiliated? . . . For the Passion of the Lord is at hand, to this day shaking the earth, opening the monuments'.[98]

Bernard recalls the events described in the Gospels, but his style dramatizes and concretizes the personal response. Gerson did not try to imitate this hyperbolic approach, for he had other concerns. In much of his sermon he expressed frustration with the state of the Church and complained especially that the number of reserved cases for confession meant that many lay people were not able to get absolution and so probably would

95. For another 'bernardine prayer', see note 32 above.
96. Gilbert Ouy, 'Trois prières françaises inédites de Jean Gerson', *Mélanges de langue et de littérature françaises du moyen âge offerts a Pierre Demarolle*, ed. Charles Brucker (Paris: Honoré Champion 1998) 27–38.
97. Gl 5:504: ' . . . *de qua dicit Bernardus quod nullum cor tam durum est quod non molliatur si passio Domini ad memoriam revocetur.*'
98. *De passione domini*, 1: SBOp 5:56: '*Quis tam irreligiosus, qui non compungatur? Quis tam insolens, ut non humilietur? Quis tam iracundus, ut non indulgeat? Quis tam deliciosus, ut non abstineat? Quis tam flagitiosus, ut non contineat? Quis tam malitiosus, ut non poeniteat his diebus? Merito quidem. Nempe adest Passio Domini, usque hodie terram movens, petras scindens, aperiens monumenta.*'

go to hell. He also attacked university teachers for their lack of concern about what to do in such cases: *Quid igitur facient scholastici nostri temporis qui materias tales nec cogitare nec legere superficietenus dignantur . . .* (Gl 5:507).

Bernard, speaking about Holy Thursday, could expect a sympathetic monastic audience to concentrate on the meaning of the Passion. Gerson in his corresponding sermon took Bernard and the Passion as his point of departure and then launched an attack on the hardened hearts of the clergy, whose members and teachers could allow so many of the faithful to be without the benefits of Christ's death. Such an approach points to Gerson's sense of frustration with his academic surroundings in the late 1390s, before he tried to leave the university for good. The sermon also shows how the chancellor could dip into Bernard and take what he wanted to make his own point.

Another brief reference to Bernard appears in one of Gerson's vernacular sermons, given on the feast of the Annunciation, perhaps in 1397. Here Mary is called our advocate and queen, 'by whose hands God ordained to give what he gives to the human creature, according to the saying of Saint Bernard'.[99] The gift of Christ comes to us through Mary, as Bernard claimed in one of his sermons on the Vigil of the Nativity.[100]

Gerson knew the work of Bernard so well that he could draw on it at will. When he wrote on nobility and spoke of the importance of *humilitas honorata*, he was borrowing a marian term from one of Bernard's sermons but using it in a different context.[101] Gerson felt no need to comment

99. Gl 7.2:541: '*Par ce Nostre dame est dicte nostre advocate, nostre moyenneresse, nostre royne, nostre empeteresse par les mains de laquelle Dieu a ordonné donner ce qu'il donne a creature humaine selon le dit saint Bernard.*'
100. Sermon 3.10 *In vigilia nativitatis*, SBOp IV, p. 219: '*Sed quia tu dignus non eras cui donaretur, datum est Mariae, ut per illam acciperes quidquid haberes.*'
101. *Tractatus de nobilitate*, Gl 9:486: '*Rarum bonum, ait Bernardus, et ideo praeclarum est humilitas honorata.*' See *De laudibus virginis matris* Homily 4.9; SBOp 4:55.

on any of Bernard's sermons in detail, but he was versed in their language and imagery.

BERNARD THE PERSON

A final aspect of Gerson's debt to Bernard is his use of stories about the saint. Gerson, who was very much concerned with chastity, whether clerical or lay, several times returned to the stories in the *Vita Prima* concerning Bernard's attempts to resist sexual temptation. Sometimes he simply includes a reference to Bernard in a list of other saints remembered for the same virtue, as is the case in Gerson's *De non esu carnium*, his defence of the carthusian prohibition against eating meat. After mentioning 'many women and virgins, not only Christian but also pagan, who because of the love of chastity punished themselves in a wondrous way', Gerson added: 'The story of Joseph is well known, and of Benedict, Bernard, and those like them.'[102] Similarly, in his little-known work on masturbation, *De confessione mollitiei*, Gerson advised the confessor to tell the penitent to avoid temptation by beating his breast, throwing cold water on himself or hurting himself physically. Here Bernard is named together with Anthony, Benedict, Thomas 'and other fathers'.[103] Gerson was almost certainly thinking of the incident in Bernard's *Vita Prima* where he is said to have cooled his desire in freezing water.[104] Finally, in Gerson's *Sermon for all Saints*, he recalled specifically the incident of Bernard's crying out 'Thief, thief' to drive away his tempter.[105] This is a

---

102. Gl 3:92: '*Vulgata est Joseph historia, necnon Benedicti, Bernardi atque similium.*'

103. Gl 8:74: ' . . . *tundendo pectus, vel etiam aliam laesionem corporalem alicubi inferendo, vel aqua frigida se spargendo, vel surgendo a lecto et similia. Solebat inducere exempla sanctorum, ut Bernardi, Antonii, Benedicti, sancti Thomae et aliorum patrum, quae commemorare longum est.*'

104. *Vita prima* I.3.6; PL 185:230C.

105. Sermon *Exsultabunt sancti in gloria* (Gl 5:277) dated to 1 November 1394: '*Conclamate cum beato Bernardo, "Ad latrones, ad latrones; ad ignem, ad ignem*'. The cry "robbers" is from *Vita prima* I.3.7; PL 185:230–31.

fascinating sermon of Gerson's, probably delivered a few months before he became chancellor and indicative of his concern about male-male sexual bonds in university life. The stories about Bernard Gerson used can usually be found in the twelfth-century *Vita Prima* and in the *Legenda Aurea*, the summary of Bernard's life compiled in the thirteenth-century collection for his feast day August 20.[106] Both sources mention how an abbot received a vision after Bernard's death, in which the new saint brought his friend to Mount Lebanon.[107] In one instance, however, Gerson tells a story about Bernard that belongs only to the *Legenda Aurea*. In his tale a peasant to whom Bernard promises a mule if he can say the 'Our Father' without being distracted, does very well until he started thinking about whether he will get the saddle as well as the animal.[108]

The story fits perfectly into Gerson's *De directione cordis*, from 1417, on the importance of total attention during prayer. Gerson's opening remark, *Exemplum legimus de Bernardo*, indicates that he had culled the story from a written source.[109] Since the *Legenda Aurea* would have been easily available to him, I have no doubt that this was his point of departure.

106. See McGuire, 'A Saint's Afterlife. Bernard in the Golden Legend and in other medieval Collections', 179–211 in *Bernhard von Clairvaux. Rezeption und Wirkung* (note 22 above).

107. *Collectorium super Magnificat*, Gl 8:213: '. . . *secundum visionem quam devotus Bernardus, cuius dies agitur, fertur insinuasse per ascensum sui post obitum in montem Libani.*' See *Vita Prima* 5.3.22; PL 185:363–64. The anecdote is at the end of the section on Bernard in *Legenda Aurea*. See the edition of Th. Graesse (Osnabrück: Otto Zeller 1890, 1965), 538. Also the assertion that oaks and beeches taught Bernard (Gl 9:424) is in both sources.

108. *Legenda Aurea*, ed. Graesse, pp. 534–35. In the early 1990s Chrysogonus Waddell encouraged me to find the origin of this story. See 'A Saint's Afterlife', pp. 197–98 in *Bernhard von Clairvaux*, note 22 above.

109. Gl 8.101–102: '*Exemplum legimus de Bernardo qui volens rusticum unum convincere de cordis instabilitate dum fit oratio, pollicitus est se daturum sibi asinum suum si posset orationem dominicam, nihil aliud actualiter cogitans, perficere. Qui mox ut ad orationem divertit, securus de asini lucro, coepit in hanc cogitationem distrahi si sellam habiturus erat cum asino. Qui tandem ad se rediens et se redarguens, instabilitatem sui cordis confessus est.*'

At times, Gerson may have been drawing on an oral as opposed to a written tradition for his stories about Bernard. In *De praeparatione ad missam* (On getting ready for Mass), whose manuscript tradition indicates it was one of his most popular latin works, Gerson discussed what to do when one is uncertain about a moral question. He referred to the advice of Bernard on this matter (*Memorandum est beati bernardi super hac re consilium*):

> There was one of his disciples who was disturbed by so many scruples that he in no way dared to celebrate Mass. The devout and thoughtful Bernard eventually reacted [by saying]: 'Go brother and celebrate the Mass with my faith'. The disciple obeyed and that general scruple disappeared for good.[110]

There is no such story in the *Vita Prima* or in the *Legenda Aurea*, but there is a similar story in the *Exordium Magnum Cisterciense*, the great collection of cistercian moralizing stories or *exempla* from the early thirteenth century.[111] It is unlikely, however, that Gerson knew the version in this source, for the *Exordium Magnum* story concerns a brother who did not have sufficient faith to take communion, not a priest who was afraid to say Mass.

Gerson may have heard the story in the version he repeats, or he may have inadvertently transformed the tale to fit his own needs. Such a transformation can take place when a narrative moves from one person to another. Stories change shape according to social and intellectual needs. What started as an assertion of cistercian solidarity under Bernard has turned into an example of how priests are to avoid scrupulosity and

---

110. Gl 9:39: '*Erat ex discipulis ejus quidam tantis inquietatus scrupulis ut ad celebrandum nullo pacto auderet accedere. Dixit ei devotus et circumspectus Bernardus postquam hoc accepit: vade frater et in fide mea celebres. Obedivit discipulus et scrupulus ille communis perpetuo discessit.*'

111. *Exordium Magnum Cisterciense*, ed. Bruno Griesser (Rome: Editiones Cistercienses, 1961) II.7, p. 102: '*De monacho, quem sacramentis altaris fidem non adhibentem iussit pater sanctus communicare fide sua.*'

trust in their duty to say the Mass, whatever their moral doubts. Such a transformation did not necessarily result from deliberate distortion of a written source. Gerson may have believed he remembered the precise story while he actually was adjusting it to suit his immediate interest. Gerson in this case and others intended to be faithful to the memory of Bernard and hold him up as an example to be followed. But in interpreting the story about celebrating mass on the basis of faith in one's superior's faith, Gerson was afraid that his listeners would go too far. They might say that there were no Bernards in their own day, and so they were excused from the duty to maintain their faith:

> Some rather naïve person might say: 'I wish I had such an abbot or prior as Bernard was. Then I could more easily believe in what he ordered. For when I consider the limited wisdom of my superior I do not dare commit my conscience and salvation to his faith in such an agreement.' Whoever you might be that says and does such a thing, you are in error and are a fool. You have not committed your salvation into the hands of a man because he is prudent or learned and devout, but because he is your superior and prelate according to a law-regulated institute.[112]

We are to obey God rather than man; the monk or priest cannot expect his abbot or prelate to be like Saint Bernard!

Gerson almost had to deconstruct his own story in order to make the necessary point that the Church functions not because of the holiness of its superiors but because

---

112. Gl 9.39: '*Dicet aliquis ex simplicioribus: utinam talis mihi esset abbas aut prior qualis erat Bernardus; crederem faciliter imperanti. Nunc vero dum subprioris mei parvam sapientiam inspicio non audeo meam conscientiam et salutem suae fidei tali pacto committere. Quisquis ita dicis et facis, erras et desipis; non enim commisisti te et salutem tuam in manus hominis quia prudens est aut plurimum litteratus aut devotus, sed quia tibi est secundum regularem institutionem praepositus et praelatus. . . .*'

of the authority given it by Christ. Here we see a fascinating meeting point between the yearning of late medieval religious life for holiness and the need to assert the independence of spiritual powers from the individual dispositions of those who held them. The memory of 'devout Bernard' could be almost subversive, for it might invite indvidious comparisons with the good old days of the twelfth century.

GERSON'S FREEDOM WITH BERNARD

Jean Gerson took what he needed from the writings of Bernard and from stories about the saint. In the latter case Gerson could draw on tales, probably both written and oral, that had expanded considerably by the fifteenth century and which can best be seen in the pictorial representations of Saint Bernard.[113] But with the works of Bernard himself, Gerson was more at home, especially in his knowledge of the *Sermons on the Song of Songs*. Gerson had his favorite passages, but he could also capture in a single line an entire bernardine argument.

Usually Gerson was loyal to what Bernard wrote. Only rarely, when he did not want to emphasize a disagreement with Bernard, did Gerson fail to show his readers what Bernard actually had written. 'Devout Bernard' or 'blessed Bernard' are more than trite titles for the saint whom Gerson recognized. He returned time and again to Bernard because the abbot had written magnificently about the contemplative life, the thirst of the soul for the coming of the Word, and the experience of that visit.

There is no doubt that Gerson sought the same kind of experience. In his attraction to the affective dimension of religion, Gerson chose for a time to leave the narrow

113. I am indebted to James France of Blewbury, Oxfordshire, whose work on the portrayal of Bernard from the late twelfth century and to the end of the Middle Ages is casting new light on links between monastic and lay spirituality.

speculative world of the university and speak to his sisters and to other women who sought religious experience.[114] At times, especially in the last years of his life, Gerson expressed skepticism about such women and what they said. He never really decided within himself whether Birgitta of Vadstena should be respected as a visionary or dismissed as a prattler.[115] But with Bernard of Clairvaux, Gerson was never in doubt. He saw the abbot as a model for combining active and contemplative life, a man who both worked for the reformation of the Church and prepared himself for the vision of God.

Gerson's Bernard was not the abbot of Clairvaux who looked after the needs of his monks, save in the one story about vicarious faith that Gerson radically altered. In this sense Gerson ignored a side of Bernard important for many scholars and monks today: Bernard the friend and affective center of a community. But Gerson still challenges us to read Bernard and reach new levels of understanding in him. I can imagine the Consoling Doctor, as the next generation called him, burning the midnight oil and poring over his tomes of Bernard. In such lonely hours the inner light of Bernard's insights could fill Gerson's mind and give him assurance of things to come. The twelfth-century abbot, the fifteenth-century scholastic, and our contemporary monk, brother and father all speak the same language of faith seeking not only intellectual understanding but also affective experience.

114. See McGuire, 'Late Medieval Care and Control of Women: Jean Gerson and his Sisters', *Revue d'histoire ecclésiastique* 92 (1997) 5–36.

115. There is the famous remark about Birgitta's canonization in *De probatione spirituum* 5, from Constance in 1415 (Gl 9:179), but also towards the end of the work, section 12 (184), Bernard is named in contrast to those who (assumedly like Birgitta) are so certain about the coming of the Word to them.

David N. Bell

Memorial University of Newfoundland

Translating the Cistercians:
Why, How, and Whom?

THE IDEAS EXPRESSED in this brief paper have their origin in a conversation with Fr Chrysogonus in the autumn of 1997. At that time, Fr Chrysogonus was staying with me and my cats in Newfoundland—we were working on his magisterial edition, translation, and study of the early cistercian documents[1]—and the task of translation led us, perhaps inevitably, to lament the quality of some recent translations of the cistercian (and other) Fathers, and to lament even more the mass of important material which remains untranslated. Having pondered the matter further over the ensuing months—a true case of *ruminatio*—I make the following comments. I am sure that many will find them uncomfortable and that many more will disagree with them, but here I stand.

Let us begin with the question of why we need translations.[2] There are two reasons. The more obvious is that, since so few people nowadays can read Latin, and fewer still can read it sufficiently well to enjoy it, without

---

1. Now published as Chrysogonus Waddell, *Legislative and Narrative Texts from Early Cîteaux: An Edition, Translation, and Commentary*, *Cîteaux: commentarii cistercienses,* Studia et Documenta 9 (Brecht, 1999).

2. In this paper I am concerned only with translations into English, and, in almost all cases, from Latin into English. Other languages pose other problems. It is, of course, unquestionable that at the time of writing, many texts hitherto untranslated are in the process of being translated, or, having been translated, are awaiting publication—I know of a number myself—but this does not affect my argument.

translations vast areas of literature must remain unread
and unexplored. The second reason is that translation
produces scholarship. Many years ago I proposed the
principle—'Bell's Law'—that the number of studies of
any latin author varies directly with the number of that
author's works available in translation,[3] and what was true
then is true now. For many people, their knowledge of
Latin is sufficiently sound for them to read a text if they
know what the text says, but not sufficient for them to
read it without a crib. Translations are therefore essential,
and as the knowledge and teaching of Latin (and even
more of Greek) continues to decline, they become ever
more essential.

If, then, translations are necessary, it is reasonable
to hope that they will be accurate. Faulty translations
must inevitably produce faulty scholarship, and although
it seems stupidly obvious to say so, medieval Latin is
not classical Latin, and patristic and medieval Greek is a
language of its own. I remember on one occasion being
asked by a publisher to check the accuracy of a certain
latin translation, and was intrigued to learn that God
sometimes spoke to people as he might speak to a horse.
This, clearly, was a novel idea of some importance—it
suggests a God with a good deal of sense—but alas! it
was not to be. The translator was unaware that classical
Latin *æquus* appears in medieval dress as *equus* and that
God sometimes spoke to us as equals, which is an entirely
different matter and not nearly so interesting. More
recently, I have come across translators who have not
realised that, in the Middle Ages, *laboro* can mean to
travel as well as to work, that a *consideratio* may be a legal
decision as well as a deliberation, and that a monk in
domus purgatoria was not in Purgatory but in the privy.
Less dramatic instances are legion, and can all too easily

3. David N. Bell, *The Image and Likeness: The Augustinian Spirituality of William of Saint Thierry* (CS 78; Kalamazoo, 1984) 13.

lead to such unreliable translations as the first volume of John of Forde's commentary on the Song of Songs published by Cistercian Publications in 1977.[4] To translate medieval Latin accurately demands wide familiarity with the language and extensive use of an ever-growing variety of dictionaries.[5] It is by no means an easy task.

Furthermore, if we are to translate an author, we should attempt to ensure—so far as is possible—that we translate, or have translated, the entire corpus of his or her writings. Works left in Latin are sure to be overlooked, and edited or abridged translations tell us more about the interests of the editors and the times in which they lived than about the author translated. Thus, among the works of William of Saint-Thierry, his *Disputatio adversus Petrum Abælardum* is still (so far as I am aware) unavailable in English and is regularly and cavalierly dismissed. It is, in fact, just as interesting as his *Speculum fidei*, but to a different audience, and I have little doubt that once it is has been translated and published, it will be re-evaluated, probably a number of times. In a similar way, it is quite indefensible that we have at least ten english translations of Bernard of Clairvaux's *De diligendo Deo*[6]— an early and over-rated work—and none of his important letter to Henry of Sens *de moribus et officio episcoporum*.[7] But this is a matter to which we shall return later. As for editing and abridgement, one need only glance at the

4. *John of Ford: Sermons on the Final Verses of the Song of Songs, I*, tr. Wendy M. Beckett (CF 29; Kalamazoo, 1977). See the devastating but just review by Simon Tugwell in *Cistercian Studies Quarterly* 13 (1978) [368]-[371].
5. The great work of Du Cange remains essential, as do the dictionaries of Souter, Blaise, and Niermeyer; but we now have dictionaries of medieval Latin from Bohemian, British, Danish, Dutch, and Hungarian sources, and more are projected. Patristic Greek is admirably served by the superb *Patristic Greek Lexicon* of G.W.H. Lampe (Oxford, 1961).
6. For translations up to 1970, see David N. Bell, 'A Bibliography of English Translations of Works By and Attributed to Saint Bernard of Clairvaux: 1496–1970', *Cîteaux: comm. cist.* 48 (1997) 125. Others have been produced since.
7. See *ibid.*, 86.

versions produced by Sr Penelope Lawson or Geoffrey
Webb and Adrian Walker[8] to see how dangerous this may
be. An author abridged is an author transformed, and it
is not, in fact, too difficult to sift through the pages of the
Marquis de Sade's *La Philosophie dans le boudoir* (*Philosophy
in the Bedroom*) and compile a brief anthology of up-lifting
quotations which would grace the shelves of any monastic
library.

But let us return for a moment to the question of
accuracy. Accurate translation is not merely a matter of
knowing what words mean; it also involves an appreciation of style. Bernard, for example, might not have been
a great theologian, but he was certainly a great latinist;
and his splendid language, redolent with cursus, cannot
and should not translated by a person whose own style has
been formed by the English of university text-books or
the quickspeak of contemporary television. We are for-
tunate, with the Cistercian Fathers, that we never have to
deal with the sort of idiosyncratic language that we find
in the coptic sermons of Shenoute the Great, but style
demands style and, furthermore, monastic style was a
style formed by and within the Bible and the liturgy.
This, indeed, is simply to state the obvious, but it has
a less obvious corollary. Medieval monastic writing is
full of biblical echoes, allusions, and quotations; and the
Latin of the latin Bible is distinctive, often peculiar, and,
by the twelfth century, decidedly old-fashioned. In fact,
listening to a sermon by, say, Baldwin of Forde, might
have been similar to listening to one of the better televan-
gelists, whose fluent modern idiom is interspersed with
a multitude of echoes, allusions, and quotations to and
from the Authorized Version, i.e. the literary language
of seventeenth-century England. In other words, the old
Douai-Reims translation of the Vulgate is a far better

---

8. For their versions of bernardine and *ps.*-bernardine treatises, see *ibid.*,
119–121.

guide to translating biblical quotations in medieval writings than, say, the Jerusalem Bible or the NRSV which, after all, are not only intended to be 'modern' but are also (for our present purposes) translated from the wrong text, *viz.*, Hebrew, Aramaic, and Greek.[9]

In any case, unless we translate biblical Latin literally, we will miss many of the key-words that provide continuity in an author's exegesis. This is particularly true of the massive sermon-literature of the Middle Ages, but it is common everywhere. Medieval exegesis is not always easy to follow—it is sometimes (to our modern minds) forced, sometimes outrageous, often unpersuasive—but it does have its own logic; and if (for example) we translate the *vetus homo* of Romans 6:6 as 'our old self' (RSV and NRSV) and a following *vetus homo* as an 'aged human being', we have lost the essential terminological connection between the two.[10]

Other key-words are more difficult to deal with. Medieval monastic Latin contains a considerable number of loaded terms, and deciding how best to translate them— or even whether to translate them at all—is no easy matter. One of the most obvious examples is the problem of *amor*, *dilectio*, and *caritas*, for although *amor* and *dilectio* may sometimes (though not always) act as synonyms, *caritas* is another matter entirely. Much of the difficulty, obviously, lies in the limitations of the english language, for although the loves with which I love my wine and my wife are not separate, they are certainly distinct. Personally, I would always translate *caritas* as charity, and work

9. See, for example, Simon Tugwell's review cited in n. 4 above, p. [369]-[370]. The Douai-Reims translation of the New Testament first appeared in 1582 and the Old Testament in 1609. A revised edition was produced by Richard Challoner in 1749–50 and it is this version which forms the basis for the modern editions.

10. I am referring here to Baldwin of Forde's exegesis in his third sermon (= Tractate XI): see *Balduini de Forda opera: Sermones, De commendatione fidei*, ed. David N. Bell (CCCM 99; Turnhout, 1991) 47–64 (CF 41: 91–115). If I were translating the text now, I would do it rather differently.

on the assumption that after one has read it a sufficient
number of times, it begins to mean what Saint Paul, Saint
Bernard, *et al*. intended it to mean, and not what it appeared to mean to Mr Perks in *The Railway Children*.[11] But
to render *dilectio* as 'dilection', while possible, is absurd,
for English should be English and not modified Latin.[12]

The problem of love and charity, however, is less
difficult than the problem of *anima*, *animus*, *spiritus*, and
mens, all of which, on occasion, may mean much the
same thing and all of which, on other occasions, must be
clearly distinguished. But even single words may pose
grave difficulties: how does one translate *affectus*, for
example, or *pietas*, or *excessus*, or *fruitio*, or *salus*? One
needs, in fact, what Sr Edith Scholl has begun to produce:
a glossary of what are, in essence, the technical terms of
monastic spirituality,[13] but one also needs similar hand-
books for medieval law, logic, rhetoric, and so on. The
task is immense, and we have only just begun.

Personally, I think a sound solution is to choose some
constant translation for these loaded terms, use that
translation—so far as is possible—throughout one's
work, and provide the reader with a note or glossary
to explain its richer meaning. Such a solution, however,
will not always work. It will not work for *affectus*, for example, and there are certain important terms for which
a single constant translation is impossible. *Virtus*, for example, must sometimes be translated as 'virtue', some-

11. Edith Nesbit, *The Railway Children*, first published 1906, ch. 9 'The Pride
of Perks'.
12. Cf. *Baldwin of Ford: Spiritual Tractates*, tr. David N. Bell (CF 39; Kalamazoo,
1986), 1: 212: it is theoretically possible to translate *O salutatio salutifera* as
'O salutiferous salutation', but who would wish to do so?
13. See Edith Scholl, 'The Cistercian Vocabulary: A Proposal', *Cistercian
Studies Quarterly* 27 (1992) 77–92. Sr Edith has so far produced six subsequent
papers, all dealing with different technical terms and all published in the
same journal. More comprehensive accounts may be found in the pages of the
Dictionnaire de spiritualité, though many of the earlier articles in that excellent
compendium are now in need of revision.

times as 'power', sometimes as 'power-and-virtue', and sometimes (in scientific and pseudo-scientific writings) as 'property', as in the properties (*virtutes*) of a metal or a mineral. My own opinion, certainly, is that as far as possible we should have the same english translation for the same latin technical term, but since this cannot always be done, we are sometimes left with the uncomfortable expedient of providing the latin term in parenthesis so that the reader can follow the author's logic, thus: 'if God is Lord of Hosts (*virtutum*), it follows that our human virtues (*virtutes*) are . . .',[14] and so on. But to take this approach too far can lead to a cumbersome translation in which one is not quite sure whether one is reading English, Latin, or Latish.

We might, for example, translate the beginning of Bernard's fifth sermon on the Song of Songs thus: 'There are four kinds (*genera*) of spirits (*spirituum*). They are known to you: [that] of an animal (*pecoris*), our own (*noster*), the angelic (*angelicus*) [spirit], and He who created [all] these.'[15] Any 'translation' of this nature should, of course, immediately be consigned to the shredder, though it does show that the ideal translation is one in which we have the latin text on one side of the page and the translation facing it. Nevertheless, there *are* problems in understanding this interesting and difficult sermon—it is much concerned with the nature of angels—for there is a substantial amount of technical vocabulary, and a number of allusions to ideas and doctrines often unfamiliar to modern readers. Notes are therefore essential, and this leads me to the question of annotation in translations.

Many years ago, a cistercian nun of my acquaintance said to me that a translation without notes was like a skeleton without flesh. True enough. Our own *Weltan-*

14. This is an invented example.
15. Bernard of Clairvaux, SC 5.1; SBOp 1: 2: 'Quatuor sunt spirituum genera; nota sunt vobis: pecoris, noster, angelicus, et qui condidit istos.'

schauung is far removed from that of the Middle Ages, and to appreciate fully the richness of most medieval writings, some sort of apparatus is essential. Sometimes, indeed, the annotations may be much longer than the text, as may be seen in Fr Chrysogonus's excellent annotated translation of Saint Stephen Harding's letter to Thurstan, abbot of Sherborne.[16] This, however, is unusual, and a better example for our present purposes is George Burch's translation, first published in 1940, of Bernard's *Steps of Humility*.[17] Here we have not only notes and two appended essays—to say nothing of the latin text opposite the english translation—but a long introduction of more than a hundred pages discussing the nature of the work and putting it in context. This, too, is important. In a splendid article on Oscar Wilde published in *The New Yorker* in 1998, Adam Gopnik observed (correctly) that in the new academic literature on Wilde, one almost never finds 'what the professors used to be drearily good at—putting a text in context, giving a sense of what was original and what was just the way they did things then.'[18] The same is true of translations and, indeed, of articles, papers, and presentations. How many times, at conferences, do we suffer through the 'X on Y' type of presentation—Bernard on war, William on charity, Guerric on anything that happens to appear in the index to his sermons—with no attempt to place the matter in context? But if what Guerric has to say on X is much the same as what Bernard, William, the Benedictines, and most other twelfth-century writers also have to say on X, then that is interesting, but no more. Similarly, any translation of any work demands an introduction which—however

16. *Noble Piety and Reformed Monasticism: Studies in Medieval Cistercian History VII*, ed. E. Rozanne Elder (CS 65; Kalamazoo, 1981) 10–39; and *The New Monastery*, ed. E. R. Elder (CF 64: Kalamazoo 1998) 90–123.
17. See Bell, 'Bibliography' (n. 6), 118.
18. Adam Gopnik, 'The Invention of Oscar Wilde', *The New Yorker*, 18 May 1998, 78.

drearily—*must* put it in context, and thereby explain (i) why one should bother translating it in the first place, and (ii) why one should bother reading the translation. One might also add that any translation should also contain, apart from notes and a sound introduction, an index of scriptural citations, certainly an index of proper names, and preferably an index of subjects.

Judging the balance of these things is not easy. Too great a preponderance of notes can be burdensome (though one does not have to read them); having to refer to a glossary of technical terms can be annoying; and I can offer no simple solutions to these difficult problems. Less difficult to deal with is the reasonable demand that translators translate the text in front of them. I mean by this that they translate what the author actually says, and that if they remove words from the text or add words to it, they inform the reader of the fact. That they should remove words seems to me indefensible;[19] and if they add them, the added words should (in general) be enclosed in square brackets.

Let us take a simple example. In what is probably the most widely read english translation of Bernard of Clairvaux's sermons on the Song and Songs,[20] the ninth sermon begins thus: 'It is time now for us to return to the book and attempt an explanation of the words of the bride and their consequence.'[21] What Bernard actually says is 'Accedamus iam ad librum, verbisque sponsae rationem demus et consequentiam.'[22] There is no mention here of time, return, or attempt; *ratio* is better translated as reason (the phrase is simply 'give a reason'); and *consequentia* does not here mean consequence, but, as

19. I do not mean the *autems*, *veros*, and so on which are often there simply to provide cursus. I mean words of any significance.
20. *Bernard of Clairvaux: On the Song of Songs I–IV*, tr. Sr Kilian Walsh and/or Irene M. Edmonds (CF 4, 7, 31, 40; Kalamazoo, 1971–80).
21. *Ibid.*, I (1971; tr. Kilian Walsh) 53.
22. SC 9.1; SBOp 1: 42.

elsewhere in medieval Latin, logical continuity or chain
of reasoning. What Bernard actually says, therefore, is
something like 'Let us now approach the Bible,[23] give
a reason for the words of the bride, and [explain their]
logic.'

Again, when Bernard writes 'Porro hominis spiritum,
qui medium quemdam inter supremum et infimum tenet
locum . . .',[24] he does not say 'We come now to the spirit
of man. This holds a middle place between the extremes
of bestial and angelic spirits . . .'[25] What he says is 'Next
[we must consider] the human spirit, which holds a sort
of middle place between the highest and the lowest . . .'
What the 'translator' has produced here is a paraphrase
of Bernard and, to my mind at least, a paraphrase is not a
translation. And lest the reader pounce on this example
as clear evidence of the need for a new translation of
Bernard's sermons *in Cantica*, I can only reply that such is
unnecessary. There are already two superior translations:
that produced by Samuel Eales in 1895 and that by Ailbe
Luddy in 1920.[26]

It would be a simple matter to continue at length in
this vein, for there are multitudes of other examples
from other translations by other translators, but to do
so would be otiose. Enough has been said, I think, to
suggest six points: (i) that there is certainly a need for
accurate translations of medieval texts; (ii) that medieval
Latin is not classical Latin, though there is obviously
a large area of overlap; (iii) that translating medieval
Latin demands wide familiarity both with medieval latin
literature and with dictionaries of medieval Latin from

23. This is not an 'interpretative translation'. *Liber* as a another term for the
Bible may certainly be traced as far as the early Middle Ages.
24. SC 5.5.; SBOp 1: 23.
25. *Bernard of Clairvaux: On the Song of Songs I* (n. 20) 28.
26. See Bell, 'Bibliography' (n. 6), 110, 114. Both translations, naturally,
need to be checked against the modern critical edition, but major differences
are very few. Mabillon was a good editor.

Du Cange onwards; (iv) that a translation needs an introduction to put it in context, notes to elucidate it, and indexes to render it useful; (v) that it is not the business of the translator either to add to, take from, or improve on the text of the author being translated; and (vi) that translation should be translation and not paraphrase.

That being said, whom or what should we translate? Much is now available in English, but there is very much more that is not. What, then, should we choose to translate? One of the greatest plagues of our time is the plague of retranslation. How many more versions of the *Confessions* of Saint Augustine do we really need? How many more translations of the *De diligendo Deo* can we really defend? As we said above, there are already at least ten of them, excluding excerpts. Furthermore, there are also a number of important instances in which we already have translations from an earlier age, and all that needs to be done with them is some modernizing of expression, and some minor amendments to the text from a modern critical edition. Let us take a specific example.

Between 1844 and 1850 there appeared an anonymous translation of the *Moralia in librum Job* of Gregory the Great.[27] The translation was part of the *Library of Fathers of the Holy Catholic Church*, published under the inspiration of the Oxford Movement, and the first volume in the series, published in 1838, was a translation of Augustine's *Confessions*. These translations, as a whole, were remarkably good. They were made from the best editions available—in the cases of Augustine and Gregory, the excellent Maurist editions[28]—and they were made by men to whom Latin and Greek were as familiar as their

---

27. *Morals on the Book of Job by S. Gregory the Great, the First Pope of that Name, Translated, with Notes and Indices* (Library of Fathers of the Holy Catholic Church 18, 21, 23, 31; Oxford, 1844–50), three volumes in four.

28. The edition of Augustine was published in eleven volumes between 1679 and 1700; that of Gregory in four volumes in 1704. Some later editions of certain works of Augustine are of decidedly inferior quality, and it must

native English.[29] There was certainly much wrong with nineteenth-century english public-school education, but it did produce a breed of scholars to whom gerundives were commonplace and to whom *oratio obliqua* or the use of *quin* offered no terrors. Their translations, therefore, may have been couched in the high style of victorian literary English, but they are solid, well-written, and accurate, and that is more than can be said for much that is now on the market.

There is therefore no need for a 'new' translation of the *Moralia* of Gregory the Great. The Victorian language may, perhaps, be brought a little more up to date (though the stately prose is a fair echo of Gregory's stately Latin) and a comparison of the Maurist edition with that published between 1979 and 1985 by *Corpus Christianorum*[30] will reveal how few significant changes need to be made to the earlier edition. What we have, therefore, is, in existence, a sound and accurate translation of a book which was to be found on the shelves of almost every monastic library, a fundamental treatise in the development of the cistercian literary tradition, and essential reading for anyone interested in the nature and development of spirituality in the medieval west. What is tragic is that it has never (so far as I know) been reprinted, that copies are not to be found in every library, and that people are still prepared to write about Bernard of Clairvaux without first having read Gregory the Great.

---

be remembered that the Maurists had access to many manuscripts which disappeared in the tumult of the French Revolution.

29. When John Gardiner Wilkinson edited Richard Burton's *Personal Narrative of a Pilgrimage to El-Medinah and Meccah*, first published in 1855 (vols. 1 and 2) and 1857 (vol. 3), he decorously translated a number of Burton's more hair-raising foot-notes into Latin; but Latin, as Edward Rice observes in his brilliant biography of Burton, was 'a language so common among educated Englishmen (and women) that it might as well have been left alone' (Edward Rice, *Captain Sir Richard Francis Burton* [New York, 1999] 202).

30. *S. Gregorii Magni Moralia in Job*, ed. Marcus Adriaen (*CCSL* 143-A-B; Turnhout, 1979–1985), three volumes.

It is time, therefore, to call a moratorium on unnecessary retranslation. It is all too often a waste of time and effort, and the fact that language changes and that translations need to be updated is really no excuse. In any case, most retranslations appear in much the same style as those they are intended to supersede, *viz.* academic literary English, slightly colloquialized. We do not have, for example, versions of the *De diligendo Deo* in Highland English, Indian English, Korean Bamboo English,[31] or teenspeak ('OK, guys', says Bernard in the fourth sermon on the Song of Songs, 'today we're gonna talk some more about sucking lip.') Furthermore, there still remain far too many texts in Latin which are not yet available in English, but which certainly should be. What texts? Here we need to go beyond the cistercian tradition, and, within the cistercian tradition, beyond Latin. It is, for example, absurd that John of Forde's long and rambling commentary on the Song of Songs should be available in its entirety in English,[32] but that Peter Lombard's *Four Books of Sentences* is not. John's commentary survives in a single manuscript and its distribution was, so far as we know, minute; Lombard's *Sentences*—the most influential theological text-book of the later Middle Ages—was read by almost everyone, was to be found in virtually every library, and was supplanted by the *Summa theologiæ* of Thomas Aquinas only in the sixteenth century. And the same is true of a host of other medieval *auctoritates* read by everyone everywhere, to say nothing of the Gloss.

But let us take a practical example. Let us glance at the early thirteenth-century library catalogue of a small cistercian abbey—Flaxley, in Gloucestershire—and see just what books the monks might have been reading for

31. These are all recognized forms of English with their own grammar and vocabulary: see *The Oxford Companion to the English Language: Abridged Edition*, ed. Tom McArthur (Oxford, 1996) 431–3, 460–5, 498, 518.
32. See n. 4 above. The complete translation, in seven volumes (CF 29, 39, 43–7), appeared between 1977 and 1984.

their *lectio divina*, and which of these books we might read today in english translation.[33] The list of eighty manuscripts begins with the Bible and Augustine's *Enarrationes in Psalmos*, both of which are available in English. We then have three volumes of Peter Lombard's commentary on the Psalms (unavailable in English), two volumes of his commentary on the Pauline Epistles (likewise unavailable), Gilbert de la Porrée's commentary on Psalms (unavailable), Lombard's *Sentences* (unavailable), Comestor's *Historia scholastica* (unavailable), a whole series of biblical glosses (all unavailable), an unidentifiable collection of decretal letters (of which we can say nothing), and the *Decretum* of Ivo of Chartres (unavailable). We are now more than a quarter of the way through the collection, and although from here on we find many more volumes that have been translated—volumes of Augustine, Gregory, Bernard, Cassian, and Hugh and Richard of Saint-Victor—that is certainly not the case for all. We do not yet have an english translation of the *Diadema monachorum* attributed to Smaragdus of Saint-Mihiel, for example, nor of the commentary on the Rule of Saint Augustine attributed to Hugh of Saint-Victor, nor of the whole of Isidore's *Etymologies*, nor of the sermons in the *Collectio Gallicana*, nor of a number of works by Richard of Saint-Victor, nor of the sermons of Ivo of Chartres, nor of Bede's commentary on the Prayer of Habakkuk, and so on.

Many of these works formed part of the standard repertoire of monastic reading, but, admittedly, none of them is cistercian. What, then, of the Cistercians? Of the four great writers whom Dom Anselme Le Bail called the 'four evangelists of Cîteaux'—Bernard, William of Saint-

---

33. For the catalogue, see David N. Bell, *The Libraries of the Cistercians, Gilbertines and Premonstratensians* (Corpus of British Medieval Library Catalogues 3; London, 1992) 15–26.

Thierry, Aelred, and Guerric—only the works of Guerric are at present available in their entirety in English. [34] How, then, can we defend yet another translation of, say, the *De gradibus humilitatis et superbiæ*—there are already four of them, three of which are good—when the important collection of *sermones de diversis* remains to be translated?

But once we move beyond these four famous names, there is a huge amount of work to be done. There is, for example, the whole series of pseudo-bernardine treatises, which, though certainly of mixed quality, were extremely popular in their day and which are of first importance for a proper appreciation of the cistercian tradition. In the fourteenth century the Cistercians of Meaux in the north of England owned five copies of the pseudo-bernardine *Meditationes piisimæ de cognitione humanæ conditionis*, [35] the Bridgettines of Syon owned seventeen copies, and the Benedictines of Peterborough owned twenty-one. [36] This little work was, in fact, one of the most widely read 'bernardine' treatises in the Middle Ages, [37] and the 'Bernard' who wrote it was the 'Bernard' most people knew. [38] But the last complete english translation appeared in 1773. [39] Often, however, pseudo-Bernard was more important than Bernard himself—the early english translations of 'Bernard's' works accurately reflect

34. *Guerric of Igny: Liturgical Sermons*, tr. by Monks of Mount Saint Bernard Abbey (CF 8, 32; Spencer, 1970–71), two volumes.

35. Bell, *Libraries* (n. 33), Z14.79d, 80c, 171d, 174d, and 177.

36. See David N. Bell, *An Index of Cistercian Authors and Works in Medieval Library Catalogues in Great Britain* (CS 132; Kalamazoo, 1994) 121–2 (Peterborough), 137–8 (Syon).

37. See *ibid.*, 28, 172–3.

38. I have a translation of this work almost completed. The actual author is unknown.

39. See Bell, 'Bibliography' (n. 6), 100–101. The 1773 version was a later edition of George Stanhope's translation, first published in 1701. In its day it was a popular work.

this fact[40]—and a glance at the interesting and important material in volume 184 of the *Patrologia Latina* will show immediately what remains to be done.[41] And then there are the 'other' Cistercians. We await english versions of important works by (for example) Adam of Perseigne, Conrad of Eberbach, Galand of Reigny, Geoffrey of Auxerre, Gilbert of Stanford, Joachim of Fiore, Richard Straddell of Dore, Thomas of Perseigne, and William Rymyngton. And once we move on a little in time, there is a wealth of material waiting: the entire works of Cipriano de la Huerga (1514–1560), for example, which are now available in an admirable bilingual latin/spanish edition, or the works of Luis de Estrada (d. 1581), or the compendious writings of Juan Crisóstomo Henriquez (1595–1632) or Ángel Manrique (1577–1649), and so on. And if we leave the world of Latin and venture into the vernaculars, there is a mighty mother-lode of cistercian literature to be read, savoured, and translated. Indeed, part of the reason for the commonly-held idea that the cistercian tradition reached its apogee on 31 December 1199 and thereafter went into permanent and irretrievable decline is due, in part, to the fact that cistercian scholars too rarely read the writings of these later authors.

In a conference held in 1998 at Ávila, Br Llorenç Sagalés Cisquella presented a fascinating and important paper on four spanish Cistercians of the sixteenth, seventeenth, and eighteenth centuries—Luis de Estrada, Ángel Manrique, Froilán de Urosa (1584–1648), and Juan Crisóstomo Benito de Olóriz (1711–1783)—and the paper was a

---

40. See David N. Bell, ' "In Their Mother Tongue": A Brief History of the English Translation of Works By and Attributed to Saint Bernard of Clairvaux: 1496–1970', in *The Joy of Learning and the Love of God: Studies in Honor of Jean Leclercq*, ed. E. Rozanne Elder (CS 160; Kalamazoo/Spencer, 1995) 291–308.
41. Some of these works are already available in English: see Bell, 'Bibliography' (n. 6), 125–128.

revelation of the riches of this later tradition.[42] But one need not go to Spain to find these treasures. What of the works of Jean d'Assignies (1560–1642)? What of the thirty-one charming *prières* of Françoise de Nerestang, abbess of la Bénisson-Dieu (1591–1652)? And what, above all, of the numerous and important writings of Armand-Jean de Rancé, the great reformer and founder of the Strict Observance? Part of the reason why he is so misunderstood is because he is not read; but the only (unsatisfactory) english translation of his seminal *De la sainteté et les devoirs de la vie monastique* appeared in 1830,[43] and apart from that, all that is available in English at the moment is a beautifully translated selection of his letters.[44]

It is unnecessary to go further. The cistercian tradition was not confined to twelfth-century England and France, and there is a huge amount of cistercian material— theological, scholastic,[45] historical, and spiritual, in a variety of languages, and of first importance—awaiting

42. Llorenç Sagalés Cisquella, 'Espirituales cistercienses en las Congregaciones de Castilla y Aragón', in *Mística Cisterciense: I Congreso Internacional sobre Mística Cisterciense, Ávila 9–12 de octubre 1998*, ed. Francisco R. de Pascual, Crescenta Mateo, and Fernando Beltrán Llavador (Zamora, 1999) 295–314. For a very brief english summary, see David N. Bell, 'Congreso Internacional sobre Mística Cisterciense (Ávila 9–12 de octubre de 1998)', *Cîteaux: comm. cist*. 49 (1998) 381.

43. *A Treatise on the Sanctity and on the Duties of the Monastic State . . . translated into English by a Religious of the Abbey of Melleray, La Trappe* (Dublin, 1830), two volumes.

44. *The Letters of Armand-Jean de Rancé, Abbot and Reformer of La Trappe*, presented by A. J. Krailsheimer (CS 80–81; Kalamazoo, 1984), two volumes. For the letters which are not translated, Krailsheimer has provided summaries.

45. Unfortunately, in the case of the cistercian scholastics—people like Guy de l'Aumône, Humbert de Prully, Jacques Fournier (later Benedict XII), Jacques de Thérines, Jean de Limoges, Jean de Mirecourt, Jean de Weerde, Pierre Ceffons—we need editions before we can hope for translations, and editions are rare. Some of the writings of Jacques Fournier are available; the *Quodlibeta* I and II of Jacques de Thérines were edited by Palémon Glorieux in 1958; and there are other bits and pieces here and there. But these are no more than a few tended trees in the neglected forest of cistercian scholasticism.

interested translators. Let us therefore have no more english versions of over-translated treatises; let us instead move forward into other realms, every bit as rich, and begin to introduce the reader who prefers to read things in English (I include myself) to a new world, unconfined by the twelfth-century latin limitations of the old. There are realms of gold out there; let us enjoy ourselves by travelling in them.

Monk of Mystery

FATHER CHRYSOGONUS WADDELL is well known as a brilliant historian of medieval history and liturgy, as a talented composer and musician, and as a very peripatetic monk. However, not as many of his friends and admirers realize that he has also played an important role in the creation of current mystery fiction.

When did Fr Chrysogonus join the company of Andrew Greely and Ralph McInerny, you ask. Does he use a pseudonym? How long has this been going on?

Brace yourselves, Gentle Readers, I am now going to reveal all!

It was Abelard and Heloise who first brought us together. While doing research on twelfth-century Paris for my first mystery, *Death Comes As Epiphany*, I happened upon the *Institutiones Nostrae* and the *Hymnal of the Paraclete*, both of which Father Waddell had transcribed and annotated. Like most medievalists, I had been fascinated by the story of the 'doomed lovers'. But I had also always wondered what happened to Heloise afterward. It seemed from most of my reading that she had entered the convent, written a few letters and vanished.

My story begins at the Paraclete, nearly twenty years after Heloise turned Abelard's retreat into a monastery for women. My main character is a young woman who is a student there. It is through her eyes that we see Heloise as a mature, confident and still passionate woman of wisdom and authority. As the story progresses, the student, Catherine, is sent back out into the world to

347

prevent an altered manuscript from the Paraclete being used to accuse the nuns of heresy.

At this point Abelard enters the story, not the brash young scholar but a man near the end of his life, 'battered, but unbowed' and still revered by his acolytes, including a young Anglo-Scot named Edgar.

Another scholar wrote me once that she thought it was lovely that I had used Catherine and Edgar to rewrite the story of Abelard and Heloise 'as it should have been', though perhaps with fewer violent deaths. It wasn't my intention to do so, for one reason because I can't envision Abelard, Heloise, and baby Astrolabe settling down to a happy domestic existence. Then, too, I find their lives as they happened far more interesting than speculation on what might have been. And the evolution of Heloise is the most fascinating part.

It was Fr Waddell's insistence on the individuality of Heloise in his commentary to the *Institutiones* that first drew me to him. Instead of seeing her as a part of Abelard with no mind of her own, Fr Chrysogonus looked at the records of the abbey she created as a reflection of her intelligence and independence.

When I first wrote him to ask an innocent question about the liturgy of the monastery, I had no idea that this was to be the beginning of what became almost a collaboration. At Gethsemani Abbey I found a kindred spirit who was enthusiastic about the possibility of a mature Heloise appearing in fiction and not at all fazed at the possibility of a number of dead bodies appearing on the scene. His response was nearly forty pages of commentary, corrections and advice.

In all my fiction, one goal that underlies all the work is to shatter the many incorrect perceptions of the Middle Ages. It wasn't until meeting Fr Chrysogonus that I realized there were a few modern misconceptions which I needed to eradicate in myself. The first one was that Trappists take a vow of silence. Fr. Chrysogonus told me in his first letter that this was false. After several years I now have come to the conclusion that they do seem to realize that silence is not a vacuum to be filled but a moment to be treasured, something we might all try to emulate.

The other image I soon rid myself of is that removing oneself from the world means being ignorant of it. Being devout and gentle does not mean being credulous. It's odd that I knew this was true for the monks of the Middle Ages. Why should it be any different today?

So, without worrying about shocking or horrifying him, I send my books to Fr Chrysogonus in manuscript. In return, he has always given me valuable suggestions, and saved me from a number of embarrassing errors. A stickler for monastic propriety, Fr Chrysogonus was firm about not allowing men to go traipsing through the cloister, no matter what the plot dictated. Instead, he offered a number of ways to keep the story on course without damaging the abbey's reputation. I feel that having to work within the same rules that governed the lives of the nuns gave the entire book more complexity as well as verisimilitude.

When I sent him the second book, *Devil's Door*, also set partially at the Paraclete, Fr Chrysogonus became even more daring, adding dialogue and a couple of plot twists. I confess that, in the heat of rewriting, I gratefully used his ready-made corrections. Very few people will not only tell a writer when she's made a factual mistake, but provide a scene, complete with conversation, by which to emend it.

More remarkably, he knew when to let me form my own conclusions. Despite his devotion to Saint Bernard, Fr Chrysogonus didn't blanch when I tackled the Council of Sens from the viewpoint of Abelard's students. Their support of their master caused many of them, particularly one Berengar, to be vituperative in denunciation of Bernard, Abelard's chief opponent. But, as long as I didn't diverge from what we know of the council, Fr Chrysogonus didn't reproach me or try to defend Bernard.

Fr. Chrysogonus also made no demure when I faced the question of Saint Bernard and the attacks on the Jews during the Second Crusade. My feeling was that Bernard, by his preaching of the Crusade, bore a great responsibility for the outbreak of those attacks. I also believe that his realization of this and his mostly successful attempts to tend the preaching against the Jews are deeds that should rank among the evidence for his sainthood.

In the same book, *The Difficult Saint*—a title stolen from Brian Patrick McGuire—Fr Chrysogonus also made a suggestion concerning a role that Bernard would have certainly wanted to play. I incorporated it into the final scenes.

Of course, I have always exercised an author's prerogative in selecting which of Fr Chrysogonus' many creative ideas to accept. The Heloise in my books does not have a squint. My jewish trader, Solomon, is destined never to convert and become a hermit. But it's quite possible that some of his other plans for my characters will find their way into future stories, so for now they won't be revealed.

Perhaps scholars reading this will feel that it's a waste of Father Chrysogonus' time to read and comment on what is, after all, only popular fiction. His work on the early records of Cîteaux, his music, his life as a monk are all of greater importance. This is true. Yet, it is also true that most people learn about the Middle Ages only through fiction. Wonderful as the transcriptions of the documents of the Paraclete, Molesme, and Cîteaux are, they are used more by other scholars than by the average reader with only a mild interest in history. This is a lamentable fault in our culture, to be sure, but one that I doubt we'll be able to overcome any time soon.

Yet, the popularity of the Middle Ages in film and literature shows that many non-specialists have a great interest in things medieval. Many, after seeing *Braveheart* and *First Knight*, for instance, are curious enough to try to discover more. Unfortunately, even many books that purport to be non-fiction have been written by either amateur historians or people whose expertise is in another period. This results in all too many people continuing to accept myths about the Middle Ages. There are the obvious ones, like belief in a flat earth and that all women wore chastity belts when their husbands left home (Put on armor, get horse shod, lock up wife?). But there are also more insidious myths; myths regarding the way people lived and perceived the world around them. Myths like, 'The Church controlled everyone's mind.', 'Women were chattel.', 'Anyone with a new idea was burnt at the stake.'. These canards are still widely promulgated in our society, even in our classrooms. They affect not only the way we view the past but also how we feel about the present. No matter what dreadful things are done we can take comfort in the fact that at least 'these are not the Middle Ages'.

Perhaps writing fiction that's not only accurate as to dress, kings, battles and dates, but also as to liturgy, theological debates, the real position of women, and, as much as can be ascertained, the immense variety in the way medieval people viewed their world seems a small step in correcting centuries of misunderstanding, but at least it is a step.

It's a pity that most of my readers will never read Fr Chrysogonus' edition of the *Institutiones* Yet, because of his assistance in making my books as accurate as possible, readers are becoming acquainted with his work, even if in a diluted state. They also have now tucked somewhere into their subconscious the fact that Heloise was more than a love-struck girl, that entering the monastery was not the end of her life, but a new beginning, and that she earned the respect of those around her without any help from Abelard.

There are also many minor details that even scholars in other fields might not notice, but all of which added texture to my text. Points of ritual and custom were explained to me so that I could make them appear natural to my characters. Nothing was too trivial, right down to the fact that Peter the Venerable rode not a horse but a mule, and a white one, at that.

Do these things make my work better? I think so. But more than that, I hope that Fr Chrysogonus' spirit also has shown through in the parts he helped with. One of the most prevalent and inaccurate impressions of the Middle Ages, and especially the practice of religion then, is that everything was dark, humorless, and cruel. The joy that Father Chrysogonus finds in the people he studies shines through his work and communicates itself. His own belief in the rightness of his choice of the communal religious life gives him a connection to the monks and nuns of the Middle Ages that few today can know.

I am so grateful that he has been willing to share, not only his knowledge, but also this sense of wonder and joy, with me. I can only hope that I've been able to pass even a bit of it along to others in my stories. For that I have Fr Chrysogonus Waddell to thank. The following story is my homage to him.

~

THE CONVENTUAL SPIRIT[1]
June 1137, the convent of the Paraclete

'Pride, Catherine! Evil, wicked pride! It will be your damnation, girl!'

Sister Bertrada glared at Catherine, their faces an inch apart. 'You'll never be allowed to become one of us unless you learn some humility,' the old nun continued. 'How dare you try to lecture me on the blessed Saint Jerome! Do you think you've received a vision of the Truth?'

Catherine bit her tongue.

'No, Sister,' she said.

Even those two words sounded impudent to Sister Bertrada, who considered the student novices under her care to be her own private purgatory. And Catherine LeVendeur, with her ready tongue and sharp mind, was her special bane.

'Abbess Heloise has a soft spot for you, though I can't see why,' Bertrada went on. 'I don't find your glib attempts at rhetoric endearing at all.'

'No, Sister.' Catherine tried to back up, but Sister Bertrada had her wedged into a corner of the refectory and there was no farther back to go.

'What you need is some serious manual labor.'

Catherine stifled a groan. Sister Bertrada did not consider sitting for hours hunched over a table laboriously copying a Psalter to be real work. Never mind that her fingers cramped, her back ached, and her eyes burned at the end of the day. Now she tried to look meek and obliging as she awaited Sister Bertrada's orders.

She succeeded about as well as most sixteen-year-old girls would.

Sister Bertrada had eyes like the Archangel Michael, which glowed with righteousness and ferreted out the

---

1. 'The Conventual Spirit' by Sharan Newman, copyright 1996: Sharan Newman. Originally published in *Malice Domestic 5: An Anthology of Original Traditional Mystery Stories*, edited Phyllis A. Whitney. New York-London-Toronto-Sydney-Tokyo-Singapore: Pocket Books, 1996.

most deeply hidden sins. Her cane tapped the wooden floor with ominous thumps as she considered an appropriate penance.

'Go find sister Felicitia,' she told Catherine at last. 'Ask her to give you a bucked and a brush. The transept of the oratory has mud all over the floor. You can easily finish scrubbing it before Vespers, if you give the labor the same passion you use to defy me.'

Catherine bowed her head, hopefully in outward submission. Sister Bertrada snorted to show that she wasn't fooled in the least, then turned and marched out, leaving Catherine once again defeated by spiritual superiority.

Outside, she was met by her friend and fellow student, Emilie. Emilie took one look at Catherine's face and started laughing.

'Why in the world did you feel you had to tell Sister Bertrada that Saint Jerome nagged poor Saint Paula to death?'

Catherine shrugged. 'I was only quoting from a letter of Saint Ambrose. I thought it was interesting that even the saints had their quarrels.'

Emilie shook her head in wonder. 'You've been here a year and you still have no sense about when to speak and when to keep silent. Sister Melisande would find it amusing, so would Mother Heloise, but sister Bertrada . . . !'

'I agree,' Catherine said sadly. 'And now I'm to pay for it on my knees, as usual.'

'And proper.' Emilie smiled at her fondly. 'Oh, Catherine, you do make lessons interesting, if more volatile. I'm so glad you came here.'

Catherine sighed, 'So am I. Now if only sister Bertrada could share our happiness.'

If meekness were the only test for judging the worthiness of a soul, then Sister Felicitia should have inherited the earth long ago. She was the only daughter of a noble family, who ought to have had to do nothing more than sing the hours, sew, and copy manuscripts. Her only distinction was that her face was marred by deep scars on both sides, running from temple to jaw. Catherine had never heard how she came by them, but assumed that this disfigurement was the reason she was in the convent instead of married to some lord. Although for the dowry Felicitia commanded, it was surprising that no one was willing to take her, no matter what she looked like. Felicitia certainly didn't behave like a pampered noblewoman. She always volunteered when the most disagreeable tasks were being assigned. She scrubbed out the reredorter, even leaning into the holes in the seats above the river to scrub the filth from the inside. She hauled wood and dug vegetables. She never lifted her eyes from the job she was doing. She never raised her voice in dispute.

Catherine didn't know what to make of her.

'I'll need the bucket later this evening,' Sister Felicitia said when Catherine stated her orders. 'I'd help you, of course, but I'm dyeing today.'

Catherine had noticed. The woman's hands were stained blue with woad. It would be days before it all washed off. Sister Felicitia didn't appear concerned by this. Nor did she seem aware that the day was soft and bright and that the other women were all sitting in the cloister, sewing and chatting softly while soaking up the June sunshine.

'Sister Bertrada wants me to do this alone, anyway,' Catherine said, picking up the bucket and brush. Sister Felicitia nodded without looking up. She did not indulge in unnecessary conversation.

Catherine spilled half the water tripping over the doorstop to the oratory. Coming in from the sunlight, it seemed to her that there were bright doves fluttering before her eyes. So she missed her step in the darkness, and then mopped up the puddles before spending the better part of the afternoon scrubbing the stone floor. But, true to Sister Bertrada's prediction, she did indeed have the job finished in time for Vespers, although her robes were still damp and stained at the hem, unsuitable attire for the Divine Office.

And that was how she knew that there had been no muddy footprints on the oratory floor when the nuns retired to the dormitory that evening.

Of course, Sister Bertrada didn't believe her.

'This time, do it properly,' she told Catherine as she handed her the bucket the next day.

Catherine fervently wanted to protest. She had scrubbed the floor thoroughly, half of it with her own skirts. It had been clean. Perhaps one of the nuns had forgotten and worn her wooden clogs to prayers instead of her slippers. It wasn't her fault.

But Catherine knew that she would never be allowed to remain here at the Paraclete if she contradicted Sister Bertrada every time she opened her mouth, and she wanted to stay at the monastery more than anything else in the world. So she took the proffered bucket and returned to the dark oratory.

She propped the door open to let the light in and knelt to begin the task.

'That's odd,' she said as she started on the marks.

"That's *very* odd,' she added as she went on to the next ones.

These had to have been made recently, after compline, when all the women had retired for the night. They were in the shape of footprints, starting at the door and running across the transept to the chapter room, stopping at the bottom of the staircase to the nun's dormitory. The marks were smudged, perhaps by the slippers of the nuns when they came down just before dawn for Vigils and Lauds. But the muddy prints had certainly been made by bare feet. And they were still damp.

Who could have entered the oratory secretly in the middle of the night?

Catherine wondered about it all the while she was

scrubbing. When she had finished, she went to the prioress, Astane, for an explanation.

'These footprints,' Astane asked. 'You already removed them?'

'Sister Bertrada told me to,' Catherine explained.

The prioress nodded. 'Very good, child. You are learning.'

'But I know they weren't there yesterday evening,' Catherine insisted. 'I did clean the floor carefully the first time. Someone was in the oratory after we went to bed.'

'That seems unlikely,' Astane did not appear alarmed by Catherine's statement. 'The door is barred on the inside, after all.'

'Then how did the footprints get there?' Catherine persisted.

The prioress raised her eyebrows. 'That is not your concern, my dear.'

'It is if I have to wipe them up,' Catherine muttered under her breath.

Not far enough under. Astane's hand gripped her chin tightly and tilted her face upward.

'I presume you were praying just then,' the prioress said.

Catherine marveled at the strength in these old women. Sister Bertrada, Prioress Astane; they both must be nearly seventy, but with hands as firm and steady as a blacksmith's. And eyes that saw the smallest lie.

'No, Sister,' Catherine said. 'But I am now. *Domine, noli me arguere in ira tua . . .*'

The prioress's lip twitched and her sharp glance softened. ' "Lord, do not rebuke me in your anger . . ." ' she translated. 'Catherine, dear, I'm not angry with you and I hope and trust that our Lord isn't, either.'

She paused. 'Sister Bertrada, on the other hand . . .'.

Catherine needed no further warning. She resolved not to mention the footprints in the oratory again.

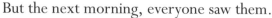

But the next morning, everyone saw them.

The light of early dawn slanted through the narrow windows of the chapter, illuminating the clumps of damp earth, a few fresh stalks still clinging to them, forming a clear trail of footprints across the room.

'How did those get there?' Emilie whispered to Catherine, peering down the stairs over the shoulders of the choir nuns.

'They're exactly the same as yesterday,' Catherine whispered back. 'But I'm sure I cleaned it all. I know I did.'

Sister Bertrada and Sister Felicitia walked through the marks, apparently without noticing, but the other women stopped. They looked at each other in confusion, pointing at the footprints, starting at the barred door to the garden, going through the oratory and ending at the steps to their sleeping room.

Sister Ursula shuddered. 'Something is coming for us!' she shrieked. 'A wild man of the woods had invaded the convent!'

A few of the others gave startled cries, but Emilie giggled, putting a hand over her mouth to stifle the sound. Behind her, Sister Bietriz bent over her shoulder.

'What is it?' she whispered.

Emilie swallowed her laughter. ' " Wild man" indeed!' she whispered back. 'Maybe Sister Bertrada has a secret lover!'

Bietriz and Catherine exploded in most unseemly mirth.

'*Quiet!*' The object of their speculation raised her cane in warning.

They composed themselves as quickly as possible, knowing that the matter would not be forgotten , but hoping to alleviate the punishment.

'Catherine,' Sister Bertrada continued. 'Since you and

Emilie find this mess so amusing, you may clean it. Bietriz, you will help them.'

Catherine opened her mouth to object that she had already removed the marks twice and it had done no good. Just as she inhaled to speak, Emilie stepped on her toe.

'Yie . . . yes, Sister,' Catherine said instead.

Privately, she agreed with both Ursula and Emilie. The marks must have been by a wild man from the forest. For who else could become enamored of Sister Bertrada?

'I agree that there is something very strange about this,' Emilie told Catherine as they scrubbed. 'Who could be getting in here every night? And why doesn't Mother Heloise say something about it? Do you think she knows who it is?'

Catherine wrung out the washrag. Bietriz, whose family was too exalted for floors, leaned against the wall and pointed out spots they had missed.

'Mother Heloise probably doesn't think this worth commenting on,' she said. 'Perhaps she thinks someone is playing a trick and doesn't want them encouraged. You don't really believe one of us is letting a man in, do you?'

'Who?' Emilie asked, 'Sister Bertrada? She and Sister Felicitia would be the most logical suspect. Since they sleep on either side of the door, they have the best chance of leaving at night without being noticed.'

Catherine tried to imagine either woman tiptoeing down the steps to let in a secret lover. In Sister Bertrada's case her imagination didn't stretch far enough.

She laughed. 'I would find it easier to believe in a monster.'

'It's not so preposterous,' Emilie continued. 'Sister Felicitia is really quite beautiful, even now. I've heard that she had a number of men eager to marry her, but she refused them all. Her father was furious when she announced that she would only wed Christ.'

Catherine leaned back on her heels and considered. 'I suppose she might have changed her mind,' she said. 'Perhaps one of them continued to pursue her even here and convinced her that he wanted her despite her looks and had no interest in her property.'

Bietriz shook her head. 'I don't think so, Catherine. Felicitia made those scars herself, with the knife she used to cut embroidery thread. She sliced right through her cheeks, purposely, so that no one would desire her. That was how her father was finally convinced to let her come here.'

Catherine sat back in shock, knocking over the bucket of soapy water.

'How do you know this?' she asked.

'It was common knowledge at the time,' Bietriz answered. 'I was about twelve then. I remember how upset my mother was about it. Felicitia threatened to cut off her own nose next. It's dreadful, but I benefitted from her example. When I said I wanted to come to the Paraclete, no one dared oppose me. Mother even refused to let me have my sewing basket unless she was present, just in case.'

'I see,' Catherine was once again reminded that she was only a merchant's daughter, at the Paraclete by virtue of her quick mind and her father's money. Bietriz was from one of the best families in Champagne, related in some way even to the count. Bietriz knew all about the life of a noble woman and all the gossip she herself would not normally be privy to. At the Paraclete they could be sisters in Christ, but not in the world.

'Very well,' Catherine said. 'I will accept that sister Felicitia is not likely to be letting a man in. But I don't see how any of the rest of us could do it without waking someone.'

'Nor do I,' Emilie agreed. 'In which case we might have to consider Ursula's theory.'

'That some half-human creature came in from the forest?' Catherine snorted.

Emilie stood, shaking out her skirts. Bietriz picked up the bucket, her contribution to the labor.

'Of course not,' Emilie said. 'Even a half-human creature would have to unbar the door. But Satan can pass through bars and locks, if someone summons him. And it's said that he often appears as a beautiful young man.'

Bietriz was skeptical. 'So we should demand to know who has been having dreams of seduction lately? Who will admit to that?'

Catherine felt a chill run down her spine. Was it possible that one of them could be inviting Evil into the monastery, perhaps unwittingly? It was well known that the devil used dreams to lure and confuse the innocent into sin. She tried to remember her dreams of the past few nights. The memories were dim, so it was likely that she had only had dreams of *ventris inanitate*, those deriving from an empty stomach and of no relevance.

They walked out into the sunlight and Catherine felt the fear diminish. While it was true that Satan used dreams to tempt weak humans, sin could only occur when one was awake. Tertullian said so. We can no more be condemned for dreaming we are sinners than rewarded for dreaming we are saints.

'And why would the devil leave footprints?' she continued the thought aloud. 'That doesn't seem very subtle.'

Emilie didn't want to give up her demon lover theory. 'There is a rock near my home with a dent in it that everyone says is the devil's toe print,' she told Catherine. 'So why not the whole foot? Satan is known to be devious. Perhaps he doesn't just want one soul. He may be trying to cause dissension among us so that he may take us all.'

Bietriz had moved on to another worry. 'Why is it that the feet are only coming in?' she asked them. 'How does this intruder get out?'

'Perhaps he turns into something else,' Emilie answered. 'Satan can do that, too.'

She seemed delighted with her conclusions, and her expression dared them to come up with a refutation.

Catherine looked at her. Was she serious? Did she now believe they were being visited by the devil as shape-changer? Emilie was usually scornful of such tales. Why was she so eager to assign a supernatural explanation to this? An answer leaped unbidden to her mind.

Emilie's bed wasn't that far from the door.

Catherine tried to suppress the thought as unworthy, but it wouldn't be put down. Emilie was blond, beautiful, and also from a noble family. Perhaps she wasn't as happy in the monastery as she pretended. It entailed a much smaller stretch of the imagination to see Emilie unbarring the door for a lover than Sister Felicitia.

But that explanation didn't satisfy her, either. It wasn't like Emilie. And Catherine was sure Mother Heloise and Prioress Astane didn't believe that one of the nuns had a secret lover, human or demon. If they did, then Brother Baldwin and the other lay brothers who lived nearby would have been set to guard the oratory entrance.

She was missing something. Catherine hated to leave a puzzle unsolved. She had to find out who was doing this. She sighed. It was either that or spend the rest of her life scrubbing the oratory floor.

It was nearly midsummer. The days were long and busy. Apart from reciting the Divine Office seven times a day, the nuns all performed manual labor. They studied, copied manuscripts for the convent library, sewed both church vestments and their own clothing, as well as doing the daily round of cleaning, cooking, and gardening necessary to keep themselves alive.

Catherine meant to stay awake that night, but after the long day, she fell asleep as soon as she lay down and didn't wake until the bell rang for Vigils.

Even in the dim light of the lamp carried by Sister Felicitia, they could all see the fresh footprints at the bottom of the stairs.

Sister Ursula retreated back up the stairs, whimpering, and had to be ordered to continue to the oratory. The others obeyed as well, but with obvious reluctance.

Mother Heloise and Prioress Astane were already waiting in the chapel. Their presence reassured the women and reminded them of their duty to pray. But Catherine was not the only one who looked to see that the bar was still across the garden door.

'Satan won't distract me,' Emilie whispered virtuously as they filed into their places. 'He can't get you while you're praying.'

Catherine wasn't so confident. Whatever was doing this had thoroughly distracted her. She missed the antiphon more than once and knew that bowing her apology to God would not save her from Sister Bertrada's rebuke.

There was an explanation for this, either natural or supernatural. Catherine didn't care which it was. She only wanted to know the truth.

The next day was the eve f the feast of the Nativity of Saint John the Baptist. There would be a special vigil that night. It was also midsummer's eve, a time of spirits crossing between worlds, a fearsome long twilight. A good Christian could be driven mad or worse by the things that walked this night. These beliefs were officially denied and forbidden, but children learned the folk takes before they were weaned and such stories were hard to uproot. The shimmering sunlight of the morning was not bright enough to dispel fear.

Each afternoon while they worked in the cloister, the women were permitted some edifying conversation. Today, the usual gentle murmurs and soft laughter had become a buzzing of wonderment, anger, and fear.

'What if this thing doesn't stop tonight at the bottom of the stairs?' Sister Ursula said, her eyes round with terror and anticipation. 'What if it climbs right up and into our beds?'

'All of ours, or just yours?' Bietriz asked.

Ursula reddened with anger. 'What are you implying?' she demanded. 'I would never bring scandal upon us. How dare you even suggest such a thing!'

Bietriz sighed and put down her sewing. She went over to Ursula and took her gently by the shoulders.

I apologize,' she said. 'It was not a kind joke. I make no accusations. But I believe you have become overwrought by these happenings. Perhaps you could sleep with Sister Melisande in the infirmary tonight.'

'Perhaps I will,' Ursula muttered. 'Better than being slandered by my sisters or murdered by demons in the dortor.'

Sister Felicitia was seated on the grass, her stained hands weaving softened reeds to mend a basket. She looked up.

'There are no demons here,' she said firmly.

They all stared at her. It would have been more surprising if a sheep in the meadow had spouted philosophy.

'How do you know?' Ursula asked.

'Mother Heloise promised me,' Felicitia answered. 'The demons won't come for me here.'

She bent again to her work. The others were silent.

'Well,' Ursula said finally. 'Perhaps I will stay in the dortor. But if anything attacks me, I'll scream so loud you'll think Judgement Day has come.'

'If you wake me,' Emilie warned, 'you'll wish it had.'

Before Vespers the Abbess Heloise gathered all the women together in the chapter room. There was a collective sigh of relief as they assembled. Finally, all would be explained.

The abbess smiled at them all fondly. Her large brown eyes studied them, and Catherine felt that Mother Heloise knew just what each of them was thinking and feeling.

'It has been brought to my attention,' she began, 'that some of you have been concerned about some mud stains in the oratory and chapel. I fear that you have allowed these queries to go beyond normal curiosity to unwholesome speculation. This saddens me greatly. If something so natural and common as wet earth can cause you to imagine demons and suspect each other of scandalous behavior, then I have not done my duty as your mentor or your mother.'

There was a rustle of surprise and denial. Heloise held up her hand for silence. There was silence.

'Therefore,' she continued, 'I apologize to you all for not providing the proper spiritual guidance. I will endeavor to do so in the future and will ask our founder, Master Abelard, for advice on how this may best be done. I hope you will forgive me.'

That was all. Heloise signaled the chantress to lead them in for Vespers.

They followed in bewildered obedience. Catherine and Emilie stared at each other, shaking their heads. As far as Catherine could see, they had just been told that the intruder in the convent was none of their business. It made no sense.

Mindful of her earlier mistakes, Catherine tried desperately to keep her mind on the service for Saint John's Eve, despite the turmoil in her mind.

'*Ecce, mitto angelum meum* . . . .' Behold, I send my angel, who will prepare the way for you before my coming. '*Vox clamitis in deserto* . . . .' A voice crying in the wilderness.

She tried to concentrate on Saint John. It was hard to imagine him as a baby, leaping for joy in his mother's womb as they visited the Virgin Mary. She always saw him as the gaunt man of the desert, living naked on a diet of locusts and honey. People must have thought him mad, preaching a savior no one had heard of.

'*Ecce, mitto angelum meum* . . . .'

All at once Catherine realized what she had been

doing. She had looked at the problem from one direction only. Mother Heloise knew the answer. That was why she wasn't worried. When one turned the proposition around, it made perfect sense. Now, if only she could stay awake tonight to prove her theory.

The night, usually too brief, seemed to stretch on forever. Catherine was beginning to believe that she had made an error in her logic.

There was a rustling from the other end of the room. Someone was getting up. Catherine waited. Whoever it was could be coming this way, to use the reredorter. No one passed her bed. She heard a creak from the end of the room as if someone else were also awake. She peered over the blanket. It was too dark to tell. There were no more sounds. Perhaps it had only been someone tossing about with a nightmare. Perhaps. But she had to know.

Carefully, Catherine eased out of bed. They all slept fully dressed, even to their slippers, to be ready for the Night Office. Catherine looked up and down the rows on either side of the room. In the dim light everyone appeared to be accounted for and asleep. Slowly, fearing even to breathe, Catherine moved down the room to the door. It was open.

All the tales of monsters and demons came rushing suddenly into her mind. Anything could be at the foot of those stairs. Who would protect her if she encountered them against orders, because of her arrogant curiosity?

She said a quick prayer to Saint Catherine of Alexandria, who had known what it was to wonder about things, and she started down the stairs.

At the bottom she nearly fainted in terror as she stepped onto a pile of something soft that moved under her foot. She bent down and touched it.

It was clothing just like her own. A shift, a long tunic, a belt, and a pair of slippers. The discovery of something so familiar terrified Catherine even more.

What had happened to the woman who had worn these clothes?

Moonlight shone through the open door of the oratory. Catherine looked down at the floor. In her fear, she had almost forgotten to test her conclusion.

She was right. The floor was clean. So far, nothing had entered. Feeling a little more confident, she stepped out into the midsummer night.

The herb garden lay tranquil under the moon. Catherine had been out once before at night, helping sister Melisande pick the plants that were most potent when gathered at the new moon. This time she was here un-invited.

There was a break in the hedge on the other side of the garden. Catherine thought she saw a flicker of something white in the grove just beyond. Before she could consider the stupidity of her actions, she hurried toward it.

Within the grove there was a small hill that was empty of trees or undergrowth. Sheep grazed there by day, but tonight . . . '*Ecce! Mitto angleum!*'

Catherine stopped at the edge of the trees. There was someone on the hill, pale skin glowing silver in the moonlight, golden curls surrounding her face like a halo. It was sister Felicitia, naked, dancing in the night, her feet covered with mud. Her arms were raised as she spun, her face to the sky, her back arched, moving to some music that Catherine couldn't hear.

A hand touched her shoulder. Catherine gasped and the hand moved to her mouth.

'Make no sound,' Abbess Heloise warned. 'You'll wake her.'

Catherine nodded and Heloise removed her hand.

'How did you find out?' the abbess whispered.

'It was the footprints,' Catherine whispered back, not taking her eyes from Felicitia. 'We all thought they were from someone being let in. But it made much more sense if they were made by someone coming back. Then only one person was needed to open the door from the inside. What I didn't understand was the prints of bare feet.'

'She always leaves her clothes at the bottom of the stairs and puts them on again before returning to bed,' Heloise explained.

'But shouldn't we stop her?' Catherine asked. 'She must be possessed to behave like this.'

'She might be,' Heloise said. 'I worried about that, too. But Sister Bertrada convinced me that if she is, it's by nothing evil and we have no right to interfere.'

'Sister Bertrada?' Catherine's voice rose in astonishment.

'Hush!' Heloise told her. 'Yes, she's on the other side of the grove, watching to be sure no one interrupts. Brother Baldwin is farther on, guarding the gate to the road. Not everyone who saw her would understand. Do you?'

Catherine shook her head. She didn't understand, but it didn't matter. She was only grateful she had been allowed to watch. Felicitia, dancing in the moonlight, wasn't licentious, but sublime. She shone like Eve on the first morning, radiant with delight at the wonder of Eden, in blissful ignorance of sin. The joy of it made Catherine weep in her own knowledge that soon the serpent would come, and with it sorrow.

Heloise guided Catherine gently away.

'She'll finish soon and go back to bed,' the abbess explained. 'Sister Bertrada will see that she gets there safely. Come with me. Astane has left some warmed cider for me. You have a cup also, before you go back.'

When they were settled in Heloise's room, drinking the herbed cider, Catherine finally asked the question.

'I figured out who and how, Mother,' she said. 'But I don't understand why.'

Heloise looked into her cider bowl for several minutes. Catherine thought that she might not answer. Perhaps she didn't know.

At last she seemed to come to a decision.

'Catherine,' she asked, 'have you ever believed that you were loved by no one? That you were completely alone?'

Catherine thought. 'Well,' she answered, 'there was about a month when I was thirteen, but . . . no, no. Even then I always knew my family loved me. I know you love me. I know God loves me, unworthy though I am of all of you.'

Heloise smiled. 'That's right, on all points. But until she came here, Felicitia believed that no one loved her, that God had abandoned her, and she had good reason. That is not a story for you to hear. I only want you to understand that I am sure Felicitia is not possessed by anything evil.'

'I believe you,' Catherine said. 'But I still don't understand.'

'I didn't either,' Heloise admitted. 'Until Sister Bertrada explained it to me. Don't make such a face, child, Sister Bertrada sees further into your heart than you know.'

'That doesn't comfort me, Mother.'

Heloise smiled. 'It should. Bertrada told me that Felicitia spent all her life being desired for her beauty, for her wealth, her family connections. In all that desire, there was no love. So she felt she wasn't worthy of love and consented to despair. She endured much to find her way to us. The scars on her face are mild compared to the ones on her soul. She struggles every day with worse demons than any Ursula can imagine. And until a week ago, she had nightmares almost every night.'

'And then . . .' Catherine said.

'And then,' Heloise smiled, 'joy came to her one night, and she danced. It has only been in her sleep so far, but if she is left in peace, we are hoping that soon she will also have joy in the morning, all through the day, and at last be healed.'

Catherine sat for a long while, until the cider went cold

and the chantress rose to ring the bell for Vigils. Heloise waited patiently.

'Are you satisfied, Catherine?' she asked. 'You assembled the evidence, arranged it properly, and solved the mystery. There is no need to tell the others.'

'Oh no, I wouldn't do that,' Catherine promised. 'I only wanted to know the truth.'

'Then why do you look so sad?' Heloise prodded.

'It's only—' Catherine stopped, embarrassed. 'I'm so clumsy, Mother. If only I could dance like Felicitia, even in my sleep.'

Heloise laughed. 'And how do you know that you don't?'

For once in her life, Catherine had no reply.

CISTERCIAN TEXTS

Bernard of Clairvaux

- Apologia to Abbot William
- Five Books on Consideration: Advice to a Pope
- Homilies in Praise of the Blessed Virgin Mary
- In Praise of the New Knighthood
- Letters of Bernard of Clairvaux / by B.S. James
- Life and Death of Saint Malachy the Irishman
- Love without Measure: Extracts from the Writings of St Bernard / by Paul Dimier
- On Grace and Free Choice
- On Loving God / Analysis by Emero Stiegman
- Parables and Sentences
- Sermons for the Summer Season
- Sermons on Conversion
- Sermons on the Song of Songs I–IV
- The Steps of Humility and Pride

William of Saint Thierry

- The Enigma of Faith
- Exposition on the Epistle to the Romans
- Exposition on the Song of Songs
- The Golden Epistle
- The Mirror of Faith
- The Nature and Dignity of Love
- On Contemplating God: Prayer & Meditations

Aelred of Rievaulx

- Dialogue on the Soul
- Liturgical Sermons, I
- The Mirror of Charity
- Spiritual Friendship
- Treatises I: On Jesus at the Age of Twelve, Rule for a Recluse, The Pastoral Prayer
- Walter Daniel: The Life of Aelred of Rievaulx

Gertrud the Great of Helfta

- Spiritual Exercises
- The Herald of God's Loving-Kindness (Books 1, 2)
- The Herald of God's Loving-Kindness (Book 3)

John of Ford

- Sermons on the Final Verses of the Songs of Songs I–VII

Gilbert of Hoyland

- Sermons on the Songs of Songs I–III
- Treatises, Sermons and Epistles

Other Early Cistercian Writers

- Adam of Perseigne, Letters of
- Alan of Lille: The Art of Preaching
- Amadeus of Lausanne: Homilies in Praise of Blessed Mary
- Baldwin of Ford: The Commendation of Faith
- Baldwin of Ford: Spiritual Tractates I–II
- Geoffrey of Auxerre: On the Apocalypse
- Guerric of Igny: Liturgical Sermons Vol. I & 2
- Helinand of Froidmont: Verses on Death
- Idung of Prüfening: Cistercians and Cluniacs: The Case for Cîteaux
- In the School of Love. An Anthology of Early Cistercian Texts
- Isaac of Stella: Sermons on the Christian Year, I–[II]
- The Life of Beatrice of Nazareth
- Serlo of Wilton & Serlo of Savigny: Seven Unpublished Works
- Stephen of Lexington: Letters from Ireland
- Stephen of Sawley: Treatises
- Three Treatises on Man: A Cistercian Anthropology

MONASTIC TEXTS

Eastern Monastic Tradition

- Abba Isaiah of Scete: Ascetic Discourses
- Besa: The Life of Shenoute
- Cyril of Scythopolis: Lives of the Monks of Palestine
- Dorotheos of Gaza: Discourses and Sayings
- Evagrius Ponticus: Praktikos and Chapters on Prayer
- Handmaids of the Lord: Lives of Holy Women in Late Antiquity & the Early Middle Ages
- Harlots of the Desert
- John Moschos: The Spiritual Meadow
- Lives of the Desert Fathers
- Lives of Simeon Stylites
- Manjava Skete
- Mena of Nikiou: Isaac of Alexandria & St Macrobius
- The Monastic Rule of Iosif Volotsky (Revised Edition)
- Pachomian Koinonia I–III
- Paphnutius: Histories/Monks of Upper Egypt
- The Sayings of the Desert Fathers
- The Spiritually Beneficial Tales of Paul, Bishop of Monembasia
- Symeon the New Theologian: The Theological and Practical Treatises & The Three Theological Discourses
- Theodoret of Cyrrhus: A History of the

Monks of Syria
- The Syriac Fathers on Prayer and the Spiritual Life

Western Monastic Tradition

- Achard of Saint Victor: Works
- Anselm of Canterbury: Letters I–III / by Walter Fröhlich
- Bede: Commentary…Acts of the Apostles
- Bede: Commentary…Seven Catholic Epistles
- Bede: Homilies on the Gospels I–II
- Bede: Excerpts from the Works of Saint Augustine on the Letters of the Blessed Apostle Paul
- The Celtic Monk
- Gregory the Great: Forty Gospel Homilies
- Life of the Jura Fathers
- The Maxims of Stephen of Muret
- Peter of Celle: Selected Works
- The Letters of Armand Jean-deRancé I–II
- Rule of the Master
- Rule of Saint Augustine

CHRISTIAN SPIRITUALITY

- A Cloud of Witnesses... The Development of Christian Doctrine / by David N. Bell
- The Call of Wild Geese / by Matthew Kelty
- The Cistercian Way / by André Louf
- The Contemplative Path
- Drinking From the Hidden Fountain / by Thomas Spidlík
- Entirely for God / by Elizabeth Isichei
- Eros and Allegory: Medieval Exegesis of the Song of Songs / by Denys Turner
- Fathers Talking / by Aelred Squire
- Friendship and Community / by Brian McGuire
- Grace Can do Moore: Spiritual Accompaniment / by André Louf
- High King of Heaven / by Benedicta Word
- How Far to Follow / by B. Olivera
- The Hermitage Within / by a Monk
- Life of St Mary Magdalene and of Her Sister St Martha / by David Mycoff
- The Luminous Eye / by Sebastian Brock
- Many Mansions / by David N. Bell
- Mercy in Weakness / by André Louf
- The Name of Jesus / by Irénée Hausherr
- No Moment Too Small / by Norvene Vest
- Penthos: The Doctrine of Compunction in the Christian East / by Irénée Hausherr
- Praying the Word / by Enzo Bianchi
- Praying with Benedict / by Korneel Vermeiren
- Russian Mystics / by Sergius Bolshakoff
- Sermons in a Monastery / by Matthew Kelty

- Silent Herald of Unity: The Life of Maria Gabrielle Sagheddu / by Martha Driscoll
- Spiritual Direction in the Early Christian East / by Irénée Hausherr
- The Spirituality of the Christian East / by Thomas Spidlík
- The Spirituality of the Medieval West / by André Vauchez
- The Spiritual World of Isaac the Syrian / by Hilarion Alfeyev
- Tuning In To Grace / by André Louf

MONASTIC STUDIES

- Community and Abbot in the Rule of St Benedict I–II / by Adalbert de Vogüé
- The Hermit Monks of Grandmont / by Carole A. Hutchison
- In the Unity of the Holy Spirit / by Sighard Kleiner
- A Life Pleasing to God: Saint Basil's Monastic Rules / By Augustine Holmes
- Memoirs [of Jean Leclercq]: From Grace to Grace
- Monastic Practices / by Charles Cummings
- The Occupation of Celtic Sites in Ireland / by Geraldine Carville
- Reading St Benedict / by Adalbert de Vogüé
- Rule of St Benedict: A Doctrinal and Spiritual Commentary / by Adalbert de Vogüé
- The Venerable Bede / by Benedicta Ward
- Western Monasticism / by Peter King
- What Nuns Read / by David N. Bell

CISTERCIAN STUDIES

- Aelred of Rievaulx: A Study / by Aelred Squire
- Athirst for God: Spiritual Desire in Bernard of Clairvaux's Sermons on the Song of Songs / by Michael Casey
- Beatrice of Nazareth in Her Context / by Roger De Ganck
- Bernard of Clairvaux: Man, Monk, Mystic / by Michael Casey [tapes and readings]
- Catalogue of Manuscripts in the Obrecht Collection of the Institute of Cistercian Studies / by Anna Kirkwood
- Christ the Way: The Christology of Guerric of Igny / by John Morson
- The Cistercians in Denmark / by Brian McGuire
- The Cistercians in Scandinavia / by James France
- A Difficult Saint / by Brian McGuire
- The Finances of the Cistercian Order in the Fourteenth Century / by Peter King

- Fountains Abbey and Its Benefactors
  / by Joan Wardrop
- A Gathering of Friends: Learning & Spirituality
  in John of Ford / by Costello and Holdsworth
- The Golden Chain...Isaac of Stella /
  byBernard Mc Ginn
- Image and Likeness: Augustinian Spirituality
  of William of St Thierry / by David Bell
- Index of Authors & Works in Cistercian
  Libraries in Great Britain I / by David Bell
- Index of Cistercian Authors and Works in
  Medieval Library Catalogues in Great Britian
  / by David Bell
- The Mystical Theology of St Bernard
  / by Étienne Gilson
- The New Monastery: Texts & Studies on the
  Earliest Cistercians
- Monastic Odyssey / by Marie Kervingant
- Nicolas Cotheret's Annals of Cîteaux
  / by Louis J. Lekai
- Pater Bernhardus: Martin Luther and
  Bernard of Clairvaux / by Franz Posset
- Pathway of Peace / by Charles Dumont
- Rancé and the Trappist Legacy
  / by A. J. Krailsheimer
- A Second Look at Saint Bernard
  / by Jean Leclercq
- The Spiritual Teachings of St Bernard of
  Clairvaux / by John R. Sommerfeldt
- Studies in Medieval Cistercian History
- Three Founders of Cîteaux
  / by Jean-Baptiste Van Damme
- Towards Unification with God (Beatrice of
  Nazareth in Her Context, 2)
- William, Abbot of St Thierry
- Women and St Bernard of Clairvaux
  / by Jean Leclercq

MEDIEVAL RELIGIOUS WOMEN

A Sub-series edited by
Lillian Thomas Shank and John A. Nichols
- Distant Echoes
- Hidden Springs: Cistercian Monastic Women
  (2 volumes)
- Peace Weavers

CARTHUSIAN TRADITION

- The Call of Silent Love / by A Carthusian
- The Freedom of Obedience / by A Carthusian
- From Advent to Pentecost / by A Carthusian
- Guigo II: The Ladder of Monks & Twelve
  Meditations / by E. Colledge & J. Walsh
- Halfway to Heaven / by R.B. Lockhart
- Interior Prayer / by A Carthusian

- Meditations of Guigo I / by A. Gordon Mursall
- The Prayer of Love and Silence / by A Carthusian
- Poor, Therefore Rich / by A Carthusian
- They Speak by Silences / by A Carthusian
- The Way of Silent Love (A Carthusian Miscellany)
- Where Silence is Praise / by A Carthusian
- The Wound of Love (A Carthusian Miscellany)

CISTERCIAN ART, ARCHITECTURE & MUSIC

- Cistercian Abbeys of Britain
- Cistercian Europe / by Terryl N. Kinder
- Cistercians in Medieval Art / by James France
- Studies in Medieval Art and Architecture
  / edited by Meredith Parsons Lillich
  (Volumes II–V are now available)
- Stones Laid Before the Lord
  / by Anselme Dimier
- Treasures Old and New: Nine Centuries of
  Cistercian Music (compact disc and cassette)

THOMAS MERTON

- The Climate of Monastic Prayer / by T. Merton
- Legacy of Thomas Merton / by P. Hart
- Message of Thomas Merton / by P. Hart
- Monastic Journey of Thomas Merton
  / by Patrick Hart
- Thomas Merton/Monk / by P. Hart
- Thomas Merton on St Bernard
- Toward an Integrated Humanity
  / edited by M. Basil Pennington

CISTERCIAN LITURGICAL DOCUMENTS SERIES

- Cistercian Liturgical Documents Series
  / edited by Chrysogonus Waddell, ocso
- Hymn Collection from the…Paraclete
- The Paraclete Statutes:: Institutiones nostrae
- Molesme Summer-Season Breviary (4 vol.)
- Old French Ordinary & Breviary of the
  Abbey of the Paraclete (2 volumes)
- Twelfth-century Cistercian Hymnal (2 vol.)
- The Twelfth-century Cistercian Psalter
- Two Early Cistercian Libelli Missarum

CISTERCIAN PUBLICATIONS • TITLES LISTING

FESTSCHRIFTS

- Bernardus Magister...Nonacentenary of the Birth of St Bernard
- The Joy of Learning & the Love of God: Essays in Honor of Jean Leclercq
- Praise no Less Than Charity in honor of C. Waddell
- Studiosorum Speculumin honor of Louis J. Lekai
- Truth As Gift... in honor of J. Sommerfeldt

BUSINESS INFORMATION

Editorial Offices & Customer Service

- Cistercian Publications
  WMU Station, 1903 West Michigan Avenue
  Kalamazoo, Michigan 49008-5415   USA

  Telephone 616 387 8920
  Fax   616 387 8390
  e-mail   cistpub@wmich.edu

Please Note: As of 13 July 2002 the 616 area code becomes 269

Canada

- Novalis
  49 Front Street East, Second Floor
  Toronto, Ontario M5E 1B3   CANADA

  Telephone 1 800 204 4140
  Fax   416 363 9409

U.K.

- Cistercian Publications UK
  Mount Saint Bernard Abbey
  Coalville, Leicestershire LE67 5UL   UK

- UK Customer Service & Book Orders
  Cistercian Publications
  97 Loughborough Road
  Thringstone, Coalville
  Leicestershire LE67 8LQ   UK

  Telephone 01530 45 27 24
  Fax   01530 45 02 10
  e-mail   MsbcistP@aol.com

Website

- www.spencerabbey.org/cistpub

Trade Accounts & Credit Applications

- Cistercian Publications / Accounting
  6219 West Kistler Road
  Ludington, Michigan 49431   USA

  Fax   231 843 8919

Cistercian Publications is a non-profit corporation. Its publishing program is restricted to monastic texts in translation and books on the monastic tradition.

A complete catalogue of texts in translation and studies on early, medieval, and modern monasticism is available, free of charge, from any of the addresses above.